Reparation and Reconciliation

Reparation and Reconciliation

The Rise and Fall of Integrated Higher Education

Christi M. Smith

The University of North Carolina Press CHAPEL HILL

*This book was published with the assistance of the
Authors Fund of the University of North Carolina Press.*

© 2016 The University of North Carolina Press
All rights reserved
Set in Espinosa Nova by Westchester Publishing Services
Manufactured in the United States of America

The University of North Carolina Press has been a member
of the Green Press Initiative since 2003.

Library of Congress Cataloging-in-Publication Data
Names: Smith, Christi Michelle, author.
Title: Reparation and reconciliation : the rise and fall of integrated higher education /
    Christi M. Smith.
Description: Chapel Hill : University of North Carolina Press, [2016] |
    Includes bibliographical references and index.
Identifiers: LCCN 2016019438 | ISBN 9781469630687 (cloth : alk. paper) |
    ISBN 9781469630694 (pbk   ) | ISBN 9781469630700 (ebook)
Subjects: LCSH: Coeducation—United States—History—19th century. | Segregation
    in higher education—United States—History—19th century. | African Americans—
    Education (Higher)—United States—History—19th century. | Women—Education
    (Higher)—United States—History—19th century.
Classification: LCC LB3066 .S55 2016 | DDC 371.822097309034—dc23
    LC record available at https://lccn.loc.gov/2016019438

Cover illustration: Collegiate graduates (Berea College), 1901. Courtesy of Berea College
Special Collections and Archives, Berea, Kentucky.

For Tim and Victor with love

Contents

Figures

Acknowledgments

Driving Route 158 in eastern North Carolina is its own history lesson: the landscape blurs cotton fields, decrepit plantation houses, and historical markers to black Reconstruction-era leaders. This is where this book was conceived, though I did not realize it at the time. I moved first to Northampton County—and later Vance County—to teach middle and high school social studies in 2001. I rented a house from the descendants of abolitionists. Their not-so-distant ancestors aided enslaved blacks on their journey to Ohio via the Underground Railroad. In cleaning out an unused front room, stacks of decades-old newspapers advertised jobs, listing race and gender as qualifications. Ninth graders saw my car parked at a local restaurant and advised me not to return; they knew I didn't know better. In the not-distant past, the restaurant served blacks at the back door only. The boundaries for daily comings and goings were not merely geographic or based on property lines, and my students and colleagues taught me to see an unmarked but deeply felt history. The county was nearly equal in black and white residents, very few white students attended public schools—the rest attended a segregationist "academy" founded in the early 1960s.

This place also has a rich legacy of black political and cultural leadership. One of the first black congressmen, Ben Turner, was born here. Among my students were descendants of Ben Chavis, one of the "Wilmington Ten," and Dr. Charlotte Hawkins Brown, one of the first black women to earn a PhD. Brown, a former American Missionary Association teacher, who later founded one of the only high schools for blacks in North Carolina in the early twentieth century. My first thank you goes to my former students, their families, and fellow educators, most especially the incomparable Maurice Crump and Victor Fenner.

War—what causes it and how it ends were everyday themes as I grew up in in a very small German village and attended U.S. army schools. The memory of the Holocaust and of war were in the path of everyday life. Sitting at a bus stop when I was fifteen years old, an elderly German woman told me of her clandestine love affair with an American pilot whose plane crashed in the fields near my home. The village grandmothers doted on my grandfather, who lived with us. The streetcars and sidewalks were devoid of old men. In the village next to ours, a grassy area in the town square remains vacant in tribute to a synagogue torched on *Kristallnacht*. Small brass markers indicated houses where Jews had been removed violently from their homes, and to which few would return. I first went to the concentration camp at Dachau, now a memorial, with my parents at the age of twelve. The potential for human cruelty and the need to commemorate and redress past horrors has remained with me since. When we moved to Newburgh, New York—shortly after the 1991 Williamsburg violence—I was shocked by the racialized poverty of my new town and the deep segregation of my new school. Army communities are far more integrated than their civilian counterparts, and I realized I knew very little about the country that issued my passport. Because of my experiences in Germany I hope that this country will heed the call made by Bryan Stevenson, of the Equal Justice Initiative, to publicly commemorate our own history of violence.

Another set of stories contributed to the questions that engendered this book. Were it not for Boston missionaries on a quest to save the Appalachian South, my grandmother and her siblings would not have attended high school. Public schools did not fully reach their county until the mid-twentieth century, and a persistent missionary named Dora Bridges convinced my great-grandfather to send the girls to a Methodist boarding settlement school. My great-grandmother, Margaret Patrick Isaac, enthralled packs of grandbabies with her adventures as a teacher in a one-room school. In the 1970s, an anthropologist collected some of her tales for the archives at the University of Kentucky's Appalachia Collection but I had the good fortune to grow up with them. She and my grandmother, Edith Isaac Smith, made the past an ever-present presence in my childhood. My father, Stephen R. Smith, continues the family story-telling tradition. My dear dad joined me in New Orleans, where I set him to work at the microfiche machine at the Amistad Research Center, and, later, we made the long commute across the Tappan Zee Bridge to the Rockefeller Archive Center, where he meticulously copied Board of Trustee minutes. His questions during the process made this a better book and I am grateful for the time we could share together.

I am deeply thankful for the many funding sources and institutional resources that made this project possible. The Herman B. Wells Graduate Fellowship from Indiana University and the Spencer Foundation Dissertation Fellowship for Research Related to Education gave me the luxury of writing time. Additional funds came through the Spencer Foundation's discipline-based scholarship in education, the Baden-Württemberg Foundation, and Indiana University's Social Science Diversity Initiative. Archive grants from the Avery Research Center for African American History and Culture at the College of Charleston, Frederick B. Artz Summer Research Grant from Oberlin College, and the Rockefeller Archive Center supported data-collection. Those with archival experience know well how much a great archivist contributes to a project. Jean Church welcomed me warmly to the Moorland-Spingarn Research Center at Howard University, and took me on a private tour of its treasures—including General Howard's desk. Jean Church, Roland Bauman (Oberlin College Archives), and Shannon Wilson (Berea College Archives) all took valuable time to share their deep knowledge of the collections under their care. Ken Grossi (Oberlin College Archives) and Christopher Harter (Amistad Research Center) have been truly extraordinary to work with. Thank you for all your assistance and expertise.

My friends and colleagues at the University of Mannheim—Sebastian and Silke Koos, Christian Hunkler, Daniel Lehnert, Nadine Reibling and Andre Schaffrin—all made Mannheim a wonderful home. Presenting work in progress at the *Mannheimer Zentrum für Europäische Sozialforschung* challenged me to look at the contemporary and international implications of this project. The sociology department at Boston University offered me a cozy place to write in Spring 2011. Emily Barman, Sigrun Olafsdottir, Catherine Connell, Japonica Brown-Saracino, Julian Go, Ashley Mears, John Stone, and David Swartz deserve special thanks. At Indiana University, Donald Warren and Pam Walters were invaluable to the development of this project, and I learned so much from them both. Gerardo Lopez and Suzanne Eckes taught me about school administration, educational law, and much more. Brian Steensland has loyally supported this project for *a very long time*, and I hope he will see his "breadcrumbs" and "spinach" throughout. At Ohio State University, Steve Lopez offered just the right advice at the right time; the peripatetic writing support offered by Cassie Pittman and Jennifer Jones made all the difference. Also at Ohio State, my gratitude goes to Heather Schoenfeld, Korie Edwards, Neha Gondal, Corinne Reczek, Hollie Nyseth Brehm, Claudia Buchmann, and Kristi Williams. I am grateful to Rune Stubager who facilitated my summer stay at the political science department at Aarhus University in Denmark, and for David Reimer and Rosa Magnusdottir's hospitality. This book was finished where the story began, at Oberlin College. My thanks to Clovis White, Daphne John, Christie Parris, Greggor Mattson, Rick Baldoz, Pablo Mitchell, Carol Lasser, and Judi Davidson for the warm welcome, and to my students who are outrageously fun thinking partners. It is a particular joy to teach at Oberlin College at a time when students are wrestling with how to reconcile this college's history with contemporary challenges.

There are others who do not fit neatly into categories. Nicola Beisel brought brilliant incisive advice and joy to this project, and great kindness too. Marc Steinberg and Brian Powell offered sage counsel at just the right times. Tamara Beauboeuf told me to write for the people I wanted to know this story, and I still lack the skill to fully bridge that divide, but I am so grateful for her wisdom and friendship. I am indebted to Matt Wray for the push to get the book proposal out and the wisdom of his advice throughout the process. David Cunningham, thank you for many years of advice on publishing and for your advice on this book, it is so much better because of you! In my undergraduate days at Smith College, Ernest Benz, Alice Julier, and Jennifer Klein were demanding teachers who set the bar high and spurred my curiosity in mixing sociological questions with historical sources. You remain my teaching heroes. I have the great joy of having my own students now, and their curiosity and questions have also shaped this book. Thank you to David Ballard and Natalie Noonan for their work in chasing historical particulars.

Thank you to my parents, Stephen and Janelle Smith, for making sure that my world was very big indeed. Bless you for encouraging independence, and letting me climb out the window when a door closed. I wish that my grandfather, Raymond Archibald Smith, could have lived to see this book. It is a joy to remember his gleaming grin. More recent additions to my family, Monica Gomez-Maqueo, Shaneka Bynum, Yaniv Word, Faye and Bill Bartley, JoAnn and the late John Hayden, each bring their own gifts. Doug and Ashley Kincaid, Rashawn and Cynthia Ray, Jessica and Scott Sprague-Jones, Amia Foston, Abigail Sewell, Oren Pizmony-Levy, Josh Garrison, Gregory Hughes, Tanya Feinberg Petrucco, Jennifer Rawlison, Evie Perry, Jeff Gold, Neda Moumtaz, Ted Sammons, Gabrielle Goodwin, and Robert Downey, thank you for your clever comments, welcome distractions, heated debates, and kindness. Nikole Hotchkiss, Tim Curtis, and Bree Marsden kept me human. Amanda Nickey, for bringing the key at dawn, you are my Lubec.

Joe Parsons at UNC Press, along with Alison Shay, have taken good care of this project—and I have been so grateful to Joe for understanding this book from the beginning. Huge thanks to the reviewers for their insightful and detailed comments. It was humbling to have such brilliant scholars to offer generous guidance on my book project. I have benefited from the wisdom of the people named in these acknowledgments, and of course the inadequacies that remain are mine.

And then there's Tim, for the laughing freedom, the fearful gamble, for the secret between the shadow and the soul, because we have a leash on love, and even if it was the 999th of July or way down at the bottom of November, I will go on choosing you. With gratitude for your love and our life together, this book is for you, and for Victor Smith-Bartley, who came into our lives just in time to be included in this dedication.

Reparation and Reconciliation

CHAPTER ONE

A Racial Reckoning on Campus?

In our work, ideas are so soon transmitted into deeds and facts
that it really becomes a very serious matter what we think.
—REVEREND SAMUEL HUNT, American Missionary
    Association, May 17, 1861

The history of this age will read, no doubt, like a romance to
future generations, and they will wonder how such things could
be. Noble schemes and philanthropy ideas have been conceived,
perfected, and hurried to glorious end. . . . This is, beyond a
doubt, set forth in the constantly increasing desire among all
nations to abhor and discontinue making capital of human
flesh, and in the establishment of great educational centers
everywhere.
—G. R. H., LINCOLN UNIVERSITY, letter to the editor
    of the *Christian Recorder*, November 22, 1872

Twenty-three years after the Civil War ended, C. Clifton Penick attended
a college commencement ceremony. "I have been there, and I have seen
it; if I had not, I would not believe it. But there is the actual thing—not
an experiment but a reality!" Penick did not know any particular graduate; nor was Berea College his alma mater. He was one of 6,000 visitors
crowding the small college campus in rural Kentucky. The visitors arrived from New Orleans and New York, Ohio, and Massachusetts. The
Lexington and Nashville Railroad prepared for the unusual traffic by
adding extra rail services for days in advance. All were there to witness
the graduation of the Berea College Class of 1888. What made this event
remarkable was that the graduating class was comprised of nearly equal
numbers of black and white students. Berea's integration was all the more
impressive for its longevity. This noteworthy annual event had drawn
crowds by the thousand for almost two decades. The men and women
graduating that day belonged to what Penick described as "a living,
thriving institution fulfilling all the conditions of the most radical lover
of coeducation."[1]

During the mid-nineteenth century, a social movement took hold to eradicate "the evil of caste." The anti-caste movement, which united American and British activists, considered all distinctions of social rank unjust, and most especially those based purely on physical characteristics—particularly race or complexion.[2] This was not a particularly American or British idea. In the mid-nineteenth century, a movement against the caste-like distinctions inherent in late-stage feudalism was gathering force. The 1848 revolutions in Europe, which swept from Sicily to Denmark and through the Austro-Hungarian Empire, temporarily united the middle and working classes to demand voting rights and just distribution of taxes, and to rally against what Karl Marx described as "half-feudal, half-bureaucratic Monarchism."[3] Abolitionists in the United States and Britain adopted the concept of caste to address not only slavery but racial and class oppression more broadly. The *New York Times* prodded its readers to understand the Civil War as "essentially a struggle between a class—the slave aristocracy and the people."[4] Many Americans had appropriated the biblical "Curse of Ham" to justify blacks' enslavement.[5] Refuting this narrow biblical interpretation, the anti-caste movement framed race as a marker in the American *caste system*, or a social order created when a stigmatized, inherited group position is locked into a system of oppression by both law and custom. In this way, they echoed critiques of inherited aristocratic positions in Europe. The anti-caste movement drew parallels between toppling European monarchs and overthrowing the Southern planter class. As Peter Stamatov has described, religious organizations have played an important role as initiators and carriers of postwar transnational and human rights organizations.[6] Anti-casteists often used historical references to white bonded labor from the colonial era and European feudalism to articulate slavery as a shared historical condition: "Race after race, people after people, have had the chains of slavery stricken from their limbs. . . . Fortunately, [blacks] are so intermingled with men from every part of the world, . . . so deeply imbued with the grand spirit of our liberty-making institutions, that a separation, an isolation like that spoken of is an absolute impossibility."[7]

Through a massive national campaign, anti-casteists encouraged Americans to understand that slavery had undermined republican governance and corrupted U.S. political, legal, and social institutions. For anti-casteists, the idea that these constituted divisible spheres would have been quite foreign.[8] From counting those enslaved as three-fifths of a person in the Constitution to slavery's role in undergirding Connecticut insurance companies, textile mills in Massachusetts, and salt cod operations in the furthest reaches of Maine, slavery was fundamental to the U.S. political and economic system.[9] Fearing that Southern secession would destroy New York's economy, Mayor Fernando Wood proposed to make New York City a "free city"—modeled after the prosperous trade cities in Northern Germany. The American Missionary Association (AMA), a leading organization in the anti-caste movement, understood slavery as economic domination. Addressing the 1867 annual meeting, one AMA member asked, "Did God create the human race to be divided into two classes; the one, a case of capitalists to luxuriate in his bounties; and the other, a caste of pariahs or laborers, to toil without hope for themselves.... We are confident it is not right or expedient so to organize society that its advantages shall be artificially confined to any class; that for instance, capital alone shall accumulate, but labor barely subsist."[10] The much-lauded distinction between the United States and the Old World was its modern break with feudalism—wherein economic arrangements, religious practice, and political decisions were determined by the ruling class. Anti-casteists called out the hypocrisy that afforded this distinct American freedom only to whites, and challenged that, for blacks held in slavery, American capitalism differed in important ways from feudalism.[11]

The AMA viewed its work in education as essential to spread the Doctrine of Social Equality and replace Southern oligarchy with republican governance. The political motivation for anti-caste "coeducation," was rooted in a belief that prejudice was a threat to republican governance and peace: "It is simply a caste feeling, a prejudice of position. This feeling controls legislation, it blinds judges and juries, it corrupts executive officers, it biases witnesses.... We can have no permanent peace ... till the race prejudice, the caste feeling, the spirit of domination is eradicated.... There is nothing, in the absence of co-education, which can secure the mutual regard, confidence and honorable deportment which must exist between the races, if we are to have a peaceful, intelligent and virtuous community."[12]

Unlike some abolitionists who saw emancipation as the culmination of their goal, the anti-caste movement viewed ending slavery as preliminary to the larger objective of "break[ing] down the barrier of caste" by obliterating whites' sense of racial superiority and entitlement.[13] In other words, anti-casteists viewed slavery as a particularly brutal product of caste-based oppression, and believed that postwar reunification of North

FIGURE 1. Oberlin College class portrait, 1900. Courtesy of Oberlin College Archives.

and South could only succeed if whites dismissed race as an arbitrary and inconsequential determinate of human value. Initially at least, anti-casteists were joined by some Radical Republicans in seeking to recast Southern blacks and poor whites as worthy citizens, in opposition to the politically suspect Southern white "planter class."

The twenty years following the Civil War were a time of radical—if sporadic and place specific—upheaval. Northerners quickly organized all manner of civic associations.[14] It was in this context that voluntary associations launched the first program for mass education in the South, starting in 1863 and funded in part by the federal Bureau of Refugees, Freedmen, and Abandoned Lands (BRFAL).[15] The largest and most influential of these voluntary associations was the AMA. How could anti-casteists tackle the bold and far-reaching goal of upending a system so deeply embedded into the foundation of a country?

Anti-casteists believed that by organizing interracial cooperation they would, in turn, effect meaningful political change. The AMA leadership envisioned a future when black Americans could be "a pastor of your churches, a president of your colleges, a leading partner of your great commercial houses, a President of the Republic."[16] The AMA's leaders thought this change could come from interpersonal transformation rather than through the imposition of laws, policies, and rules from above. This stemmed from a deep unwillingness to see government-run social institutions, particularly in the South. As a Protestant organization, the AMA believed the secular state was inappropriate for the moral work required to transform Southern values and beliefs.

The AMA coordinated the placement of teachers in BRFAL schools and launched a network of colleges committed to racial and gender co-education. The hope was that graduates would go on to work in professions foundational to the anti-caste vision of modern society—teaching, law, medicine, clergy—in the South. This would create a Southern middle class, black and white, saturated with anti-caste egalitarianism. The AMA advocated creating small, bounded communities—college campuses—where blacks and whites would come to "recognize each others' humanity."[17] Though a few anti-caste colleges were founded in the 1830s, by the end of the Civil War, anti-casteists launched a network of coeducational colleges as an organized political project. Among these was Berea College, whose founder explained to the *New York Times* that "practical, impartial education—coeducation . . . is the only way to prevent a 'war of the races.' Those who pray together and study together will not fight."[18] Put differently, the AMA imagined that caste-breaking experiences on college campuses could open what Pierre Bourdieu has called "space for symbolic strategies aimed at exploiting the discrepancies between the nominal and the real" and thereby disrupt students' individual *habitus*—the dispositions, preferences, and sensibilities formed through an accumulation of life experiences.[19] To the founders of Berea College and the anti-caste movement more broadly, C. Clifton Penick's reaction was as important an accomplishment, if not more than the academic achievements of the men and women who graduated that summer day. A Confederate veteran, Penick was precisely who the anti-caste mission endeavored to reach. The AMA insisted that culpability for racial oppression rested on whites and that whites' reeducation was the necessary first step toward national unity and lasting peace.

At AMA-sponsored colleges, trustees, administrators, faculty, and students worked out the challenges of implementation in classrooms, dining halls, dorm rooms, work programs, and campus activities. Oberlin College, founded in 1833, predated the AMA, but Oberlin's faculty, trustees, and alumni were tightly intertwined with AMA leadership. As early as 1852, Oberlin faculty petitioned the Board of Trustees to adopt affirmative-action-style hiring policies. Howard University's first class was comprised of five white women, but the university boasted black and white trustees, deans, and faculty members from its start in 1867. Students at these colleges shared bedrooms, classrooms, extracurricular activities, and a few even fell in love "across the color line."[20] Berea's Board of Trustees adopted a policy in 1872 that explicitly allowed interracial dating.

For over twenty years, Berea maintained equal enrollment of black and white students; Oberlin's black enrollment ranged from 5–10 percent, and Howard's white enrollment ranged from 5–20 percent.[21] Berea administrators decided that the only way to truly transform students' ideas about race was to create an immersive environment in which every activity—whether debate teams, public speeches, or on-campus jobs—was comprised of equal numbers of black and white students. At Oberlin and Howard, the integration of student life was perhaps less formally structured, but black and white students shared classrooms, chapel activities, and work duties. Like Howard, Berea had both black and white trustees, faculty, and administrators. Women attended all three schools, and Oberlin was one of the top producers of black women college graduates.

Major news outlets endorsed higher education as a political training ground. In August of 1865, the *Chicago Tribune* encouraged its readers to take inspiration from Oberlin because it had "solved the social problem of the nation."[22] By 1884, journalists joined cultural, political and military elites in heralding these colleges as a model ready for mass replication, proclaiming that "equality is achieved. . . . What has been done there can be done everywhere in the South, and must be."[23]

Yet by 1900, Berea, Howard, and Oberlin no longer placed interracial coeducation at the center of their institutional missions. Berea transformed into a college dedicated to a new cultural group, the Appalachians, after cultivating support for "mountain education" in the Southern Appalachians. Howard and Oberlin differentiated themselves by claiming a unique ability to educate male leaders. In Howard's case, this meant chiseling a last foothold for liberal arts education for a black elite, in the midst of the rise of industrial colleges for blacks. Oberlin modeled itself on elite universities but drew upon its moral heritage to cast Oberlin as ideal preparation for leaders in the burgeoning U.S. colonial empire.

In short, the project to create racial integration shifted into a segmented system—elite white colleges for men and for women, gender-integrated industrial colleges for African Americans and for Appalachians, and a few elite universities for African Americans.

As we will see, this retrenchment occurred without pressure by the courts. Why and how did educational organizations, deeply committed to coeducation, shift to an approach that, while different in its specific contours, reinscribed racial categories?

Making Sense of "Redemption"

From the vantage point of the twenty-first century, with our knowledge of the long, bloody, and unfinished struggle for civil rights and racial justice, it is easy to imagine that the egalitarian goals of Radical Reconstruction and the anti-caste movement were doomed from the start. Yet we must try to read past events without presuming that that the victories of Reconstruction would necessarily be subsumed by the violence of Jim Crow.[24] As Ann Mische argues, we must "refocus attention on the open, indeterminate, 'polythetic' perception of the field from the point of view of the actor surveying the future in terms of multiple possibilities."[25] This means using a processual approach that reconstructs the hope, possibilities, and hardships of the historical moment. And this demands making sense of the largely ignored and complex 1880s, what has been called "Redemption," when white Southerners were symbolically "redeemed" at the expense of black rights.[26]

Four million black Americans rejoiced for emancipation, even as they and white Americans grieved for loved ones who had died in battle, suffered in prison camps, or returned home emotionally and physically scarred. Millions were displaced, without the means to meet their most basic needs. Refugees crowded into cities, desperate for aid, and inadequate public sanitation led to public health crises in Nashville, Washington, D.C., and elsewhere. Charitable organizations struggled to dispense meager rations. For a reader in the twenty-first century, such indicators give us cause for pessimism, but for an American in 1865, these terrible conditions made painfully clear the necessity of breaking with past customs and policies. Journalists expressed the need for creativity in brokering lasting peace: "We are living in an hour when there are no precedents, and no traditions by which politicians can be guided, when they will fail us if we attempt to follow them."[27]

This book examines how higher education took on a symbolic status deeply entwined with political rights. Racially integrated higher education became the "solution" to Reconstruction, and this book takes us on campus to understand how integration was practiced at specific colleges. These colleges were founded to develop a more just society, and to that end they began by refusing to acknowledge old racial hierarchies in building more democratic and more moral ideals of citizenship and society. My focus is on three AMA-affiliated colleges—Berea College, Oberlin College, and Howard University—from their founding through 1915. In addition to founding hundreds of primary schools across the South, the AMA helped establish or maintain eleven colleges or universities during Reconstruction, including Atlanta University (Georgia), Fisk University (Tennessee), Hampton Institute (Virginia), LeMoyne/LeMoyne-Owen College (Tennessee), Tougaloo College (Mississippi), Straight University (now Dillard) (Louisiana), Talladega College (Alabama), Huston-Tillotson University (Texas), and Avery Normal Institute (now part of the College of Charleston, South Carolina). My three colleges were chosen from this larger set for their national prominence, variation in demographic composition, and differences in campus policies. They illustrate different variants of the project to create racial coeducation.

These are certainly not the only cases that illustrate the liminality of race in nineteenth-century education. Roughly thirty colleges and universities were open to blacks by 1870. By limiting the scope to several deliberately integrated institutions, I did not include Georgetown, where the son of a former slave "passing" as white became the university president in 1874. Nor does this book focus on the admission of very small numbers of black students to West Point, Harvard, Cornell, Vassar, and other campuses.

To understand the rise and fall of racially integrated higher education, I have analyzed personal letters and diaries, financial records, speeches, Boards of Trustees minutes, and administrative documents independently collected from nine archives.[28] These archival materials allow for a view of the positions of politicians, elites, and social movements. I have also collected press data from many nineteenth-century newspapers and magazines. I used these press sources in a few different ways. Periodicals illustrate how information about particular issues or organizations was communicated to the broader public.[29] I then attempted to triangulate information gained through the press with other archival materials. In other cases, newspapers help to fill in for incomplete archival records.

This is particularly true for Howard University, which suffered various losses to its collection. I use these sources to examine interactions within colleges and charitable organizations, the institutional structures that facilitated and/or constrained integration, and support for interracial cooperation at the state and federal levels.

As described in the chapters that follow, the Republican supermajority in Congress was able to demand new constitutions and pass important civil rights legislation during Reconstruction. But these victories lacked enforcement power, and many were overturned within a decade.[30] Since the American state had yet to include social welfare provisions, it is perhaps not surprising that federal efforts to develop educational infrastructures in the South were short-lived.[31] Whether fearful of inciting further violence in the South or as a result of financial strain, by time Reconstruction ended in 1877, federal resources were diverted to expansion efforts in the West and new colonial projects. There was little enforcement of the requirements demanded by the federal government for former Confederate states to gain readmission to the Union. This allows us to consider what happens when the state steps away from obligations in the public realm. Could the charitable or philanthropic sector take on the challenge of creating a racially integrated society?

I argue that the reliance on private organizations to manage nation-rebuilding efforts—with education as a primary domain—eroded opportunities for the durable transformation of racial structures. Though originally promoted to inculcate republican beliefs across the South, the expansion of higher education soon led to racialized forms of organizational competition. The field of higher education became competitive as it grew, and colleges' attempts to garner support in this environment led them to shift away from their initial commitment to racial coeducation. Organizations—in this case, colleges, universities, and voluntary associations—must constantly navigate their environments. Yet as scholars of "inhabited institutionalism" remind us, organizational actions also depend on the people who live and work within them.[32] In this case, the competitive environment, combined with the particular strategies of actors within the AMA and the colleges, led to the demise of racial coeducation.[33]

It is useful to draw here on Elisabeth Clemens's concept of "obligation hoarding," or the process by which aspiring elites position themselves as the best agents to control social provisions for a given sector. Actors engage in obligation hoarding not to secure a valued resource for their own use, as in Charles Tilly's concept of opportunity hoarding or Max Weber's idea of social closure. Instead, actors engage in obligation hoarding to engender trust, loyalty, respect, and dependence from outside their own social class. The AMA, scornful of government's role in the moral sphere and fearing that the planter class could too easily find its way back to the halls of power, engaged in obligation hoarding. It embarked on a project to take on the challenge of social reconstruction, launching colleges to promote anti-caste values and staking a claim that Protestant organizations should have substantial sway in matters of education. As noted historian C. Vann Woodward argued, "the church was a serious competitor of the state and the philanthropic capitalist for influence over higher education in the South."[34] Though the AMA was nondenominational, many Congregationalists were in positions of influence within the organization. Baptists, Catholics, Presbyterians, and Methodists all had their own educational projects in the South. I argue that these dynamics sapped the potential to transform racial structures.

Contemporary explanations assume that the power to segregate lies with the state, whether through laws that mandate *de jure* segregation, or more contemporary district boundaries that allocate students to schools producing *de facto* segregation. In the cases studied here, legal action did not initiate segregation on any of the campuses. Yet, most often racial formation scholars have focused at macro-level forces. As Omi and Winant define racial formation as "the sociohistorical process by which racial identities are created, lived out, transformed, and destroyed." The term racial structure means that race is not merely ideological, or a set of beliefs, but that racial differences are created, acted upon, and enforced by political, cultural, and economic institutions and organizations. Powerfully, they deny that race is an essence or an illusion. Race is socially constructed but central to structuring daily experiences. As Ta-Nahisi Coates writes, "difference in hue and hair is old. But the belief that these factors can correctly organize a society and that they signify deeper attributes, which are indelible—this is the new idea."[35] Race is an idea, but it takes actors within organizations to translate ideas into action.[36] We know that race is not biological or bounded as a category and yet, the degree to which actors are enabled or constrained in defining, choosing, or activating racial identities remains under-theorized, particularly for whites.[37] This book builds upon many elements—most particularly the idea of "racial projects"—identified by racial formation theorists.[38] But it also focuses on the work of actors who patrol the boundaries between public and private sectors. These actors saw their influence as connecting interpersonal interactions with organizational decision-making, and examining how macro-level forces supported or thwarted these endeavors. Social movement actors frame social problems, encouraging others to take on their perspective, and embedded in these acts of framing are proposals for who and how the problems should be solved.[39]

This book offers a multilevel analysis of racial segregation, examining the interplay between various levels of influence—from the political arena, to the national organization of the AMA, and the local campus level. This gives us a view to how organizations disrupt or advance racial structures. My hope is that understanding retrenchment through these cases can help universities in our contemporary moment to create truly inclusive campuses. This historical moment holds lessons for multi-institutional theories of power and current efforts to implement egalitarian and anti-racist reforms.

To understand segregation, it is useful to return to Pierre Bourdieu's question: What makes a social class? How are social groups made to seem real and natural? And who can produce such misrecognition? Symbolic power—the power to define and to have the definitions of 'groupness' created by one group dominate over the definitions of others—is at the heart of Bourdieu's answer. As Loïc Wacquant elaborated, making groups "real" is an act of "sociosymbolic alchemy whereby a mental construct is turned into a historical reality through the inculcation of schemata of perception and their deployment to draw, enforce, or contest social boundaries."[40] Segregation by race depends upon, foundationally, schemas that impose a hierarchy and articulate why some belong together and others do not. Segregation also depends on a host of social acts to build and maintain a social system in accordance with these cognitive frames. In building integrated colleges, anti-casteists attempted to disrupt old schemas by building spaces where outmoded schemas would be challenged and ideally wither.

While recent scholarship in ethnic boundaries has begun to acknowledge the role organizations play in creating, defining, and defending boundaries, race scholars have favored studies of either macro-level racial formation or micro-level scholarship of attitudes and social distance; few studies bridge levels of analysis or address organizations at the meso-level.[41] Organizations are dependent on the people who live and work within them. When racial structures are conceptualized in this way—as a structure that is ever-changing and in need of constant reinforcement to maintain its potency—we are forced to think about who perpetuates racial boundaries and the incentives for doing so. These structures are not devoid of actors or interests. At the heart of investigations into processes of segregation and integration are issues of schematic understandings of in-groups and out-groups and how the boundaries between these are drawn.

In the pages that follow, *Reparation and Reconciliation* tells the forgotten story of an early struggle for racial integration. The book shows how Republicans looked to education for reconstruction, and how the AMA amassed support for a remarkable interracial coeducation project. But it also shows how what began as a concerted effort to revise the widely-shared American meanings of race and status, ended by creating a competitive system of higher education that projected types of education on a matrix of race, gender, and social status. Through a detailed exploration of administrative decisions at Berea, Oberlin, and Howard, we can see the interplay of internal and external pressures that led to this configuration of organizational and symbolic boundaries. Despite deep ties among a close network of like-minded college administrators and social movement actors, we see a variety of forms of engagement that extend far beyond the college campus. Private, state, and voluntary sector actors all produced new strategies for increasing access, standardizing quality controls, and embedding their desired logics in a rapidly changing institutional environment. As higher education transformed from individual colleges into a field, individual organizations were increasingly pressured to conform to particular rules and logics in order to establish and maintain their legitimacy. Rising competition in higher education spawned new organizational boundaries and new categorizations of people. These groupings activated particular ideas about the civic value of particular groups; once consecrated, they had grave consequences for accessing complete rights of citizenship.[42] At a historical moment when actors dared to reinvent the social order, they ended up inscribing race as the most salient of social boundaries.

Reparations and Reconciliation

Could the United States overcome racism? Is it possible to dislodge racist ideas and practices that have been woven into national institutions? How can a nation reckon with the specter of slavery? Today, these questions remain as relevant and challenging as they were in 1865, when the AMA took up the enormous challenge of remaking cultural beliefs around race in the United States. To be sure, many things have changed. Thousands of activists have risked—and some lost—their lives in the battle for Civil rights and racial justice. Blacks can legally vote, hold political office, and seek remedy through the courts; discrimination based on race is illegal. Yet mass incarceration and police brutality have signaled what Michelle Alexander terms the "new Jim Crow"; in 2013, the U.S. Supreme Court overturned key provisions in the 1965 Voting Rights Act. Schools—at all levels, whether public or private—are undeniably segregated.[43]

The United States has never broached a thorough reckoning of racial injustice. Unlike Germany and South Africa, where "truth and reconciliation" campaigns forced painful examinations of national brutality, the United States has yet to undertake a similar investigation and make reparations. This is not to suggest that Americans have not wrestled with the question of atonement.

While not to detract from the importance of the contemporary debate, for the purposes of this book it is important to understand the context of reparations for actors during Reconstruction. The idea of financial compensation for the unrequited work of enslaved persons would have been quite unimaginable. Southern planters did press upon the U.S. government for compensation of their "loss of property," and were quickly rebuffed. Far from creative hubris, Southern planters drew on the decision made by British Parliament in the 1830s to provide compensation to slave owners upon the abolition of slavery. Though most modern discussion of reparations suggest financial compensation paid to those wronged, the term is rooted in "to repair." It is in this spirit that the AMA could conceive of providing assistance—through schools and social relief—as reparation. Members of the AMA argued forcefully that white Americans owed former slaves for past wrongs, and that their work would help repay an incommensurable debt. If slavery created a logic of race as a marker of status inequality, the AMA viewed its reparative work as correcting that imbalance; they viewed education as essential to secure mutual respect.

When BRFAL closed in 1872, the AMA recognized that the federal government would not attempt any reparations, and certainly Southern states would not either. The AMA recognized the daunting task before them as an economic challenge: "Our work hereafter among the Freedmen will lack the efficient aid of the Freedmen's Bureau; our diminished list of teachers will strike the popular eye with less force; our need of increased salaries for teachers and professors, nay, our imperative need of endowments for colleges and seminaries, will render our wants greater."[44] Yet the AMA also saw that the shuttering of the BRFAL opened space for Protestant organizations. The AMA publicly declared it would have to do the work of a state in righting injustice, and it would do so through providing education: "We believe the American people owe, and recognize that they owe, *a vast debt yet unpaid* to these ex-slaves . . . [and] that this Association is doing just the work needed at the South."[45]

The AMA and its affiliated colleges encouraged donors to provide student scholarships as their contribution to reparations. The AMA sought to inspire individual transformations rather than legal-political remedies. Speaking before the 1872 commencement at Berea College, Kentucky State Legislator William Brown, a former slave owner, testified to the audience that "to slave labor he owed his education, his wealth . . . and that there was a solemn obligation resting upon him to repay, as far as possible, the debt he owed the race."[46] The AMA positioned itself as an arbiter of reparations. It would begin to make amends through the creation of coeducational colleges and the larger project of building primary schools throughout the South. The establishment of college campuses could also help whites and blacks develop the habits they would need to participate in an integrated democracy. If race is a caste system where our everyday actions, customs, and manners all contribute to the perpetuation of racial inequality, then no slight adjustment could hope to accomplish a radical transformation. The AMA hoped that the controlled environment of a college campus, sheltered from outside influences, and with the opportunity for making close friendships across the color line, would indelibly mark each student's racial attitude.

With emancipation, 4 million people were legally recategorized from slaves to persons. The great problem of reconstruction was quickly defined by the challenge of incorporating blacks into the citizenry—that is, a challenge of status transformation. Congress rapidly enacted the Thirteenth, Fourteenth, and Fifteenth Amendments, which recognized blacks as citizens and protected voting rights. But the recognition of these rights remained (and remains) a trenchant problem.[47] While we often think about this as a problem of the state—including law-making, court decisions, and census categorization—the AMA had different ideas.[48] Because Confederates were only briefly and haphazardly barred from voting, and because barriers were quickly put in place to limit (and eventually deny) black voters, the AMA rightly felt that political institutions in the South were not to be trusted. Even when laws were in place to counter voter discrimination, federal enforcement was severely limited.

Unlike many social movements, the anti-caste movement and its colleges did not plead their case to the state directly. They did not call for changes in the legal system or in policy directly. In fact, the AMA was quite explicit that "top-down" efforts to change social mores through legal mandates would only incite greater resistance. Instead, the AMA's approach to reparations and reconciliation focused on dismantling the American caste system through education. They developed an extra-democratic solution to a deeply democratic problem. Their schools in the South would create opportunities for blacks without bending to the planter class. Their colleges would allow them to staff professions essential to democracy in the South, and transform the status and identify of both white and black students, recasting citizenship in new terms.

Explaining the Rise and Demise of Interracial Coeducation

The Expanding Field of Higher Education

Few scholars have taken an intersectional approach to understand how the educational opportunities (or lack thereof) of a particular group affects the opportunities for other groups or the field of higher education as a whole. For instance, dominant historical accounts describe the rise of women's education and black education as largely without impact on colleges and universities for white men.[49] Yet, the rise of a higher education system built on particular forms of education matched to particular types of people can only be understood through examining contention between fields—legal, political, educational, charitable—that produced these distinctions. By the end of the nineteenth century, this meant that a rather chaotic field of higher education was distilled into a singular logic: To compete against an ever-increasing number of colleges, types of education should be matched to particular groupings of people as a means to attract donors. Characterized in broad strokes, this resulted in a systemic stratification by race, class, and gender.

This diffusion of differentiated higher education excluded integration as a model for higher education. Berea, Howard, and Oberlin, three integrated colleges, aligned policies and practices to match expectations in the broader field of higher education. Not only are curricula standardized through isomorphism, but so too are the groups of people considered relevant for certain forms of education. Schools restructure whole populations, create and expand elites, and redefine the rights and responsibilities of social groups.[50] Indeed, as comparisons among colleges increased and colleges competed for donors (as well as students), the boundaries of legitimate models for higher education and matching between racial groups and educational form concentrated. In their examination of the global expansion on higher education in the twentieth century, Evan Schofer and John Meyer briefly suggest that competition leads to disenfranchisement and/or exclusion of particular groups.[51] We find the roots of this persistent trend in the late nineteenth century.

Organizational foundings differ between education and other types of organizations; educational innovation rarely responds to "structural holes" and needs.[52] Organizational emergence is most often conceptualized as a count process, but the alignment and variation in higher education illustrates that to examine emergence only through the number of new organizations misses powerful contests over meanings and logics. Some new organizations—some variations—carry more weight, more status, and through their creation, they in turn powerfully shape the future of group interactions. This reveals the causal relationship between racial and status boundary processes and the production and diffusion of educational forms.

To understand how educational segregation was legitimated and normalized, this book traces how higher education became a competitive field that produced not only particular types of education but also consecrated group differences. The Civil War pushed college expansion, with enrollment increasing by 278 percent in the three decades between the end of the war and the dawn of the twentieth century.[53] Civil War and Reconstruction policy-makers viewed the expansion and democratization of higher education as essential to a secure national reunification. In 1862, Congress passed the Morrill Act to extend higher education to the "laboring classes." To gain readmission to the Union, ex-Confederate states were required to write new constitutions that pledged public funds for the education of blacks and whites, including the maintenance of colleges or universities. This played out differently across the States. South Carolina, bolstered by a majority black legislature, removed the "tuition barrier" and integrated its state university. The

University of North Carolina, by contrast, refused integration and shuttered its doors until the end of federal Reconstruction. Between 1837 and 1905, private organizations founded at least one hundred colleges either designated for blacks or with policies of racial nondiscrimination. Even more predominately white colleges occasionally admitted a few black students.

Despite the growth in higher education, few blacks were able to access publicly funded colleges or universities until the second Morrill Act of 1890, which recognized the limits of educational expansion. Rather than suggesting that blacks needed to be better prepared for college—as some continue to do—the second Morrill Act recognized racial prejudice as the source of unequal access. It allowed for the use of federal funds for "historically black colleges and universities"—spurring an enduring nomenclature.

Scholars and policy-makers have typically thought of the expansion of higher education as serving several purposes. From a development and modernization perspective, increasing educational access is supposed to accompany political and economic growth and stability. As the population increases in education and skills, so too grows the economy. Additionally, as John Meyer and colleagues have argued, access to higher education has become an important symbolic indicator for recognition as a modern state. Furthermore, expanding access is thought to ameliorate class gaps by fostering greater social mobility.[54] While the state of the United States expanded rapidly after the Civil War—offering, for instance, the first social welfare programs[55]—increasing higher education enrollment did not translate into greater social equality. More doors were opened, but they did not lead to equal opportunities.

One reason is that the emergence of competitive spirit between colleges diverged dramatically from the intentions behind the energetic project of expanding higher education in the 1870s. As Max Weber argued, in democratic societies—and particularly those transitioning away from inherited status hierarchies (such as aristocracy)—education becomes an arena where merit is consecrated. This bureaucratization of merit can be of great value, but it can also serve to legitimate the reproduction of privilege. In describing the interconnectivity of cultural and educational ideals with systems of social status, Weber remarks that the educational ideal of the "cultivated man" was "stamped by the structure of domination and by the social condition for membership in the ruling stratum."[56] Merit is subjective, and what is *valued* and deemed meritorious is often at the heart of conflicts in unsettled times. Higher education replaced forms of social hierarchy that depended upon familial ties, and thus individuals were "certified." Carrying this forward, Pierre Bourdieu argued that the state consecration of elites through education is a direct legacy of the *noblesse de robe* of aristocratic orders of the past.[57] He argues that elite universities accomplish "a rite of institution," whereby the consecrated elite are not only made separate and distinct but are also recognized by others—and by themselves—as deserving of their special categorization. Merit contests often spur social closure, or what Bourdieu called "the magical efficacy of institutional dubbing."[58] The illusion of higher education as a merit contest among individuals leads us to what Shamus Khan describes as a "democratic conundrum"; in times of increasing access, individualistic merit-based status contests reduce the potential for collectivist mobilization, and poses a challenge to democratic education more broadly.[59]

Weber and Bourdieu argue that the power of consecration lies with the state and cannot be claimed by private entities. While elites in many European countries are educated almost exclusively in state universities, most U.S. elites are educated in private colleges and universities.[60] Without the symbolic power of the state to accomplish these rites of institution, how do colleges procure and gain wide recognition for their ability to confer status? And does the absence of state control over elite higher education matter for the ways in which racial, gender, and ethnic categories are bound in the consecration of elites through higher education?

Especially in the United States, the field of higher education is composed of an array of public and private actors. As Paul DiMaggio and Walter Powell have argued, organizational fields are made up of organizations that share a common enterprise, including resource-suppliers and regulators of the focal set of organization (e.g., colleges and universities). DiMaggio and Powell argue that fields develop when there is increasing interaction among organizations, including the sharing of practical information, and recognition among participants that they share a common enterprise. As Neil Fligstein proposes, we can locate fields when we see groups of actors frame their actions vis-à-vis one another.[61] Yet as Mustafa Emirbayer and Victoria Johnson have detailed, the legitimate definition of the field is quite often at the heart of the contests between participants.[62]

As we will see, the growing field of higher education in the United States was structured by cohesion and conflict. Initially, the ambitious

AMA viewed its sphere of influence as nearly limitless. Its goals ranged from the transformation of individual mores across all levels of education, to the highest political chambers and global missionary actions. As other organizations built barriers and imposed constraints to solidify the field of higher education, the AMA was forced to ratchet down its boundless ambitions and orient its work to the particular arena of higher education. Benevolent societies like the AMA, philanthropic foundations like John D. Rockefeller's General Education Board, higher-level organizations like the American Association of Collegiate Alumnae and the American Medical Association, and enterprising "ethnographic experts" at private colleges sought to define the field as they built it. Colleges are dependent for resources, and this is all the more true for private colleges whose donor base and student population are unstable. Moreover, the growing field of higher education was dynamic because its actors were constantly shifting; administrators and faculty moved from one campus to another and new generations of students arrived. In so doing, as I will show, the administrators of private organizations—whether colleges, religious benevolent associations, philanthropies, or professional associations—managed the differentiation and exclusion of blacks, Appalachian whites, and white women from higher education.

As much as the AMA had hoped that colleges would filter out the racist beliefs students brought to campus and launch them into positions of professional influence, the AMA also neglected to attend to the ways in which on-campus integration would face resistance from external organizations. For instance, the American Medical Association erected barriers to white women and black doctors, which effectively segregated Howard's medical department by the end of the 1880s. Organized efforts to rank and rate higher education—whether by the Alumnae Association of Collegiate Women or the 1910 Flexner Report sponsored by the Carnegie Foundation—further institutionalized barriers to integration and access to professions.[63] The rise of the research university as a dominant model of elite higher education, and its quest for increasing elite status, pushed out forms of higher education that were more inclusive.[64] Rather like the failings of colorblindness familiar to twenty-first century readers, these exclusions were quite often accomplished without explicit demands for segregation.[65] One of the failings of anti-caste administrators was their belief that college campuses could constitute "total institutions." Their colleges—and the success of their graduates—were vulnerable to changes in the legal realm. For instance, though blacks were legally granted civil rights, implementation was poorly enforced, and anti-caste leaders actively spoke out against using the law to combat racial segregation.

Contact, Coeducation, and Organizational Activation

Racial logics are not stable. Anti-casteists hoped to seize a moment of great uncertainty, and force a new moral logic, built on a belief in a common humanity, into debates over racial hierarchies. They endeavored to rebuild American ideas about what merited status (social, political, and moral) and to do so they needed to dismantle existing racial structures. Before delving into understanding integration, it is useful to introduce the concept of race using Edward Bonilla-Silva's term *racial social systems*. In this view, "economic, political, social, and ideological levels are partially structured by the placement of actors in racial categories or race. Races typically are identified by their phenotype, but . . . the selection of certain human traits to designate a racial group is always socially rather than biologically based."[66] Anti-caste efforts attempted to diminish wide-spread essentialist notions of race and they planned to do so by organizing interracial contact on college campuses. Like anti-caste activists of the nineteenth century, scholars of race have often understood educational integration through the lens of some version of "contact theory," which emphasizes interpersonal interaction as the key to overcoming prejudice.[67] Scholars have argued that schools and other organizations can produce racial integration if the conditions for interracial contact are appropriately specified.[68] For many, the hope is that by reducing individual prejudice, schools can foster new attitudes to produce change beyond the schoolhouse gate.

To quantify the degree of contact in schools and other social settings, scholars usually rely on compositional measures, such as the number of students identifying as from particular racial backgrounds attending the same school or district.[69] For instance, in K–12 schools, the Harvard Civil Rights Project (now at UCLA) compared extremely segregated minority schools (where more than 99 percent of students are minorities), intensely segregated minority schools (more than 90 percent), and predominantly minority schools (over 50 percent).[70] For neighborhoods, the most popular measures of segregation and integration include the index of dissimilarity, which captures the distribution of groups, and the exposure index, which measures the likelihood of intergroup contact.[71]

These demographic measures are powerful for measuring racial isolation, but they explain little about the shape of contact or the dynamics of integration. For instance, they do not tell us about values, beliefs, ideals, and other cognitive or symbolic shifts. Further, tools from cultural sociology help us understand the contestation around racial meanings that makes integration difficult to implement. Race is neither a stable set of essential qualities nor is it is as malleable as some theorists of social constructivism have argued. Nor are the lessons gained from integrated settings easy to quantify. What do we learn from experiences within integrated schools, and are these lessons apparent immediately or do they take years to distill?[72]

"Coeducation," as used by the anti-caste movement, involved more than just opportunities for interracial contact. It signified a commitment to place interracial contact at the center of collegiate missions and to consider the informal, interactional learning that takes place in a college as essential to the overall educational purpose of higher education. At times, this model of interracial coeducation overlapped with gender coeducation, although as we will see, gender and race were intertwined in complex ways. As I delve into the cases, I use the term "coeducation" where there is robust evidence that the speaker or organization professed allegiance to the anti-caste model. I use the term "integration" to refer to adjustments to demographic composition. Integration tells us about access but does not signify a deeper commitment to include the transformation of racial schemas as part of the mission of the college or university.

In line with contact theory, we certainly need to look closely at what happens on campus, as I will do in chapter 3. Students, faculty, and Boards of Trustees all make decisions that shape the culture of the college. Yet an incomplete picture emerges if we look only within schools. Rules and resources that determine many college policies often lie far from campus life, in legislatures, courts, and philanthropies, for instance. In addition, private bodies that oversee or evaluate schools, including rating bodies and professional associations, may wittingly or unwittingly support or undermine integration. Inter-organizational competition for resources and status can also dampen the importance of internal structures of contact.

Looking at interracial coeducation in the nineteenth century, we see that the successes and failures of racial integration depended on much more than simply contact. Instead, interactions between colleges—and the emergence of a competitive field of higher education—undermined even successfully integrated campuses. At Oberlin, for instance, coeducation went from being both a political goal and an organizational practice, to being shunted aside as competition intensified. Both integration and segregation are organizational accomplishments, rather than merely aggregated individual choices or implemented legal decisions. Organizational actors attach particular meanings to race, ethnicity, or sex, and thus activate these over other social boundary divisions—for instance, religion, class, or political orientation.

In other words, organizations activate both the salience of race as well as particular meanings about race when it is advantageous for them to do so. But how do organizations determine what will be advantageous?[73] I will show that this depends on leaders' understanding of their sphere of influence and their field of operation. The decisions about activating difference—whether by race, ethnicity, and/or sex—described in this book were undertaken by organizational leaders who were navigating an emerging field. They engaged in "boundary work" to investigate the changing boundaries around them and to produce new ones. In this way, they defined their position in an emerging field and made claims of "ethnographic expertise" about race and gender.[74]

Such processes can help explain how racial and gender differences emerge as key principles for social organization. More broadly, as others have argued, to understand the structure of formal political arrangements, we must examine processes of cultural status ordering and boundary formation.[75]

Historical Roots of Contemporary Debates

Education and the Achievement of Citizenship

Under slavery, the rules governing citizenship and race were painfully defined. What would replace this old order? For many white Americans, the question was how to maintain supremacy. In contrast, the anti-caste movement demanded the eradication of the old divisions based on race, and proposed replacing these with distinctions of civic and moral valor.

In this historical moment, a tension emerged between the legal system and the education system as the locus for producing and ensuring social and political status. In the aftermath of the Civil War, politicians debated the qualifications for citizenship and, for the first time, established federal requirements for citizenship. Scholars have long understood *jus sanguinis* and *jus soli* as the primary foundations for citizenship. Some nations have elected to define the bounds of citizenship based on "blood"—for instance, Italy and Germany—and others by where a child is born. Yet neither of these models of citizenship accurately fit the U.S. case. The United States has never fully attached citizenship rights to ethnic heritage, as have many European countries.[76] Nor have all persons born in the United States been guaranteed these rights. Most glaringly, blacks were largely denied citizenship rights and the protection it offers, Native Americans were explicitly excluded from the Fourteenth Amendment, and women did not win the right to vote until 1919. Between 1890 and 1915, many Southern states used educational requirements to exclude black voters.[77] The following were used to disqualify black voters. Reading and writing tests were instituted by Mississippi (1890), South Carolina (1895), North Carolina (1900), Alabama (1901), Virginia (1902), Georgia (1908), Oklahoma (1910), and in Louisiana (1921). Other states mandated "understanding tests" of the United States (or state) Constitution, including Mississippi (1890), South Carolina (1895), Virginia (1902), and Louisiana (1921). A few tacked on elaborate questions regarding the obligations and rights of citizenship to their "understanding tests," including Alabama (1901), Georgia (1908), Louisiana (1921), and Mississippi (1954). To circumvent the problem that these tests would in fact disqualify large numbers of whites, the following exemptions were made to include white voters who might not otherwise have passed the educational requirements. Whites could vote if they could claim a "voting grandfather" in North Carolina (1876), Louisiana (1898), and Oklahoma 1907 (amended 1910), or if they could claim a civil war veteran—the "fighting grandfather clause"—in Georgia (1877), Alabama (1901), and Virginia (1902).[78] In short, these states were quite explicit that race was not the cause for exclusion, that their voting requirements were colorblind, but that active citizenship demanded educational prerequisites. Of course, in practice, there is no dispute that race was central to who could vote and who could not. But it is because education became so deeply intertwined as a signifier of capacity and eligibility for the full rights of citizenship, that higher education became a competitive domain for adjudicating racial hierarchy.

I argue that between the rise of nationhood in the nineteenth century, we see the rise of a new foundation for citizenship—what one might call *jus laurea*—or civic and social inclusion based on educational accomplishment. As the civil rights victories of the 1870s were chiseled away during the 1880s and 1890s, many within the anti-caste network saw a college education as the best and last hope for securing the rights of citizenship through demonstrating blacks' civic value. The struggle over education shaped ideas about the cultural deservedness of different groups, and these played into political adjudication of rights and opportunities based on group membership. The anti-caste movement intended for interracial coeducation to eradicate whites' prejudice; but by the end of the nineteenth century, the AMA and others focused on proving that blacks were worthy of citizenship.

Education has been called both "the guardian and cultivator of a democratic and egalitarian political culture in the U.S." and the most important institution for improving U.S. race relations.[79] Yet, without careful attention to justice in the administration of education, schooling can prove a powerful legitimating force for inequality and exclusion.[80]

Segregation in Higher Education

This book offers a little-known prequel to the desegregation and resegregation of U.S. education in the twentieth century. The majority of American students once again attend intensely segregated schools. This is true not only of primary and secondary schools, but also in higher education.[81] Yet segregation is largely masked by our faith that academic merit is class and color-blind. It is sobering that few selective universities today achieve the diverse enrollment of Oberlin in the 1860s, and they lag far behind either Howard or Berea during this period. As of 2014–2015, blacks make up 11 percent of the student body at Harvard, 9 percent at Yale, 7 percent at Wellesley, and 5 percent at Smith.[82] Many colleges and universities publicize only enrollment figures for students of color as a group, hiding the low enrollments of U.S.-born blacks. Berea College, impressively, boasts black enrollment of 21 percent of its student body (and a higher endowment than Oberlin College), but this is still less than half of what it was in the 1880s. The figures for flagship public universities are rarely more encouraging. Blacks made up 3.5 percent of the student body at The Ohio State University, 4.25 percent at the University of Texas, and 4 percent at the University of California at Los Angeles; Rates are higher in Southern states with large black populations, such as 12 percent at the University of Alabama, 13.4 percent at University of Mississippi, and 17 percent at the University of South Carolina.

In spite of a dramatic increase in college enrollment, there is a deep fractionalization by race and class in the type of higher education institutions students attend. Between 1995 and 2009, freshman enrollments of black students increased by 73 percent. Despite this, white and black students attend dramatically different types of higher education institutions. Roughly 70 percent of black students entered open enrollment or two-year college programs, while 82 percent of new white students entered the 448 most selective colleges in the United States.[83] We see a dramatic increase in access to higher education, but this occurs in a dual system of racially separate pathways. These dual pathways quietly determine graduates' access to occupational sectors, professional prestige, and economic prosperity. This is hardly a new trend, however, and we can find its roots in the very development of higher education from 1865 to 1900.

Contemporary court cases like *Fisher v. the University of Texas-Austin* remind us that higher education remains a high-stakes political arena. In 2012, the U.S. Supreme Court heard arguments for Abigail Fisher, a white petitioner who sued on the grounds that the University of Texas violated the Equal Protection Clause of the Fourteenth Amendment when it denied her admission. In its 2013 ruling, the Supreme Court noted that "racial classifications are constitutional only if they are narrowly tailored to further compelling governmental interests," and outlined the possibility for racial inclusivity to foster dialog and break down stereotypes (Grutter 539 U. S., at 326).[84] The question of who benefits from racially integrated schools is old indeed, and can be traced back to the 1850 case of *Roberts v. Boston* (59 Mass. 5 Cush. 198), in which Benjamin Roberts sued to allow his five-year-old daughter Sarah to attend an all-white school much closer to her home. Charles Sumner, a powerful Radical Republican, joined with Robert Morris, one of the first black lawyers to practice in the United States, and their efforts succeeded in legally banning segregation in Massachusetts public schools. Like future school desegregation cases, Sumner and Morris argued that segregation caused individual anguish.[85]

Yet the importance of Fisher and previous cases is not limited to the trajectories of individual college graduates. The University of Texas, for instance, defends its use of race-conscious admissions by invoking civic values, arguing that there is an "expectation that many of its graduates will become state and national leaders."[86] In this view, university education is foundational for a pluralistic society because, without integrated higher educational opportunities, pathways to power and professional status are also segregated.

Recent resegregation of primary and secondary schools is most often explained by districts' release from court orders or residential segregation.[87] These explanations are important for understanding the degree of influence exerted downward from political institutions to local practice. Yet the cases studied here remind us that segregation can occur independent of legal action or demographic shifts.

Too often, policy-makers, journalists, and scholars address the challenges of educational segregation by focusing on *access*—whether by increasing the "pipeline" to college or encouraging "grit" in low-income students and students of color. Addressing diversity only through a lens of "increasing access" obscures the deep roots of segregationist organizational structures in higher education. In this book, I will show how some of these structures came about. In addition, this examination of interracial coeducation in the late nineteenth century suggests some much-needed lessons for how integrated organizations *can* be developed and maintained. In particular, as discussed above, these cases suggest that interracial *contact* is not the same as more thoroughgoing coeducation. In addition, we will see how the search for resources in a competitive environment can lead private organizations to abandon practices of integration. At the very least, these cases remind us that segregated schools should not be a taken-for-granted feature of American education.

Moving Forward

Why did integrated education generate so much interest after the Civil War? The next chapter contextualizes the anti-caste movement and the postwar rush to launch a mass education system in the South. Integrationists argued that segregation—and maintaining two separate school systems—demanded an irrational and excessive cost. But by filling the void, charitable funds enabled this disparity.[88] Benevolent organizations relieved Southern states of their responsibilities to enforce constitutional commitments to public education. As the following chapters will show, this reliance on private largesse—whether through benevolent organizations or the capitalist philanthropy that followed in subsequent years—had profound consequences for the kind of education groups were able to access.

Chapter 3 provides a local analysis of lived experiences on three integrated college campuses. Berea, Howard, and Oberlin differed in racial composition, recruitment strategies, and black representation in faculty and administration. This shaped the forms of interracial cooperation on campus. Nevertheless, all three colleges struggled to resist segregationist pressures from beyond the campus gates.

Chapter 4 explains how racial coeducation at Berea, Howard, and Oberlin was undermined when, for the first time, colleges began to compete with one another. As education for blacks and mountain whites was increasingly defined as "charity," the colleges faced increasingly stiff competition for donations, as well as the attention of the AMA. Whereas students' higher education choices had previously been organized around religious disciplines and familial legacies, by the mid-1880s a competitive field of higher education emerged. As the chapter shows, law, migration, and external organizations played important roles in diffusing particular models of higher education. In response to competition in this growing field, Berea, Howard, and Oberlin differentiated their positions to maintain resource streams while activating unique articulations of race, class, and gender.

In an era prior to selective admissions, colleges began to distinguish themselves on two dimensions in the 1880s—by curriculum and as appropriate for certain "types" of people. This had gendered, as well as racialized dimensions. Chapter 5 explores the intersection of racial and sexual politics in structuring various forms of higher education for women. A particular private organization—the Association of Collegiate Alumnae (ACA), now the American Association of University Women—played an important role in structuring women's higher education. For the first time, the ACA initiated an evaluative campaign to measure the quality of higher education opportunities. This produced the first systematic efforts to commensurate educational offerings across colleges. Like contemporary rankings, this system exerted discipline on both coeducational and single-sex colleges.

Chapter 6 explores the paths Howard and Oberlin took to attain elite status. The field of higher education increasingly emphasized liberal arts education for white elites and industrial training for blacks.[89] Yet both Howard and Oberlin framed their students as having a unique capacity for leadership. Indeed, until the early 1900s, Howard was more likely than Oberlin to be linked in the press to the universities that have since been dubbed "the Ivy League" than to other predominately black schools.

Both Howard and Oberlin prioritized masculinity. While neither banned women, as did other universities, women were deprioritized in their ascension to elite status.

In chapter 7, we follow Berea's leaders as they constructed Appalachians as a particular brand of poor whites, and without the stigma of the Confederacy attached to other Southern whites. By the mid-1880s, a new wave of benevolent agencies launched a new form of colleges designed for this newly categorized group—"mountain education." The mountain education movement treated poor white Southerners as deserving of Northern philanthropic aid by arguing that class oppression could rival racial oppression. Here we see how competitive dynamics, as navigated by organizational leaders, produced not only particular types of education but also consecrated groups of people.

From the democratization of the Morrill Act and the anti-caste colleges to President Obama's push to expand universal free community colleges, and at many moments in between, campus life has been a place of unparalleled optimism. This book provides one story of both the possibility of social change through higher education and the real limits of this approach. Tracing out the implications of efforts to realize ambitious ideas from the private sector remind us of the importance of the state and democratic process. Big ideas abounded, whether in the AMA's mission to undo caste-based foundations of American society, the ACA's charge to securing rigorous standards for women's higher education, or efforts by Rockefeller's General Education Board to structure the field of higher education. In the case of the AMA, we can feel sympathetic to their impulse to circumnavigate the state. After all, the Southern states were often dominated by the racist ideologies. And large contributions by wealthy capitalists are often interpreted as generosity—whether oil and railway magnates of the Gilded Age or the Silicon Valley set of today. Yet, if education is a key power to shape democratic institutions, then protecting transparency and the democratic process in making decisions around education is essential for creating a society that is not just generous, but also just.

CHAPTER TWO

Education Follows the Flag

> We have stayed and rebuked the spirit of Southern barbarism
> by military power, but the schoolmaster must finish what the
> sword has so well begun.
>
> —*CHICAGO TRIBUNE*, May 20, 1865

> I am not asking for sympathy at the hands of abolitionists,
> sympathy at the hands of any. I think the American people are
> disposed often to be generous rather than just. I look over this
> country at the present time, and I see Educational Societies,
> Sanitary Commissions, Freedmen's Associations, and the
> like—all very good: but in regard to the colored people there is
> always more that is benevolent, I perceive, than just, manifested
> towards us. What I ask for the Negro is not benevolence, not
> pity, not sympathy, but simply justice.
>
> —FREDERICK DOUGLASS, "What the Black Man Wants,"
> April 1865, Annual Meeting of the Massachusetts
> Anti-Slavery Society in Boston

Peace felt fragile. Politicians believed that the policies for Reconstruction—
that is, the conditions under which the former Confederate States could
rejoin the Union—would either create lasting peace or reignite violent
conflict. Congressman Thaddeus Stevens described the demands of brokering a reunion: "Holding [the ex-Confederacy] like clay in the hands
of the potter, we must see that no vessel is made for destruction."[1] Despite widespread distrust and anger, few pushed to have Confederates
stand trial. In fact, only two Confederates were charged with war crimes.[2]
Instead, Republicans struggled to create policies to safely reunite the nation and honor Lincoln's wish of brokering peace "with malice toward
none." In his second inaugural address, Abraham Lincoln pledged to
"bind up the nation's wounds," but his assassination laid bare the depth
of that challenge. The daunting challenge was to reconcile hostile ene-
mies and build a new social order—one that would secure lasting peace.[3]

This chapter investigates four popular proposals for Reconstruction
policy—the importation of Northern immigrants to manage agricultural

labor, land redistribution, voting rights, and military occupation. Each of these proposals promoted particular goals for reorganizing the social order. It explains how school-building triumphed over all of them.

Between April and December 1865, when Congress was in an eight-month recess, important debates occurred about how exactly to reconcile deep intraparty differences. There was broad support for some form of Northern tutelary power over the South. Tutelary governance has wider latitude in exercising control and, in exchange, political subjects learn how to fulfill their obligations as citizens.[4] The new federal BRFAL set out to structure this tutelary control of the former Confederacy. The *Chicago Tribune* reported that BRFAL operated as a "school of education in the practical administration and in the value of government."[5] The BRFAL "school" instructed Southerners by managing the extension of civil and social rights to black citizens—through court proceedings, by monitoring labor contract negotiations and disputes, by legally consecrating marriages, and by policing against white-on-black violence.

For the first time, rights were made available to blacks and secured with state protection. Southern whites, predictably, were hostile to the new mandate that empowered the state to govern both the civil rights of blacks and black-white interactions. That rights of any sort should flow from the state to black citizens, unfiltered through white intermediaries, ran contrary to the exclusive control to which Southern whites'—and many Northern whites—were accustomed.[6]

Yet, there were contradictory opinions among legislators and journalists as to who should be the focus of this tutelage. As Americans debated the best path for Reconstruction, the discussion quickly centered on the types of rights appropriate and necessary for the "imagined futures" of three Southern groups—the planter class, poor whites, and blacks. Journalists, politicians, and leaders of influential voluntary associations weighed the comparative merits of these three groups. Though the historical record has largely focused on whites' skepticism about blacks' capability for citizenship, many Northerners were equally concerned by the political choices that poor whites might make. In fact, Reform Republicans believed blacks were the best guardians of republican values in the South, as evidenced by the service of 200,000 black Union veterans and their likely allegiance to the Lincoln party and emancipation. By contrast, Conservatives did not view race-based hierarchy as fundamentally incompatible with republican governance, and they pushed for "qualified suffrage," or restricting the vote to only those who were educated.

All agreed, however, that poor whites posed a substantial challenge. They were derided as recalcitrant, uneducated, and aligned with the planter class out of "race pride." Conservative and reform-minded Northern Republican elites were split over the forms of citizenship to offer black and white Southerners. There were three main factions within the Republican Party after the Civil War: Conservatives, Moderates, and Radicals. Conservatives were tied to President Johnson and prioritized economic stabilization. Moderates followed Lincoln, and Radicals were linked to William Henry Seward and Charles Sumner. For the purposes of this chapter, Moderates and Radicals are collapsed to "Reform" Republicans, following the terms used by the newspaper sources for this chapter, the *New York Times* and the *Chicago Tribune*. Conservatives feared exacting punitive measures against white planters while Reformists—both Moderate and Radical Republicans—saw disrupting planter class power as the only path to safe reunion. The wealthy planter class was a small fraction of the Southern population and few imagined it truly possible to constrain their rights for any length of time. Conceptualizing democracy as truly representative, political debates focused largely on winning the loyalty of poor whites and blacks.[7]

These debates explored what it meant to be a citizen—that is, what rights citizens have, how they gain them, and how they lose them. But these debates also reveal the instrumental use of categorical groupings to adjudicate questions about citizenship. Citizenship rights are one outcome of a variety of possible configurations of national membership rules rather than "ready-made" by the state and attached to individuals.[8] The most expansive mode of citizenship allows for an array of rights—political, social, civil—and limited mediation by supervisory agents. Citizens leverage different degrees of access to these rights, in large part because of their social status or symbolic value. Child citizens have few rights for political participation and limited social rights; they may access education but not work. Adult citizens, too, access citizenship differently, dependent upon class or race.[9] In different political contexts, prisoners are stripped of their right to vote, either for the period of their incarceration or permanently. The political rights of women have been, at different times and places, filtered through male heads of household. Political and social rights are distributed differently, not individually; they are based on constructions of the value of different groups to the nation. How are such delineations of rights made legitimate?

Americans debated the rights of citizenship during a historical moment when there was little consensus regarding the boundaries between social groups or what made those boundaries valid.[10] When Congress resumed session, a Republican supermajority enabled them to sweep aside presidential Reconstruction measures and institute policy in accordance with their ideological interests.

Since no government agencies had the capacity for Reconstruction, Congress created the BRFAL as a subunit of the U.S. Department of War on March 3, 1865.[11] Congress, however, recessed before outlining a precise directive for BRFAL intervention. BRFAL agents became "street-level bureaucrats"—adjudicating directives and creating new programs at the local level. Actors negotiated the reach of the state through debates over imposing martial law on the South, whether to allow benevolent societies to administer education systems, and under what conditions federal intervention was justified in imposing requirements for civil society and labor agreements. In June 1865, the BRFAL commander, General O. O. Howard, stated, "the task before the bureau is already so great that it will not undertake the establishment and conduct of any system of schools."[12] Despite this reluctance, within a matter of months Howard saw education as the cornerstone of BRFAL efforts.[13] As commissioner of the BRFAL, General Howard initially supported land redistribution, as proposed by black leaders on the Georgia Sea Islands. When that option was revoked, Howard considered freedmen's education as the most possible form of compensation for unrequited labor and military service. As Howard described the duty of the BRFAL to the AMA: "The Freedmen's Bureau (is) an institution demanded alike by the wants of Freedmen and the best interests of the country. . . . This bureau has been to the Freedman a wall of defense in danger, a source of prudent supply in a time of sore need, an efficient help in the paths of knowledge; to the country, it has been a wise expenditure in payment of the vast debt due to the colored man."[14]

Pursuant to the 1867 Reconstruction Act, Congress required that ex-Confederate States write new constitutions including provisions for public education as part of their reapplication to the Union.[15] This called for a dramatic expansion of social policy in the South. Only forty years earlier in New England, the first secretary of the Massachusetts State Board of Education, Horace Mann, led the charge for common schools—publicly available, tax-funded primary education.[16] The development of mass education had yet to take hold throughout the South. But through the work of BRFAL and the AMA southern education was set to expand greatly.

Republican Tutelage or Racialized Tutelage for the South?

Policy adoption required entrepreneurs to craft administrative systems that complimented federal efforts or depended on others to supply needed resources. Many powerful actors preferred other options: securing Northerners to manage Southern agricultural production, land redistribution, extended military occupation, or expanded voting rights. Surprisingly, however, these debates rarely referenced the financial cost of programs. Instead, the debates centered on the authority of the state to intervene—whether in confiscating land or requiring proof of literacy to vote—and moral characterizations of the groups in the South. Who required reformation? What measures would best produce the desired changes in behavior and attitudes to ensure national unity?

It is easy to dismiss the potential for state intervention during Reconstruction by falling back on the familiar trope of the American state as weak. Yet as Desmond King has argued, this depiction ignores the state's strength in protecting the rights of the white planter class. Indeed, efforts to reform the South were constrained in deference to Southern white demands for a particular type of government. As King argues, "Southern-type segregation was more integral and universal to the U.S. Federal government and to governmental programmes than commonly recognized."[17] Similarly, Ira Katznelson highlights the embedded nature of racial segregation into the workings of the state, shaping who the state chooses to champion or neglect.[18]

By analyzing thematic clusters of policy recommendations and logics in 1865, two dominant models emerge: Conservative "Racialized Tutelage" and Reformist "Republican Tutelage." These models differed in the types of rights they proposed to allocate to different groups. Understanding these fundamental concerns, embedded in the policy proposals, is critical to understanding how schooling triumphed as the most pervasive program in Reconstruction policy. The struggles surrounding the various "rights packages" embedded in the four policy options illuminate how discursive, evaluative processes of categorization structure modes of citizenship. The campaigns for various rights packages depended heavily on "equalization strategies," or discerning appropriate comparisons between groups.[19] Importantly, antebellum voting rights were locally determined with no federal directive in place, and proof of citizenship was often not required to vote.[20]

Republican Tutelage Reformists highlighted the need for social recognition as a precursor to political rights. The question of Southern blacks' social status was tightly coupled to the question of citizenship; to retreat from the promise of Southern blacks' inclusion would divorce Reconstruction from ideals many Republicans deemed essential to establishing a peaceful Republican society. They pushed for a class-based society to replace the racialized caste hierarchy. For instance, a journalist for the *New York Times* compared blacks and poor whites to European serfs to highlight slavery as a barrier to modern governance: "Looking back to the old social positions of the South, we find a landed aristocracy controlling its policy. Without the formal titles of rank, they had all the essentials of a class nobility. They were the magnates of the land, holding the "poor-whites" in a political subjugation designed to keep them ignorant and debased, and maintaining this subjugation by the strong contrast afforded by the condition of the enslaved blacks."[21]

Republican Tutelage Reformists saw the planter class as the greatest threat to creating a lasting peace, believing that empowering Southern blacks would temper the political might of the planter class. Reformists argued that the entire region required a political education that used courts, labor arrangements, and local governance as "classrooms" for training in civil, political and social relations—a Republican Tutelage model. This view maintained that white Southerners constituted the greatest threat to political stability: "The interest of both State and of the nation would be better subserved by excluding the white rebel minority than by excluding the loyal black majority of the people of the State."[22] Radical Republicans, black and white abolitionists, and many other progressive Northern elites shared these views. Discursively, Reformists used color conscious language to draw attention to the planter-class oppression of blacks and poor whites.

A second frame package, Racialized Tutelage, prioritized revitalizing the Southern economy, viewing radical interventions to the social hierarchy as threatening political stability. Conservatives advocated a program of Racialized Tutelage to retain the racial hierarchy while reincorporating the South. Blacks were depicted as "wards of the State," requiring "friendship" and "counsel" to school them in the "values of industry, self-reliance, and all the manly virtues."[23] This view underscored that blacks were ill-prepared for political rights. Advocates embraced a discursive strategy centered on individualistic merit and embraced colorblind language: "He who is most meritorious, and virtuous and intellectual, must stand highest, without regard to color."[24] This stance articulated that whites would naturally recognize blacks' merits, and negated the likelihood of racial discrimination. Reluctant to undermine state sovereignty, Racialized Tutelage supporters disavowed federal interventions writ large. Above all, they advocated differentiated citizenship rights for Southern whites and blacks by arguing that Northern intervention threatened Southern economic activity and risked provoking whites to further violence. At every turn, Conservatives opposed proposals that risked angering the planter class.

As these options were debated, the discussions shaped both how actors viewed particular groups of people in the South—namely freed blacks, poor whites, and the white planter class—and how these assumptions and representations were incorporated into policy programs. As Marc Steinberg argues, "Discourse mediates power by facilitating the social action of control and exploitation. It is a form of power, for through it consciousness is shaped and possibilities for action and change are culturally constituted."[25] Through these proposals—some adopted, some dismissed—we see how Reform and Conservative Republicans built on their expectations about groups to broker a compromise for Reconstruction strategy. Understanding the process by which education became a major force in reconstructing the South also reveals why particular types of education became available and linked to political and citizenship status, as explained in the chapters that follow.

Proposed Reconstruction Strategies and Divergent Ideas of Citizen Incorporation

During the 1865 congressional recess, President Johnson set his course for Reconstruction into action. While Republicans turned to Europe to envision a post-emancipation future without the vestiges of monarchial rule, some planters envisioned new lives in Latin America—in Brazil, Cuba, Venezuela, or Mexico. But most returned quickly, disenchanted by the strangeness of their new surroundings and without fear of federal reprisal.[26] Johnson's program of extending pardons was roundly mocked for allowing wholesale admission of former Confederates. Johnson allowed unexpected levels of state-controlled policy, including allowing former Confederates to hold federal office. His policies prioritized reunification, remaining neutral when Southern whites enacted "black codes" that closely replicated the conditions of slavery. A report to the president and Congress lambasted codes enacted in Vicksburg, Mississippi as a "striking embodiment of the idea that although the former owner has lost the individual right of property in the former slave, 'the blacks at large belong to the whites at large.'"[27] Such codes were often set at the municipal level, and ranged from imposing curfews to restricting travel or imposing forced labor—unpaid "apprenticeships"—on "idle" black youth. The moral undertone of Confederate pardons and black codes structured the debates and the interpretation of various policy proposals crafted at the time and put forth in the media.

There was widespread dissatisfaction with President Johnson's Reconstruction program. The media offers a window to understand how Northern elites envisioned the work of Reconstruction. Such "eventful" moments make visible the multiple matrices actors use in establishing "competing grammars of worth" as legitimate and viable during evaluative stages of policy deliberation.[28] The political process of policy deliberation has been conceptualized as one of choice and constraint, with choices narrowing, funnel-like, through the deliberative process. Critical events offer opportunities to witness how policy choices crystalize. Adam Slez and John Levi Martin describe the importance of studying these types of political events as a chance to understand "political choice unencumbered by existing political structures," which "gives us the chance to witness the encumbering process itself."[29] This characterization is also apt for media deliberations. During the mid-nineteenth century, newspapers were tightly wed to political parties, and journalists freely offered opinions as part of their reportage.[30] These debates rendered certain policy options legitimate for consideration when Congress resumed in December 1865, while deflating others. The policy options were complex packages of ideas about the types of rights necessary for building a strong citizenry. Embedded within these rights packages were a mix of hopes, fears, assumptions, and expectations for particular divisions of citizens. The debates in major newspapers uncloak discursive strategies used to structure policy options, describe appropriate rights, and decide on the role of the state.[31]

Four options garnered the largest share of media discourse, which I call "Northern Masters," "Land Redistribution," "Political Rights," and "Military Occupation." These represent a continuum of rights and autonomy that Northern elites considered extending to Southern whites and blacks. The Northern Masters program advocated enticing Northern immigrants to manage Southern agricultural production. Land Redistribution extended the right to control one's labor and establish a baseline of self-sufficiency. Proponents asserted the primacy of land rights for blacks to leverage security and disrupt the plantation elite's land monopoly. Others prioritized Political Rights, arguing "there is a power in citizenship that can touch, as with a rod of magic, the status of the freedmen."[32] This view advanced that the eligibility to vote engendered expansive status changes as the new status would force politicians to work for new voters' interests. Finally, the fourth option, Military Occupation, favored military supervision to supervise interracial labor negotiations, courts, governance, and social relations. As this chapter will show, school-building proved an unexpected compromise between these four options.

Importing Northern Masters

In 1861, New York City mayor Fernando Wood proposed that the city secede from the Union. New York City would model its status on the "free cities" of Northern Germany. Though Wood's drastic suggestion was not adopted, it reveals the North's dependence on the Southern economy. Wood feared that without Southern trade, New York City's economy would crash. Northerners were desperate to quickly revitalize the Southern agricultural economy because the broader American economy depended so heavily on the South. Conservatives feared that provocative reforms would only exacerbate racial hostility and "repel capital."[33] Blacks' labor would be controlled by others. "There is no choice but for the government *both to protect and to direct*" former slaves, opined the *New York Times*.[34] Finding little support for making the federal government an overseer, Conservatives settled on a new course with volunteers in lieu of federal agents: "We must find employment for them in the Southern States, and if it can be done in no other way, it must be done by giving them new masters. If the Southern landowners will not give the negroes an opportunity to work, northern employers will be found to colonize the South."[35]

The Northern Masters plan encountered staunch resistance, both from Southern whites and blacks who wanted labor conditions similar to those of Northern white workers. The press reported gruesome attacks by white Southerners against these Northern migrants, and blacks often resisted employment that too closely mimicked the conditions of slavery.[36] Many fled to urban areas, where increased military surveillance offered greater protection from white reprisal. Conservatives described their flight as shirking from labor. Reform journalists and politicians responded that if blacks were unwilling to resume agricultural labor, it was due to unfair labor conditions: "In educating the freedmen to the habits of industry, the North must be the teacher. The South is committed to the belief that they will not work except under the lash, and it is not to be expected that they will prove apt scholars under such instruction."[37] The Northern Masters proposal urged postponing decisions on political rights for both blacks and former Confederate whites. Northern intermediates would temper social relations between whites and blacks in order to regenerate the Southern agricultural economy. Whites were unfit until they yielded their domination over blacks, and many worried that slavery had ill-prepared blacks for independence. Only Northern colonialism could stabilize the South and revive the economy.

Land Redistribution

When General Sherman met with black leaders in January 1865, their recommendation unanimously called for black land ownership. Impressed by the black communities on the Georgia Sea Islands, where for several years blacks had organized self-sustaining agricultural communities, Sherman penned Special Field Order 15 to reserve land in Georgia and South Carolina for black farmers. Newspapers frequently reported on the success of autonomous black farming communities. Davis Bend Plantation was a particular media favorite. Following military confiscation, 7,000 acres were redistributed to black farmers in 1864. Journalists highlighted the poetic justice of a well-organized black farming community on a plantation formerly owned by the family of Jefferson Davis, former president of the Confederacy, "the place where 'foulest treason had had its chosen seat.'"[38] Another such community in Virginia was hailed for its "industrious, self-supporting black population of some eight hundred families" with farms, local stores, and trade unions. Calling for barriers to safeguard against returning white planters repossessing their lands, the *Chicago Tribune* rejoiced that "these freedmen so far from being a weight upon the Government or their neighbors show a property roll of $51,000 in their own right." Praising such communities as important for undermining oligarchy, the *Tribune* added, "nor is this all in the hands of a few fortunate owners."[39] Reports of autonomous black communities countered claims that blacks were not "prepared for freedom." They emphasized that the true obstacle to economic revitalization—and a stable middle class—was the planter class monopoly.

In the mid-nineteenth century federal land disbursement was common practice. Multiple federal land redistribution programs were in operation, including the 1862 Homestead Act and the disbursement of 100 million acres of Western land to any citizen or "intended citizen."[40] Land ownership seemed to promise the security and an economic foundation for a future as autonomous citizens. Most Americans lived in rural areas or small towns, where owning land enabled self-sufficiency. Confiscating lands would break the planters' monopoly and forge a new middle class in the South.

During the summer of 1865, President Johnson dispatched General Carl Schurz on a tour to assess the situation in the South. Over three months he traveled through Alabama, Georgia, Louisiana, Mississippi, and South Carolina. Schurz was particularly well-suited for the job. Schurz was one of more than 4,000 Germans who fled after the failed revolution of 1848. A political exile, Schurz found refuge in Switzerland, Scotland, England, and France before arriving in the United States. Seeing a similar struggle for freedom in his new country, he passionately joined the abolitionist cause. He found himself in Europe again when, in 1861, Lincoln dispatched him as minister to Spain, but he soon returned to serve in the Union Army. By the time he embarked on his tour, he had been a keen political observer for over twenty years. His experiences in post-revolution Europe gave him a unique perspective for understanding the crisis in the United States. Schurz described the difficulty in persuading the planter class to accept compensated labor and blacks' rights to choose their employers: "Every irregularity that occurred was directly charged against the system of free labor. If negroes walked away from the plantations, it was conclusive proof of the incorrigible instability of the negro, and the impracticability of free negro labor."[41]

Schurz's travels impressed upon him the importance of giving blacks the means to self-sufficiency. The intransigent racial hostility Schurz witnessed sensitized him to the improbability of Southern whites accepting blacks as equals for many years to come. Schurz found Southern whites irrational: "It frequently struck me that persons who conversed about every other subject calmly and sensibly would lose their temper as soon as the negro question was touched."[42] Schurz's tour—combined with similar reports from Northern news correspondents—negated hope that even the most modest plans for black-white cooperation might endure absent federal intervention.

In his assessment report to President Johnson and the Senate, General Schurz recommended breaking the planters' monopoly.[43] Schurz's recommendations were endorsed as promising a "more wholesome sense of change from the old order of things among whites."[44] Even this would be insufficient, Schurz argued, to lasting peace unless planter class whites were displaced from their position of influence. Confiscation was framed as fitting punishment to planters' noncompliance with federal requirements to pay black workers: "This bigoted and stupid determination of the late rebels to impoverish themselves and let their plantations go to ruin rather than to employ labor ... is open rebellion against the emancipation policy of the Federal Government, not by armed force but by individual force, and should be met and treated as such—by confiscation of the property of the individuals who are responsible for these outrages."[45]

There were a number of factions within the Republican Party after the Civil War, and their differences were pronounced on the issue of land redistribution. Conservatives within the Republican party who opposed land redistribution were charged as "determin[ed] that the negroes must never become independent freeholders, but must remain homeless, landless plantation laborers forever."[46] Moderate Republicans marshaled congressional support but failed to make confiscation of Confederate lands part of the 1866 Southern Homestead Act. While 2.9 million acres were transferred, the path to accessing these lands was difficult. Without confiscation policies, white planters retained ownership of the best lands. Land redistribution advocates agreed "these people can take care of themselves, and, under Liberty, bring forth all the fruits of a prosperous and peaceful community."[47] Yet, land redistribution—and the autonomy it offered—threatened Conservatives' preference for segmented citizenship rights.

Radical Republicans viewed slavery as a problem of oligarchy, and considered the redistribution of Southern lands the best way of breaking up the planter class monopoly. The BRFAL initially included a charge to allocate abandoned Confederate lands. However, once it became clear that President Johnson would not pursue harsh punishment of Confederates, many planters returned to claim their lands—often forcing blacks who had worked the lands in their absence into new and unfair terms of labor. In 1866, Congress passed the Southern Homestead Act specifically for blacks and loyal (Unionist) whites to purchase lands in Alabama, Arkansas, Florida, Louisiana, and Mississippi. After the Civil War, many blacks also applied for Homestead Lands as an exit route from the South. By 1869, 4,000 blacks initiated the application process to gain land through the Southern Homestead Act.[48] The application process entailed many obstacles—application sites were difficult to reach and even relatively modest application fees were high for all but a few. Though it did not explicate political or civil rights, this option provided unmediated access to a basic social right, the control of one's labor.

Unlike the other dominant policy suggestions, journalists never discussed land redistribution as a means for the North to educate Southerners. Though many black activists deemed land ownership essential to their freedom, it was difficult to cultivate white support in either the South or the North. The 1865 legislation authorizing the BRFAL included a redistribution plan but did not confiscate land or inhibit exiled Confederates from returning to claim their abandoned lands.[49] In short, land redistribution was perhaps the best hope for blacks to begin autonomous lives as free citizens. It would position them in a similar status to many whites as self-sufficient farmers. And perhaps for exactly this reason, the plan failed to win broad support.

Military Occupation

The most frequently discussed plan for Reconstruction was military occupation. Most of the military battles were fought on Southern soil, and the Union Army carried out the work of the BRFAL across the South after the war. BRFAL agents were at work deciding how best to maintain peace, allocate rations, and foster fair working conditions. Many proposed expanding their powers. Military occupation was viewed in part as a Republican Tutelage project to educate Southerners. Military occupation would teach blacks to "wear the mantle of freedom" while whites learned respect for black personhood. General Schurz described, "When Southern people speak of the insolence of the negro . . . it is but very rarely what would be called insolence among equals. . . . A negro is called insolent whenever his conduct varies in any manner from what a southern man was accustomed to when slavery existed."[50] Schurz relayed to Congress the necessity of systematically cultivating Southern respect for blacks in order to secure any lasting change. Increasingly, Reformers sought plans that would engender a cognitive shift in whites' appraisals of blacks. They wanted to activate new meanings of race. Troop occupation would restrain whites and liberate blacks to freely exercise their rights: "A regiment of uniformed black men is a living gospel of political right to the black race around them. The very sight of it causes the black man to feel that he has or ought to have equal rights to life, liberty and the pursuit of happiness with the white. If this is the slaveholder's objection, and we think it is, then instead of removing the black regiments, double the number immediately. . . . If the presence of negro troops lends any additional confidence to the timid and long-suffering slave, to maintain his freedom and protect his rights, we are glad of it. By all means they must stay there—be increased and new armies of them, if need be, recruited till every slave in the South has shouldered a musket."[51]

Reformists also asserted that military occupation would suppress white violence against blacks while legitimating federal authority. Those promoting Republican Tutelage viewed attempts by the planter class to create unfair labor arrangements as in defiance of federal authority. They urged that blacks should be seen as the embodiment of the federal government. When blacks were attacked or harassed, it should be understood that "every such act is an act of war against the military authority of the Government. They should be taught that inasmuch as they have done unto the last of these black citizens, made free by Federal power, they have done it unto the Federal Government."[52] Reconstruction, Reformists argued, was the next stage of warfare: "It is no longer a war for the domestic, but [against] the social and political enslavement of the black race."[53] Military Occupation advocates promoted military force as necessary to restrain Southern whites. Without decisive federal intervention, emancipation without enforcement opened "the floodgates of slaveholding cruelty and rage without raising any barrier for his protection. It has given him the promise of liberty only to endanger his life."[54] Military occupation met both goals of the Reformist model of Reconstruction—securing the peace and providing an intermediary supervisory power over whites until they learned to conduct and respect Republican institutions.

Federal agents needed sophisticated diplomacy skills to mediate interracial contact. Where agents defended black rights, military occupation often yielded impressive results. An event in May 1865, however, illustrates the demands for diplomatic skill and for supervisory control in punishing Union agents who failed to live up to O. O. Howard's demands for enacting fairness. A public meeting was held in Charleston, South Carolina to discuss possibilities for reorganizing the state government. Several hundred white and black citizens gathered in Hibernian Hall, an impressive Greek Revival structure in the heart of Charleston. Union Army Lieutenant Bodine of the 127th New York Regiment asked that all blacks clear the hall, and as they withdrew, the whites cheered boisterously. After leaving for a few minutes, the blacks soon returned—this time cheering for themselves as they entered. In the commotion, a man stood and called for all "Union men" to remain in the hall and the meeting resumed and continued peacefully and produced a list of recommendations. The Union men numbered 40 whites and 150 blacks.[55] For his part in attempting to exclude black citizens from political participation, Lieutenant Bodine was found to have acted without authority and was arrested that same day.

Military occupation mediated whites' exercise of power by controlling whites' interactions with blacks. The success of military occupation often depended heavily on both troop density to suppress Southern whites and the attitudes of the Union officers in command. The *Chicago Tribune* explained: "One thing, however, is certain. In the work of reconstruction no mere theory or paper plan is so important as it is to build on the sure foundation of unconditional Unionism in the men selected or permitted to engage in the work."[56] Military occupation provided a system of checks and balances while whites learned to respect blacks' new social status. When the 1867 Military Reconstruction Act passed, it provided some resources but not the troop density needed to guarantee security throughout the South. All too quickly, Union troops were deployed to new battles in the West.

Political Rights

Not all citizens held the right to vote; as such, the question of black voting rights hinged on "equalization strategies," adjudicating whether groups were perceived as more similar to citizens who did not have voting rights or to citizens who did.[57] Even prior to emancipation in the

South, members of the 1853 Colored National Convention asserted that blacks' political rights precede immigrants': "We ask that in our native land we shall not be treated as strangers, and worse than strangers."[58] Conservatives wrestled for the appropriate comparison group for Southern blacks. Broadly speaking, three categories of citizens existed: enfranchised white males, "protected" citizens whose political representation was held by the family patriarch (white women and children) and "apprenticed" voters, generally immigrants, who were often delayed from voting for five years. In many states, however, noncitizens could vote.

Conservatives dismissed claims for universal male suffrage: "Mr. (Wendell) Phillips thinks that unless the negroes are at once admitted to vote, slavery will again be reestablished. . . . Every woman, every youth under twenty-one, every unnaturalized foreigner in Massachusetts is a slave, in that sense."[59] Some Republicans proposed an alternative pathway to citizenship that retained the selectivity of the franchise by proposing a merit clause. This proposal limited voting rights to those who could demonstrate proven loyalty to the Union through military service, rooting suffrage in the same masculine privilege through which many white colonial-era indentured servants acquired citizenship rights. While supporters of Land Redistribution and Military Occupation often supported black male suffrage as part of a larger policy package, this proposal addressed black suffrage as a stand-alone policy.

Reformists balked at reinstating ex-Confederates as voters unless blacks were granted the vote. The antebellum Constitution counted enslaved blacks as three-fifths of a person. If blacks were counted but ineligible to vote, the South would be awarded more seats—and thus, more power—in Congress. Most politicians assumed that blacks would remain loyal to the Party of Lincoln, and projected voting estimates accordingly. Delaying black voting rights raised fears of Confederate reprisal: "It is hard to see how the reconstruction of the State, on the basis of placing the feet of the white rebels on the necks of the black Unionists, can be safe either for emancipation or the Union."[60] Tactical-minded Republicans viewed black voters as critical to wresting political power away from the Democrats, the party which garnered the votes of the slaveocracy after the demise of the Whig party: "It follows then that in all the great former slaveholding counties and districts the old barons will still hold the sway that Slavery gave them and that the oppression of the poor-whites will be as grievous as ever before, and *the regeneration of the coun-*

try impossible."[61] Reformists required ex-Confederates to say shibboleth in some fashion. The acceptance of "universal freedom and equal human rights" was deemed a reasonable test of readiness for political sovereignty, and they demanded deeds, not verbal promises.[62] President Johnson pardoned individual Confederates who renewed their loyalty to the Union. Even Conservatives largely ceded that Johnson's "loyalty oath" pardons were meaningless but still rejected the Reform agenda that demanded proof of Southern contrition through the extension of rights to blacks. Conservatives refused to see blacks as the embodiment of federal authority in the South: "*Devotion to the negro, regardless of everything else, affords no proof of loyalty.* An anti-slavery man may be as thoroughly disloyal as a pro-slavery man; and if he holds the constitution and the Union—the authority and the supremacy of the government of the United States subordinate to his friendship for any class or race of men, and acts accordingly, he has no claim to be considered a loyal citizen—and still less has he any right to dictate a policy to the government."[63]

Conservatives, who initially viewed black suffrage as impossibly radical, softened their stance as the debate shifted from immediate, universal suffrage to qualified suffrage. Conservatives countered Reformist demands for universal male suffrage with "qualified male suffrage." Reformers offered a multifaceted assessment of desirable qualifications for voting rights, including literacy, property ownership, or demonstrated patriotism. As the idea of qualified suffrage took hold, the debate increasingly hinged on the educational achievement of Southern blacks and poor whites. Despite General Schurz's warning, policy options to suppress the planter-class oligarchy were losing support. Instead, Reformists demanded greater transparency for qualification for suffrage and equal application to blacks and whites: "We only ask that whatever qualified a white man to vote, whether it be property, knowledge, or patriotic blood shed in the service of country, shall also, if possessed by a colored man, qualify him."[64] In addition, as the *Chicago Tribune* wrote, "In deciding this question [Congress] themselves must determine the status of the four million of [sic] slaves whom they have made citizens of the United States, and must give some sound reason, why, as citizens, they are to be excluded from voting. If it be ignorance—exclude the ignorant. If it be poverty—exclude the paupers. If it be color—that is no sound reason. The path of justice is the path of safety."[65]

Qualified suffrage gained favor because it could be equally applied to whites. John Stuart Mill appealed to Republicans of both stripes when he enjoined, "I have no objection to requiring, as a condition of the suffrage, education up to the point of reading and writing; but upon condition that this shall be required equally from the whites. The poor-whites of the South are understood to need education quite as much as the negroes, and are certainly quite as unfit for the exercise of the suffrage without it."[66] If poor whites proved recalcitrant regarding school attendance, then their obstinacy would be understood as a rejection of the new culture of the Union. A literacy test would thus also eliminate white voters deemed uncooperative in the "new order of things." A literacy requirement would not disenfranchise the planter class, but their numbers were few. If blacks' school attendance and rapidly increasing literacy rates persisted, black voters would rapidly become a powerful Republican voting bloc. This was particularly true because blacks often far outnumbered planter-class whites in voting districts where the planter class held the most power.

This voting power could be strengthened if poor whites were encouraged to see their interests as aligned with blacks rather than with the planter class. Many, including President Johnson, considered the poor white class an important part of rebuilding the South. Andrew Johnson envisioned expanded opportunities for poor whites in a reconstructed South. As the *New York Times* reported, "The President means to build up a new and loyal class from the poor whites."[67] Journalists argued that blacks were not the only victims, and that poor whites had been excluded from the labor market by slavery and that slavery, as an institution, devalued educated, free workers: "The effect of two centuries of slavery on the 'poor whites' of the South has been terrible. When the war began they numbered four million, just about as numerous as the slaves—showing that to make a chattel of a black man required that a white man should be ruined. Shut out from the rich lands and impressed with the plantation idea that all manual labor degrades free people."[68] If poor whites could be impressed that their interests were consistent with those of Republicans, formal politics in the South would change dramatically.

These differences in adjudicating qualified suffrage reveal the deep impasse between Conservatives and Reformists. Conservatives imagined a logical foundation for whites' prejudice that blacks could overcome through hard work and education. Radical Republicans, on the other hand, viewed blacks as superior to Southern whites in political loyalty and educational ambition. They saw blacks—and potentially poor whites, if "converted"—as ballast to the planter class. The question of suffrage opened the door to debates over education. As other policy options faded—either for failing to offer sufficient grounds for compromise or due to resistance—education as a prerequisite to universal suffrage took hold as a reasonable compromise. But mass education in the South was severely underdeveloped and resistance to state expansion of social provisions remained a substantial barrier.

The Convergence of Policy Options and the Triumph of Education

Actors made sense of the process *temporis momentum*, and international comparisons helped make sense of an unsettled time. The international wave of revolutions in 1848 ushered in nationhood and republicanism, combating the vestiges of feudalism, including the abolition of peonage, colonial slavery, and monarchial rule. In Austro-Hungary, Brazil, France, Germany, New Grenada and elsewhere, revolutions rejected caste barriers as inconsistent with modern state-building.[69] The internationalization of anti-caste discourse was consecrated in new constitutions, for example, Germany (1849, 1871), Italy (1870), Panama (1863, 1865). This bolstered universal male citizenship as an important legitimatizing achievement. The international diffusion of abolitionism—whether from late-stage feudalism or slavery—discursively linked black Americans with broader peasant uprisings in a shared experience of oppression. Lincoln strategically issued the Emancipation Proclamation, leveraging European class politics to block England and France from contributing troops to the Confederacy. British workers held hundreds of meetings across the country to support black rights, which included important addresses by John Stuart Mill and Karl Marx.[70] These international comparisons encouraged an understanding of U.S. slavery as an institution that, like feudalism, was an outdated caste hierarchy.

American journalists and politicians frequently compared the Southern slave-holding class and French Bourbons, who overthrew post-revolution republican governance and replaced it with a constitutional monarchy. For instance, in the 1866 Joint Congressional Committee on Reconstruction hearing, General O. O. Howard interrogated a former Virginia legislator, who crystallized the comparison: "[White southerners] are waiting and hoping for a restoration of the Bourbons . . . to take possession of the United States government."[71] The comparison to France offered a cautionary tale that victories born of revolution could prove short-lived without strict enforcement. If the Southern oligarchy retained its political power, peace would be short lived. Extending the vote—and using black voters to stabilize the region politically—seemed to many Republicans the best protection against the feared resurgence of Southern oligarchy. In order to modernize the South and unite blacks and poor whites on Republican governance, Reformers argued it was necessary to break the racial caste system. They came to see schooling as a policy conducive to this goal, and to compromise with Conservatives.

Reformists testified that schools could foster republican governance in two ways. First, schools reduced white prejudice: "Marked influence of these schools is seen upon the white people in the lessening prejudice, in the admission of the African's ability to learn, and his consequent fitness for places in the world from which we have hitherto excluded him."[72] Not even the most optimistic imagined that these schools would reach children of the elite, however, wealthy planters were few in numbers. Still, schools could serve as a space to cultivate an alliance between blacks and poor whites by correcting for poor whites' misdirected racial animosity, a cleavage fostered by the planter class. Both Reformists and Conservatives were optimistic that that Southern whites' prejudice toward blacks would diminish as blacks demonstrated their intellectual capability and "merit" through educational achievement. School-building would encourage literacy among poor Southerners: "Not only the 4 million blacks, but the great body of the poor-whites of that section, have always been in densest ignorance."[73] These arguments assumed merit evaluation processes as objective: whites would rationally recognize blacks' achievements. Reformists supported measures ensuring blacks' access to schools, representation on juries and in politics, while Conservatives advocated gradual advances in economic and educational attainment. Education would ameliorate wealth inequality, racial prejudice, and regional differences. Furthermore, Racialized Tutelagists were comforted to see schools as a site where blacks remained under white supervision: "One thing is certain: [blacks] must be with white people and under their best influence and fostering care to attain their best state."[74] Unconvinced that black autonomy suited their economic interests, Conservative observers viewed schooling as part of a program to condition blacks into continued subservient status: "Give him teaching and education in every sense, and *discipline* too, good and thorough."[75] Absent a universal labor policy enforcing black agricultural labor, education could provide a means of "discipline" and white control over blacks. Schooling provided an arena of control, unlike land redistribution or universal male suffrage. By 1866, the *New York Times* interpreted John Stuart Mill's endorsement for school-building: "No better solution, than this of putting education with the reach of the freedmen, can be found for the serious problem of reorganizing society at the South in conforming with the new order of things, and of restoring something like real harmony of feeling and sympathy between North and South."[76] The *New York Times* attested that education served the "industrial interests of both races" by aligning expectations for the new social order, similar to the "master and servant relationships" found in the North. In this conservative formulation, education inculcated appropriate respect for a hierarchical social order.

Second, schools could address deficiencies among poor whites. This point was widely agreed on. The *Chicago Tribune* expressed that "in half of our country it has educated one class to be tyrants, another to be slaves, and a third to be barbarians. We must have free schools everywhere. Both for the blacks—whose enthusiasm to learn establishes their right to an education—and for the poor whites, whose contended solidity the nation must cure, because it cannot endure."[77] Analogizing the slaveholding South to European feudalism, one popular argument attributed secession to the absence of common schools in the South: "Many do not, we imagine, fully realize the issues of our democratic theories—see clearly the radical distinction between the American and the old world idea of government. Such discrimination is essential to conscious citizenship. The duties of maintaining and continually improving our public schools system cannot be too strongly urged upon the public attention.... *The real work of permanent Southern rehabilitation lies in this direction*. We have stayed and rebuked the spirit of Southern barbarism by military power, but the schoolmaster must finish what the sword so well began. Had the Northern system of public school instruction been adopted at the South, this late horrid rebellion would have been averted."[78]

Johnson, like Lincoln, drew upon his log-cabin childhood. Raised in eastern Tennessee, he championed self-sufficient rural America. In contrast to the "labor-stealing" planter class, self-sufficient yeoman farmers were championed as a group that might have been similar to staunch New Englanders, were it not for the contaminating effects wrought by the institution of slavery. The *Chicago Tribune* declared Northern and European immigrants, blacks, and Unionist poor whites the "new race of thorough Union men."[79] Johnson and others felt that the independent yeoman represented the Union ideal. But there were none who objected that this "new race" of Union men would benefit from more schoolhouses.

This would cultivate status competition among poor whites who, most imagined, would not wish to "fall behind" blacks' achievements. Schools organized by benevolent societies were overwhelmed by demand, and it was not uncommon for a single teacher to instruct a school of several hundred students of all ages. Although open to both races, benevolent societies like the AMA reported struggling to enroll whites who resisted integrated schools. Given this disparity in school attendance, some argued for deliberately leveraging whites' status anxieties: "The only means of keeping the freedmen from gaining upon the white race is by adopting the free school system of the Northern States, and arousing in the poor whites a new spirit that would prompt them to avail themselves of its facilities. It remains to be seen whether Southern legislators will have the wisdom and the energy to carry out this policy, and thus give the poor white masses a fresh impulse, or whether they will content themselves with simply seeking to plant obstructions in the path of the freedmen."[80]

In sum, schools proved less radical than alternative proposals that explicitly punished white Southerners and less aggressive than importing Northerners to supervise black laborers. Whereas land confiscation programs yielded no compromises, benevolent societies reported converting white planters to support schools as an incentive to retain black laborers.[81] Those who advocated Northern colonization as the best means to reorder social relations were often surprised to find that schools were a mutually agreeable compromise. Schooling was articulated as a means to produce a new class of voters and as a site to encourage and organize competition between blacks and poor whites. Thus, from its origins, Reconstruction school-building contained deep tensions about its goals.

A New Alliance: Public-Private Partners in Southern Education

In 1862, the Union Army captured and occupied New Orleans, the largest city in the South and home to more than 12,000 *gens de couleur libre*, as they were called. "Free persons of color" organized a broad range of civic and benevolent associations and owned nearly 3 million dollars in property. Many sent their children to private schools, while others were enrolled in integrated schools. When more than 10,000 blacks fled rural plantations for the safety of Union-occupied New Orleans, they were met by numerous voluntary associations—run by blacks and whites—who launched the first effort to organize schools for children previously enslaved. General Nathaniel Banks, who held command of occupied New Orleans, lent his authority to organizing eight "freedmen's schools" beginning in 1863. Banks had himself only attended school until the age of fourteen, at which time his family's circumstances compelled him to work as a "bobbin boy" in a textile factory in his Massachusetts hometown. The *Chicago Tribune* praised Banks for initiating a Board of Education to create the first interracial public schools in the territory under his command. The *Tribune* urged: "This is, however, but the beginning of a work which must spread over the entire Southern States, until both freed blacks, and the almost equally ignorant and even more degraded and vicious 'poor-whites' have been brought within its Christianizing and civilizing influences."[82]

Reformists also drew policy ideas from abroad in formulating education as a reunification strategy. Famed preacher Henry Ward Beecher addressed the AMA, the largest voluntary association in partnership with the BRFAL: "After the first Napoleon had crushed Germany like an egg shell, she did not commence fortifying by building castles and forts on her frontier; no, but a thorough and most extensive system of education for the people was soon inaugurated."[83] When Germany first inaugurated mass education, the first schools were created through religious orders and gradually transferred to the state. Many argued that a similar process could unfold in the South. Scant provisions for mass education existed in the South. The push for mass education in the region relied upon private voluntary associations.

At the war's end, benevolent organizations began a mass school-building project: "The Schoolmaster . . . should not wait till Southerners call them but they should go as good men go to India or Africa, bearing with them the light of intelligence, freedom, and civilization."[84] A cadre of volunteers was already in the field operating schools: "Wherever our armies have penetrated, the schoolmaster has followed close in their rear, . . . and (if) the government should decide that the education of blacks and 'white trash' at the South was a necessary part of the work of pacification and settlement, it would find the machinery already in place, and the work almost half done."[85] Private organizations entered the field of Southern education, expanding school-building projects begun by Union officers in 1863. The African Methodist Episcopal Church, the American Baptist Home Missionary Society, and the United Methodist

FIGURE 2. Emancipated slaves, white and colored: Wilson Chin, Charles Taylor, Augusta Boujey, Mary Johnson, Isaac White, Rebecca Huger, Robert Whitehead, and Rosina Downs, 1863. Photographer: Myron Kimball. Courtesy of the Charles L. Blockson Afro-American Collection, Temple University Libraries, Philadelphia, Pennsylvania.

Church also opened multiple colleges. The largest of these, the AMA, received the majority of the funding allocated by the BRFAL. The AMA, more than any other society, was eager to create interracial colleges as a contained space where blacks and whites could learn to interact as social equals.

In May 1865, BRFAL Commissioner General O. O. Howard insisted that creating a public school system in the South lay outside the purview of his organization. Yet, by the end of that summer, Howard pledged to 1,300 delegates of the American Institute of Instruction that the BRFAL would provide material support and military protection to benevolent associations undertaking Southern education projects at all levels—from adult education and primary schools to higher education.[86] General Howard prioritized teachers' beliefs about race in hiring to such a degree that he corresponded extensively with the benevolent associations organizing freedmen's schools. Howard personally evaluated individual teacher applications and rejected many who did not clearly express views consistent with the Republican Tutelage model.[87] The BRFAL was authorized to allocate funds to private organizations if they educated "loyal Refugees and Freedmen," that is, Unionist whites and blacks.[88]

The BRFAL provided material and logistical support to benevolent associations operating freedmen's schools in the South. In 1865–1866, despite terrible conditions, 1,293 Northern teachers arrived in the South.[89] These schools were funded largely by Northern church tithes and Southern blacks' donations.[90] This dependence left school-funding vulnerable, as donations depended upon depicting black personhood in accordance with Northern expectations. Freedmen's aid societies sold pictures of Southern slave children as a way to bring in donations. These images showed adults and children grouped together, reading diligently from their primers. Teachers testified to their convictions: "I defy any Northern skeptic to spend an hour in my school, and depart unconvinced that Southern negroes are endowed with not merely common but very noble manhood."[91] These testimonies to blacks' moral worth—and superiority over poor whites—were frequently reprinted in major newspapers, magazines, and fundraising campaigns. The romantic imagery of the Northern schoolmarm resonated strongly with Northern audiences who thrilled to stories of heroic black "children [who] come to school barefooted over the frozen ground" or "how earnestly those gray-haired men bend their wrinkled faces over the Freedmen's primers and how their countenances light up with joy."[92] Images of the freedmen learning to read and pictures of aged men and little children reading the Bible were morally compelling. Benevolent societies had decades of experience in mounting emotionally persuasive public abolitionist campaigns, and their experiences enabled them to again create a compelling case, activating widely shared moral beliefs that opponents could not fight. As later chapters will show, these campaigns were not without consequence. Such descriptions presented a picture of post-emancipation social relations many whites imagined appropriate, but left little space for black autonomy.

Local schools often expressed preference for black teachers, though this was shielded from most public campaigns. In a rare admission of the cooperation between the BRFAL, benevolent aid societies, and blacks, *Harper's Weekly* reflected on the first two years of education work in the South. *Harper's* advocated increasing the numbers of black teachers and preachers "as the only possible way of meeting the constantly increasing demand for them. With the aid of the Freedmen's Bureau, and by making all the use it can of the co-operation of the colored people, it has

FIGURE 3. *Emancipation* by Thomas Nash. King & Baird Printers, Philadelphia, circa 1865. Courtesy of the Historical Society of Pennsylvania.

already secured a large number of sites and buildings for high schools, normal schools, and incorporated colleges."[93] Press coverage of the education of the freedmen usually obscured the fact that, by 1868, the number of black teachers exceeded the number of white Northern teachers, and when the BRFAL shuttered, black teachers remained the majority of the teaching force.[94]

Benevolent societies largely appeared as the public face of the Southern school-building project. Though the BRFAL was quite involved in hiring teachers and logistical support, its role was largely shielded from public view. As such, the federal government took on a new dimension of welfare provision—establishing a new social obligation for education—while allowing opponents to see school-building as a charitable endeavor. As Elisabeth Clemens describes, "conflict over the role of public and private efforts in the relief of poverty is a durable feature of American history" whereby "discursive linking of economic independence and citizenship rights positioned relief and charity as key sites for struggles over political membership."[95] The AMA and other voluntary associations engaged in what Clemens has called obligation hoarding, by pushing for certain social responsibilities to fall under voluntary associations rather than the state. In doing so, they could control the scope and delivery of social programs. While the BRFAL provided limited material resources, the associations contributed staff, partial funds, and public campaigns to generate support for black education. As a result, a mix of public-private organization of mass education gained legitimacy as an acceptable mechanism for meeting the requirements of state duties. As federal occupation and federal oversight diminished, former Confederate states provided little in the way of material resources for mass education. Private organizations—churches and charities—staked an ever-increasing claim for the private administration of public goods.

From Primary to Higher Education

Scholarship on higher education has often assumed segregated education as a starting point.[96] More than a historical inaccuracy, this oversight has important theoretical consequences. If we instead examine the series of chain reactions through which a model grows, we can better examine the emergence of new types of organizations and larger fields.[97] Postwar higher education expansion did not lead to the diffusion and reproduction of a single model for higher education. Rather, educational entrepreneurs launched a host of experiments with new educational forms. Different schooling projects were not on separate tracks. Rather, they were connected in an increasingly competitive web. More generally, organizations do not emerge *ex nihilo*, but through the coevolution of multiple social networks.

The Civil War pushed college expansion with enrollment, which increased by 278 percent between 1869–1870 and 1899–1900.[98] Some of this growth can be explained by the influence of expanding educational opportunities for black students. Between 1834 and 1905, more than 100 colleges opened their doors as either colleges designated for blacks or proclaiming a welcome to both blacks and whites. Though blacks' access to educational opportunities beyond common schools in the South was largely restricted to private, religious colleges, the dramatic shift in college attendance also drove white enrollment.[99] Between 1865 and 1900 the proportion of women enrolled in college grew from one-fifth to over one-third, and a decade later 5,000 African Americans were college graduates.[100]

In addition to the BRFAL, the federal government directed the expansion of higher education through other means. Even before the war, Congress encouraged higher education expansion through the 1862 Morrill Act, which provided federal provisions for the creation of colleges to educate "the laboring classes." The Morrill Act apportioned 30,000 acres per each Senator and representative, which the states could sell to establish colleges. This was the first effort by the federal government to provide resources for the state support of higher education. These universities posed a distinct challenge to the existing form of higher education, because the Morrill Act proposed something quite new altogether: education for the laboring classes. The Act declared its purpose that each state should sponsor "at least one college where the leading object shall be, without excluding other scientific and classical studies, and including military tactics, to teach such branches of learning as are related to agriculture and the mechanic arts, in such manner as the legislatures of the States may respectively prescribe, in order to promote the liberal and practical education of the industrial classes in the several pursuits and professions in life."[101] This represented a bold new democratization of higher education and a substantial expansion of states' responsibilities.

When the Morrill Act passed, a substantial number of state universities were already in operation. Though contemporary politicians drew sharp lines between North and South, in fact, New England held an advantage in its private but not state-sponsored colleges. In the South, the University of North Carolina—founded in 1789—is the oldest public university. In 1801, South Carolina organized South Carolina College as part of a push championed by Thomas Jefferson to encourage Southern states to invest in public education as a means to unify citizens after the American Revolution. Thomas Jefferson designed the University of Virginia in 1819 to develop civic-minded public leaders, rather than clergy. North Carolina, South Carolina, Georgia, and Virginia all founded state-supported universities within twenty years of one another. After a few years of difficulty, the University of Alabama opened in 1831 with fifty-two students. Mississippi, too, had established a university prior to the Morrill Act. The Legislature chartered the University of Mississippi in 1844 and its first class matriculated in 1848. The federal government authorized the Alabama Territory to set aside land for a university prior to statehood. Florida founded a state-funded seminary in 1853 that would, following the Morrill Act, become the University of Florida. The University of Maryland—chartered in 1858 as Maryland Agricultural College—preceded the act by only a few years and awarded degrees to its first two graduates in 1862. In fact, only Kentucky and Louisiana were without some preexisting public university. In the Northeast, New Hampshire, Connecticut, Massachusetts, Maine, Rhode Island all founded state universities after the Morrill Act. New York founded Cornell University as its land grant university. These states were all home to well-established colleges and universities, but these were largely private and originally founded to educate clergy. A rare exception, the University of Pennsylvania, was founded as a private university to educate the business and ruling classes. Benjamin Franklin was influential in this aspect of the university's design. In New England, only Vermont had an existing public university when the 1862 Morrill Act passed.[102] By 1867, the federal government launched for the first time a federal Department of Education to regularly collect data and work in partnership with others to improve access to primary schools, high schools, colleges, and universities.

In summary, the difference between North and South prior to the Morrill Act was one of state funding for education, with private higher education taking center stage in the North and public higher education gaining greater support in the South. This neat distinction, however, could easily misconstrue the accessibility of these types of higher education. Just as Massachusetts denizens launched public high schools to funnel public funds to schools for which only children of the elite could access, in the South public universities were largely restricted to the sons of the white planter class.[103] While some states, most notably South Carolina, effectively though temporarily integrated public universities, these policies depended upon robust black political power.[104]

In South Carolina, where blacks comprised more than half of the representatives at the 1868 Constitutional Convention, provisions were also required for a state university. For instance, Representative Benjamin Randolph, who studied classics at Oberlin College, was instrumental in shaping higher education in South Carolina. As a Union Army chaplain, Randolph was the only black soldier in his unit. After the war, he was salaried by the AMA and the BRFAL as assistant superintendent of education for a large district headquartered in Charleston, South Carolina. This gave him opportunity to survey the conditions in the freedmen's schools. He drew upon these experiences in authoring the first provision for publicly funded education in South Carolina for the 1868 Constitutional Convention. The following year, South Carolina's legislature created an interracial, tuition-free university.[105] By contrast, the University of North Carolina shuttered its doors from 1871 to 1875 rather than integrate. It reopened as a white-only institution only after federal oversight of the state ended.[106]

This kind of resistance to public education encouraged many to support benevolent society-sponsored private colleges. Recognizing that Southern whites both lacked a tax base and largely resisted efforts to educate blacks, the AMA added privately funded colleges to their program. Many Republicans favored private organizations—like the AMA—to expand higher education in the South. Supporting private colleges allowed for the circumnavigation of democratic politics and depended on donor support rather than taxation. As we will see, this institution-building was contradictory. More doors opened, but they did not lead to equal opportunities.

Given that so few Americans graduated from college during the mid-nineteenth century, why would anti-caste organizers choose colleges as a home for their project? One reason is that private colleges did not require political consensus or local support. Reformers had seen Congress's failed attempts to promote integrated primary education. Extra-democratic autonomy in higher education meant that AMA colleges could appeal for donations outside of their local or regional base. Indeed, without donors in New York, Massachusetts, and various parts of England for instance, neither Berea nor Oberlin would have survived for even a decade. As part of their efforts to raise and maintain funding, college leaders launched vigorous public relations campaigns to place their schools in the media.

The second reason for the AMA to launch a network of colleges was that campus life provided a sheltered, controlled space where college administrators could realize their visions for the future. On campus, administrators could manage student relationships in classrooms and in extracurricular activities. They controlled hiring, scholarship, and curricula. As long as they could attract and retain students and donors, college administrators were free to mold their own social world. Advocates for the anti-caste colleges argued that campuses were best positioned to increase interracial social contact. Friendships fostered in the dining hall, classroom, or in work-study programs would make prejudice feel irrational. The president of Oberlin College described the campus' success in shaping common experiences that melted feelings of superiority. White students learned that "a supercilious air seems out of place. The lip that at first curled with contempt, will at length smile a recognition of a common humanity."[107] Coeducation, as initially designed by the anti-caste movement, intended to foster trust reciprocally among whites and blacks. At a time when so few Americans attained higher education, colleges seemed an unlikely place to build an anti-caste future, but founders and supporters envisioned that colleges—unlike primary and secondary schools—could operate outside the local context. This was important for organizations facing formidable local resistance.

The American Union Commission (AUC), like the AMA, was an anti-caste organization intent on "recognizing no distinctions of caste or color, [and] proffering its assistance to all men upon the score of a common humanity alone." General Howard endorsed the AUC in 1865: "Everything that you, as a commission, can do to facilitate industrial pursuits, to encourage education, and meet the wants of the suffering amongst the poor white people, who have been degraded by slavery, is collateral with my specialty, and meets my hearty sympathy and support."[108] However, the AUC made special efforts to avoid duplicating services with freedmen's aid societies and as such often enrolled more white students in its schools. Both organizations shared many members in common and viewed their work as building a cooperative network of schools in the South. In the aftermath of the war, and particularly with the victory of black male citizenship secured, the AMA emphasized the political importance of its anti-caste agenda. The AUC similarly declared: "This work is one not only of charity, but of patriotism. We have but one country. In the welfare of every part of America, all Americans possess an equal interest. Especially it is clear even to the least thoughtful that popular education is essential to the perpetuity of popular government."

The AMA evaluated the worth of groups by their past contributions—by military service rendered, "stolen" or uncompensated labor during slavery, and allegiance to Republican values. An AUC publication detailed how it allocated aid with descriptions of individuals. Among those who were provided "social relief" were "a very worthy colored woman, 75 years old; master turned her off; makes a little by washing; hasn't asked anything of the government. Says government set her free; thinks she ought to support herself now;" another woman with "five brothers in the Union army; three other relatives in the United States service; daughters took care of sick Union prisoners; 10 in family; no means. Husband ran off to avoid conscription; wouldn't fight, he said, against the old flag." In contrast to a list of the deserving, the AUC issued only one description of the sort of person they refused to assist: "Some came dressed in silks and furs, set off with jewelry, still clinging to their *effete* aristocracy. When they demanded assistance, we advised them to

sell their jewelry . . . they insisted that 'you have taken away our property [slaves] who used to support us, and now you are bound to feed
us.' "[109] The dividing lines in the immediate aftermath of the Civil War
were relatively straightforward and even expected: those who fought
against the Union as undeserving of Northern aid and those who defended the Union, as well as those harmed by the enemy of the Union,
were categorized as deserving.

By Reconstruction's end in 1877, at least sixty colleges were founded
explicitly for black students, and more were chartered as open to "all,"
and by the end of the century, nearly one hundred colleges reached thousands of students. In rare cases, colleges began recruiting black students
prior to the Civil War. For instance, its Board of Trustees asked Otterbein College to recruit black students in 1854. Otterbein's Board wanted
to align college practices with its religious values. More common, however, were new colleges founded after the Civil War that enrolled blacks
and whites together as part of a larger social mission. While many of
these predominately enrolled blacks, their charters stressed inclusivity
("open to all") and "useful" curricula to expand the middle class. The
language from the charter of Washburn College in Topeka, Kansas is
typical of these colleges. Founded in 1865 as Lincoln College, Washburn
garnered its funding through a New York abolitionist and pledged in its
charter "to afford to all classes, without distinction of color, the advantages of a liberal education, thus fitting them for positions of responsibility and usefulness."[110] These were not colleges to cultivate elites but—like
the Morrill Act—emphasized the importance of training a new middle
class.[111] Among colleges with anti-discrimination charters, demographic
enrollment varied widely. In some cases, like Washburn for instance,
very few black students enrolled; at others, like Hampton University,
very few whites enrolled.

Conclusion: School-Building as a Compromise of Tutelary Regimes

As the United States rebuilt its vision of the nation, not all citizens
emerged with the same degree of rights and freedoms; rather, varying
degrees of citizenship were created based on group membership. The historical moment that this chapter examines reveals the transparency with
which the rights of civic participation were deliberately linked to group

categories. It was widely understood that the political rights of groups would determine the form and style of governance available in the Republic. Policy choices were debated through narratives about the economic and political worth of Southern blacks and whites. When the Thirty-Ninth Congress resumed session on December 4, 1865, it rapidly passed more legislation than any prior Congress. The Thirteenth Amendment, abolishing slavery, was ratified two days after Congress resumed session on December 6, 1865.[112]

Activating and manipulating moral categories proved influential in shaping Reconstruction policy, leading to school-building rather than military occupation or the redistribution of material resources. Three of the policy packages required steep investments of resources. Northern Masters hinged upon black cooperation and Northern migration. Beyond troops to maintain peace, Military Occupation required staff skilled in the particular bureaucratic demands of their assignment (labor negotiation, adjudication of courts) and prepared to treat blacks as citizens. Land Redistribution required confiscation programs to dislodge the planter class from power. As debates turned to voting rights, both Conservatives and Reformists imagined a merit-tested franchise would permit the exclusion of "unfit" voters and spur interest in institutionalizing public schooling.

Reconstruction actors differed in how they imagined the importance of timing for various forms of citizenship rights. Reformists championed immediate universal male suffrage on the basis that blacks had already earned their political rights—that is, blacks' rights were earned by military service and loyalty to the Republic. Conservatives argued for delayed suffrage, and, failing in that effort, they called for qualifications to temper citizens' access to political rights. Education triumphed over alternative policies because Conservatives and Reformists each feared a different population in the South, imagining schools as a disciplinary force for that group. Conservatives feared that empowering blacks, who could command fair wages, would crush the economy. Conservatives also worried that blacks were ill-equipped for the responsibilities of voting. Reformists feared a revival of the white planter class, which could quickly monopolize power in the South. The push for mass education was successful because it allowed opposing political advocacy groups to support education, albeit while holding radically different conceptualizations of its purpose and aims.

Mass education, as organized by voluntary associations, satisfied the concerns and visions of both Conservatives and Reformists for the political and social reconstruction of the South. Conservatives imagined education as a disciplinary force to maintain white supremacy; Reformers envisioned mass education as a great liberating force for blacks and a containment mechanism for whites. A private-public alliance to structure mass education offered a uniquely legitimate mode of continued Northern oversight of Southern politics. Schools were a mechanism of political containment—a means to restrict the rights of certain groups. Education proponents were entrepreneurial in designing an organizational form governed by elites, but sufficiently elastic to provisionally include federal agents who lent bureaucratic and logistic support. Education systems in the South emerged as a site of conflict over control and social closure.

While federal Reconstruction spending lasted only a few years, voluntary associations entered the Southern field—founding schools as early as 1862—and maintained racially integrated schools until the early 1890s. While formal politics played a role in legally inscribing requirements to make education widely available, voluntary associations claimed responsibility for organizing education. Many voluntary associations were involved primarily through "freedmen's schools," yet these schools were limited in advancing the kinds of changes many progressives desired. As a result, a new movement to launch higher education—including interracial campuses—was pushed to the fore. The antebellum status hierarchy was made visible by skin color and labor status; in remaking the status hierarchy, educational achievement might prove a means to create a level playing field whereby loyalty and accomplishment determined social rank.

Rather than conceptualizing education as a social right accessible through citizenship, as described by T. H. Marshall, I have argued that education gained support because elites viewed schools as a sorting device to distribute certain forms of citizenship rights to certain groups.[113] Schools provided a central site where the North felt it could extend tutelary power—a political education—over the region. Whether in freedmen's schools or on college campuses, education was organized with the mandate that schools produce the right kinds of citizens for a new, stable and unified republic.

The next chapter examines the policies and practices that shaped campus life of the nineteenth-century integrated colleges, which were created as spaces to live out the anti-caste ideals at the heart of the Republican Tutelage model. These colleges remind us that segregation was not inevitable. Given the tribulations of Reconstruction, were anti-caste educators able to realize their political goals in action? Who attended these colleges and what motivations brought students to these campuses?

CHAPTER THREE

Inside Interracial Colleges, 1837–1880

> Oberlin claims to have solved the social problem of the
> nation.... For a whole generation [blacks] have enjoyed equal
> rights and privileges of the institution.... They sit side by side
> in the classes, the lecture halls and the public assemblies. The
> teachers assure me that they find no difference in their abilities.
>
> —"COMMENCEMENT WEEK AT OBERLIN," *Chicago Tribune*,
>   August 29, 1865

> That in this Institution, as in no other in the land, it is believed,
> the Anglo-Saxon, the Celt, the Indian, the Mongolian, the
> Greek and the African already sit side by side on the same
> benches. All races and sexes and both have here, in the pursuit
> of knowledge, a fair field and equal favor."
>
> —THE ANNUAL REPORT OF THE PRESIDENT, 1870,
>   Howard University

> Equality is achieved.... What has been done there can be done
> everywhere in the South, and must be.
>
> —"BEREA COLLEGE," *The Independent*, July 3, 1884

Moving in for a closer look at life on campus, this chapter investigates
the decisions these interracial colleges made in structuring policies
around race and integration, and the impact of these decisions at Oberlin, Berea, and Howard. Howard secured congressional funding and benefited from a supportive local black middle class. Berea and Oberlin
were each located in communities founded purposively to support their
mission. All three were well-connected to important donors, politicians,
and well-established in abolitionist circles. As twenty-first century political debates highlight, admissions practices are a critical site for exploring
how race organizes college campus life.[1] Each of the colleges designed
strategies for and responded to changes in enrollments. The Board of
Trustees also exerted considerable decision-making power in structuring campus life. By venturing on campus, we evaluate whether college
administrators were able to realize their goals for students to share in trans-

formative, "caste-breaking" daily experiences. Contemporary explanations assume that the power to segregate lies with the state, whether through laws that mandate *de jure* segregation or more contemporary district boundaries that allocate students to schools producing *de facto* segregation. In the cases studied here, none of the schools were segregated by legal action.

For over sixty years, contact theory has remained the standard solution for the problem of racial segregation.[2] In this theoretical tradition, interpersonal contact is the key to integration. This theory poses that racial integration can be achieved within schools if the conditions for interracial contact are appropriately specified. School experiences reduce individual prejudice and spur social change, radiating from the school outward to broader society. Contact theory emphasizes that not only do students need to come into close proximity and work toward shared goals, but also learn from teachers from diverse racial backgrounds. The anticaste colleges described here—Oberlin, Berea, and Howard—put into practice many of the tenets of contact theory. How did the colleges fare? The question here is not whether making campus-level changes mattered for individuals—because there is ample testimony that for many students, it did. Graduates of these colleges were among the first women (black and white) to attend medical school and law school, practice medicine and law, and among the first black men to hold public office and lead universities. Graduates—white, black, male, and female—left these campuses with a desire for racial justice, and many dedicated their working lives to that pursuit. Yet, the anti-caste mission was something more than mere individual advancement. The goal was nothing short of radical social transformation. Following a discussion of the foundational beliefs and founding stories of these three colleges, this chapter describes how administrators, faculty, and students organized new modes of interaction on interracial colleges. How did the colleges live up to their bold goal?

Foundational Beliefs

In 1835, abolitionist and New York City silk merchant Lewis Tappan made a substantial donation to Oberlin College that helped establish the first college publicly committed to "racial coeducation." The following year, William Lloyd Garrison founded the American Anti-Slavery Society and, within four years, it united 1,200 auxiliary societies and 125,000 members. Though abolitionists were quickly mobilizing, it was clear that there were deep divides over the methods abolitionists should pursue. By 1840, the American Anti-Slavery Society splintered when some members found that Garrison's Society "repudiated a hostile attitude toward the churches and unsound positions respecting the Constitution and the government."[3] Brothers Lewis and Arthur Tappan helped to organize the splinter group into the Foreign Anti-Slavery Society, later the AMA.[4] From its inception, the AMA was a racially integrated organization. Its first board included eight white and four black men.

Though the abolitionist movement was growing rapidly in the 1830s, a pivotal event helped galvanize support for the cause. In 1839, fifty-three Mende people were captured from the Kaw-Mendi territory in Sierra Leone and traded to Portuguese slave-traders. Sold in Havana, Cuba, the Mende were then transported on a Spanish slave ship. When their captors failed to secure the prisoners one night, Sengbe Pieh led his compatriots to rise up in mutiny. When the ship landed on Long Island, near Montauk Point, the authorities took the mutineers to New Haven where they were charged with murder and piracy and jailed. Future AMA secretary, Reverend Simeon S. Jocelyn, expressed how the event inspired him: "Here on the soil of a free state were a body of men in confinement on a charge of murder because when kidnapped against law on a Spanish vessel, they had risked life for liberty."[5] Less than a decade earlier, Jocelyn had been dissuaded from opening a college for blacks in New Haven, first by order of a town meeting and later, more violently, by a mob visit to his home. Jocelyn's long-time friend and fellow activist, Lewis Tappan, helped form a legal defense committee for the mutineers. At the age of seventy-three, former U.S. president John Quincy Adams accepted Tappan's request that he serve as counsel. The trial exposed the lawlessness of the slave trade. The Supreme Court ruled that the slave ship had violated international slave trade agreements signed by the United States, Spain, and Britain.

Out of this event, the AMA was born. This rebellion stirred many Americans to view enslaved Africans as human and to recognize the brutality of the slave trade. It also forced a new recognition of New England's complicity. After the trial, the Mende lived in Farmington, Connecticut for over a year before they—in concert with the AMA—raised sufficient funds to transport the thirty-five surviving Mende home to present-day Sierra Leone. One of the Mende girls, Sarah Margru

Kinson, crossed the Atlantic again to enroll in Oberlin College in 1846. Lewis Tappan provided her scholarship. The officials who organized the AMA—and the colleges they founded—had early and profound experiences that led them to believe in the importance of close social contact across racial boundaries. Most held Protestant religious beliefs that valorized social justice and rooted the righteousness of equality in Biblical scripture, professing: "God hath made of one blood all nations of men for to dwell on all the face of the earth."[6]

After the Civil War, like Republican Tutelage supporters more broadly, AMA leaders believed deeply that there were no past precedents to follow. American society required a thorough transformation in order to avoid another outbreak of war. To make these cultural changes, they envisioned the college campus as a site to test the boundaries of interracial living. On contained campuses, they could diminish the resistance their radical break with racial hierarchy would no doubt incur. In order to effect deep and lasting change, AMA officials knew they needed to subvert deeply entrenched moral and cultural codes. As AMA official Samuel Hunt confidently explained: "In our work, ideas are so soon transmitted into deeds and facts that it really becomes a very serious matter what we think."[7] Only through finding appropriate new practices to produce new cognitive patterns could they remake the meanings of race. It was with this in mind that the colleges designed virtually every aspect of campus life to support the development of deep interracial friendships.

The three colleges discussed at length in this chapter—Berea (Kentucky), Howard (Washington, D.C.), and Oberlin (Ohio)—shared an organizational affiliation in the AMA. The AMA created a cohesive network of shared beliefs about civil rights and social inclusion by organizing local chapters and maintaining communications through publications and conferences. The AMA was the largest benevolent association with operations in nearly every state and multiple foreign countries. The AMA also worked closely with the BRFAL before it finally shuttered in 1872. In addition to hundreds of primary schools, the AMA backed eleven colleges and explicitly promoted them as replicable models. As one speaker at Berea College argued: "Let there be Bereas planted throughout the nation, institutions in which the youth of the land, white and colored, shall study together, play together, sing together, worship together, and there will be no war of races. If Berea shall be a success there will be a demonstration of practical utility to the South."[8] Their goal was to create a new form of higher education that could be reproduced across the country. Culture is often considered a repertoire—a set of practices that can encompass schemas, scripts, narratives, cognitive frames, and classification systems. College campuses—AMA officials reasoned—provided a space to locate and develop cultural practices that could foster republican governance and interracial cooperation more broadly. The campuses could put the AMA's anti-caste ideas into practice and become models for other colleges.

The colleges represented a range of enrollments and policy choices. Berea enrolled equal numbers of black and white students, while Howard enrolled more black students and Oberlin enrolled more whites. These colleges attracted private investors from afar, as well as leadership, faculty, and students who shared their ideological framework, so they were able to set up schools even where there was local resistance. Though not located in the former Confederacy, the colleges shared aspirations that their graduates would use their careers to help reshape Southern society: "The War was a war of ideas. Thirty years of constant, earnest, persistent discussion by lectures, preachers, and political speakers, prepared the North to demand for all portions of our country under the exclusive control of the United States equal rights for all men. . . . The war of ideas is still in progress, and will continue till harmony of thought and feeling between the North and the South is essentially secured. . . . The North and the South must meet and reason together, kindly, earnestly, patiently, persistently. The pulpit, the press, the school, the rostrum, should all be employed to the utmost capacity of the friends of equal rights and universal education."[9]

AMA leadership believed that whites would abandon their prejudices if they were able to develop egalitarian relationships across the color line. To effect such dramatic transformations in whites' racial attitudes, the AMA believed that shared daily experiences in interracial colleges would generate, in the words of President James H. Fairchild of Oberlin College, "the wide-spread influence which these must exert in the family, the school, in the church, and in the State."[10] Above all, they hoped to revise Americans's assumptions about the meanings of skin color: race had, through generations of slavery, become an indicator of caste, but this meaning of race was an ideological tool of the Southern "slavocracy" rather than biologically determined. The AMA charged that the South had built up a pervasive social system wherein clergy, scholars, and politicians colluded to socially construct a set of meanings about race that served the institutional interests of slavery.

Anti-casteists considered egalitarian social and political relations as foundational for securing peace and stable governance. The AMA argued that the institution of slavery produced feelings of white superiority that inhibited the enactment of Republican governance in the South. Berea College president, Edward H. Fairchild, argued that caste prejudice threatened the foundations of the legal system.

> White and colored people must be perfectly equal before the law. They must have the same civil rights, and be protected alike in the enjoyment of them. . . . These distinctions are kept up not because colored people are personally disagreeable to the white people. . . . It is simply a caste feeling, a prejudice of position. This feeling controls legislation, it blinds judges and juries, it corrupts executive officers, it biases witnesses [and] . . . we can have no permanent peace, nor, what is more important, any exalted sense of honor and virtue, till this is effectually secured; and it can never be secured till the race prejudice, the caste feeling, the spirit of domination is eradicated. . . . There is nothing, in the absence of co-education, which can secure the mutual regard, confidence and honorable deportment which must exist between the races, if we are to have a peaceful, intelligent and virtuous community.[11]

The AMA believed that for such transformations to take place, Americans needed to learn to see the world without "color." For this reason, the colleges largely refused to record racial demographics. Abolitionist discourse drew heavily on the fallacy of color as a signifier of moral character. Unlike the most common users of colorblind language in the twenty-first century, who often mute critiques of injustice, during its first 30 years the AMA was bold in confronting racial injustice. Abolitionists often referenced the cruelty of slave owners who raped and enslaved women and then left the children they fathered to endure a lifetime of bondage. They also disseminated pictures illustrating the wide range of slaves' skin shades to emphasize this point. For instance, in 1864, the most widely circulated periodical in the United States, *Harper's Weekly*, published an illustration titled "White and Colored Slaves" depicting a group of children attending a New Orleans freedmen's school. The author, an officer of the National Freedmen's Relief Association, provided a detailed history of each child's parentage, and described their complexion and hair texture (see figure 2 in chapter 2). Rebecca, enslaved in her father's house, was described as "perfectly white" while Rosina had a "blonde complexion and silky hair."[12] The intention was to force recognition of the mutability of race and deny that racial differences were concrete or meaningful. At the annual meeting of the AMA in Hartford, Connecticut in October of 1871, President Edward Fairchild of Berea College disabused his listeners of their faith in a color-coded social hierarchy: "The two races, *if there are two races of men*, have got on together without friction and without impediment. If any evils have grown out of the arrangement, they have been felt elsewhere, not here. The ratio of white to colored has been two to three, so far as we could ascertain by their looks and their testimony. Should we undertake to separate the races, as we never shall, we should be obliged to apply to somebody more skilled in 'visible admixtures' than we are, to accomplish the task."[13]

Berea's founder, Reverend Fee, was convinced that "the matter of the essential equality of the negro people . . . could not even give the status of a 'question;' all men are equal in the sight of God and therefore equal in the sight of all 'Godly' men."[14] In 1860, while principal of the preparatory department at Oberlin, the future Berea president Edward Fairchild articulated that only integrated schools could affect real change in individual attitudes: "However high its literary character, it must lie on the other side of that barrier of caste, which a false system has reared between the races. To furnish such a school, might be a good work; but it was a far more difficult task to make a breach in that division wall, to found a school in the breach itself, and secure such influences as that the student from either side should feel at home. The gratifying success which has attended the effort, is the result of a combination of influences, literary, social, and religious, the absence of any of which would have caused a failure."[15]

In describing education "at the breach" between whites and blacks, Fairchild clearly articulated that integration existed only when "the student from either side should feel at home." Anti-caste educators struggled to ensure that the schools did not—in any aspect—favor one group of students over another. The ideal of racial coeducation went beyond a particular demographic composition formula and required that students not only attended class together, but developed real friendships with those whose backgrounds differed from their own.

The AMA believed that students would learn to see one another as equals and leave their campuses to lead the nation to integrated civic life. AMA-affiliated colleges envisioned their role as addressing a social problem rather than providing education for individual advancement. Reverend Fee, saw the "chief aim was always to save the souls of southern whites from the sin of complicity in slaveholding and prejudice."[16] This was wholly different from the "uplift ideology" made famous by Booker T. Washington in later years. In Washington's model, blacks needed to demonstrate their value and accept a complementary but subordinate existence to whites. The most fitting form of education would "uplift" blacks by training them in the trades and establishing a solid economic footing. Anti-caste education focused explicitly on eradicating whites' prejudice rather than on the elevation of blacks: "In the twenty-five years past more than ten thousand students have been connected with the Institution, and few of these have been here so short a time as not to have their prejudices removed, their feelings liberalized, and their interest quickened in reference to the colored race."[17] By building interpersonal relationships, whites would find their assumptions of racial superiority unfounded. Anti-caste advocates imagined that by transforming individuals through shared educational experiences, they could diminish racial separatist practices for the good of the nation.

Founding Stories

Organizational affiliation in the AMA allowed college leaders to participate in common forums of discussion and a social network that supported their bold practices. While the worlds they were building on their respective campuses may have seemed radical to those outside the dense network of the AMA, by fostering relationships with others who shared their vision, these colleges were able to draw upon the collective resources of like-minded educators and activists. While Oberlin was integrated within two years of its founding, Berea and Howard were founded as interracial schools. These three colleges were strategic in their geographic location. Both Berea and Oberlin were situated in remote, rural locations to create new communities where they could live according to the rules of their own design. Families moved from afar to be a part of these unique communities. Howard, by contrast, was located strategically in Washington, D.C., close to the South but buffered by a strong federal presence.

The colleges shared administrators and faculty with significant experience in politics, higher education leadership, and social movement work. Faculty members at Oberlin went on to administrative posts at Berea and Howard. Many had been administrators in the BRFAL, and some held positions as BRFAL school district supervisors. In this capacity, they traveled across large districts touring ill-equipped schools. Witnessing the desire of so many met by such a paucity of resources motivated them to work toward creating better education options. In addition to experience as BRFAL agents and administrators, many were deeply involved in the AMA. Oberlin College claimed the AMA as a product of its students: "Its leading founders and officers were from the early friends and supporters of Oberlin."[18] For instance, Reverend Michael Strieby was active in the Underground Railroad that traversed Oberlin, from which he graduated in 1838. In 1864, he became secretary for the AMA and later a trustee at Howard University.[19] Berea trustees, black and white, worked together at Camp Nelson refugee camp in Kentucky. During the war, Camp Nelson was the third-largest training depot for black Union soldiers. After the war, many soldiers brought their families to the camp where the AMA helped the BRFAL provide housing and schooling. It was here that Berea's reverend Fee met a black chaplain, Reverent Gabriel Burdett, and the two formed a close partnership. Both worked the next two decades together at Berea College.

Edward H. Fairchild, president of Oberlin's preparatory department (1853–1869), later became Berea's president (1869–1889); his brother, James Fairchild, was president at Oberlin College. Edward Fairchild's son, Charles, also worked in promoting the AMA's mission by helping organize fundraising tours of Europe with the Fisk University Jubilee Singers. He also aided Berea and Oberlin in their fundraising. The son of staunch abolitionists who raised him in the Oberlin community, William Goodell Frost spent his early career as professor of Greek at Oberlin before being named president of Berea (1893–1920). Oberlin-educated John Mercer Langston, was professor of law and Howard's interim president (1873–1875), before being elected to the Fifty-First Congress. Berea College graduate Carter G. Woodson later became dean of liberal arts at Howard University, where he established the Association for the Study of Negro Life and History. Through personal connections and AMA meetings, colleges benefited by communicating strategies for funding challenges, adjudicating policies, and managing enrollment trends. Together, they were engaged in creating a model interracial college for replication.

A "Peculiar People" on the Western Reserve: Oberlin College

The Oberlin commune, from which the college grew, required all members to agree to a covenant of piety and plain living on the western frontier. Oberlin was a small town—a close-knit community created to embrace a particularly strident practice of Protestant faith. Its first class of students, however, came from New England, "not children of the colonists, but young people who on their own account had made their way to the school in the wilderness."[20] Dancing, fine clothing, and certainly the use of stimulating drink or tobacco violated the moral tenets of the community. By the early 1860s, approximately 25 percent of the 2,915 residents were black.

While a few Northern colleges on rare occasion admitted black students, Oberlin was remarkable because it publicly espoused a belief in racial coeducation.[21] Oberlin came to its anti-slavery convictions due to two related factors: first, a change in political thinking among abolitionist activists on the issue of slavery and second, the financial opportunity this new generation of abolitionists offered institutions willing to take up the abolitionist cause. Abolitionist faculty and students had been expelled from Cincinnati's Lane Seminary. Lane Seminary was dominated by Presbyterians and supported colonization, not emancipation. Supporters of colonization argued that blacks and whites could never coexist in the United States and the best solution to ending slavery was to send emancipated blacks to Liberia. In December 1834, 51 Lane students submitted a letter outlining their grievances with the Seminary. Chief among these was the suppression of "free discussion" of slavery and abolition.[22] The "Lane Rebels" were invited to Oberlin. Reverend John Shipherd, one of Oberlin's founders, sensed a moment of opportunity whereby the fledgling college could capitalize on increasing abolitionist mobilization in the Northeast: "Because thus doing right, we gain the confidence of benevolent and able men, who probably will furnish us some thousands." Shipherd appealed for equal opportunity admissions rather than an admissions policy that required significant outreach efforts. He emphasized that the plan would create opportunity for the few blacks whose situation would allow them to elect "the Oberlin option." Though nearly half of the students initially objected, the trustees, "Resolved, that students shall be received into this Institution irrespective of color." Oberlin's president James Fairchild boasted that no further actions were taken after this initial decision by the college to negotiate race relations at Oberlin:

This vote "determined the policy of the Institution on the question of slavery, and no other action has been needed on the subject from that day to this. It was a word of invitation and welcome to the colored man, as opposed to the spirit of exclusion which was then dominant in the land."[23] While a few white students left when the school inaugurated its new policy in 1837, about half the student body supported racial integration and the new students from Lane mitigated the drop in enrollment.

Slavery was the question of the day and Oberlin was often viewed as a test case, a model of what was possible, if slavery were outlawed. Even a few black students at Oberlin, combined with a policy of racial tolerance and abolitionist fervor, brought national attention to the small college. Oberlin's unique commitment attracted wealthy donors from Great Britain and Northern abolitionists who contributed to fund the fight for equal rights: Southerners and Northern Democrats viewed blacks as less than human; coeducation forced the recognition of black humanity through daily, observable practice. This put Oberlin College at the center of a political storm, and the college was harshly decried by Conservative critics. Oberlin president James Fairchild described how the offensive term "nigger" "was exchanged for the prefix 'Oberlin,' as embodying all that was odious in abolitionism, and pernicious in religious heresy."[24] This stigma proved a saving grace for Oberlin's financial woes. Oberlin's policy of accepting students "without regard to race," was rewarded with financial support from the wealthy New York abolitionist brothers, Alfred and Lewis Tappan. This mission of education across the color line continued to prove a useful motivator for outside funders to support the college. "From time to time, a load of debt accumulated, and special efforts were made to lift the burden. In 1838, when debts were pressing and friends in this country seemed discouraged or exhausted, Messrs. Keep and Dawes undertook a mission to England. They went, sustained by the commendations of distinguished philanthropists in this country, and were cordially received by men of similar spirit there. By untiring diligence, they raised, in the course of eighteen months, $30,000, sufficient to cancel the debt. *It was chiefly the fidelity of Oberlin to anti-slavery principles that brought forth such a response from British Christians.*"[25]

Upon his death in 1858, Charles Avery, a Pittsburgh-based cotton merchant who came to abolitionism after a horrifying tour to the South, donated $25,000 to Oberlin for a professorship on the condition that "the college shall (enroll) needy colored students free of tuition on the same conditions as whites, to the number of fifty at a time if so many should apply and if at any time the College shall refuse to receive colored students on the same terms as whites, the fund shall revert to the heirs or to such person or persons as shall be authorized to receive it."[26] The Avery Fund was "devoted as a permanent fund for promoting the education and elevation of the colored people of the United States and Canada . . . and to confer upon them without prejudice on account of color all the educational advantages."[27] As such, maintaining black student enrollment was critical for the college's financial funding. According to the president's report of 1871, student enrollment was "abundant" but Oberlin's tuition was intentionally kept too modest to survive on tuition alone. The college built a dependence upon donors into its organizational structure.

There were surprisingly few scandals, particularly given the visibility Oberlin attained in a short time. Of course, the college also needed to maintain a pristine image given its public scrutiny. However, in 1862, a scandal threatened Oberlin's community. Two white women fell mysteriously ill, and their housemate, Edmonia Lewis, was accused of poisoning their drinks. Of Native American and black ancestry, Lewis arrived at Oberlin in 1859 after preparatory studies at another progressive, interracial school, New York Central College. Together with a dozen other female students, Lewis boarded at the home of Reverend John Keep, an Oberlin trustee. Early in the afternoon, Lewis and two white friends visited in one of their rooms. Perhaps they talked about their studies or the young men who would soon arrive to take the girls for a sleigh-ride that snowy day. Despite the strict temperance policy, Lewis offered her housemates a forbidden treat of mulled wine. When the girls fell ill later that day, Lewis was accused of poisoning her friends. Angered that Oberlin officials failed to arrest the suspect, vigilantes attacked Lewis outside her home. The *Cleveland Plain Dealer* mocked the trial as a "dark affair" for allowing black witnesses and court officers.[28] The local Oberlin paper—edited by Oberlin professor Henry Peck—defended Lewis "whose character has been exemplary . . . and whose color subjects her to prejudice."[29] Lewis was defended by Oberlin's only black attorney, John M. Langston, Oberlin class of 1848. Forensic evidence uncovered the presence of a naturopathic aphrodisiac (canthardin) associated with harsh side effects. Langston persuaded the court that insufficient evidence was found to convict Lewis, who soon left the United States to study sculpture in Rome.

The case is illustrative of the differences between Oberlin and its neighboring communities. The *Cleveland Plain Dealer* attacked the Oberlin community, charging that its radical beliefs in social equality provoked white wrath. The newspaper charged that by encouraging interracial social relationships, Oberlin held responsibility for angering whites and endangered blacks' safety. Many conservatives imagined that if the racial hierarchy requiring blacks' deference to whites remained intact, then peace and social stability would prevail. While the college faulted Lewis for violating the strict code of temperance, the Oberlin community supported her by charging that others were too quick to assess her guilt by the color of her skin. Though a painful event for Lewis, as well as the Oberlin students and residents, scandal at any of the colleges was a rare event. The Lewis's trial seemed to hold no lasting consequences for the college—no new policies were written by the Board of Trustees, no students called for changes in housing policies or moral codes, nor did the event diminish black enrollment. At the end of the Civil War, philanthropists saw Oberlin as an ideal location to build on the educational work for the freedmen. By then, Oberlin had nearly forty years of experience in interracial education.

A Loyalist Reserve in the Mountains: Berea College

Though Kentucky never joined the Confederacy, it was a state divided by slavery. During Reconstruction, Republican politicians and journalists condemned the South for failing to address vigilante violence through civil institutions of justice. Because of broad disagreement over the bounds of federal sovereignty, insufficient numbers of Union troops occupied the South. As a result, the North lacked resources to effectively quell Southern hostilities. Although it never seceded, Kentucky was central to the Civil War. Presidents of both the United States and the Confederate States were Kentuckians. That most famous of abolitionist works, *Uncle Tom's Cabin*, which Abraham Lincoln famously suggested helped start the war, highlighted the cruelty of slavery in Kentucky. Lincoln retained the border states by excluding "states not in rebellion" from the abolition of slavery outlined in the Emancipation Proclamation of 1862. To position Kentucky as isolated from the war would have been likely incongruous to many Americans. As noted Reconstruction historian C. Vann Woodward argued, "Despite Kentucky's failure to secede and join the Confederacy, no state below the Ohio

River presented a more solidly Confederate-Democrat front in the decade after Appomattox."[30]

Two influential events transformed the son of a wealthy Kentucky slave-holder into an abolitionist and secured Berea much-needed funding. During his studies at Yale, Cassius Clay heard William Lloyd Garrison speak against slavery and was moved when Simeon Jocelyn—who later helped organize legal defense for the Amistad mutineers—attempted to found a college for blacks in New Haven.[31] Clay argued against slavery not because it was immoral or unjust, but because it impeded Kentucky's economic progress and diminished opportunities for poor whites to enter the labor market. Clay met Reverend Fee when they were both speakers at an abolitionist event. Fee was a strident abolitionist with close ties to Oberlin College and the AMA. Kentucky legislator Clay deeded Fee a large portion of land to establish Berea College.

Shortly thereafter, in 1856, Fee successfully appealed to the AMA for financial support. From its inception, Berea's mission was to serve the abolitionist cause: "We ought to have a good school here in central Kentucky, which should be to Kentucky what Oberlin is to Ohio, anti-slavery, anti-caste, anti-rum, anti-secret societies, anti-sin. . . . Could we have even a good academy, in the mountainous and non-slaveholding districts, we could do much, and that too most effectively, for the overthrow of slavery. And as Kansas will soon be a free State, may we not expect the eastern and northern friends to turn their attention and means to Kentucky, and by a constant influx of teachers, preachers, and emigrants, in a legal, peaceful and yet most effective manner, make this fertile and healthful State the 'home of the free and land of the brave.'"[32]

After Fee's speech to the AMA, Oberlin benefactor Lewis Tappan proposed to Henry Ward Beecher that Fee should be invited to New York to speak on the topic of Berea. Touted as the "most famous man in America," Beecher was an acclaimed abolitionist, preacher, and younger brother of Harriet Beecher Stowe. The invitation to Brooklyn launched Berea into the abolitionist limelight. Far from Brooklyn, in Harper's Ferry, West Virginia, abolitionist John Brown had recently led a raid on a federal depot. The raid party included three men from Oberlin, among them one who was a refugee from slavery. Brown was, in fact, the son of a former Oberlin trustee.[33] Fee described his speech: "The country was in a state of intense excitement. In my address before the church I said, 'We want more John Browns; not in manner of action, but in spirit of consecration.'" The nuance of this distinction was lost on the angry pro-slavery forces in Kentucky, and mob violence quickly escalated. While he and his young daughter made their way back from New York, mob search parties demanded Fee's capture. In Kentucky, over 800 thronged the county courthouse to protest his return. Rather than face the mob, his wife and son joined him in Cincinnati. The relief of their reunion was brief. Their four-year-old son, Tappan, died from exposure due to what Fee called their "exodus" in mid-winter.[34] In 1864, eager to return to his work, Fee and his family made their way through Confederate lines with a Union flag painted on his carriage. His wife, Matilda, drove the carriage through the most dangerous stretches of their journey. Fee worked at Camp Nelson until he could reopen his school after the war.

After the war, General Howard, commissioner of the BRFAL, awarded Berea College the princely sum of $7,000 to help reopen the school. Berea, like Oberlin, had members who relocated to create a new community built on their shared belief in social equality, and both schools offered preparatory and collegiate divisions. Fee purchased large tracts of land with a grand plan. By 1870, 200 black families moved to Berea, and four years later Fee's land allotment plan allowed 74 white and 40 black families to purchase land.[35] As described in chapter 2, after the war, many black leaders prioritized land ownership as the best path for future safety and social mobility. By intervening and first purchasing land from whites and then reselling the land to black families, Fee's program allowed black families to purchase land in a state where they would likely have faced formidable barriers to land ownership. Fee sold his tracts of land in patterns that guaranteed blacks and whites would live near each other. Fee had, perhaps, designed the first planned interracial residential community.

Yet, despite the close-knit local community, Berea's principles were sharply opposed by residents in adjacent counties. In 1871, a white Berea trustee, W. W. Wheeler, traveled with his wife and daughter to neighboring Estill County where they dined at the home of an old friend, who was black. The media did not disclose the friend's name, revealing only that the two had begun their friendship in Berea. Upon leaving town that evening, a group of whites fired several shots before Wheeler escaped. In the middle of the night, his attackers found him at his hotel. This time they found him with his wife and young daughter. Beaten and whipped, Wheeler was accused of bringing "Northern principles" to start a school for blacks.[36] Berea president Edward Fairchild, Fee, and two Berea professors submitted the story to several newspapers, "hoping it may impress good citizens of both sections with the necessity of maintaining law and order." In doing so, they hoped to secure donations by making the political work of the college visible.

There had been widespread violence against many schools in Kentucky. The BRFAL supported 6,000 students in 136 schools but they did so against persistent local resistance.[37] By 1871, the BRFAL was diminishing in capacity but Berea viewed its successes as stronger than the resistance it faced. The trustee did not abandon his post, nor his principles, and the college interpreted conflict as an indicator of the need for anti-caste education. Above all, the college emphasized the forging of close interracial relationships that persisted even through grave threats. Berea's resistance to local opposition garnered national attention. The *Chicago Tribune* described Berea as "a school which has been antagonized by many of the natives, and whose officers and teachers a few years ago were mobbed and repeatedly driven from their homes for doing a work which Kentuckians generally commend."[38]

Northern newspapers occasionally showcased hostile commentary toward interracial colleges from Southern newspapers. These reprinted columns depict the fierce resistance provoked among Southern whites. In 1874, the *Independent* and the *Kentucky Register* debated Berea's mission. Mockingly, the *Register* presented a view that Berea empowered blacks to assume social liberties that undermined the established social hierarchy of white over black: "'We's gwine to ride free on the railroads, smoke in de ladies' car, and put our feet on the percushions of the seats whenever we damn please. We's gwine to be allowed to stop at de hotels, and set at the head of de table, and hab de biggest slice ob de chickens . . . and make de white trash hustle themselves and wait on us without grumblin.' We's gwine to be allowed to go to de white schools." Like Oberlin, the area around Berea was hostile but this press showcased the importance of their work and helped bring in Northern donations.

Berea's critics in the South articulated its efforts as undermining whites' rights. This view revealed a zero-sum assumption whereby increasing rights for blacks necessarily eroded the rights of whites. The *Kentucky Register* complained that as blacks gained in status, the status of whites diminished: "Have white folks no rights in Kentucky? . . . We still adhere to our old faith that white men are just as good as negroes so long as they behave themselves."[39] Dismantling white supremacist attitudes was the *raison d'être* for AMA colleges. Reports of hostile Southern reactions helped spur fundraising campaigns. The issue of anti-caste education raised hackles in Kentucky, and "a prominent Democrat" offered President Edward Fairchild $10,000 "if he would restrict the work to either race." Though a substantial amount at the time, it was nonetheless paltry compared to the funds raised from Northern and British abolitionist groups and individual donors who celebrated the victories of the rebellious colleges fighting back Southern racism. Overwhelmingly the Northern press declared Berea a success.

As described in chapter 2, education became a favored solution for Reconstruction, in part because it could serve as reparation. The nation should repay those who had sacrificed for the Union and the currency of that reparation could be education. The AMA usually framed this form of repayment as specific to black veterans. However, Berea argued that there was a small, but geographically substantial "reserve" of loyal, white Unionists in eastern Kentucky. Berea's leaders proposed that it was an ideal starting point for the anti-caste educational movement in the South. Poor white Union veterans and their descendants in the mountain region seemed the most likely group of white Southerners to enroll in an integrated college. The first college catalog (1866–1867) expounded on this rationale.

[Education] is needed scarcely less for the loyal white people of the mountainous portion of Eastern Kentucky and the similar regions in other States adjoining, not a few of whom are eager to secure its advantages. The "hill country" of Eastern Kentucky alone, upon the confines of which Berea is situated, has an area equal to that of Massachusetts and Connecticut combined, and though occupied by hardy and loyal men, is singularly destitute of educational advantages, which hitherto in the South have been monopolized by the wealthy class of planters. Several of these counties, not far from Berea, sent more men to the Union army, than were subject to military service. Can any part of the North show so good a record? Now that these men, their ideas enlarged and energies developed by the War, are asking for the key of knowledge, their wants must be met. Having periled their lives for the Union, the least their grateful countrymen can do is to give them those Christian seminaries necessary to the full development of their manhood.

Berea and its anti-caste advocates, faithful to the ideals of Republican Tutelage, implored potential donors to view the poor whites in eastern Kentucky as a special group. This group should be seen as deserving of Berea's opportunities because of their faithfulness to the Union. Given the mob violence only years before, this was not an uncontroversial case to make. Still, the unusual numbers of poor whites enrolled lent credibility to the endeavor even though the college had to expend great efforts to recruit local white students. Berea, they argued, held a special advantage in forging a sense of solidarity between poor whites and blacks. Berea appealed to the North: "There is no other large school in the country where in so nearly equal numbers white and colored students are gathered."[40] By 1868, Berea enrolled more than 300 students.

Overlooking the Capitol: Howard University

When Howard University was founded in 1866, its trustees declared their ambition to "make the Howard University a University indeed, as broad and catholic as it is possible for an institution to be—no less so than Harvard, Dartmouth, Yale, Oberlin, or any other institution of worth in this country," which would "be open to all persons without distinction of race, sex or former condition, who possess the requisite qualifications."[41] Howard's congressional charter mandated it "serve youth" in Washington, D.C. but did not mention any racial designation. Unlike the older universities, Howard opened its doors to all students, regardless of race and gender. While black leaders had organized for integrated education since at least the 1830s, Howard University offered a new, well-funded structure within which to advance integrated education as an organizational form.[42] The university was incorporated by an act of Congress approved on March 24, 1867. General O. O. Howard, head of the BRFAL and AMA ally, was appointed president. By locating in Washington, D.C., Howard bypassed contentious state-level politics.

In antebellum Washington, D.C., blacks were restricted from meeting unless organized through religious or fraternal associations. As a result, there were many well-organized black civic associations. John Francis Cook, a political activist whose two sons would serve as Howard trustees, described the city's black population: "We are intelligent enough to be industrious; to have accumulated property; to build, and sustain churches, and institutions of learning. We are and have been educating our children without the aid of any school-fund, and, until recently, have for many years been furnishing unjustly as we deemed, a portion of the means for the education of the white children of the District. . . . Out of a population of less than 15.000, we have contributed three full regiments, over 3.500 enlisted men, while the white citizens out of a population of upwards 60.000 sent only about 1.500 enlisted men for the support of the Union, the Constitution and the Laws. In all our Country's trials, our loyalty has never been questioned—our patriotism is unbounded."[43]

After the war, new refugees arrived daily from the South, and physical conditions were nearing desperation for many. Many fleeing the South imagined finding a safe harbor in the nation's capital. Most refugees lived in Freedmen's Village in Arlington, on the former plantation land of Confederate general Robert E. Lee. By 1880, about one-third of Washington, D.C.'s population was black, though deep divisions persisted between those who had been free before the war and the newly arrived Southern refugees.[44] Still, the strong presence of black associations in Washington, D.C. provided a deep base of support for Howard University. Trustees and faculty often had substantial experience in activism, deep political knowledge, and they could rely on well-organized networks for communicating information.

The location in the nation's capital was strategic for its proximity to the federal center of power and the protection the trustees hoped the federal government offered. Many viewed its location as equally salient symbolically: "If a stranger would see the magical results of war, how the God of battles has lifted up into the light of freedom, and intelligence present and to come, the African race, let him take the 7th-street car, and visit this institution. Externally it is built like a palace, crowned with its glistening dome in the center and with the stars and stripes floating above it. From it cupola—nay, from its lower rooms—it commands one the widest and finest views in the whole region. To the south lies the spread-out city, with its broad avenues. . . . There hangs the white dome of Capitol, as though let down from heaven to moderate the strong light of so many brilliant legislators. . . . There too, sweeping round its royal bend past the graves of the nation's defenders on Arlington Heights."[45]

Though the university desired to enroll both whites and blacks, its promotional work down-played anti-caste education as central to its mission. Howard began a campaign in the style of "stealth politics," by quietly balancing a progressive political agenda while projecting a moderate message to secure broad support. This practice was also utilized at other AMA colleges, including Straight University in New Orleans (now

Dillard), where no mention was made in college catalogs to indicate its anti-caste aims, nor any allusion to race or color.[46] During his time as commissioner of the BRFAL, O. O. Howard advised district supervisors under his command to persuade hostile Southerners with kindness and perhaps a little deception. His supervisors learned to tailor their message to particular audiences, revealing more about their "radical" aims to some while providing limited reassurances to more conservative groups. Howard's experiences in supervising his subordinates in these negotiations proved valuable in his leadership of the university.

The administration used anti-caste principles to guide policy decisions. Yet, Howard, unlike Berea, did not want external audiences to view its work as political or in opposition to Southern whites. While the congressional charter that founded the university provided some relief from fundraising, it also brought additional constraints. O. O. Howard aspired that the university would gain recognition for its exceptional educational opportunities, rather than for enrollment practices. O. O. Howard published a lengthy article in a leading magazine of the day describing that the university would provide "to the general student . . . the means of a general education."[47] Buried at the end of a lengthy publicity piece highlighting the elegance of the university buildings, the scientific collections available to aid study, and the expertise of its faculty, Howard finally broached the topic of the university's admissions policy: "The scope of the university is broad, and its aims must meet the approval and co-operation with the liberal mind everywhere. *It opens wide its portals to the student of whatever belief, color, or sex.* It offers them the training necessary for commencing any legitimate business, to fit them to teach others in the schools and in the professions, or to fill with credit any position which duty, necessity, or inclination may lead them to undertake."[48]

General Howard negotiated the sale of a large tract of land for the university; purchased from a farmer, the property was near the Freedmen's Hospital on a hill with an expansive view of the nation's capital.[49] Andrew Wylie, a judge on the Supreme Court of Washington, D.C., and his wife were angered when they learned of plans to build a school for blacks near their home. Mrs. Wylie threatened Colonel John Easton, the assistant commissioner for the BRFAL and future Howard University trustee, saying that his career would be jeopardized if plans continued. The protests of a few, however, were insufficient compared to the might of the Howard trustees.

Howard's commitment to open admissions brought severe financial consequences and a congressional investigation. While commissioner of the BRFAL, Howard made allocations to Howard University. The BRFAL was only authorized to grant funds to private organizations for the "education of loyal Refugees and Freedmen." Because the university charter stipulated that its mission was for the "education of youth," Howard was accused of improperly allocating BRFAL funding to the university. The *New York Times* printed a lengthy defense of General Howard, and reproduced the university's financial records for its readers. The *New York Times* asserted that the scandal impugned an honorable man.

> It comes from the same bitter spirit of calumny which has never ceased to follow him from the hour he openly planted himself upon the broad principle of complete human equality until now. While in the army, while at the head of the Freedmen's Bureau, no man dared utter aught in disparagement of Gen. O. O. Howard; but so soon as he took the ground that both the church and the school should be thrown open to his colored fellow-citizens, he combined against himself the sleepless malice of an old and relentless persecution. ... There is nothing mysterious or difficult to explain in the present financial conditions of Howard University. Notwithstanding the hue and cry now raised in different quarters, there is nothing which ought either to alarm its friends or give satisfaction to its enemies. It is true that the President and trustees of Howard University possessed large means; but it is also true that they have bravely attempted and accomplished a very large work. ... It has been attempted to accomplish in a year what in ordinary times might require a century. ... Howard University, fully equipped, completely organized and in vigorous operation is now a noble feature of Washington, worthy of the nation.[50]

Though the ordeal stretched over several years, the scandal led to Howard's resignation as president in 1874, the same year the BRFAL officially shuttered. Previously in 1872, Howard was dispatched to negotiate a treaty with the Apache in Arizona. During the first two years of Howard's western assignment an interim president took the helm. The interim president was John Mercer Langston, the Oberlin graduate and lawyer who had defended Edmonia Lewis against charges of poisoning her college roommates. Langston's administration was praised by trustees and the *Washington Post* alike. Despite wide admiration, the school's board ultimately lacked faith that a black president would succeed in raising funds from white donors. Howard would not have an official black president until Mordecai Johnson in 1926.

Living Coeducation at the Three Colleges?

For over sixty years, when scholars study school integration and its challenges they, implicitly or explicitly, turn to some variation of Gordon Allport's contact theory. Allport asserted that schools can produce racial integration if the conditions for interracial contact are appropriately specified. By reducing individual prejudice, schools foster new attitudes to produce change beyond the schoolhouse gate. Allport theorized that positive integration results from equal status, authoritative support and cooperation and shared goals. This view articulates schools as something akin to total institutions, bounded from the prejudices, power relations, and inequalities of broader society. In Erving Goffman's articulation of total institutions, however, there are "inmates" whose lives are wholly structured and ordered within the institution and there are "caretakers" who leave and interact with the outside world. As the inmates adapt and are rehabilitated they internalize wholly the values of the institution. In the most extreme depiction of the process of education, students are also asked to give up much of their identity in exchange for various rewards—social and cultural capital, for instance.[51] Such a view was all the more dominant for mission-driven campuses like Berea, Howard, and Oberlin. For anti-casteists and adherents to contact theory, schools have the power to not just rehabilitate individuals but also—and more potently—to translate within-school relations upwards to macro-level social change. Yet, to exert such influence required perfecting integration at the local level.

How thoroughly did anti-caste philosophy permeate daily life? What actions did administrators and faculty take to realize their professed goals? Recent work on organizations by Amy Binder and Tim Hallett, among others, focuses on disjunctures between local-level practices and macro-level "myths" or "logics." Such accounts suggest organizations may fail to live out their professed ideals because of a disjuncture between the realm of local practice and the macro-level ideals. As this section shows, the three schools were tightly wed to their logics in daily practices and policies. But the three schools interpreted anti-caste logics differently at the campus level. Amy Binder emphasizes attending to "creativity at the local level, as well as the rules of the game, to understand how organizations work."[52] Oberlin adopted strict colorblind practices while Berea and Howard administrators were flexible to changes in their enrollment. How did each college craft its own approach to integrationist practices in student life experiences, enrollment policy and practices, and representation in faculty and administration? On each campus, there are compelling reasons to imagine that the colleges could resist external pressures to segregate. Evidence of the colleges' logics and commitment to interracial education are analyzed through examination of two measures: student enrollment policies and representation at the level of faculty and administration. Scholars typically measure *authoritative support* by the presence of minority teachers. Administrators and trustees designed curriculum, policy, and the demographic composition of faculty and students. Enrollment and minority representation provide evidence of the colleges' strategies for organizing integration.

As scholars of racial integration demonstrate, within-school practices that shape student experiences are a key factor in shaping attitudes about racial performance. Thus, "gate-keeping" mechanisms, including tracking, can produce racial divisions even within a school boasting robust demographic variation.[53] Did these daily experiences and close friendships produce durable transformations for individual students? How did students, faculty and board members contribute to practices of integration? Did the experiences they shared in dormitories and dining halls prove as transformative as their founders hoped?

Enrollment Strategies

The three colleges differed in their enrollment strategies. Oberlin's black enrollment hovered between 5 and 10 percent, blacks constituted a majority at Howard, and Berea maintained equal enrollment of black and white students. All three enrolled students from multiple states.[54] Though most students came from Kentucky, Ohio, and Tennessee, Berea students came from as far as Rhode Island and Oregon. Howard and Oberlin also boasted international enrollment. In addition to students from the Northeast and upper South, Howard enrolled Native Americans and students from Japan, China, and unspecified African countries. By 1908, Oberlin claimed alumni from every state and over 100 countries, including Micronesia, Peru, and Austria.[55] Fewer blacks attended Oberlin and fewer whites attended Howard than the equal enrollment of blacks and whites at Berea. Still, Oberlin and Howard enrolled more minority students than do most selective colleges in the twenty-first century. Although all three achieved impressively diverse student bodies, each adopted different enrollment strategies. Oberlin students often came from communities with large free black populations, such as Rochester or Oneida in New York. Many first enrolled in the preparatory division and later matriculated in the college. An "Annual Circular to Alumni and Friends from 1880" provides a historical overview of Oberlin's enrollment: "The proportionate number of colored students is probably greater than of any other class. It is impossible to obtain an exact statement of the facts; because our catalogues and record books do not reveal the color and no man's memory is reliable on this question for a period of several years. In the last catalogue the proportion of colored students is 5 and one-third per cent. This is exactly the ration for the decade preceding the war. For the decade following it was about eight per cent. This class of students would feel more than others the financial pressure and yet we are better provided with means to aid such students than any other class, having fifty scholarships covering tuition to give to them, and the interest of $6,000 to distribute to them in addition."[56]

President James Fairchild argued that through common experiences at Oberlin College, feelings of superiority fell away as white students learned that "a supercilious air seems out of place. The lip that at first curled with contempt, will at length smile a recognition of a common humanity."[57] Fairchild asserted that schools established only for black students might offer fine facilities and excellent faculty, indeed they might offer better resources, but without the opportunity for whites and blacks to attend school together, such schools could not match the transformative "caste-breaking power" available at Oberlin. In doing so, Oberlin denied that there should be any matching between the type of education offered and the types of students who enrolled: "Oberlin College was never designed to be a colored school; that is, to furnish facilities peculiarly adapted to the wants of the colored people; nor has there ever been an effort on the part of its managers, so to modify it as to meet these wants. It has aimed to offer to the colored student one advantage, as pressing as any other—that is, to the extent of its influence, to break down the barrier of caste, and to elevate him to a common platform of intellectual, social, and religious life. This result it aims to secure, by admitting him, without any reservation or distinction, to all the advantages of a school, having a fair standing among the colleges of the land. Such a work, a distinctively colored school could not effect."[58]

Oberlin professor Henry Cowles compiled a list of the black students who had attended the college between 1835 and 1863. He found far more had, unsurprisingly, attended the preparatory division. Despite irregularity in recording racial identification, Cowles found somewhere between 245 and 310 black students in its first twenty-eight years.[59] Blacks made up between 20 and 30 percent of the small town, and in addition to an integrated private college, the public school—less than a block south of the college—was also integrated.

Berea took a more radical approach. Its administrators decided that for interracial contact to have transformative effects, the college needed equal numbers of black and white students. After the war, it reopened in 1865 with ninety-five black students and ninety-one whites and it maintained this enrollment ratio into the early 1890s. In 1867, Reverend Fee reported to the AMA that Berea achieved equal enrollment of black and white students: "This is the first day of the term. There were present this morning nearly 200 pupils. . . . During the last term, the school was about equally divided—colored and white. Though there is yet in the State much prejudice against impartial education, yet in many instances this is giving way. . . . The precedent will do good. The work here we regard as of great importance."[60]

An early fundraising campaign described Berea students as "manifesting such a degree of energy, perseverance and self denial in getting an education that they cannot fail to become a great power in the South. . . . Every room in the college buildings is overflowing, and some are crawling up into the attic where they can scarcely stand erect. Shelter for this class of earnest, self-reliant young men, white and colored, must be provided without delay."[61] Increasingly, Berea hedged away from its earlier insistence that race could not be recognized visually. Determined that Berea should attract white and black students equally, college administrators and faculty agreed that deliberate color-conscious recruitment efforts were needed. By 1880, the college decided it needed to actively recruit black students to formally ensure racial balance. To do so required a two-part approach: "Sometimes (outreach) needs to be in the mountain counties to increase their interest in education and draw large numbers of white students to Berea. Sometimes the blue grass counties should be visited, that the colored people of the State may not be allowed to abate their interest in higher education, nor the number of colored students fall off."[62] Faculty committed to grueling outreach activities. Through lecture tours and correspondence, they appealed to donors in the North. Berea's need to send faculty on fundraising speaking tours proved successful in attracting funds but came at a significant cost. Addressing the Board of Trustees, an exhausted Professor V. I. Dodge pleaded, "Such is the relation of Berea toward the outer world as well as toward its students, that an efficient worker here must be more than a class instructor.... Since the last meeting of the Board of Trustees I have delivered 56 addresses on various public occasions, attended 436 meetings, and written 96 letters for the College.... I hope that in my 18 years service I have not shown much disposition to shirk work. But I find it is my duty to inform the Board that the effects of the years are urging upon me a readjustment of the hours of labor and rest."[63]

The intensity of their ideals might suggest that these colleges were utopian communities, but they did not wish to shut themselves off from broader society. Instead, they viewed their existence as critically tied to communicating the necessity and feasibility of interracial cooperation. They were, above all, promoting a model for living in interracial solidarity as citizens. Taxing though this was on the faculty, it proved successful. The national news magazine, the *Independent* reported, "As these fathers fought side by side with the colored man on the battle-field, so now the sons of these white men are willing to stand side by side with the colored boy in the school-room."[64] Nearing the twenty-fifth anniversary of its founding, Berea's Board of Trustees celebrated that the "marvelous thing in Berea's history has been the nearly equal division of our students between white and colored."[65] In 1881, the *New York Times* announced that Berea had received a number of large donations. The largest, a sum of $50,000, was donated by "a Western Massachusetts friend," an abolitionist who had secured a fortune as a successful merchant. A journalist heralded Berea as extraordinary, as a little school in a rural area that had attracted widespread donor attention, for which "six different States should unite in aiding a school shows the wide-spread interest which the North has in the general education and impartial treatment of the masses at the South."[66] Advocating anti-caste coeducation had attracted generous donors and media attention, both during the Reconstruction years and the decade that followed.

Howard University elected a policy of colorblind admissions. In fundraising, General Howard and others did not make mention of the unique mission of the school.[67] Howard enrolled a majority of black students and attracted white students predominately to teacher education, law, and medical programs. It is important to note that these three programs of study enrolled far more students than the school's liberal arts course. Howard sought to attract white students by offering exceptional advantages in facilities and courses of study at a price more affordable than comparable local colleges. Howard would be a "school so well mannered and so thoroughly furnished that the white youth in its vicinity would also seek its advantages."[68] Howard's administration invested heavily in physical infrastructure, assuming whites were rational actors who would enroll at the best-equipped institution. By 1868, Howard added a medical department, and in 1869 added a department of law, growing the faculty substantially.

In 1870, a Howard observer pointed to the additional challenges that Howard faced in managing its growth.

> This last great enterprise of General Howard and his coadjutors was from the start beset with peculiar difficulties. They purposed to found in the very heart of the nation an institution which in all the details of its work would necessarily confront the most deeply-rooted prejudices of the people and yet should offer an attractive example of broad Christian benevolence. They designed to provide the highest possible culture for the freedmen of both sexes, in a school so well mannered and so thoroughly furnished that the white youth in its vicinity would also seek its advantages. Such a university could not begin small and grow slowly to large proportions as do others. The number and violence of its enemies would be fatal to it in its incipiency. Nor could the zeal of its friends brook delay. To achieve success it must from the first exhibit such strength and health as to compel admiration and override opposition. This determined the policy of its foundation.[69]

Howard grew quickly indeed. Two years after it opened, the university boasted law and medical schools. During that same time, enrollment skyrocketed from five white women students to a population of several hundred students. On farm fields where cattle once grazed, Howard quickly erected an impressive campus with handsome brick buildings. Journalists found Howard's diversity remarkable: "We were impressed.... There were students of both sexes, of all colors, and many races—there were pure negroes, mulattoes of every tint, Indians, Chinese, and a sprinkling of Anglo-Saxons."[70] Howard president Patton, in 1877, commented that the university affords the "opportunity to pursue normal school and collegiate studies, and also to obtain a theological, medical, or legal education. Its charter has no restriction (and forbids any) as to race, color, or sex, and it always has had more or less white students."[71]

Howard's medical college enrolled the largest number of white students. In its efforts to attract both white and black students, every effort was made "to place it, in respect to lecture rooms, apparatus, and all other necessary appliances, upon a par with the most advanced medical schools of the day."[72] Yet it was also the scarcity of medical schools nationwide and the attractively low comparative costs that drew white students to the medical college. The profession of medicine was relatively young and few universities offered medical training, and Howard alone offered an on-site training hospital. This was particularly true for women whose opportunities to pursue medical degrees were limited to a handful of programs. Between 1870 and 1880, women made up about 15 percent of medical students. Out of Victorian modesty, the dissection laboratories were single-sex but men and women studied together in their other classes. Enrolled at Howard's medical school were 103 women—30 black, 57 white, and 16 without a racial designation.[73] The professions of law and medicine—and the need for specialized training schools—were maturing alongside Howard.

The combination of excellent facilities and low tuition managed to attract white students for over fifteen years. Fewer students were sufficiently enticed by the low costs in other departments to enroll in the liberal arts divisions. An 1879 publication averred, "The caste feeling has been so conquered that two-thirds of the medical students are white— owing partly to the fact that this is the cheapest medical school in the land, and has a connected hospital of three hundred beds."[74] Oberlin and Howard operated on a model of "equality of opportunity." This assumed that whites would cross status divides in search of affordable high-quality education. Berea, by contrast, took a more skeptical view of whites' propensity to risk crossing racial divides and deliberately structured its enrollment policy to ensure equal enrollment of ethno-racial groups.

Representation among Faculty and Administration

The colleges differed greatly in sharing faculty and administrative roles among blacks and whites. Black and white trustees and faculty helped shaped college policy at Berea and Howard while Oberlin lacked black representation in either of these positions. From 1852 to1853, Oberlin's Board of Trustees considered a faculty petition to encourage hiring black faculty members. The faculty felt strongly that students should see blacks in positions of authority as well as in peer relationships. The board "resolved that in the choice of Professors and teachers of all grades we are governed by intrinsic merit irrespective of color," which did not lead to a single affirmative hiring decision.[75] Oberlin did employ a few black graduates as instructors. It was common practice to ask the most talented college students to teach in the preparatory division after their third year. Born into slavery in 1837, Fanny Coppin Jackson completed both college preparatory studies and later the collegiate ("literary") course at Oberlin, where she graduated in 1865. The college recognized her talents and employed her to teach a class of white students which took, as she explained, "more than a little courage" on the part of the faculty.[76] The historical record obscures the identity of most instructors, however, so it is difficult to know how many other black instructors taught in the preparatory division.

Oberlin faculty and trustees had extraordinary political connections. When an Oberlin professor was advised to seek a warmer climate for his health condition, the *Chicago Tribune* reported that, "President Lincoln was consulted and he at once tendered the Professor the Consulship at Hayti."[77] Oberlin graduate Jacob Dolson Cox, who married the daughter of Oberlin president C. G. Finney, served as governor of Ohio and was later appointed secretary of the interior by President Ulysses Grant. Political candidates often included a stop in Oberlin on campaign trails. Cox was also connected to President Garfield, who favored Oberlin as well.

Berea had only two black faculty members and six black board members during the nineteenth century. Its administration boldly wrote policy that challenged their staunchest critics. In 1872, the Board of Trustees wrote into policy that Berea College allowed interracial dating and marriage. This radical policy directly challenged the charge often used by critics: that integrated education would lead to interracial marriage. Berea boldly responded by affirming its commitment to thorough integration. Though the college had fewer black faculty and administrators, its community included many blacks with long careers in abolitionist and civil rights work.

Of the three, Howard University had the most diverse faculty, administration, and Board of Trustees. General Howard, BRFAL commissioner, was appointed Howard's president. Howard's Board of Trustees was comprised of prominent white and black leaders from a variety of professions. Among the white board members were Georgetown University professor and scientist Silas Loomis, several AMA officers, and Kansas senator Samuel Pomeroy. General Howard was largely commended for his policy of appointing blacks in "controlling positions," but subsequent administrations were more hesitant to do so. These appointments were not only important for representational issues, but Howard's black faculty and trustees brought essential skills from decades of negotiating contentious racial politics and leading major reform campaigns. These included black politicians and lawyers who lived abroad during the final decades of slavery, returning with international experience. Among the widely known board members were Frederick Douglas and lawyer John Mercer Langston. Another board member, Lieutenant Colonel Alexander Augusta, was one of only eight Union surgeons commissioned during the Civil War. Augusta, denied entrance to the University of Pennsylvania due to his race, pursued his medical training in Canada. An AMA agent, Francis L. Cardozo, educated in Scotland, and Henry Highland Garnet, an abolitionist activist whose success garnered him speaking engagements in Britain, both also held positions as college presidents. Similarly, Howard's first black professor, George B. Vashon, an 1844 Oberlin graduate, previously worked for the BRFAL and served as president of Avery College in Pittsburgh. Blacks served as faculty and deans of the theology and law departments.[78] For instance, Vashon's administrative and political experience proved influential in launching Howard's law school. Importantly, the greater representation of blacks on the board, combined with their considerable skills in negotiating conflict, enabled Howard's board to deal more openly with contentious issues than either Berea or Oberlin. In addition to both black and white faculty members across the campus, Howard also boasted four women instructors—three white and one black—in Howard's medical department during the nineteenth century.

Student Life

Student life in the mid-nineteenth century was austere. Students lived humbly, many interrupted their studies to teach in Southern schools to afford college, and there was little time for leisure after fulfilling their academic and work duties. Students at Berea, Howard, and Oberlin all engaged in "learning and labor" programs, earning their tuition and board. This stemmed from the manual labor movement that began in the 1830s. Proponents worried that too much studying would rob young men of their physical prowess and that the inaccessibility of university training for anyone but the elite ran counter to Jacksonian democratic ideals. In response, some colleges augmented their "literary" or academic studies with requirements for manual labor. At Oberlin and Berea, in particular, administrators believed these experiences would liberate students from feelings of class superiority. These self-support programs allowed students of lesser financial means to attend college. Students might work in the kitchen, maintain buildings, or grow food in the gardens. Still, student labor positions did not financially support a college. Since the colleges prioritized enrolling students of limited means, they had to find other means to finance their operating costs. A common practice was to allow donors to provide "subscriptions" that financially supported individual students' tuition. Prior to the rise of foundations in subsequent years, small individual donors constituted the majority of financial support for these colleges, primarily from political allies abroad and in the North.

Like many contemporary universities, the colleges included high school education in addition to college programs. By the mid-nineteenth century, Oberlin's preparatory division enrolled several hundred students and students could elect a "classical" education. Access to high school education was beyond consideration for many Americans, and exceedingly rare in rural areas. Like those at Berea and Howard, Oberlin's preparatory division proved popular even during trying financial times, such as after the war when "the new admissions show no falling off of students."[79] Because there were no standardized college admissions criteria, preparatory divisions also offered a prime pathway for the recruitment of college students. For example, in 1867, Howard's preparatory division, as it was called, required three years of Latin and two years of classical Greek. Many of the students who enrolled in the preparatory divisions continued their collegiate studies at the same college. But a few Howard preparatory graduates pursued higher education in the Northeast: Inman Page (Howard 1872) graduated from Brown University, and Wiley Lane (Howard 1873) was elected Phi Beta Kappa at Amherst College. After studying at Berea, Carter G. Woodson pursued advanced degrees at the University of Chicago and Harvard before joining the faculty at Howard.

The curriculum was shaped by the educational experiences of the faculty. Many administrators and trustees hoped graduates would become leaders in the South.[80] Supporters of Howard University argued, "We do not know [how] money could be more judiciously and productively invested than by endowing Howard University to supply the present and future, urgent and constantly-increasing demand for educated teachers, physicians, lawyers and ministers, to labor for the people of the South."[81] The clearest path for students at Berea, Howard, and Oberlin was to become preachers and teachers, and Howard added lawyers, doctors and pharmacists. At Oberlin and Howard, students could find work as teachers after completing the preparatory course. The bachelor's degree had yet to become a unified degree of study; as such, there were a variety of educational programs. For students equipped with a classical preparatory education, the "literary course" offered coursework leading to the equivalent of a bachelor's degree. The "ladies course" at Oberlin offered coursework comparable to a modern bachelor's degree but did not require knowledge of classical languages. The colleges differentiated between literary courses, which required classical languages, and ladies' courses, which did not. At all three colleges, several women enrolled in the classical literary courses. All three offered theological and teacher-training courses as well as liberal arts programs. The literary course at Howard was similarly classical in curriculum, perhaps a reflection of the faculty's educational experiences; of the five founding faculty members, three were educated at Yale, Princeton, and Harvard.

From Howard University's earliest hours, it was evident that the challenge was less the capacity of the university to provide a first-rate education. Rather, the university's main challenge was gaining broad recognition for its students as equals in intellectual potential with students at the elite, white universities. Mastering the classics was regarded as the highest scholarly achievement. As such, the colleges were quick to highlight the success of black students in these courses: "The freshman who ranked highest in the preparatory department was born a slave; and, under a very strict teacher, his marks were perfect in Greek, and failed only once in being perfect in Latin."[82] Black students were hyper-visible at Oberlin, where they were few in numbers, and in Washington, D.C., where Howard's black students were often compared to neighboring students at Columbia College (now George Washington University) and especially Cornell University. Cornell made a nice comparison for many observers because it was founded in the same year as Howard and shared an appreciation for "self help" through manual labor. Their classroom achievements were broadcast not only within the school, but even made national news. By contrast, Berea focused on collective accomplishment and ensured that blacks and whites were equally represented, whether in delivering public speeches or classroom exercises. Regardless of the activity, black and white students were consistently and deliberately paired. Berea maintained that the true achievement of the college was in working toward social harmony. While Howard broadcast its mission as centered on academic and professional excellence, Berea and Oberlin both regularly affirmed that the learning environment and process were as important as what students learned.

Yet, students' experiences were filled with contradictions. As college students, they were young and often away from their families for the first time and their actions were under unusually close observation. Fanny Coppin Jackson remembered, "I never rose to recite in my classes at Oberlin but I felt that I had the honor of the whole African race upon my shoulders. I felt that, should I fail, it would be ascribed to the fact that I was colored."[83] Yet at the same time, she reported feeling "part of the family" at her boarding house. Her overall recollections of her life on campus were positive: "I was elected class poet for the Class Day exercises, and have the kindest remembrance of the dear ones who were my classmates. I never can forget the courtesies of the three Wright brothers; of Professor Pond, of Dr. Lucien C. Warner, of Doctor Kincaid, the Chamberland girls, and others, who seemed determined that I should carry away from Oberlin nothing but most pleasant memories of my life there."[84] After graduating in 1865 and beginning her career as a classics teacher, she reported finding life in Philadelphia a bruising experience: "I had been so long in Oberlin that I had forgotten about my color."[85] While administrators and journalists were eager to convey the ease with which coeducation was accomplished, Fanny Coppin Jackson's recollections remind us that black students must have felt enormous pressure. This pressure, however, was also not limited to their time on campus. The *Washington Post* reported the unfair standards to which Howard students were held. Upon graduating from the preparatory division, a group of six rising first-year Howard students were celebrating their accomplishment boisterously. The *Post* condemned police for arresting the students, charging that it is a blunder to discriminate in the execution of the law. If Harvard, Princeton, Yale and other college boys are permitted to give their class "yells" in the public streets here, . . . the Howard University boys have the same rights as other boys and should be permitted to enjoy them."[86] Every action—every mistake and every accomplishment—was viewed as representative of blacks' suitability for freedom, for inclusion, and for citizenship.

Students shared other campus experiences, beyond those of the classroom. Alcohol, smoking, and other vices were strictly scorned and chapel attendance was an important part of daily life. All three colleges erected impressive brick dormitories within a few years of their founding, and students shared rooms and dined together. At all three colleges, it was common for students to live in either dormitories or in boarding houses. Howard's first dormitory had rooms available for 300 students, as well as space for some faculty. Indeed, at Berea and Oberlin students were, for some periods of time, assigned dining tables to inhibit cliquish behavior. After his first year on campus, a Berea professor, who lived in the male dormitory, described campus life: "Here throughout the year, the Negro, the Mountaineer, and the Northerner fraternized in the most cordial way. . . . Having lived with the men, and having made a careful study of that specific point during the year, it is my unqualified opinion that this mixing up of men from different sections and of different races, is good, and only good. . . . The game-room, the baseball diamond are . . . social foci of high value."[87]

At Oberlin, several faculty and local families took in black and white students as lodgers. Sepia-tinged photographs in the Oberlin College archives show residents posed outside their boarding houses, groups of ten to fifteen young women, usually with only one or two black students among them. Boarders ate their meals with the family and often reported feeling very much at home. One black student, who described herself as naturally quite thin—"like two matchsticks"—felt her health declining in the dormitory but happily gained healthy weight once she moved in with a family.[88] Letters between students and among alumni reveal the tight connections and ideological commitment of the college.[89]

Organized student activities were few. Students were treated as young members of the community. Berea and Oberlin, especially, went to great effort to avoid "town-gown" distinctions. Of course, unlike Washington, D.C., both the towns of Berea and Oberlin were so small that campus and community were easily melded together. Popular among adults as well as students, literary societies were social events for the discussion of political issues, philosophical ideas, or literature. Students created their

FIGURE 4. Berea College graduates, 1901. Courtesy of Berea College Special Collections and Archives, Berea, Kentucky.

own literary societies—popular at nearly all nineteenth century colleges—where students read a selected writing, often political or philosophical in nature, and spent the evening debating ideas. Literary societies were a high-status campus activity for debating philosophy and politics.[90] Berea's literary society annually shifted between black and white society presidents and its debate teams were structured as interracial pairings.[91] Yearbook portraits of the literary societies at Oberlin show that some had more black students than others, but it appears that most Oberlin students took part in one debate club or the other.

The pressure to maintain white enrollment had the undesirable effect of stifling some discussions, at least on campus. Howard's literary society was formed in 1872 and many other literary societies formed off-campus in Washington, D.C., drawing students and faculty alike. Howard student were incorporated into Washington, D.C.'s black elite society, taking part in off-campus church and literary societies, where they had greater freedom to express political beliefs.[92]

Despite differences between the campuses, records from the literary societies indicate that debates on racial equality were frequent for all three campuses. Students readily engaged with potentially divisive topics even if—as at Howard—they did not always do so in integrated club settings. Aside from the rare festivity or literary society meeting, most students were busy with chapel, their work obligations, and their studies. Students had the luxury of time to study but were not given license to engage in "frivolous" activities.

Students and faculty forged close relationships at all three colleges. During their studies and in reflection later in life, students remembered their campus experiences as rare. As Frances ("Fanny") Coppin Jackson remembered, "Prejudice at Oberlin is preached against, prayed against, sung against, and lived against."[93] A personal letter between Anna Julia Cooper, who graduated in 1884, and a white alumnus friend reveals that both remembered Oberlin as more egalitarian in their college days: "There were giants in those days, big hearted, high towered giants of spiritual elevation."[94] The letter was written nearly sixty years after their graduation and offers testimony to the depth of interracial friendships that were possible at Oberlin. By several accounts, a serious shift occurred in the mid-1880s that left many black alumni hurt and puzzled by the changing social climate on campus.

The "Knotty Problem" Solved?

The accomplishment of these schools bringing together blacks and whites was indeed remarkable. The colleges published appeals for donations in leading Northern newspapers and news magazines and were endorsed by major cultural figures, politicians, and journalists. College presidents were invited to speak at high-profile public lectures in the North. For instance, in 1869, Berea's reverend Fee spoke, along with contemporary celebrity Reverend Henry Ward Beecher. Beecher was the most famous American entertainer in an era when entertainment—including opera and theatre—were scorned by "respectable" people.[95] At the height of Beecher's fame, Frost took the stage alongside him at New York City's Cooper Institute to deliver a lecture on the subject of "Education at the South and in the Special Interest of Berea College," which the New York Times reported as "of great interest."[96] Berea, Edward Fairchild argued, would be a beacon to the rest of the nation "by (its) constant exhibition of perfect equality."[97] The New York Times, Chicago Tribune, and other news outlets regularly reviewed commencement activities at large schools such as Yale, Michigan, and Wisconsin. Though much smaller in size, Berea, Oberlin, and Howard were featured in the same press coverage of commencement exercises. During the 1870s and 1880s, Berea reported attracted several thousand visitors to witness commencement exercises. Attendees included nationally known visitors from New Orleans, Chicago, and New York. George Washington Cable, a literary figure whose popularity rivaled that of Mark Twain, was a frequent visitor and supporter. Similarly, John Greenleaf Whittier, celebrated poet, abolitionist, and a founding contributor to the *Atlantic Monthly*, also supported Berea.

The colleges hoped their successes in interracial living would inspire others to adopt their practices for building interracial solidarity. The *Chicago Tribune* heralded that Oberlin had solved "the social problem" a mere five months after the Civil War ended. The *Chicago Tribune* applauded the effects of interracial education as important for reducing white prejudices: "Another almost immediate and marked influence of these schools is seen upon the white people in the lessening prejudice, in the admission of the African's ability to learn, and his consequent fitness for places in the world from which we have hitherto excluded him."[98] Another publication praised Berea for its eighteen years of success: "Looking at the success of this school the question that naturally arises is this: Will this school lead to the establishment of other mixed schools?"[99] The colleges were praised for educating blacks and whites together, and their students' accomplishments were used as testimony in a broader debate over whether blacks and whites were equal in intellectual potential. In 1880, forty-three years after Oberlin voted to admit black students and fifteen years after the end of the Civil War, the *New York Times* declared, "Oberlin has clearly solved that knotty problem of the respective mental capacity of the races."[100]

Together, these glimpses into campus life reveal an unexpectedly high level of interracial contact that challenges contemporary depictions of the era as wholly segregated. Students ate their meals at integrated dining tables, sat together in classes, and worked together in the garden and in the laundry. Despite pervasive racism, all three colleges enrolled black and white students who became close friends, roommates, and classroom peers. Education "at the breach" was not without its challenges. Students like Fanny Coppin Jackson reported feeling enormous pressure; at the same time, it was a far more liberated space than the world students would enter upon graduation. They sang together in chapel choirs and shared their ideas about politics and literature through literary societies. They prepared together for careers in medicine, law, teaching, and as scholars.

A few fell in love, some stayed on to join the faculty of their alma maters, and many became preachers, lawyers, or teachers. For more than twenty years, the anti-caste dream was realized on campuses in Washington, D.C., rural Kentucky, and Ohio. While administrations differed in their visions for how best to foster and maintain interracial contact, administrators shared deep personal convictions in equality and social justice. In many ways, these administrators designed organizations that aligned remarkably well with the conditions that contemporary sociologists have found essential for integration, and they did so a century earlier. How then were these advances thwarted? It is to this question that the following chapter turns.

CHAPTER FOUR

From Cause to Common Charity
Off-Campus Pressures

> The nation took time to breathe and think; and then was heard
> another voice saying, "You are our creditors, by reason of years
> of unredressed wrong; and you are our comrades, because you
> fought with us and for us in this war."
>
> —HENRY MARTYN SCUDDER, D.D. to the AMA National
>   Conference, 1871

> The race is to be tested by results.... The only way the
> friends of the black man can permanently protect him is to
> help him gain this inward power.... The grammar schools
> and colleges, the industrial and theological schools, and the
> churches will do more to secure their rights as freemen than
> a standing army can do.
>
> —C. H. RICHARDS, *The American Missionary*, 1878

Postwar Organization of Higher Education

In 1873, the new National Bureau of Education published the first com-
prehensive list of higher education institutions. Education commissioner
General John Eaton, a former BRFAL administrator, viewed the importance of the document as "giving a view of the influence upon the community of the colleges as a class; whereas now each college is looked upon
measurably as an institution standing by itself alone."[1] Prior to this, colleges largely determined their own rules. Indeed, there was very little
that was uniform among colleges. Individual colleges set their admissions
and graduation requirements, evaluated faculty quality by a variety of
metrics, and issued an absolute hodgepodge of diplomas. An analysis of
439 newspaper articles focused on Oberlin, Berea, or Howard reveals
that, prior to 1880, colleges were rarely discussed in conjunction with
other schools, whereas in the decades that followed, journalists regularly
clustered colleges and universities in reportage.

The allocation of resources by the BRFAL and AMA, combined with
increasing legislative deliberation over Southern education, focused at-

tention on the entire landscape of higher education. This brought into focus an understanding of the many colleges and universities—public and private, state-run, and denominational—as constituting a field of higher education. This new field orientation was at odds with the governing logics at anti-caste colleges. Anti-caste colleges were not initially oriented toward other colleges but rather articulated their importance in relation to broader society—to the future communities where graduates would teach or minister, to the political debates that united the citizenry, and to the theological concerns within their religious communities.

These colleges had little tolerance for students who indulged in leisure activities. Rather, students' time could be better spent contributing to the greater good, or at least preparing themselves to do so. There was very little concern for other colleges and the notion of creating a separate campus life was viewed with disdain. "College life with us is not peculiar, occupied with its own exclusive interests, pursuing its own separate schemes, and governed by its own code of duty and of honor," Oberlin president Fairchild explained in his inaugural address in 1866, but rather, "each student belongs to the world, not isolated from its sympathies, obligation and activities.... The student still shares in the responsibilities of common life, and is here for the purpose of a better outfit for the work before him."[2] In short, the colleges were not refuges from the responsibilities of adult life, and as Fairchild looked out at his students one year after the end of the Civil War, he must also have remembered the many students who had left Oberlin to fight for the Union Army and the many who never returned.[3] Of the 166 young men enrolled in 1861, 100 students volunteered to enlist and more than 800 men left Oberlin to fight for the Union cause.[4] Oberlin was very much engaged with the political and civic challenges of the day, and students were afforded no protected status. Fairchild had grown up in Oberlin, he attended the preparatory division, worked his way through as a "manual labor student" and began teaching at the preparatory division already during the latter two years of college. If anyone might have thought of Oberlin—or a college education more broadly—as isolated, it would have been Fairchild.

Rather than isolated, the colleges were self-sufficient. Because many colleges—including Berea, Howard, and Oberlin—had preparatory divisions attached to the college, there was a very clear trajectory and a seamless curriculum that bridged secondary and collegiate education. Individual colleges often held their own on-campus admissions examinations.

Not only did more colleges open after the war, but the nature of the college curriculum and degrees awarded also underwent a transformation. In the early nineteenth century, the strict and uniform curriculum prevalent in many colleges before the war focused on ancient languages, mathematics, moral philosophy, natural philosophy, and chemistry.[5] After the Civil War, curricular changes opened to offer a wider range of programs of study. The Morrill Act pushed to democratize higher education by including technical studies. For instance, Cornell University took as its motto in 1868, "an institution where any person can find instruction in any study."[6] In this regard, Ezra Cornell articulated his belief that Cornell should be open to anyone, especially to poor men and women. He also believed that the education at Cornell should include the mechanical and industrial pursuits and apply broadly to the students' chosen future endeavor.

Some colleges, including Oberlin and Howard, created a range of diploma options to reflect this opportunity for specialization. The National Bureau of Education reported no fewer than thirty-five distinct college degrees awarded across the United States. The agency remarked that this range was overwhelmingly complex, noting an alphabet soup of degrees "embracing abbreviations not to be found in some dictionaries."[7] As governmental tabulations increased, publications like the U.S. Commissioner of Education Reports streamlined the types of degrees tracked. By 1878, the U.S. Commissioner of Education Reports recorded twenty-five separate degrees, not including feminized degrees such as "mistress of arts." The Howard Alumni Catalog includes graduates awarded the following degrees: BS, BA, BL, LLB, LLD, AM, MS, and more.[8] Though the U.S. Commissioner of Education Reports kept track of the number of colleges, number of graduates, tuition, and sometimes even the number of books, the quality of the education afforded was not under scrutiny.[9] The commission seemed to carefully count all manner of things but had yet to determine a way to quantify something so elusive as the quality of an education. Colleges were able to determine their requirements independent of external oversight.

By the early 1880s, Oberlin, Berea, and Howard had been implementing innovative policies to ensure coeducation for nearly twenty years. All had received national recognition. Berea and Oberlin were both established communities—in addition to college campuses—and that seemed to offer an important buffer from social tension. These communities imagined themselves as laboratories for creating a model society. Even as violence against blacks raged from New Jersey to South Carolina, Howard found security in its location in the nation's capital.[10] Seemingly assured of federal protection and surrounded by an elite black community, Howard felt protected. Yet college campuses were far from isolated or protected from the dangers of the outside world. None had imagined they were building reclusive utopias. All proclaimed their triumphs and encouraged others to follow their lead. This chapter examines these changes across the fields that the AMA envisioned as within its reach— law, migration, charity, and higher education—and the impact these had on the AMA as an organization. Through this examination of the external environments of the schools, we see how the legal field, migration, new private philanthropic projects, and increasing intercollegiate competition coevolved to undermine interracial cooperation.

The colleges—and the AMA connections that united them—imagined their graduates exerting multi-level influence in social relations. Anti-caste organizers believed that interpersonal contact and heterogeneous group experiences could shatter prejudices imported to campus from early life experiences, and that these individual transformations would affect students' beliefs and actions even after they left college. Interracial contact and familiarity—particularly as fostered through schools and churches—were conceptualized as more powerful than legal structures in the durable transformation of norms. As one speaker noted at the annual meeting of the AMA, "The primer and the Testament, well used, will be a better palladium than Congressional enactments."[11] While still commissioner of the BRFAL, General Howard articulated prejudice as "a conventionalism . . . and all conventionalisms are liable to change."[12] In their view, the tenets of anti-caste beliefs would spread across domains vertically—from individuals up through organizations to the political realm. The AMA believed colleges were a protected setting for young citizens to practice interracial cooperation. College campuses would act as a filtering station where students would arrive, likely with certain prejudices, and the anti-caste ideas students learned at college would be transmitted to and purify other fields. The colleges had not, however, considered the influence of other fields—both meso- and macro-level forces—that would exert pressure on them.

The AMA built up a dense network of actors and projects, imagining that the organization could exert substantial control over the actions of member projects and their connections to society. The AMA and its member colleges often articulated that they were autonomous from broader social influences, but that their accomplishments would succeed in transforming the social and political realm. As Gary Alan Fine and Tim Hallett note, however, "every ongoing group is an outpost of society."[13] Organizations rely on collective input to shape their goals and actions, but the demands and pressures of the larger environment reverberate through inter-organizational choices, including shifting logics. While interracial colleges gained support as a postwar reunification strategy, by the turn of the century colleges were increasingly valued for their ability to elevate individual social status. Increasingly, colleges were forced to recognize and respond to influences from beyond the campus gates. The challenges of negotiating between fields held important—if not always straightforward—challenges for anti-caste colleges.

The AMA negotiated a rapidly changing environment by drawing on a particular form of expertise to assert their legitimacy to influence social policy. The AMA made changing deeply ingrained institutional logics—most specifically, the logic of race as a basis for social status—the center of all its projects. Such narratives were promulgated as ethnographic expertise. Different types of discourse lead to different types of interventions. George Steinmetz has described ethnographic discourse as that which claims to represent a fundamental or essential character of a given population by another group which seeks to increase its power. These interventions are efforts to stabilize representations of particular groups and isolate the right conditions for power over particular groups or sectors.[14] The AMA referenced their experience as a long-standing anti-caste organization to situate their view of how best to respond to challenges for civil and social rights.

Perhaps even more important than direct funding, the AMA connected its affiliated colleges to a national organization and published stories and fundraising pleas through its publications. It also connected supporters and funders through national conferences. In its publications and through AMA-fostered speaking engagements, the colleges were able to issue certain narratives about their mission and practices. These narratives regularly drew on the American debt to former slaves and asserted that education offered a viable means of healing wounds caused by slavery. As the memory of the war faded, however, the colleges and the AMA invented new narratives to champion their cause and focused on matching types of education with ideas about particular groups of people.

The next section of this chapter examines legal and demographic changes that shaped the potential for maintaining integration. Changes in the legal environment decreased civil rights enforcement and permitted institutional discrimination by private organizations. Responses to demographic changes affected the network of allies available to the anticaste movement. New immigrant groups arrived from Southern and Eastern Europe and East Asia and this, coupled with the first large-scale black migration to the North and West, aroused both widespread hostility and piqued the interest of the AMA. The demographic changes were interpreted as a status threat by white elites and resulted in changing resource streams. The AMA had organized small missions for Chinese immigrants in California for many years and, with increasing focus on immigration, the AMA saw this as a burgeoning attraction for donors. The following section examines the importance of external organizations in mediating status contests. External organizations—benevolent associations like the AMA, professional organizations, and philanthropic foundations—were constitutive in transforming the field of higher education by spurring intercollegiate competition. The final section of this chapter provides an overview of the changing landscape of higher education. How these shifts in the educational landscape shaped Howard, Oberlin, and Berea are further elaborated in chapters 5, 6, and 7.

As the remaining chapters in this book will show, the dependency upon donors shaped college practices and ideas about groups of people. Comparisons across colleges grew increasingly important as colleges competed for philanthropic support and other resources (including student enrollment). The emergence of commensuration as a mechanism for governing the field of higher education and the introduction of new actors—namely industrial philanthropists—initiated new standards for adjudicating status. As industrialists amassed vast fortunes in the South, they too wanted a hand in organizing Southern race relations. Relatedly, a new organization—the Association of Collegiate Alumnae—emerged in the 1880s and exerted pressure to reform women's educational opportunities at mixed-gender colleges and universities and women's colleges. This will be discussed in the context of sex segregation in chapter 6. Together, focusing on these external organizations helps us understand how even colleges that had been integrated for decades eventually segregated.

Legal Gains and Setbacks

Transforming the Higher Levels of Government

When Radical Republicans gained congressional control in December 1865, Southern whites were briefly barred from voting and office-holding, and subject to federal occupation. Though this was widely lamented by Democrats, such restrictions were sparsely and inconsistently practiced. As part of their application for readmission to the Union, former Confederate states were required to establish public schools for all children. Often the new Constitutions included provisions for supporting a state university, and the abolition of property requirements for voting. That these conditions were implemented sporadically—if at all—is now historical fact. Yet, however briefly, and despite intimidation, blacks gained unprecedented political power in the South.[15] Political representation was more dramatic at the state level, particularly in South Carolina where blacks made up 60 percent of the state legislature. Blacks also held a considerable number of local and state-level political offices and diplomatic posts abroad. To name a few, Dartmouth-educated Jonathan Gibbs served as secretary of state and later as superintendent of education in Florida, and P. B. S. Pinchback was the only black governor in U.S. history until Douglas Wilder's election in Virginia in 1989. Yale-educated Ebenezer Bassett represented the United States to Haiti, and James Milton Turner, briefly educated at Oberlin's preparatory department, was appointed Ambassador to Liberia. Local-level black political organizing took place both through formal political offices, as well as private organizations such as Union Leagues.[16]

On February 25, 1870, Hiram Rhodes Revels was elected the first black member of the U.S. Senate. *Harper's Weekly* published a cartoon titled "Time Works Wonders" depicting Jefferson Davis, former president of the Confederacy and Hiram Revels cast in Shakespeare's *Othello*. In the cartoon, Senator Revels deliberates with colleagues while Davis lurks around a corner quoting: "For that I do suspect the lusty Moor hath lead'd into my seat: though whereof doth like a poisonous mineral gnaw at my inwards."[17] Revels' election signaled to Radical Republicans precisely the shift in politics they hoped to see in the South: Black Republicans ousting white oligarchs. Hiram Revels was joined in the Senate by Blanche Bruce (Mississippi, Republican). Another twenty-one black men served in Congress between 1870 and 1900. Though seemingly a small number, it was not until 1970 that the percentage of black representatives and senators elected during Reconstruction would be repeated.

Black political leaders pressed for fair treatment by the courts, in labor contracts, and in education. The proceedings of the Convention of Colored Men held in Columbia, South Carolina on October 18, 1871, reveals a simple request. An anonymous speaker affirmed that his constituents desired to share in "interests common to the whole people" and rejected that civil rights legislation represented a desire for consideration as a special class. "We do not ask the Government or people of the United States to treat us with peculiar favor, but that, in the policy of the laws, our interest may be grouped with those that receive the consideration of our legislative bodies, and that, in the administration of the laws, no invidious distinctions be made to our prejudice." In particular, black Republicans and their political allies focused most heavily on securing non-discrimination legislation to integrate courts and schools and the enforcement of existing laws to prosecute perpetrators of violent crimes against blacks. Blacks organized political conventions that focused on increasing their influence and representation in politics and schools. These most often occurred at the state level. For instance, at the 1883 Convention of Colored Men in Georgia, delegates pledged to mobilize political canvasing in neighborhoods and counties—particularly predominately black counties—to support black legislative candidates. Delegates also passed a resolution with a set of proposals to secure black representation on local boards of education.[18]

In retaliation against increasing black political and social power, white Southerners formed societies promoting white supremacy and intimidating blacks from exercising political rights. These organizations included the White League, the Ku Klux Klan, and the Knights of the White Camelia. Though woefully insufficient, in 1871, Congress passed the Ku Klux Klan Act to contain white violence against blacks. Southern whites largely adopted a policy of "masterly inactivity" whereby they abstained from participating in formal political elections in protest over the inclusion of blacks as candidates and voters.

Recall that the AMA initiated its program of building a network of colleges in the hopes that relationships forged on campus would influence graduates' later lives, transforming other social institutions. The influence would move from the individual to common schools and churches until it would transform the highest levels of government. The reach of the anti-caste project was evident in the testimony presented in favor of a civil rights bill to prohibit discrimination from private spaces such as restaurants and hotels. In his testimony before Congress, Representative Alonzo Ransier (Florida, Republican) pointed to "schools where black and white are taught in the North and East as well as in the South, it does not appear that either race is injured, or that the cause of general education suffers." Ransier drew on schools with fractional levels of racial diversity—Harvard, Yale, and Wilberforce—as well as Berea and Oberlin.

> At Yale, Harvard, Wilberforce, Cornell, Oberlin, the testimony is that both races get along well together. Nor is the South without such schools. In Madison, Kentucky, there is the Berea College.... The fact that southern-born whites and blacks, in nearly equal proportion and in large numbers, have, for the past six years, recited together and in perfect harmony, makes this institution typical of what may be accomplished throughout the nation, and makes it of more than local importance. It requires no argument to show how much the colored people will be benefitted by such an education. There is nothing like just such a school as this to teach mutual respect and forbearance, to dignify labor, to enforce a regard for the person and property of all classes, and to take away some of the arrogant superciliousness of caste and race.[19]

Nor was Ransier the only congressional representative using integrated universities and colleges as evidence of their potential for realizing social integration more broadly. The University of South Carolina was integrated by the state legislature and publicly funded. In response to charges by Representative Robert Vance (North Carolina, Democrat) that integration had "destroyed" the university, Representative Harvey Cain (South Carolina, Republican) replied:

> It is true that a small number of students left the institution, but the institution still remains. The buildings are there as erect as ever; the faculty are there as attentive to their duties as ever they were; the students are coming in as they did before. It is true, sir, that there is a mixture of students now; that there are colored and white students of law and medicine sitting side by side; it is true, sir, that the prejudice of some of the professors was so strong that it drove them out of the institution; but the philanthropy and good sense of others were such that they remained; and thus we have

still the institution going on, and because some students have left, it cannot be reasonably argued that the usefulness of the institution has been destroyed. The University of South Carolina has not been destroyed.[20]

Consistent with the founding intentions of the AMA colleges, legislators described interracial colleges as available microcosms where legislators could see living examples of the potential for interracial governance and cooperation. In this way, the colleges were described as both predictive—a view of a world that might be—and generative in producing graduates who could draw on their experiences to more broadly diffuse egalitarian practices.

Early Civil Rights Legislation

Few resources were allocated to enforce the laws, but many blacks and whites were encouraged that these laws were written and expected them to hold a durable power over any challenges. The AMA, however, disagreed: "Hostile peoples cannot be pinned together by bayonets, nor bound in harmony by mere laws."[21] For the AMA, only individual conversion—through shared experiences—could create a foundation for civic equality. This work, the AMA held, required the moral guidance of the Protestant churches. The Civil Rights Bills of 1866, 1870, 1871 and 1875 protected rights to property, jurisprudence, and suffrage. Representatives Charles Sumner and Benjamin Butler, both Massachusetts Republicans, first sponsored a bill in 1870 to prohibit discrimination in courts, schools, and private facilities (including transportation). Anti-discrimination legislation pertaining to schooling was heatedly debated. Representative Harvey Cain (South Carolina, Republican) forcefully argued for integrated schools. "Some think it would be better to modify it, to strike out the school clause, or to so modify it that some of the State constitutions should not be infringed. I regard it essential to us and the people of this country that we should be secured in this if in nothing else. I cannot regard that our rights will be secured until the jury-box and the school-room, those great palladiums of our liberty, shall have been opened to us. Then we will be willing to take our chances with other men."[22] Black legislators avoided the term "social equality" but they nonetheless lobbied for a socially integrated future, complete with racially integrated schools.

When Representative Cain spoke before Congress in 1874, he responded to the Conservative clamor over social equality. Like many—including the AMA—he concurred that laws alone could not force social relationships. But Cain drew the boundaries around social relationships as pertaining to shared social institutions, not interpersonal ties: "Sir, social equality is a right which every man, every woman, and every class of persons have within their own control. They have a right to form their own acquaintances, to establish their own social relationships. Its establishment and regulation is not within the province of legislation. No laws enacted by legislators can compel social equality. Now, what is it we desire? What we desire is this: inasmuch as we have been raised to the dignity, to the honor, to the position of our manhood, we ask that the laws of this country should guarantee all the rights and immunities belonging to that proud position, to be enforced all over this broad land."[23]

Cain avoided attempts to legislate relationships and focused on institutional resources—schools, representation on juries, etc. His goal was to match the symbolic value of citizenship with concrete resources to build pathways for social mobility. Representative Cain made clear that without equal access to schools, there could be no objective merit contests. Cain was joined in his call for equal rights by many black legislators.[24]

After five years of debate, Sumner and Butlers' Civil Rights Bill of 1875 was accepted with a vote of 162 to 99, but without provisions for integrated public education.[25] This bill guaranteed that blacks share "full and equal enjoyment of the accommodations, advantages, facilities, and privileges of inns, public conveyances on land or water, theaters, and other places of public amusement." Importantly, this short-lived measure legislated integrating private social spaces. *Harper's Weekly*, the most widely circulated American periodical, affirmed the importance of the bill arguing that it "forbids distinctions founded upon a system of caste which the law has abolished. It prohibits, within its sphere, making an American citizen a pariah because of his color."[26]

Yet, without enforcement, these changes in legislation were difficult to secure on the ground. Federal troops, charged with peace-keeping, were the sole enforcers trusted to adjudicate when blacks were denied rights. The BRFAL, as described in chapter 2, was not authorized sufficient troop density to enforce legal protections. Even at the height of Union occupation, BRFAL agents were responsible for huge territories that were impossible to effectively govern. As military action against Native Americans increased during the 1870s, Union troops were increasingly reassigned from the South to the West. The Compromise of 1877, as it came to be called, followed the contested Hayes-Tilden election of 1876. The 1876 election ended with disputed results in Florida, Louisiana, Oregon, and South Carolina. Democratic leaders accepted Rutherford B. Hayes' victory in exchange for the removal of the last federal troops from the South.

By 1878, the AMA announced its acceptance of the defeat of civil rights legislation. "Now this outward guardianship of law and force has been needed; just as the transplanted flower needs special shelter and the upholding aid of the stick to which it is tied, until its vital power can build it into independent strength. It is still necessary, to a certain degree, though God's providence is fast showing us that law and force can do but a transient work for the race, and must soon be superseded by something better; and that something better is the development of the colored man himself into wisdom, and capability, and moral power." The AMA determined that their educational work remained the single best hope for cultivating a just society. The attention to coeducation through which whites would learn to respect blacks as equals had faded from the AMA's program. By contrast, the AMA articulated an expectation of justice that no longer demanded concessions by whites, arguing that, "when the colored man shows by his deeds that he is able to do all that a white man can do, he will hold his footing of equality secure."[27]

The Invisibility of Racial Discrimination in Law and on Campus

As historian John Hope Franklin has described, Reconstruction waned between 1875 and 1877 and blacks pressed the boundaries of social equality. "There was a new dignity, a new pride, a new self-respect by which African Americans gave evidence of understanding the marked change in their status . . . [by] their quiet, undramatic attempts to assume responsibilities as members of an advanced and changing social order."[28] Though these rights were enshrined in law, could blacks enjoy the full use of shared spaces? Following challenges in multiple states, five court cases advanced to the U.S. Supreme Court (109 US 3 (1883)) that challenged the integration of private service industry and entertainment facilities. Four of these cases were brought outside the South: restaurant service (Kansas), hotel lodging (Missouri), exclusion from an opera house (New York), and theatre (California). In the fifth case, *Robinson v. Memphis and Charleston Railroad Company*, the court deliberated whether a black woman named Sallie Robinson was wrongfully refused admission to the ladies' car. The majority opinion held that because "she was in company with a young man whom he [the claimant] supposed to be a white man, and, on that account, inferred that there was some improper connection between them."[29] In other words, because planter-class mores were challenged—as evidenced through an interracial companionship—Robinson's presumed "immorality" made her unsuitable for the ladies' car.

The Supreme Court ruled that private organizations were able to impose discrimination if there were some bona fide reason—including suspicions surrounding moral character—for doing so. The court reconsidered and decided that Congress lacked the authority under the enforcement provisions of the Fourteenth Amendment to outlaw discrimination by private individuals and organizations. Editor of the *New York Globe*, T. Thomas Fortune, wrote, "The colored people of the United States feel to-day as if they had been baptized in ice water."[30] Private owners—it was decided—had the right to determine whether they found particular individuals fitting as customers. The court declared that this kind of decision was to be individually applied, "not being made for any reasons by law applicable to citizens of every race and color, and regardless of any previous condition of servitude." In other words, the court decided individual (but not categorical) discrimination would not necessarily universally dispossess all blacks access. As the court expressed: "The XIIIth Amendment relates only to slavery and involuntary servitude (which it abolishes), and, although, by its reflex action, it establishes universal freedom in the United States, and Congress may probably pass laws directly enforcing its provisions, yet such legislative power extends only to the subject of slavery and its incidents, and the denial of equal accommodations in inns, public conveyances, and places of public amusement, imposes no badge of slavery or involuntary servitude upon the party but at most, infringes rights which are protected from State aggression by the XIVth Amendment."[31]

Opponents viewed additional protections unnecessary, claiming that blacks did not need "special treatment" to access private facilities. Representative Robert Vance (North Carolina, Democrat), a former Confederate colonel, testified that blacks could freely "enjoy all their rights" in railroad cars, hotels, and places of leisure, that indeed "they have all the rights and all the immunities accorded to any other class of citizens of the United States." Vance in particular, and whites more generally, were accustomed to seeing race selectively. Because no explicit notifications of discrimination were posted, Vance could claim that railway cars were integrated.

Representative Cain disputed his testimony: "Now, it may not have come under his observation, but it has under mine, that such really is not the case; and the reason why I know and feel it more than he does is because my face is painted black and his is painted white. We who have the color—I may say the objectionable color—know and feel all this."[32] The disconnect between lived experiences and legal equality that plagued Reconstruction politics also frustrated some anti-caste college administrators. Despite mounting evidence of racial violence and the retrenchment of blacks' rights to exercise legal rights, even many anti-caste whites struggled to believe that words and ideas were failing to transform into action. In 1885, the celebrated author George Washington Cable, a strong supporter of Berea College and anti-caste politics, called for recognition that despite the constitutional amendments and various laws, justice remained elusive: "For years many of us have carelessly taken for granted that these laws were being carried out in some shape that removed all just ground of complaint."[33] Cable called for recognition of the vast divide between legal equality and lived segregation.

On paper, many establishments did not have official discriminatory clauses. This was true of higher education as well. College catalogs were largely devoid of discriminatory language. Individual black students might enroll, leaving the broader public to interpret their scant numbers as a lack of qualified black applicants rather than an indicator of institutional discrimination. Many colleges had unofficial quotas that allowed an individual black student to enroll, while another common practice was for college officials to respond to letters of inquiry from black applicants and suggest that they might be "more comfortable" at another college.

The 1902 Report of the U.S. Commissioner of Education included a number of notes from college presidents who had been asked to give their opinion on the usefulness of college education for blacks. Of the thirteen schools responding to the poll, eight responded affirmatively. These colleges included Bates College, Bowdoin College, Boston University, the University of Iowa, the University of Michigan, Stanford, and Indiana University. Though both had enrolled more black students than most of their peer institutions, Amherst and Harvard maintained that social prejudice in the North was greater than in the South and therefore black students would find Southern colleges more comfortable. Clark University and Williams College negated the need for blacks to attend college, while Yale president Arthur Hadley found the question too difficult to answer. While espousing his belief that "no race or color is entitled to monopolize the benefits of higher education," the president of Boston University suggested that, "if any race is entitled to be specially favored in this respect I should say it is the one that has by the agency of others been longest deprived thereof."[34] While there was considerable variation among college presidents, black alumni responded to the same question with resounding and universal affirmation for the importance of higher education. Upon asking 626 black college graduates if college training had benefited them, only one respondent responded in the negative.

Yet because there were no official restrictions to black enrollment at many Northern colleges, many whites were unwilling to recognize barriers that signaled danger to many blacks. Even the unflinching abolitionist leader William Lloyd Garrison imagined that social equality would flow naturally from civic equality—that emancipation and voting rights would cause whites to rationally accept blacks as fellow citizens.[35] Indeed some abolitionists opposed involving the judicial branch in securing equal rights imagining that the abolition of slavery and constitutional amendments ensured permanent protection against future injustice. Addressing a graduating class at Howard University, Senator George Hoar touched on the 1883 decision. Even Hoar, a Radical Republican and dear friend to the fierce equal rights advocate Charles Sumner, counseled graduates to remember that they had achieved constitutional rights "whereas the forces arrayed against them were only temporary."[36] Despite mounting evidence, many of the most sympathetic whites failed to heed the warning signs of rights retrenchment.

In opposition to calls for patience, the Equal Rights League opted for legal action. The Equal Rights League was a predominately black association that organized the first state constitutional conventions. The conventions were large state-level gatherings where blacks discussed obstacles and strategies to civic inclusion and social mobility. They sued for equal transportation rights and hired lawyers to secure black soldiers their veterans' benefits.[37]

Anti-casteists held tightly to their belief that legal remediation was an inappropriate path to transforming the attitudes and behaviors of individuals. As George Washington Cable exhorted his readers, racial integration could only be accomplished through individual transformation and was not appropriate for governmental action: "We ask not Congress, nor the Legislature, nor any other power, to remedy these evils, but we ask the people among whom we live. Those who *can* remedy them if they *will*. Those who have a high sense of honor and a deep moral feeling. Those who have one vestige of human sympathy left. . . . Those are the ones we ask to protect us in our weakness and ill-treatments. . . . As soon as the colored man is treated by the white man as a *man*, that harmony and pleasant feeling which should characterize all races which dwell together, shall be the bond of peace between them."[38]

To the Land of Freedom: Responses to Migration and Immigration

> Thousands more were congregating along the banks of the Mississippi River, hailing the passing steamers, and imploring them for a passage to the land of freedom, where the rights of citizens are respected and honest toil rewarded by honest compensation. The newspapers were filled with accounts of their destitution, and the very air was burdened with the cry of distress from a class of American citizens fleeing from persecutions they could no longer endure.
>
> —Report and Testimony of the Select Committee of the United States Senate to Investigate the Cause of the Removal of the Negroes from the Southern States to the Northern States, 46th Cong., 2nd sess., 1880

Another response to the fading hope of Reconstruction—and the violence and desperation that accompanied it—was for blacks to leave the South. Despite securing the fervent support of several Union generals, land redistribution in the former Confederate states was short lived. As described in chapter 2, black leaders had argued for land rights as essential to safeguard all other freedoms. In 1862, Congress passed the Homestead Act, which allowed those who had never borne arms against the United States to purchase tracts of 160 acres provided that they lived and worked the land. Land distribution was a major policy goal after the Civil War. Before the act was repealed in 1876, approximately 1,000 blacks—out of a population of 4 million—were able to claim land through homesteading. As Union troops left the South and civil rights retrenchment increased, many black leaders once again argued that the best path for political and economic security was to extend homestead rights to blacks similar to those regularly made to whites in the Western territories.

The post-emancipation era saw dramatic changes in migration, with both new immigrant groups to the East and West Coasts and Southern blacks exiting the South. Howard University faculty and trustees were actively involved in organizing the first mass migration out of the South. As white Southern violence intensified, many blacks migrated North and West. At reportedly the "largest assemblage of colored people ever seen in this (New York) City" at Cooper Union Hall, Howard University trustee reverend Highland Garnet read a series of resolutions approving black migration to the West. He stated that as a result of "the unparalleled atrocities of their former masters, that they have been mercilessly robbed and murdered, education denied them, and the Federal protection withdrawn from them." He continued by appealing "to every man, woman and child in this community to lend a helping hand."[39] Several faculty members at Howard appealed to legislators for new land policy to facilitate migration. Richard Greener, Howard law professor, represented a delegation of black citizens who met with Senator Windom to discuss the Minnesota senator's proposal that blacks migrate from the hostile conditions of the South to the West.[40]

By 1879, the Senate launched an investigation into the cause for the mass migration. One hundred fifty-three blacks of wide ranging education and occupational status testified to terrifying conditions. Blacks testified that white violence was retaliation for black political mobilization. The *Chicago Tribune* affirmed the need, comparing migrating blacks to the oppressed of the Bible as a "great Exodus of Negroes."[41] The *Chicago Tribune* contended, "The negro in the South has been reduced to serfdom by another name. He has been stripped of his political rights and robbed of his citizenship. He has been cheated out of his wages and hunted down with shotgun and rifle. . . . He goes where he can have the right to labor and to live."[42] Though many whites adhered to the belief that legal protections offered by the constitution provided adequate protection, the Southern states (and municipalities therein) refused to enact protections. Southern states launched vigorous campaigns of disfranchisement and incarceration and faced little opposition from federal authorities.[43]

When blacks were denied rights, AMA officials sometimes drew upon their political and personal connections to challenge injustices. Lewis Tappan—a major donor to Oberlin College—lobbied for a Pennsylvania bill to desegregate railway cars before the Civil War had even ended. When Fisk College's Jubilee Singers were denied passage on a Pullman railcar while traveling for a performance, the AMA's Erastus Cravath angrily telegraphed railway magnate George Pullman who promptly overturned the ticket master's decision. The *American Missionary Magazine* kept its readers informed of challenges to political, economic, and social equality. The AMA remained largely silent on the efforts of black self-advocacy organizations, nor did it appear to coalesce with other organizations. The AMA was a committed, albeit highly imperfect, partner in the struggle for both civil rights and social rights.[44]

In 1880, the Senate resolved that blacks were "induced to [migrate] by the unjust and cruel conduct of their white fellow-citizens . . . and by the denial or abridgment of their personal and political rights and privileges."[45] The reactions among black leaders and elites varied. Frederick Douglass, former Howard trustee, and Richard Greener, Howard law school dean, debated the best options at the 1879 meeting of the American Social Science Association. Douglass, like many in the AMA called the exodus "a surrender, a premature, disheartening surrender, since it would make freedom and free institutions depend on migration rather than protection; by flight, rather than right."[46] Douglass was clear that blacks should not in any way be held in the South if they wished to migrate, but argued for increased enforcement of blacks' legal rights. Richard Greener expressed no less disappointment in the swift and harsh return of planter-class rule and terror after the departure of federal troops. Educated in the North at Oberlin, Andover, and Harvard, Greener had been a professor of philosophy at the University of South Carolina. In 1877, South Carolina's General Assembly segregated the university and Greener moved to Howard University. Given his own recent forced departure from South Carolina, Greener helped organize black churches to collect funds and coordinated communication between blacks in the North and West and those planning migration.[47]

Many from Berea's black community joined the "exoduster movement" of Southern blacks moving westward in search of better social conditions. For this reason, Berea trustee Reverend Gabriel Burdett, explained his view to Berea administrators that Kentucky could not be made safe for black families. To truly experience the freedom promised by emancipation, he explained, leaving home was required. Reverend Burdett had been a part of Berea since he met Berea founder John Fee while working together with black refugees and soldiers at Camp Nelson.

He had devoted nearly twenty years to building the Berea community. Multiple letters between Reverend Gabriel Burdett to the AMA national secretary relate black Kentuckians' growing frustration with the AMA's method of patience rather than active resistance to white intimidation.[48] Reverend Burdett wrote, "It will be hard for the colored man to do anything in this county unless there is a great change in this State and I do not see what that will be unless the colored man makes it himself."[49] Burdett argued that the only chance for blacks' safety and prosperity was to deny the Southern economy black labor and "leave this land where the foot of the slave has marked the soil and go to a land where all men are regarded as men."[50]

Anti-caste rhetoric, hampered by its colorblind focus on the individual, provided few resources to address race-based injustices. Berea's administration and the AMA leadership reported feeling abandoned in the work they had long viewed as in partnership with blacks. The departure from Berea, however, was not complete. While many black families left the Berea community, black student enrollment actually increased. Though migration westward was of chief interest to policymakers and journalists, a sizable percentage of black college graduates remained in or moved to the South. The 1901 Report of the U.S. Commissioner of Education analyzed the places of birth and places of work among 600 black college graduates. It estimated that 50 percent of "Northern born college men come South to work among the masses of their people at a personal sacrifice and bitter cost which few people realize; that nearly 90 percent of the Southern-born graduates, instead of seeking that personal freedom and broader intellectual atmosphere which their training has led them in some degree to conceive, stay and labor and wait in the midst of their black neighbors and relatives."[51] Where college-educated blacks chose to live and work was a matter of deep interest to a variety of governmental and voluntary sector actors. In allocating federal funding and raising funds from private donors for higher education for blacks, the dominant discourse centered on educating black teachers for the South—not on educating black professionals who might seek a less hostile climate in the North or West. The disappointing response by the AMA to the increasing hostility in the South meant that the organization's number of black leaders—like Richard Greener and Gabriel Burdett—decreased.

The AMA remained confident in its powers to effect change. While its self-important tone unabashedly claimed that whites conferred citizenship upon blacks, AMA members nonetheless argued for black self-determination and unrestricted ambitions—if that determination and ambition meshed with the AMA's goals. Northerners grew increasingly fearful of new immigrant groups arriving from Southern and Eastern Europe to the East Coast and from East Asia on the West Coast. At the same time, the AMA promoted a view of blacks as "native" voters who would balance the perceived negative influence of the "foreign" vote. Indeed, not only would black suffrage cure the white violence and political tyranny that threatened the South's peaceful reunion with the nation, it might also prove a safeguard against the perceived political dangers that accompanied increased immigration. "Will it shape itself in such a way as to neutralize the turbulent immigration that flows in upon us from abroad? Will it prove a home alkali to receive and antidote this foreign acid?"[52]

These changes in the political domain held important implications for the colleges. As the next section will show, the political backdrop changed how the AMA viewed blacks and the mission of racial cooperation. Some within the AMA, for instance, saw continued discrimination and violence in the South as evidence that integration had been tried but failed due to Southern whites' resistance. As many blacks fled the South for the West or points North to avoid violence and secure work, whites increasingly viewed black migration as a status threat. The traditional logic of the AMA was political. Anti-caste values were held as essential to undergird republican governance. As opportunities to influence Southern politics—particularly through federal Reconstruction policy—diminished, and the AMA's membership rolls whitened, the AMA increasingly viewed its work as charitable and palliative rather than political and transformative. The next section describes these changes.

The Changing Nature of Benevolent Organizations

Changes in legal rights and shifting demographic patterns shaped how the colleges—and the AMA—defined their mission and interests. The AMA began to activate racial difference—and the organization's special ethnographic expertise—as justification for its continued relevance and legitimacy. The AMA had long claimed special knowledge about race relations. Indeed, after military occupation ended, the struggle for control of Southern education lay largely in a contest for "home rule" between Southerners and benevolent, religious organizations. The AMA rooted its legitimacy in the organization's multi-decade history of inter-racial cooperation and abolitionist activism. Because it counted blacks in positions of organizational power, aided refugees from slavery and supported black-led churches in the North, and its foundation lay in interracial relationships, the AMA argued it was uniquely qualified to set precedents for establishing a new model of postwar higher education. In his widely reprinted 1873 speech titled "Educated Labor," General Howard invoked the AMA's ethnographic expertise: "We have been accustomed for half a century to hear it said by slaveholders—'You do not understand the negro.' But what was about him so difficult to understand I never could discover. . . . We judged the black man as a man; [Southern whites] judged him as chattel. . . . We know him, and we know his aspirations, his capacities, his real worth to the country; what he might become to himself and to the nation, if the artificial pressure of the powerful hand of avarice were removed from him."[53]

From 1870 to 1872, the BRFAL lost considerable funding and presidential support. In response, the AMA began to diversify its missions to survive financially. The AMA used different measurements to assess the value of groups to the nation and frame their campaigns around the particular qualifications and needs of the groups. In doing so, the AMA no longer adhered to a strict dichotomy of traitors and heroes. The temporal dimension of group evaluation shifted from past contributions to the Union to expectations for future, contingent contributions. The AMA and its affiliated colleges were in constant struggle to remain operational—and to do so they needed to interpret a shifting political climate. This was their challenge.[54] They hoped to maintain and gain legitimacy. They also hoped to shut out Southern oligarchs by establishing that the primacy of obligation in higher education belonged to private organizations rather than state actors. Increasingly, they framed their mission as one of providing social provisions and they expanded these services to new groups—new immigrants and Native Americans. As they had in the past, the AMA continued to promote its mission as legitimated through the ethnographic expertise of its members. During this time, Berea and Howard both distanced themselves from the AMA, though social ties among them remained important.

The AMA shifted some of its resources to new immigrant groups, providing scholarships to immigrants from China, Japan, and Korea. Several of these students enrolled at Howard. The AMA also sponsored new charitable missions and schools in California, and increased its missions in China. Addressing the AMA at the 1870 annual meeting, Henry Ward Beecher suggested that the organization embrace new immigrant groups with the same spirit of amalgamation that the AMA proposed for black inclusion: "I would to every one, *everywhere*, come to our shores.... Their foreignness, with God's blessing, will be of short duration. They will see that our institutions are no less beneficent to them than they are to others."[55] The broader reaction was quite different. Many Northern municipalities and states passed discriminatory codes and statues that reproduced many of the same civil rights violations as the South. These demographic changes constituted a status threat to the old elite. To create a buffer, elites formed new institutions including art museums and private boarding schools.[56]

At the same time, in the wake of military conflict, the AMA launched educational and missionary work among the Arapaho, Comanche, Cheyenne, Lakota, Kiowa, and Sioux tribes. As Union troops—including General O. O. Howard—moved from South to West, many within the AMA grew increasingly concerned over the slaughter of native peoples. Unlike arguments made for black education, Native Americans' prospects for citizenship were not initially offered as a reason for AMA intervention.[57]

Key AMA leaders began to articulate a new character for the AMA, absent the BRFAL, as moral and humanitarian rather than civic and political, and drew attention to suffering rather than repayment. Reverend Henry Ward Beecher articulated new concerns at the 1870 AMA annual meeting: "In the closing of this decade, a new candidate for popular odium and Christian sympathy came before the American people. The tawny Mongolians came from China in such numbers to California as to attract attention, and soon the Chinese stood side by side with the negro, in the hatred of the same set of politicians and mobocrats.... The Indian, too, so long sunk in his own degradation, and crushed under the apathy of the government and the rascality of agents, once more arose to the surface."[58]

Beecher's address was the first to express a view where blacks were linked to lower status groups and it would take a few more years before Beecher's sentiments were fully embraced by the AMA. By the end of the 1870s, the AMA still claimed a shared humanity, but it no longer framed blacks as the best hope for republicanism and virtuous governance in the South. Rather, the AMA linked white oppression against Native Americans, Chinese immigrants, and blacks as tied to a hierarchy of social development. In doing so, the AMA offered an air of rationality to the irrationality of prejudice by suggesting that oppressed groups were developmentally inferior.

The AMA helped to clarify an ambiguous status arrangement. Native Americans and Chinese immigrants in California had both been shut out of voting rights because of their ambiguous civic status. The Fourteenth Amendment clarified which persons were eligible for citizenship and omitted Native American men. Federal treaties with the Chinese government—namely the Tianjin Treaty of 1858 and the Burlingame-Seward Treaty of 1868—established some protections and rights for Chinese immigrants. Despite this, California law enacted wide-reaching measures ranging from barriers to naturalization and special require-ments for the employ of Chinese workers. The California state mea-sures resembled the black codes of the South, leading the AMA to draw parallels: "There is no people, however obscure or degraded, or decimated and dwindled, that does not belong to the solidarity of humanity. . . . Every outrage upon them is one of another. Each time an Indian is corrupted or defrauded, each instance of the brutal abuse of Chinese, each assassination of a freedman, bring home to us our duty afresh."[59] The AMA, despite equivocating on the question of social equality, was vocal against the rising terror in the South. Yet decrying the most violent forms of oppression was but a faint shadow of the AMA's original commitment to full and immediate citizenship for black men and social equality for all.

This represented a marked departure from earlier admonitions to see blacks as citizens, and attacks on blacks' rights as attacks on the sov-ereignty of the federal government. Recall the *Chicago Tribune*'s 1865 admonition that "every such [attack on blacks] is an act of war against the military authority of the Government. They should be taught that inasmuch as they have done until the last of these black citizens, made free by Federal power, they have done it unto the Federal Govern-ment."[60] In 1871, Reverend Henry Martyn Scudder addressed the AMA annual meeting. Scudder, while promoting education as a fitting form of reparations, emphasized military service as evidence for inclusion within the bounds of citizenship: "You are no longer slaves; you are as free as any other Americans. No one, hereafter, shall be lord over you; you are made lords over yourselves. This was the voice of war. The nation took time to breathe and think; and then was heard another voice saying, 'You are our creditors, by reason of years of unredressed wrong; and you are our comrades, because you fought with us and for us in this war.' "[61] Importantly, the AMA conceptualized its work as repayment for an owed debt. The AMA positioned itself as an arbiter of reparations. Scudder and others within the AMA linked their work in building schools—and the path schools would open for social mobility—as compensatory for the "unredressed wrongs" of enslavement and in recognition of blacks' service in defense of the Union. Scudder spoke for the AMA, saying "We confer upon you citizenship, and we open to you the path of ambition; you may become alderman, mayor, representative, senator, governor, vice-president or president."[62] In doing so, the AMA also articulated it held the power to confer citizenship, a power that is reserved for the state.

In the immediate postwar years, the AMA had pushed for an understanding of blacks as integral to the American nation and frequently cited the enlistment of thousands of black soldiers in the Union Army as essential to the preservation of the Union. Black leaders from the National Equal Rights League also insisted upon blacks' claim to "native" status. They did so by citing black military service in the Revolutionary and Civil Wars: "While the devotion, the gallantry, and the heroism displayed by our sons, brothers, and fathers at Port Hudson, Fort Wagner, Petersburg, New Market Heights are fresh in the minds of the American people, let us spare no pains, let us not fail to make every effort in our power to secure for ourselves and our children all those rights, natural and political, which belong to us as men and as native-born citizens of America."[63] This had presented an impressive discursive convergence. Important black-organized civil rights groups, Radical Republicans, and the AMA all promoted Southern blacks as Union veterans, who had served valiantly and earned citizenship.

By 1874, the AMA clarified that its mission was race-specific. This mission specified the dividing line between groups in the U.S. and made a clear argument about the nature of the relationship between power and race. It identified that the key boundary between groups lay in those who had been oppressed and those who had oppressed others, and it no longer included poor whites among those oppressed by the planter class. Furthermore, it linked power and prestige to immorality and greed: "Three races stand out in history as the victims of atrocious wrong on the part of the Anglo-Saxon race, and atrocious sin against the ordinances of heaven, the savages from whom in many cases American soil has been violently or fraudulently alienated, the Chinese whose land was forced open with awful demoralization and blood, the African whom English slave-holders' cupidity robbed and spoiled for 200 years."[64] In doing so, the AMA drew new boundary distinctions uniting blacks, Chinese immigrants, and Native Americans, making the defining boundary characteristic victimization by white oppressors. By expanding the AMA mission to include all who suffered indignation, without specifying patriotic merit, blacks were attached to other groups who were deemed worthy of charity only for their sufferings and not valued for their contributions. The boundary characteristics—"the thing of boundaries" to invoke Andrew Abbot's phrasing—were manipulated by actors with the capacity to articulate boundary distinctions and make such distinctions meaningful through the differentiated allocation of resources.

This new approach was quite different from the AMA's earlier claims that white plantation owners oppressed blacks out of avarice and greed. For instance, in 1867 General Howard had described the importance of education to the BRFAL's mission of rebuilding the Union: "The intelligent citizen, operative, or laborer, knows what his rights are, and will make no contracts that ignore those rights. His increased self-respect, also, is a guaranty against the crushing arrogance and avarice of the capitalist."[65] As Joseph Gerteis has described, interracial labor organizing united some blacks and whites during Reconstruction. However, increasingly the AMA's mission shifted away from economic oppression by oligarchs and capitalists and instead focused on particular groups. Similar to Gerteis' account, how interracial organizers drew boundary lines around their work held deep consequences for producing racial difference as natural and inevitable rather than as a boundary constructed by actors in service to particular interests and motives.

This new focus on racial difference also shifted the motivation for building a system of higher education from one of reparation, of paying a debt owed for unrequited labor and military service, to one of charitable outreach. The AMA had historically operated on a political logic that coeducation would secure republican governance. It was predicated on beliefs that coeducation was mutually beneficial, in that whites' racist attitudes were immoral. Further, the AMA argued for viewing blacks as the morally superior element in the South by not only decrying the injustice of slavery but by holding up blacks as patriots, war heroes, and politically important to the nation. In shifting the logic to one of aid rather than reparation or political development, the AMA undermined its earlier position that blacks had made important contributions to the country and their contributions merited equal status.

While Chinese immigrants and Native Americans shared experiences of discrimination and persecution with Southern blacks, no advocates had yet attempted to claim rights for these groups on their centrality to the American nation. By expanding the AMA mission to include all who were stigmatized, without specifying patriotic merit, blacks underwent a process of what Mary Douglas has called "symbolic pollution," whereby they were linked to other oppressed groups.[66] By 1878 the AMA declared: "The only caste-oppressed races in America are the Negroes, Indians and Chinamen."[67] The AMA drew clear boundary lines between whites, regardless of class status, and Southern blacks, Chinese immigrants, Native Americans.

This demarcated a new boundary distinction for the AMA's focus and moved away from conceptualizing the mission as one of building a strong foundation for a multi-racial social and political union. This new strategy focused attention to injustice by linking groups together based on experiences of racialized oppression by whites. By 1878, the AMA described slavery as a "debt that can never be repaid." The greed of slavery was compared to "the greed . . . the white man has pursued [against Native Americans] from that day to this. From place to place they have been driven. Bargains have been broken and treaties violated, in almost every instance, first by the white man. The true history of almost every Indian war (so called) has been begun by the violence or provoked by the faithlessness of the white man. . . . Shall we run in debt to the Chinaman, as we have to the Negro and the Indian?"[68] As the AMA shifted its emphasis to the oppressed, it backed away from its passionate insistence that the only path to building a just democracy and lasting peace required ridding whites of their prejudice and organizing integrated communities. Instead, the AMA turned away from work among poor whites and increasingly saw its future in charity among the oppressed. Doing so placed the onus of responsibility on blacks to prove their civic value to whites.

The hard line drawn in 1874 turned the AMA's attention away from poor whites almost entirely. It shifted the AMA's interest away from coeducation—which focused on dispelling whites of their prejudices— and toward the "uplift" of groups oppressed on the basis of race or ethnicity. Despite this, Berea, Howard, and Oberlin continued their programs based on coeducation. The AMA affiliation to the colleges persisted but the AMA increasingly pursued more direct aid services without attending to changing attitudes and behaviors among whites.

This could have been a critical moment for the AMA to deepen its critique of white supremacist ideology and recognize the disparity between the AMA's ideals, on the one hand, and the unfinished work of Reconstruction. Could the AMA, for instance, have used its massive transcontinental membership roll and its close ties to elites to demand federal assistance to support expanding its work? Despite the legal architecture that had constructed an ideal of racial equality through constitutional amendments and civil rights legislation, and despite the interpersonal transformations accomplished in particular places—among white Southerners who testified that witnessing black students in the Freedmen's Schools and on AMA campuses changed their views about blacks' intellectual or moral potential—huge swaths of the United States were left unreformed. Too many within the AMA failed to recognize the limits of their work. Often arguing against legal and state action, the AMA failed to acknowledge that their accomplishments depended upon concurrent legal and political change.

In the face of rising violence and rights retrenchment, the AMA viewed its past work as monumentally successful. Leaders within the AMA continued to draw upon AMA success as evidence of the organization's ethnographic expertise and superior understanding of race relations. AMA officer Reverend Lathrop reminded members of the success the AMA had achieved among the thousands of freedmen who became editors, teachers, lawyers, dentists, and physicians, boasting that these men and women were educated almost exclusively in AMA schools. Nor was this claim wholly exaggerated—the AMA had indeed succeeded in opening classroom doors to thousands of Southern blacks, and many were pillars of their communities.[69] The AMA took credit for black success in "steadily acquiring property, building homes and improving their surroundings," including over eighty black-owned newspapers in the former slave states of the South.[70] An elite class of blacks attained unprecedented economic, educational, professional, and political success. These achievements were particularly visible in selected pockets—Charleston, New Orleans, Philadelphia, and Washington, D.C.[71]

The emphasis on achievement, however, was not limited to the AMA. Many black-owned newspapers—including Washington D.C.'s *The Afro-American*—featured regular columns dedicated to sharing success stories.[72] It was these success stories that the AMA focused on rather than the harsh realities of most Southern black lives, trapped in serf-like conditions, subjected to violence, intimidation, and the rapid retrenchment of their constitutional rights. These were, of course, not unrelated. As blacks were able to make gains in professions, education, and securing rights, many whites increasingly viewed these accomplishments not as proof of merit as co-citizens, but as a status threat. Legal rulings that decreased racial barriers increased white-against-black violence.[73] The AMA struggled to reconcile that a worthy and moral group could be the continued victims of Southern violence. The AMA honed its focus on respectability politics, convinced that the trappings of the middle class would ensure safety and cultivate white support.[74]

The AMA depicted the failed project of Reconstruction not as the failure of state intervention to subdue violent whites, but of blacks' moral failing to leverage legal rights to attain economic and social success. The AMA increasingly advocated for religious (albeit strictly Protestant) influence and control in restructuring the social and political order. In 1877, the AMA recognized a *quid pro quo* exchange of political rights for a reduction in violence: "But for the present the offence of the ballot has ceased; and from our knowledge of the field we endorse the words of President Hayes, that there have been fewer outrages and oppressions heard of in the past six months than during any like period since the war ended."[75] Overwhelming evidence indicated that, absent the governmental enforcement of civil and social rights, anti-caste efforts were failing to transform white Southerners' attitudes toward blacks. The principles upon which the AMA had structured all its efforts were failing. The withdrawal of federal troops had unleashed the vindictive anger of the white South that interpreted every black accomplishment as a threat to their dominant status. Regardless of this growing recognition, the AMA affirmed its commitment to interpersonal conversions rather than state action, declaring that "a legal injustice can be done away by law; a moral dealt with by law; but a taste, a sentiment, a feeling, an instinct, a prejudice—there pass the bounds of all legislation; and by the attempt to rectify or regulate these by law serves only to irritate opposition. At these points, human nature has much in common with the porcupine."[76]

By the late 1870s, the AMA retreated from its commitment to full racial equality; it would no longer argue that black and whites were equals. The AMA amended its "principles" of equality: "This Association does not affirm that races, any more than individuals, are equal in physical or mental fiber and development. Some races, as well as individuals, are manifestly below others in some respects."[77] The AMA no longer advocated leveling the antebellum topography of racial distinction.

The AMA's new dispirited program lacked the political fervor of its earlier days. At the 1878 annual meeting, AMA president Buckham announced a change in its "principles and plans," saying that "the negro, it must be confessed, has lost the place he once held as an attractive object of philanthropy. Invested with the legal rights of a man, and thus by necessity thrust forward into comparison and competition with other men, he not only exhibits his inferiority on a conspicuous stage. . . . The negro cause has thus sunk from an impassioned crusade to a commonplace charity."[78] Not only did this shift the AMA's commitment to the anti-caste belief in social equality but it also altered their *raison d'être* from one of political activism to charity. The AMA explained the shift as declining "zeal . . . slackened when they found that the work among the Freedmen could not all be finished in fifteen or twenty years. . . . The well-ordered citizen . . . (had) been so long under the strain of anxiety about the war that he was weary of it and of everything that reminded him of it."[79]

Members of the AMA were motivated by status concerns. Status cannot be independently produced or claimed, it is inherently relational and hierarchical. At its core, status is a process of recognition and acknowledgement. Third party organizations like the AMA are intermediaries among actors in status systems and external audiences, encouraging particular representations, understandings, and metrics.[80] The AMA needed to continue to secure public recognition of its legitimacy and one way to accomplish this was through successfully encouraging others to recognize the AMAs group-making power. As the AMA expanded its aims—both to secure donations and to increase its share in controlling social provisions—it did so with some risks to the groups within its purview. As status competitions increased in the professional and political realms, these competing status hierarchies and metrics of status lead to changes in the very rules that defined status hierarchy.

Philanthropists and the Reorganization of Southern Education

Northern philanthropists turned to the problem of Southern education at the turn of the century. While others, such as the Peabody Foundation, focused more heavily on primary (or "common") schools, J. D. Rockefeller's General Education Board (GEB) allocated resources to colleges and universities.[81] Foundations directed organizational logics and immense financial resources to consecrate segregated higher education as legitimate and appropriate. As described above, the relationship between private organizations and the state in organizing public education began at the end of the Civil War when the BRFAL provided funds, security forces, and logistical support to private organizations, including the AMA, to establish a mass educational system in the South. By the early 1890s, new private organizations announced their vision for reforming and systematizing education in the South.

In 1890, the Mohonk Conference on the Question of the Negro gathered many white elites at an upstate New York resort. Neither AMA affiliates nor black educational leaders were invited. Former U.S. president Hayes and Peabody Fund agent J. M. L. Curry sat on the dais before an audience filled with the most prominent education reformers in the country. In his speech, former Emory University president and Slater Fund agent Bishop Atticus Haygood claimed—against all evidence—that spending for black education exceeded what was available for white students: "In law, the Negro children share equally with white children. In fact, the Negro children receive more and more benefit from the public school systems in the South."[82]

The new philanthropies were overtly hostile to blacks' desires to influence schools and colleges with sizable black enrollments. Haygood revealed the discomfort with which white reformers experienced self-sufficiency among blacks: "Much of whatever inequality there may be grows out of the condition of the colored people themselves. It is not strange that a race so circumstanced fails to secure the best results from their schools. The Negroes are as determined to teach their public schools as Southern white people are not to teach them. Indeed, the Negroes show so marked a desire to control the colleges built for their benefit that their best friends are anxious lest the impatience of the very people they labor for should marr their best planned efforts to help them."[83] Booker T. Washington shared his fear with famed author (and Berea supporter) George W. Cable that "the disposition of many of our friends to consult *about* the Negro instead of *with*—to work *for* him instead of *with* him."[84] Blacks were almost wholly excluded from the conferences and foundation work.

In 1898, a group of industrialists organized the first Conference for Education in the South (CES) held in Capon Springs, West Virginia.

The conference brought together educational reformers and those with economic interests in the South who considered the blending of philanthropic and business interests as the best means to steer social reform and develop social institutions in accordance with capitalist logics. As a result of the CES, in 1901 Robert Ogden organized a train trip for leading industrialists to witness first-hand the South's educational plight.[85] After the train trip, John D. Rockefeller Jr. spoke to his father. The senior Rockefeller supplied him with 1 million dollars to found the GEB. Rockefeller soon increased his pledge to 10 million.

Among the founding members of the GEB were some of the most influential and wealthy men in America. Morris K. Jessup, long involved in Protestant benevolent societies, had helped found the Museum of Natural History. Harvard graduate and railway executive, William Baldwin Jr. served on the board at Tuskegee Institute. Investor and a board member for General Electric, George Foster Peabody also served on the board for Hampton and Tuskegee Institutes, as did wealthy merchant Robert Ogden. Former Southern legislator and Confederate officer, J. L. M. Curry was the Southerner in the room. Baptist minister William Buttrick became acquainted with J. D. Rockefeller through Baptist missionary societies; Buttrick soon came to serve the GEB as a general agent and later as a trustee. These were the men who gathered at Morris Jessup's Madison Avenue home, just down the street from J. P. Morgan's mansion, on a cold January day in 1902. The group possessed enormous wealth, far-reaching political connections, and a deep desire to cultivate goodwill and trust among those who might otherwise question their vast fortunes. As Elisabeth Clemens writes, businessmen sought civic influence to create a culture where philanthropy was valued more than civic taxation.[86]

The GEB's mission would "promote education with the United States of America, without distinction of race, sex or creed and cooperate with existing educational organizations and attempt to cultivate tax-based public schools."[87] Yet none of these goals could be located in the GEB's actions. The foundations explicitly organized types of education to match particular groupings of persons. In fact, the GEB separated its funding streams so that some focused on industrial and rudimentary education for Southern blacks, while others funded higher education for whites. Separate white and black field agents were employed to oversee these projects.[88] In its first few years, the GEB made a small one-time donation of $7,000 to Berea. But once the GEB trustees deliberated on their funding priorities, further appeals for funding from Berea were consistently denied.[89] Most GEB-managed funds for black education were diverted to primary and high schools. There were a few exceptions. For instance, Laura Spelman Rockefeller was the daughter of an abolitionist family who endowed Spelman Seminary, a college initially for domestic training for black women.[90] The GEB also prioritized supporting universities located in cities, citing that doing so would strengthen ties between education and commerce. Rockefeller's first venture was in co-founding the University of Chicago, and a decade later he founded the Rockefeller University. Following these, Rockefeller invested in existing schools rather than founding new ones.

Like the AMA before it, the GEB ambitiously planned to systematically restructure the entire field of higher education. Unlike the AMA, however, the GEB did not lack for financial funding. Whereas the AMA relied on small donations from many individual donors, the GEB gathered large donations from a few wealthy industrialists. Its trustees launched a survey into the existing range of colleges and their locations to develop its goals. Within a few years, the board had designed a far-reaching, multi-tiered investment plan and coordinated with the most important existing educational foundations. It provided limited funds to industrial colleges for blacks, with more dollars going to black primary schools and a few high schools. While many small liberal arts colleges benefited from GEB matching campaigns to build their endowments, schools serving blacks were almost exclusively awarded small annual awards. Hampton and Tuskegee were never offered more than $10,000, and only rarely were funds made available to women's colleges. By contrast, Princeton and Yale were granted $200,000 and $300,000 respectively. Though not technically in major cities, their historical status met the GEB's requirements. Increasingly, Rockefeller's agency made clear that to maintain resources and status, it was almost a necessity for private colleges to seek GEB aid. Unlike the ethnographic expertise the AMA deployed to signal its legitimacy, the GEB seemingly relied on *argumentum ad crumenam*, and never made its case for its legitimacy in intervening based on knowledge or superior skill.[91]

Both the AMA and the GEB viewed their role as a means to ensure that the private sector—whether religious, commercial, or philanthropic—could exert substantial influence in social institutions. Like the AMA before it, the GEB played on the poverty of the South to dictate the right of private organizations in directing the Southern education system. The

AMA had articulated its legitimacy by claiming that a moral force was necessary for promoting republican governance in the South. Unlike the AMA, which built its claims by focusing on the *moral* poverty of the white slave-owning class, the GEB focused on the *economic* poverty of the South and used its accumulation of wealth through industry as evidence of its qualification to shape Southern educational policy. For instance, the mayor of Little Rock, Arkansas sent a telegram asking if the GEB would assist in relocating the State University to Little Rock. The mayor cabled in advance of legislative debate on the issue to relay that there was no appropriation funding available. The GEB wired its reply: "The GEB does not wish to influence action of Legislature, but if state itself decides to remove, we are favorably interested in the project." In short, the GEB would provide funding for projects that fit its goals but wished to appear outside the democratic process.[92] Like the AMA, the GEB wanted to impose an educational system that would further the interests of its members rather than garner consensus.

The GEB secured access to the highest levels of federal government. The board's secretary communicated the value of the GEB's many important connections to Commissioner Claxton of the U.S. Department of the Interior (then overseeing the Bureau of Education). In a 1912 letter, Claxton responded by welcoming this cadre into his office, believing that "we can easily find ways by which the Board of Education may be more helpful to these Boards and Foundations.... I know they may be helpful in many ways to this Bureau."[93] In a letter to President William Taft, Rockefeller's secretary underscored the guidance private philanthropy provided in shaping higher education as a service to the nation. Rockefeller submitted that all funding choices made by his Board of Trustees were subject to some level of review in that "the authority to veto each and every choice is given to the President of the United States, the Chief Justice of the Supreme Court, the President of the Senate, the Speaker of the House and the Presidents of Harvard, Yale, Columbia, Johns Hopkins and the University of Chicago."[94] Rockefeller would limit his visible involvement only to private colleges, arguing that to do otherwise might suggest to citizens that their state universities were "less theirs" and evoke charges of elitism against the universities.

The GEB prided itself in its systemic approach. It mapped out all high schools, colleges and universities across the United States. In 1906 it undertook a massive project to "see at a glance the distribution of colleges of the state ... the relative size of the cities, their railroad communications . . . and the relative importance of the colleges both as to students and productive funds . . . [providing] a bird's eye view of the educational condition of the whole state [that] will assist materially in our great work of developing a system of education."[95]

Rockefeller and other industrial elites were interested in concentrating political power in cities and circumnavigating federal authority. The Board of Trustees resolved to prioritize endowments for colleges and universities "in the centers of population and wealth."[96] Corporate actors increasingly used philanthropic giving as a means to cultivate loyalty, trust, and gratitude. This provided a barrier to mobilization by dissatisfied workers and others that might otherwise take collective action to contain the deepening stratification of wealth and privilege. As Elisabeth Clemens describes, "Local government posed significant challenges, but the requirements of defending urban resources from state and federal governments were greater still. A solution was urgently needed as capital itself took on increasingly national and transnational scale, further threatening the capacity of local industry and commerce to control their own destinies."[97] Rockefeller was keenly interested in strengthening the political power of cities, and one of his first efforts to this end was encouraging elite urban universities. Rockefeller's GEB possessed "monopolistic control of education" in the South, and further reduced opportunities for blacks.[98] This created an inequitable advantage for select predominately white private colleges that rarely enrolled women or black students. Further, by incurring the dependence of private colleges—and blacks were educated more often at privately funded colleges—Rockefeller was able to shape the curriculum and determine professional pathways for generations. Industrial interests—coal mining operations, cotton mills, and the charity movement that accompanied it— were gaining control in the South. By 1909, the GEB had $53 million dollars and by 1921 Rockefeller had personally donated $129 million dollars to the organization.

The Changing Field of Higher Education: An Overview

This chapter provided an in-depth analysis of *how* competition between fields affects status transfers. Pierre Bourdieu describes the power of political actors to make and unmake groups by manipulating representations in accordance with political interests.[99] Political actors gain currency for their ability to speak to and speak with constituents in lower-status positions. This is not the same for actors who are being evaluated by other actors with greater power than themselves. Joel Podolny conceptualizes status as two-sided, as both indicator of quality and that its transmission occurs through network relations.[100] This includes understanding network status as the centrality of an actor to other high-status organizations. As Mary Douglas has theorized, higher status actors risk dilution or status pollution as they interact with lower status groups.[101] Status can be maintained and even enhanced through particular types of interaction with lower-status groups, but only where the hierarchy is established and unquestioned. Thus the AMA stood to gain in reputation and power if it succeeded in making its vision of social rankings and boundaries visible and actionable to others. In its attempt to expand its mission beyond that of a postwar organization, it engaged in activating particular ideas about the characteristics that made some groups targets of voluntary association intervention. Comparisons between colleges pushed schools to differentiate themselves from competitors.

Whereas AMA affiliates had initially been part of a network to expand higher education, they increasingly found themselves competing for status and resources. Berea and Howard adopted paths of exceptionalism by claiming "ethnographic capital," or a uniquely legitimate position of authority gained through specialized knowledge about a specific ethnic category. Colleges developed ethno-racial expertise as a legitimizing strategy to leverage donations and bolster their reputation. Group-making projects are inherently bound to particular organizational interests and power. While most scholarship has focused on ethno-racial group-making as part of state- or nation-making projects, private organizations have also mobilized to produce meaning about ethno-racial difference to serve organizational goals. As Emily Barman has described, to make claims of difference, organizations construct a hierarchical relationship between themselves and their competitors based on particular criteria.[102] Claiming superior knowledge of a particular groups is a strategic move on the part of elite actors engaged in an "elite standoff" to claim jurisdiction over a particular domain of state policy.

Southern states were decreasingly subjected to federal monitoring, and private colleges increased in number. This unmoored obligations and left private colleges subject to the changing interests of private donors. Meanwhile, Southern state universities were woefully underfunded. Funding disparities between Northern and Southern colleges were stark. Of the eighteen U.S. colleges and universities with endowments of $1.5 million or more in 1900, none were in the South and only Tulane and Vanderbilt had endowments over $1 million. Indeed, the *total* available annual income for the sixty-six colleges and universities of Virginia, North Carolina, South Carolina, Georgia, Alabama, Mississippi, and Arkansas was $65,843—less than that of Harvard in 1901. Furthermore, these records excluded women's colleges and industrial colleges, thereby excluding most of the historically black colleges in the South.[103] The AMA's initial project of building colleges in the South—and the broader postwar push by a host of private organizations to spread higher education after the war—had effectively created a buffer that allowed for Southern states to only fund higher education for whites. By the turn of the twentieth century, industrialist-sponsored philanthropic organizations built on the legacy of public-private partnerships to instantiate their ideas about social organization by race and gender. Absent rules inhibiting private interference in public education, these powerful foundations were able to effectively control the types of education offered to different groups.

As this chapter illustrates, the declining availability of liberal arts and professional training for blacks resulted from the changing composition of donors and the entrance of enormously wealthy private philanthropists into higher education funding. Podolny emphasizes the importance of third-party actors in status transfers. In this model, all parties enter into exchange situations aware of the flow of goods and services that constitute the exchange relationship. The philanthropic relationship, however, is not one of explicit exchange. By 1900, a new large, well-funded foundation entered the field. John D. Rockefeller designated $10 million to create the GEB to redesign Southern education. Referencing AMA- and black-organized colleges, the GEB stated: "The General Education Board therefore resolved that, while certain privately managed institutions must be aided, its main purpose required that it cooperate with progressive Southern sentiment in creating publicly supported educational systems."[104] In other words, Rockefeller's foundation dedicated its enormous financial resources to publicly funded segregated education at the primary and secondary levels; its commitment to honor community standards extended to promoting particular forms of higher education in the South. To avoid antagonizing Southerners, Rockefeller's foundation only supported colleges for blacks that offered industrial education programs. The foundation organized its scholarships and charitable giving to promote research universities in major metropolitan centers and industrial education for Southern blacks. It is important to note that such foundations provided resources supporting segregated education, rather than equalized or integrated education.[105]

Changes for Anti-Caste Colleges

College administrators and external organizations negotiated divergent logics around the motivation for higher education, the metrics for evaluating the social worth of groups, and the commensuration of both groups of people and colleges. Two features of anti-caste colleges are important to remember. First, these colleges had defined their value through their ability to change social and political attitudes, both among their students and through their graduates' work in education, politics, and missionary fields. Second, before the 1880s, anti-caste colleges drew students from limited networks. Anti-caste college students were most likely to arrive at Oberlin, Berea or—to a lesser degree—Howard through networks established in shared abolitionist heritage. As higher education developed as a competitive field, colleges articulated their value by their position within the field, as the cases of Oberlin and Howard (chapter 5) and Berea (chapter 7) will show. Anti-caste education had initially endeavored to create a model for replication. As the field of higher education began to take form, Anti-Caste colleges increasingly needed to curry support for the individuality and special expertise of their particular model. In this way, we see how competition consecrated groups of people and a set of beliefs about the meaning and purpose of higher education.

In addition, new external organizations implemented systematic methods of ranking and allocating resources according to private interests (see chapter 5). Initially, the BRFAL cooperated with private benevolent organizations to build an educational system in the South. This strategic maneuver circumnavigated local opposition to black education and interracial cooperation. The AMA had an additional motivation—it wanted to keep governance over civil rights matters outside the realm of state involvement. The AMA engaged in obligation hoarding. The AMA claimed special expertise in organizing Southern education to keep black education from falling under the control of untrustworthy Southern governments unlikely to provide reasonable education facilities for black students. As Elisabeth Clemens has described, "conflict over the role of public and private efforts in the relief of poverty is a durable feature of American history" whereby "discursive linking of economic independence and citizenship rights positioned relief and charity as key sites for struggles over political membership."[106] This public-private hybrid of higher education was a postwar reconstruction policy. It bridged Republicans' interests in transforming social structures to secure republican governance, while allowing private Northern organizations some control in a region hostile to federal or Northern involvement.

The AMA kept its work under private control—funded by Northern and British dollars—to make certain social responsibilities fell under voluntary associations rather than the state. It did so out of fear that Southern states were hostile to extending citizenship to blacks. But the vulnerability of higher education to the changing winds of donor interests proved to have profound consequences. By the late 1890s, as the final section of the chapter describes, new sets of elites competed against the AMA for control. By having largely wrested private control over Southern education, there were no legal measures to inhibit private investment—regardless of how it impacted blacks' social rights. The following three chapters illustrate the development and diffusion of new forms that couple groups of people with groups of colleges and types of educations.

As the next three chapters will show, not all colleges and universities aspired to the same model. Educational organizations are not solely characterized by the unidirectional transferal of knowledge and increased status. Rather, educational environments are abuzz with status interactions—from faculty, among students, and through the place itself.[107] Increasingly, college administrators recognized that to claim special status, they would need to develop a particular niche—whether through creating a unique constituency or a unique curriculum. As elaborated in chapter 5, Oberlin's trustees set the goal to become an elite college on par with exclusive schools on the East Coast. Trustees made decisions to align curricular programs and certification practices in accordance with other colleges: for the first time, boards determined the criteria for peer organizations and, particularly at Oberlin, set their goals to meet the practices of those schools. In 1894, Oberlin aligned the degrees, certificates, and courses of study to match competitors' offerings, even voting to retroactively grant bachelor's degrees to students who had received a variety of outmoded programs. The new competitive spirit reached students through new pedagogical practices. Many colleges and universities—including Stanford, Oberlin, Smith, Wellesley, and others—did not grade students. By 1912 most colleges marked student work, signaling an increasing acceptance of competition on every campus, whether coeducational or single-sex.[108]

Berea articulated its place as a "Tuskegee" for poor whites and modeled a new industrial training program on Hampton and Tuskegee. As discussed in greater detail in chapter 5, Berea appraised its ability to maintain its donor base with trepidation. Yet a new president, W. G. Frost, saw a strategic opening. Despite increasing industrial education for blacks, few whites were educated for trades at college. Frost attempted to revive the interest in "the laboring classes" legislated through the Morrill Act and transform Berea's mission to white industrial education. In an era prior to selective admissions, colleges began to distinguish themselves as appropriate for certain types of people in the 1880s. Frost's construction of a new cultural category—the Appalachian—as a differentiation strategy for Berea is discussed in chapter 7.

These changes, as mentioned, expanded higher education but produced categorically dependent pathways of educational opportunity. For white students of means, the experience of higher education was rapidly changing. Students began to compare a wider array of possible college options. While previous generations would likely have selected their college by religious denomination, declining emphasis on college as preparation for the ministry meant that college students could elect to pursue a range of professions and enjoy campus activities—including sports—during their campus years. Leisure increasingly replaced stern religious and political devotion as a defining collegiate experience. Mission-driven colleges were suddenly in competition with a wider array of college options. While small numbers of women had attended most land-grant colleges, new elite women's colleges were founded and increased in acceptability for wealthy women.[109] Predominately white colleges increasingly emphasized nonacademic components of the college experience; opaque personal qualities such as "character" and "personality" were prioritized in admissions and campus life centered on activities like athletics and debate.[110]

For black students, in contrast, available courses of study diminished. The population of colleges expanded rapidly but the overwhelming majority of these only offered industrial (vocational) programs, with training in trades like brick masonry or carpentry for men and domestic training for women. Northern schools enrolled very small numbers of black students and Southern colleges offering nonindustrial education were diminishing. As the colleges aligned to particular rules of the field, protests from black constituents—alumni, students, faculty, and administrators—were largely ignored. To understand how status closure processes worked through higher education—including the reconstitution of race as a legitimate social barrier—the next sections provide an analysis that encompasses multiple bases of status distinctions across different sectors.

The higher education field developed wholly without state regulation. Lifschitz, Sauder, and Stevens aptly characterize the era from 1870 to 1910 as a condition of status anarchy; colleges constituted a competitive organizational sector without a coherent status hierarchy.[111] As the higher education field crowded with new colleges, Oberlin, Berea, and Howard all endeavored to maintain their legitimacy and exceptionalism. Other external agencies competed for expertise status, whether for their knowledge of interracial cooperation, particular ethnicities, or expertise in gendered education. The use of ethnographic capital is a strategic move on the part of actors engaged in "elite standoffs" to claim jurisdiction in a particular domain of state policy. In higher education, these actors competed for jurisdiction over particular groups as a means to differentiate their campus from others.

The remaining three chapters of the book describe how intercollegiate comparisons fueled competition for resources beginning in the 1880s. Higher education developed as a semiautonomous field with its own rules and unique stakes in competition. It was during this time that colleges first compared themselves to others and later, with the emergence of external monitoring by the Association of Collegiate Alumna (see chapter 5), were subjected to intercollegiate comparisons and the rise of rankings. Prior to third-party evaluations, however, we can consider press data as one way that comparisons were drawn across colleges. Status is, of course, a relational game and colleges had two somewhat competing challenges. As administrators and trustees changed and responded to new external demands, these colleges reoriented their strategy. As discussed in greater depth later, this new competitive field of higher education pushed colleges to differentiate their missions while adopting bridging strategies to align with the field generally.

CHAPTER FIVE

The "Perils" of Gender Coeducation

It was generally predicted that none but coarse-grained, loud-voiced, brawny "shriekers" in bloomers and short hair would dare enter the University. Time has shown how false were the predictions.... The women are here. And from all that I can learn and observe, I do not see that the women ... [are] in any danger of becoming masculine, or "unwomanly," by reason of the broader intellectual culture and discipline she is gaining day-by-day, nor that the students have been injured by her presence, nor that the standard of scholarship has been lowered.

—"MICHIGAN UNIVERSITY: Result of Six Years of Coeducation of the Sexes," *Chicago Daily Tribune*, February 20, 1875

Anti-caste colleges and colleges for black students in the South almost always enrolled men and women. Anti-casteists never argued that sex differences were a fallacy, yet they maintained a place for women in higher education. Gender divisions were maintained more strictly than those around race. But as more doors opened to women, and female students began to outpace their male peers, harsh critiques—by academics and social critics—pushed against further gender integration. Instead, biological arguments emphasized the harm that might come from gender-integrated education and new forms of "sex-designed" education were created.

The push for mass higher education—beginning with the Morrill Act—was largely framed as a mission for educating voters and workers. Women did not fall easily into either category. While very small numbers of women were able to enroll in male colleges and universities since the 1840s, the post-Civil War expansion created a political opportunity for increasing women's access to higher education. Their claim to access, however, was complicated by the prevalent logics at work in the democratization of public higher education—after all, women would not be able to vote until 1919 and women were largely excluded from the professions. Advocates continued to face difficulties in framing the need for women's education. The importance of providing some base level of education to the "mothers of the Republic" was not new. Women's education had been considered largely compensatory to the education of men: women should enjoy a moral education, suitable to raising children, providing moral direction in a community, and even some medical skills to care for the sick and elderly. When the first coeducation colleges were founded in the 1830s, they largely followed this pattern of women's education as compensatory: educating women for futures as help-mates to missionaries, preachers, and teachers.

This chapter underscores the fallacy of equating educational *access* with greater inclusivity and egalitarian progress. Throughout the history of higher education, access has not secured inclusion, rather—as this book argues—early "success" in coeducation was followed by calls for segregation and organizational pressure to provide a "biologically appropriate" form of education in place of coeducation. By bringing in standardized measurements of quality, certain groups were brought into view as worthy of certain types of education. These projects all endeavored to commensurate a field in which previously, as the first survey of U.S. higher education described in 1873, "each college is looked upon measurably as an institution standing by itself alone."[1] This chapter helps to reveal how gender and class distinctions helped to impose a legible hierarchy to make sense of the "status anarchy" that characterized the emergent higher educational field.[2]

Two new organizational forms grew out of the conflict over gender coeducation in the 1870s and 1880s. First, sex-designed colleges emerged in response to social critiques of coeducation. Secondly, in response to conflict over coeducation—both in coeducational universities and in the growth of new women's colleges—a new privately organized monitoring organization emerged. Because women's educational options differed dramatically even at coeducational universities, the Association of Collegiate Alumnae (ACA)—a group of college-educated alumnae—formed the first evaluative organization to monitor against discrimination.

This first section of this chapter examines three forms of higher education for women: sex-integrated, sex-segregated, and sex-designed. First, sex-integrated colleges permitted women to attend the same classes and pursue the same degrees as men. I have termed this sex-integration rather than coeducation because these colleges and universities did not claim gender coeducation as a matter of the social or political importance or that inter-gender education was itself an important aspect of the education provided. Unlike anti-caste coeducational colleges that framed racial coeducation as the first step toward greater political and social equality, most support for sex-integrated colleges and universities came from state legislatures eager to reduce costs. While some universities—Michigan, for example—initially requested separate colleges for women, state legislatures often found the cost of providing dual systems prohibitive. Others, like the University of Delaware, initially welcomed women enthusiastically—after all, more students meant more funding—and only later banned women's enrollment.

Sex-segregated education largely resulted from the first wave of women who petitioned for access to elite private universities. These schools—Columbia, Harvard, Brown, and others—responded to demands for inclusion by providing "annexes." Annexes were separate from the larger college or university. Women students were permitted to take exams and gain limited recognition for intellectual accomplishment but were barred from regular academic life. For instance, Barnard and Radcliffe Colleges grew out of annex programs. A third program, sex-designed colleges, emerged when efforts to secure equal access to rigorous academic programs in coeducational settings were met with critics who charged that women were harmed by higher education. To secure greater resources for women's higher education, sex-segregated colleges played upon contemporary fears that higher education would hinder women's reproductive capacity. Vassar and Smith established a unique market niche by brokering a compromise. Acknowledging backlash critiques based on faulty science, Vassar and Smith implemented a collegiate program expressly designed for the "unique biological needs" of women. Their campaigns assured prospective parents and other interested parties that female students were not permitted the same liberties as male college students, but women were allowed access to intellectually rigorous coursework.

In addition to new forms of education, women's increasing participation in higher education also produced a new technology for and a logic of commensuration. The U.S. commissioner of education first began tabulating the number of colleges in 1870—including the number of colleges open to women. Support for women's access to higher education was quickly cultivated; the more contentious questions were for what purpose and in what setting. In 1870, the commissioner of education reported 11,000 women attending higher education institutions, though only 3,000 women were enrolled in colleges rather than "seminaries."[3] It was not until the birth of the ACA that colleges were compared and evaluated for their academic quality. This chapter explores both the transformations of forms of education and the emergence of a new organization to make sense of a rapidly changing, heterogeneous field—and how single-sex education emerged from these changes.

The Context of Women's Education, Work, and Politics

New forms of higher education for women emerged in response to the growing population of colleges. Access to higher education has been conceptualized as occurring both horizontally (field of study) and vertically (level of study). Universalistic mandates more directly undermine vertical rather than horizontal inequalities.[4] This was true in the nineteenth century as well. Many supported the call for universal education but this did not produce widely shared understandings of the appropriate fields of study or settings for women's higher education. Thus, while women were increasingly gaining access to tertiary education, obstacles to the professions remained firmly in place. Access to elite education proved, unsurprisingly, to be the most contested realm; women's access to liberal arts education was won only through severe restrictions on both form and purpose. Elite colleges designed gendered organizational forms to educate women in strictly monitored settings and demanded discursive allegiance to traditional gender roles.

The postwar generation of women college students benefited from greater opportunities for educational, political, and professional participation. These opportunities stemmed from feminist and abolitionist activism, which grew steadily since the 1840s, as well as the need for women's participation in the war effort and Reconstruction as community educators, nurses, and teachers, among other roles. Following the Civil War, women assumed new professional opportunities, most notably in teaching and medicine. For example, the U.S. Sanitary Commission trained women for new roles as volunteers and women organized councils across the Union. In addition to training in basic nursing skills, the commission offered a wide-scale chance for women to forge organizations collectively and develop administrative skills. As one report described, "These Councils, or conventions of representative women, were held from time to time, as the changing circumstances of the war seemed to require them, and they always resulted in perfecting the details of the general organization, in stimulating those engaged to work for the soldier to renewed zeal."[5] Such organizations—part of a patriotic war effort—allowed women to organize outside the home or church without the charges of radicalism faced by those in feminist organizations.

Anti-caste colleges and universities funded through the Morrill Act claimed that higher education mattered for an increasingly inclusive democracy; while faced with many barricades, women advocated for their rights in the professional and economic realms. During the twenty years prior to the Civil War, activists had mobilized impressive campaigns supporting voting rights for women and blacks, though the suffrage question also proved deeply divisive when the constitutional amendments of Reconstruction left women behind. Still, some gains were made. The territories of Wyoming and Utah both granted voting rights to women, while Sojourner Truth and Susan B. Anthony dramatically attempted to vote in Michigan and New York. Virginia Minor, president of the Woman Suffrage Association of Missouri, would test the right of individual states to bar women from voting in an 1874 Supreme Court case.[6] Women's social movement organization had increased, with pro-suffrage organizations existing in many states. While political representation proved a more protracted struggle, women were successful in opening doors to higher education opportunities. The *New York Times* proclaimed "the educational advantages of young men and women in the Western States, at least, are very nearly equal for a majority of all the Western colleges have thrown open their doors to students of both sexes." In these Western states, the *Times* counted the numbers of colleges by state that did not discriminate by sex: four in Wisconsin, three in Iowa, four in Missouri, ten in Ohio, and nine in Indiana.[7] The *New York Times* was enthusiastic, if not precise, in suggesting that the absence of absolute exclusion might be claimed as "very nearly equal" opportunities.

Most dramatically, the enormous demand for teachers during Reconstruction fractured men's monopoly on the teaching profession, with more women than men teaching for the first time. By 1874, nearly 60 percent of students pursuing teaching careers were women. Thousands of teachers ventured far from their home communities to teach in the new freedmen's schools.[8] These experiences were often isolating and harrowing, as Northern teachers were frequently met with stark resistance by Southern whites.

Though the initial impetus for expanding medical training to women began in the late 1840s, increasing numbers of women also enrolled in medical programs after the Civil War. Prior to that, medical colleges for women provided health practitioners who could attend to gynecological health concerns without subjecting women to male view. Boston and Philadelphia opened women's medical colleges in the early 1850s and New York legislature chartered a similar college in 1863. As some historians argue, these schools constituted "the original 'Alma Mater,' or the inauguration of separate women's educational programs, and fostered friendships and female identity."[9] Like teacher training programs, which were called normal departments, women's medical colleges offered a limited professional curriculum.

In 1870, the cover of *Frank Leslie's Illustrated*, a widely read publication, featured an illustration of a female medical student practicing surgery at the New York Medical College for Women.[10] The illustration challenged widespread views that women were too delicate for the gory practice of medicine. In that year, the U.S. Census counted 525 trained women doctors. By 1890, that number grew to 4,557 and increased to 7,399 by 1900.[11] In 1897, Howard University's medical school graduated a class of thirty-four doctors, dentists, and pharmacists. Among them were three white women and three black women. The *Washington Post* congratulated the graduates, viewing their accomplishment as one for the greater good that would "cure many ills."[12] Between 1864 and 1900, 115 black women—30 of whom were trained at Howard—and roughly 7,000 white women earned medical degrees, compared to 132,000 white men.[13] Women were increasingly mobilizing for entrée into professions and politics, and activists viewed the postwar boom in higher education as a critical juncture to expand women's opportunities.

Early Success and Growing Backlash

The Oberlin model lead the way for gender integration, spreading in the 1840s–1860s to Olivet (Michigan), Ripon (Wisconsin), Grinnell (Iowa), Knox (Illinois), Northfield (Minnesota), and Antioch and Wilberforce (Ohio), before expanding further after the Civil War to nine AMA-sponsored colleges.[14] While anti-caste schools all admitted women, non-affiliated colleges and universities were also increasingly opening their classrooms to women. It was not uncommon, however, that women were only allowed to attend lectures if they sat behind screens to keep them from distracting males.

Prior to the 1890s, many of these schools differentiated programs of study between male "literary courses" and "ladies' courses." As the *New York Times* described in 1873, "degrees seem to have been usually modified in name when conferred on women, who are called 'Mistresses,' 'Maids,' and 'Sisters' of Arts, and 'Mistresses' of English Literature."[15] Because most colleges were initially founded for the purpose of divinity training, classical languages remained an artifact in both admissions requirements and the collegiate curriculum. Because these languages were needed for careers that excluded women, few high schools in the United States offered girls the opportunity to study Latin or Greek. Nonetheless, there were some exceptions and small numbers of women completed literary degrees. At Oberlin, for instance, the ladies' course did not require knowledge of classical language, but such distinctions between ladies' courses and literary courses were not uniformly drawn across all colleges. Indeed, there was very little that was uniform across colleges. Individual colleges set their admissions requirements and graduation requirements, appointed faculty based on a range of qualifications, and granted a range of diplomas. What was common, however, was that women were almost never treated the same as male students.

Pressured by legislatures for economic reasons, public universities funded through the Morrill Act were the most likely to admit white women. Religiously funded colleges in the South were nearly the only access to higher education available to black women. While most of the land-grant colleges that grew from the 1862 Morrill Act offered opportunities of some form to white women from their inception, they often compromised by offering ladies' courses and insulated normal departments. This was not limited to public universities: the University of Wisconsin, Grinnell, Northwestern, and the University of Missouri also followed this form.[16] The original charter of the University of Michigan, the largest university in the country at the time, provided for a female department but the legislature balked at the expense.[17] The Morrill Act of 1862 was an important policy in expanding higher education opportunities for white women and nonelites more broadly. The majority of college-educated women of the nineteenth and early twentieth centuries benefitted from the movement that encouraged the laboring classes to enter higher education.

Anti-caste schools founded in the antebellum period and during the height of Reconstruction—Antioch, Oberlin, Berea, Howard, Fisk, Wilberforce, and others—all enrolled black and white women. The exclusion of white women from many private colleges enabled colleges like Howard to maintain racial diversity. Barred from elite male colleges and universities, some white women enrolled at predominately black colleges to study medicine and law. But by the mid-1880s, many public and private colleges disincentivized women's enrollment.

Yet even in universities with supportive administrators, women faced stark pressures to defer to the established hierarchy. At the University of Delaware, for example, President Purnell pushed for coeducation to increase enrollment as part of his vision for growing the university with Morrill Act funds. Enrollment efforts were successful and soon there was a sizeable cohort of women students. Women students organized a feminist literary club to sponsor discussions of controversial political issues and invited activists including Belva Lockwood—the second woman to campaign for president of the United States—and Susan B. Anthony. Resentment among male students increased as women students claimed many of the academic prizes during the 1870s and 1880s. By 1885, the Board of Trustees, bolstered by alumni protest, abolished coeducation and President Purnell left the college.[18]

Though Oberlin had educated women for more than fifty years, by the 1890s the college took measures to encourage female applicants to seek admission among the many newly formed women's colleges. Oberlin made symbolic gestures toward women's education but these were not always put into practice. In a discussion by the board of trustees over the distribution of funds across departments at Oberlin, one trustee, confused by the lack of consistency between practice and policy asked: "We have a Dean of the Woman's Department. What is the Woman's Department?"[19] As discussed in the next chapter, when Oberlin launched a new agenda to compete with elite colleges in the early 1890s, the Board of Trustees aligned the admissions practices with its perceived competition. This included encouraging women and blacks to attend segregated colleges. While it did not wholly abandon coeducation, like Delaware and others, the Board of Trustees repeatedly redirected financial resources from women and black students and funneled these funds toward white men.

Few of the elite sex-designed colleges knowingly enrolled black women, though in rare instances some black women matriculated. None of the colleges had an explicit policy for race in admissions, though many had unspoken quotas.[20] Black women were often denied on-campus housing and boarded with faculty instead. At Vassar, the father of Anita Florence Hemmings' roommate hired a private detective to uncover Hemmings' racial background. Despite such hostility, Hemmings graduated in 1897. Black women faced much greater constraints than other students, including black men. In W. E. B. DuBois' survey of 107 predominately white colleges, 549 (79 percent) black graduates were male and 144 (21 percent) female. At the thirty-four predominately black colleges surveyed, black women fared worse, with 2,964 (83 percent) male graduates and 514 (17 percent) women.[21] Oberlin graduate Anna Julia Cooper described additional barriers: "I fear the majority of colored men do not yet think it worthwhile that women aspire to higher education."[22] Cooper chided black male reformers for imagining that "race uplift" could be complete so long as women were excluded.[23] As Linda Perkins describes, many black leaders preferred to focus first on securing positions of status for black men on par with those of whites, too often limiting their vision of a new social order to prevailing discriminatory patterns of white society that made subordination of women appear natural and unchallenged.[24]

By 1890, women made up nearly one-third of U.S. college students, and unlike black students, increased access to higher education was not limited to particular educational settings for white women. By 1897, the majority of women attended gender-integrated institutions, a figure that continued to rise in the twentieth century before the Servicemen's Readjustment Act of 1944 (P.L. 78–346, 58 Stat. 284m), or the G. I. Bill, offered a unique college pathway for men.[25]

Women were admitted to the Oberlin Collegiate Course in 1837, with the first woman graduate awarded a baccalaureate in 1841. Even in this time, women at Oberlin agitated to have their contributions recognized. Women students at Oberlin participated in a raid to rescue a refugee slave, and helped repeal the 1850 Fugitive Slave Act at the Ohio Republican Convention. In the face of this act, Oberlin student Frances Hazen argued, "Our enthusiasm differs from that of young men only in that it is less demonstrative—still, we would have its existence acknowledged."[26] Women were included for the service they might provide men—to help cheer up the somber student life on campus and with the expectation that their education would benefit service-focused marriages. But women students were eager to prove they were capable of more, and that their political engagement was equal to their male classmates. Despite this desire to have their political consciousness recognized, Hazen drew on the compensatory framework to articulate women's place at Oberlin: "Without the young women's hands to supply this great want, and to rectify that evil, without their voice to cheer the loneliness there would be something lacking, at least the fuel with which to kindle youthful enthusiasm. In short, from the gown and slippers to the higher calls of the moral nature, all speak of the desolation that would ensue if all the young women should turn their back upon the world and make their exit."[27]

While J. H. Fairchild's administration claimed that there were no impediments to women taking the classical course, this did not mean that the college wholly endorsed women claiming equal status with men. J. H. Fairchild delivered a lecture on "Women's Rights and Duties" that made clear he viewed the primary duties of women as domestic, and not in the public sphere as women's rights advocates claimed. One student was so upset by his speech that she cried for two days before her roommate related how deeply Fairchild's views had pained her. Fairchild responded that he hoped by speaking his mind he would "save the bright and happy girls from leaving their own appropriate sphere."[28] What is perhaps most surprising here is that the female student had, in 1849, believed that her college held equal expectations for the intellectual development of male and female students. Indeed, so deeply embedded were these gendered norms that, in its first decades, Oberlin women were kept out of classes on Mondays to do laundry for male students.[29] At graduation, a public event and therefore deemed by administrators as inappropriate for women's voices, women's graduation speeches were read by male faculty.[30] This would not change until 1858 or 1859. Campus administrators boasted that women's presence benefited the health and stability of the collegiate environment for men, though as Jill Ker Conway states, "Women's minds during and after college education were thus considered only from the point of view of the services they might provide for men."[31] A number of Oberlin women persisted in pushing the limits of acceptability by completing the collegiate course, rather than the ladies course.

During the 1870s, journalists, academic administrators, and others described gender coeducation as successful when women's participation neither caused women to transgress feminine docility, nor challenged university settings as masculine domains. Similar to the debates over the appropriate form of higher education for blacks, the most successful campaigns were those that protected firm status boundaries between blacks and whites, men and women.

Advocates for women's inclusion struggled to articulate a purpose for women in higher education on any other rationale than "fairness." The well-known and outspoken advocate for women's equality, Thomas Higginsworth argued: "We eat our breakfast as human beings, not as men and women; it is the same with nine tenths of our interests and duties in life. In legislating or philosophizing for woman, we must neither forget that she has an organization distinct from that of a man, nor must we exaggerate the fact. Not "first the womanly and then the human," but first the human and then the womanly, is to be the order of her training."[32] How should advocates make the case for increasing and equalizing women's educational access? What narrative would resonate best with the most powerful actors?[33] This was an important and difficult determination.

The reasons that had stirred support for higher education for blacks were not applicable to women. They had not "earned" compensation for military bravery, and women had failed to secure the right to vote by the recent constitutional amendments. Women's education was not framed as repayment for a social debt, nor as preparation for political participation. Despite the importance of women's service as teachers and nurses during the Civil War, this was not a reason deployed in calling for women's education. Similar to the framing used in the 1850 Roberts v. Boston school desegregation case, supporters argued that women suffered psychologically from their exclusion. "The Press and the pulpit abound with exhortations on the necessity of opening new paths of labor to women. All who have daughters to provide for feel how limited is the field in which they must hereafter earn their own living. At present, for girls of the higher class, teaching and keeping boarding houses seem to be almost the only two "professions" open. And even those who can reasonably hope to be able to secure a support for their daughters, must see how much more dignified and useful a position it is for a woman to be engaged in some work demanding the employment of mind and requiring education. Merely to be waiting for marriage is not a very satisfactory calling for a woman of powers and culture."[34] However sympathetic, these arguments were focused on the individual. There was no discussion of what broader contributions were lost by excluding women professionally and politically. Neither the inclusion nor exclusion of women was argued to have implications for the state or national development, as was the case with education for black men. Nor was women's education framed as a status threat or as professional competition, at least not yet.

Is an Annex "Access"?

As a member of the Vassar class of 1870 wrote nine years after the college's founding, "Not only is Vassar College a success, but the serious consideration of the question, whether their doors shall not be opened to women is agitating every college in the land."[35] As described, Vassar was not an early mover. By 1870, 3,000 women were already college students—and most of them on campuses with male classmates. Vassar was successful in that it offered a rigorous education, but it did not necessarily facilitate opening more doors to higher education. When women pressed for entry into elite colleges, few managed to matriculate.

In response to the mobilization by women for access, a few universities responded with annex programs in separate facilities near the universities. Though some classes met, more commonly annexes allowed students the privilege of sitting for exams rather than learning from lectures. This project yielded early success for a few but depended upon the goodwill of faculty to provide free labor. This produced limited success, both in the United States and internationally. *Woman's Work*, an American journal for working women, reported on increasing educational access in Russia where, in 1867, a group of women petitioned to have access to medical education. Though the minister of public instruction denied the petition, faculty members "taking advantage of their right to lecture in public" taught courses that were open to women and men. These courses were not part of their university duties, rather, sympathetic faculty members offered general education courses to the public. Because the courses required students to invest without any likely return, the courses enrolled almost exclusively female students. Within ten years, the ministry acquiesced and women in St. Petersburg were able to access medical education.[36] Within a few years, women in the United States lobbied for similar access. Through this unlikely strategy, some elite colleges were eventually forced to create annexes after prolonged battles.

The process that unfolded at Columbia University, and followed a similar pattern at Harvard and Brown, is illustrative. Trustee Morgan Dix imagined coeducation as "a passing fashion, a part of the radicalism spawned by the Civil War and Reconstruction."[37] To appease Lillie

Devereaux Blake, descendant of two Columbia presidents, Dix proposed coeducation to the board. They declined unanimously in 1873. Blake took her case to Elizabeth Cady Stanton, president of the National Woman Suffrage Association. Stanton included an appeal for coeducation at Columbia in her address to the 1873 Woman's Congress. Bolstered by this support, Sorosis, a New York City women's organization originally formed to protest discrimination by the New York Press Club, took up the campaign. In his annual report, Columbia's president Barnard affirmed that the new colleges for women could not possibly provide the same quality of "long-established and well-endowed colleges," and furthermore, women would prove a steadying influence for men. Offering data from Cornell as evidence, President Barnard argued that the admission of women "raised the standard of scholarship" and reduced attrition by 10 percent.[38] Barnard made requests on three occasions for the trustees attention to the matter. Finally, in 1883, with a petition signed by over 1,300 New Yorkers and Barnard's appeal to the New York Board of Regents, the trustees conceded to allow for a "Collegiate Course for Women," which permitted women to sit for exams but not attend classes with men. Beginning in 1889, Columbia faculty taught classes to women at the new Barnard College in a nearby townhouse. Few were satisfied with annex programs. Coeducation supporters found the annex model insufficient for providing women with rigorous academic programs. Indeed it would take nearly another century for some of the most selective and most prestigious universities to adapt. Yale and Princeton did not admit women as undergraduates until 1969, Dartmouth not until 1972, and Columbia delayed until 1983.

Opponents resented women's claims to share the same resources. Alumni complained that even admitting women to annexed programming reduced male student's access to resources. Harvard students complained that women "seriously incommoded" male students "by using these books of reference kept in the library."[39] The *Chicago Tribune* described that even though the women at the Harvard Annex were scarcely granted more than the opportunity to sit for exams, coeducation threatened the "usefulness of the university, and its failure as an educational institution will only be a question of time."[40] As more women enrolled, critics used a new argument against gender coeducation by claiming that coeducation challenged the purpose of university education. Suggesting that university education held a utility value linked to future employment and status, allowing women to prepare for professional life challenged the dominant functionalist logic of the time. The most common critique was that access to literary education—or liberal arts education—would "give women a distaste for the pleasures of domestic life and would disqualify them for their duties in both family and society."[41] Critics used a range of arguments against gender coeducation, claiming that it diminished the status and quality of education, depleted material resources, and served no utility value. These arguments were largely unsuccessful. As the next section will discuss, opposition to women's inclusion in elite higher education was mobilized by framing coeducation—in even its weakest form—as a threat to the reproductive capacity of the upper classes. It was with this rationale that coeducation critics found success in excluding women from elite education.

Women's entrée into higher education, however, threatened men's monopoly on professional employment. More often, sociologists have viewed women's changing role in the late nineteenth and early twentieth century quite narrowly. Most work on the professions during this era has focused on men.[42] Standard accounts imply a quasi-functionalist argument: as women gained in education, new and gendered professional pathways opened to them. From the emphasis on social settlement work, one might imagine that women's professional aspirations and accomplishments were limited to the growing bureaucratization of social welfare projects. While the numbers of women in the professions were small, they nonetheless comprised a greater threat than most sociologists have acknowledged. This leaves us with a view of women's gains in higher education—and later professional work—as wholly separated from conflict or struggles over resources. Contemporary actors, however, viewed the swelling enrollment of women in colleges and universities through a wholly different lens. In 1904, Harvard professor Hugo Münsterberg expressed his alarm that women would soon prove more desirable for academic positions because, unlike men, they would not have family obligations: "In the colleges and universities men still dominate, but soon will not if things are not changed; the great numbers of young women who pass their doctoral examinations and become specialists in science will have more and more to seek university professorships, or else they will have studied in vain. And here, as in the school, the economic conditions strongly favor the woman; since she has no family to support, she can accept a position so much smaller that the man. . . . If social factors do not change, women will enter as competitors in every field where the labor does not require specifically masculine strength. So it has been in the factories, so in the schools, and so, in a few decades, it may be in the universities."[43]

What is critical to recognize is the degree to which educated women were increasingly perceived as legitimate challengers to the established social hierarchy. High status professional and philanthropic organizations mounted formidable resistance. The American Medical Association refused to open its membership to any school where women were instructors or admit female physicians to its ranks until 1915. The Flexner Report, funded by the Carnegie Foundation for the Advancement of Teaching, closed doors to many medical programs open to women and black men.[44] Münsterberg argued that women's increasing presence crossed class divides and spurred competition in nonmanual labor fields. There are a number of similarities between the rise of gender coeducation, predominately among white women, and the rise of college opportunities for blacks. In both cases, early access was achieved with much less resistance than reasonably expected. After limited success—as measured in enrollment, graduation, and professional achievement—both faced a low threshold before they were perceived as a status threat to white men. Despite these similarities, very different outcomes followed.

As women's education became an independent form of higher education and a social project, it was placed in competition with other forms of higher education as colleges competed for students, donors, and legitimacy. Arguments for women's access were received as threats to male dominance, in the work force and within marriages. Absent wifely duties—as educated women were considered unsuitable to family life—they would be better equipped to compete in the labor market. Not only that, but if they married, they would as Anna Julia Cooper (Oberlin 1884) asserted, pose a useful challenge to the accepted conventions of marriage: "Her standards have undoubtedly gone up. . . . The question is not now with the woman 'How shall I cramp, stunt, simplify, and nullify myself as to make me eligible to the honor of being swallowed up into some little man?' but the problem, I trow, now rests with the man as to how he can develop his God-given powers as to reach the ideal of a generation of women who demand the noblest, grandest, and best achievements of which he is capable. . . . Nature never meant that the standards and ideals of the world should be dwarfing and minimizing ones, and the men should thank us for requiring of them the richest fruits which they can grow. If it makes them work, all the better for them.[45]"

Activating Difference: From Coeducation to "Sex Designed" Colleges

> Identical education, or identical coeducation, of the sexes defrauds one sex or the other, or perhaps both. It defies the Roman maxim, which physiology has fully justified, *mens sana in corpore sano.* The sustained regimen, regular recitation, erect posture, daily walk, persistent exercise, and unintermitted labor that toughens a boy, and makes a man of him, can only be partially applied to a girl."
>
> —Edward H. Clarke, *Sex in Education*, 1875, 128

Though the fundamental premise was shared, the emerging sex-segregated colleges of New England initially differed in dramatic ways. These colleges also posed a particular paradox. In exchange for adhering to strict social rules for maintaining "decorum," the colleges also provided women—administrators, faculty, and students alike—with a rare experience of autonomy. We will see a similar dilemma emerge at Howard University in the next chapter. As Vassar prepared to open, it quickly became mired in controversy over its plans for an exclusively male faculty. Attacked in a leading periodical, its founder was persuaded to hire female faculty. Matthew Vassar printed additional copies of the article and declared his earlier decision folly, "for it is vain to educate woman's powers of thought and then limit their operation."[46] A Vassar student urged her peers and alumnae to agitate for a woman to fill a vacancy on the Board of Trustees: "It is a patent absurdity that a college for women should have no representation for women, unless the Trustees are willingly open to take the position that they should be as 'clay in the hands of the potter.' That seems hardly consistent with that honoring of their intellects which the Founder showed, when he gave them a chance for education."[47] Wellesley, for example, created an "Adamless Eden" by exclusively hiring women faculty and administration. The new sex-designed colleges often portrayed students as pioneers and the founders as benevolently supportive of educating women. This reduced the changes in higher education to one of mere access, even though more women gained access to higher education through coeducation than sex-designed colleges. The central conflict was not over whether to educate women but over the form of higher education to make available. These colleges were part of a larger push to specify particular types of education for particular type of people.

As women made gains in higher education, their increasing presence was perceived by some as a threat to the pervasive, exclusionary masculine control of a key social institution for categorizing privilege and status. When elites were pressured to vary established admissions practices, a new campaign was launched to rearticulate the rules governing women's access to symbolic and material resources for upward status mobility: sharp class distinction, biological difference, and racial competition. Just as rising "scientific racism" articulated a theory of polygenism, or the belief that different races developed on separate tracks, academics applied a similar logic to women. Women would be harmed by forms of higher education not designed with their particularly, unique biological development at its core. Race, class, and gender are understood as sustained patterns of interlocking inequality, a matrix of domination, deeply embedded in the most personal aspects of both individual and social life.[48]

Many critics had long voiced concerns that student life was hazardous to health, as were the professions college students would likely enter. Studying entailed long periods of sitting, thinking, and reading, depriving the body of fresh air and strenuous physical labor. The manual labor movement launched in the 1820s increasingly linked health and mental development. Education reformers Thomas Higginson and Horace Mann, among others, warned that without physical exertion, students risked "premature physical collapse and early death."[49] These concerns, however, were largely for male students. Many women were already under pressure to restrict physical activity. Feminists, including the philosopher Mary Wollstonecraft, had long argued that women needed vigorous activity to stimulate their minds. For such reasons some colleges—including Antioch, Berea, and Oberlin—emphasized physical activity for both men and women. These colleges framed physical exertion through manual labor an important component in college education. Not only would manual labor allow poor students to afford college and inculcate respect for labor among the future white-collar professionals, but labor programs would also develop students' bodies and inculcate healthy habits for their future in sedentary professions. By the 1870s, however, health concerns were rarely voiced for men and manual labor programs largely faded from predominately white campuses.

When, in 1873, Harvard medical professor, Edward H. Clarke, published his appeal against gender coeducation, his arguments built on long-established widespread concerns that too much study threatened a healthy body. Clarke extended the familiar concern that education posed a health risk for men and reframed the threat in to include female students' reproductive organs. Clarke believed in a five-year peak period of female reproductive development, or *catemenia*. He claimed if women were stressed during this developmental phase, their future reproductive capacity would be invariably and irreversibly harmed. His book was widely received and reprinted twelve times in its first year.[50] The debate shifted from health to biological determinism. Clarke argued that women's reproductive system "organized" the development of body and mind, which "lends to her development and to all her work a rhythmical or periodical order, which must be recognized and obeyed."

Biological differences in physical development, Clarke asserted, required appropriate educational settings: "Periodicity characterizes the female organization, and develops feminine force. Persistence characterizes the male organization, and develops masculine force. Education will draw the best out of each by adjusting its methods to the periodicity of one and the persistence of the other."[51] The *New York Times* endorsed changing how women students were graded in accordance with Clarke's admonitions: "The great change to be made in women's colleges is the method of grading or marking. The evil complained of in Wisconsin would be partially obviated if the students were tested by examinations, not daily recitations . . . then no young woman would be obliged to work when she ought to be at home resting."[52] In other words, both instructional and evaluative design needed to be tailored to the particular biological needs of men and women. Men required training in persistence and benefited from attending regularly scheduled lectures. By contrast, women could demonstrate their learning through exams, thereby providing them more control over their study schedule since they were unable to control their menstrual cycle. Though highly influential, Clarke's view was countered by powerful critics from social movements and higher education.

Julia Ward Howe compiled papers from leading social thinkers, male and female, in her 1875 rebuttal to Clarke. Protesting an education that prepared women solely for motherhood at the expense of broader intellectual development, one coeducation advocate argued: "Nothing is so absurd as to press upon a young woman's thought the idea that she is to become a mother. What if she is? Let her make herself a healthy, happy human being, and what will may befall. What would be thought of a community which definitely undertook to train young men to the functions and duties of fathers? A shout of derision would be raised at once. 'Let us have citizens!' they would cry. I echo the demand."[53] Six years after the admission of women, the *Chicago Tribune* tabulated enrollment reports for the University of Michigan. Though noting that the numbers of women studying law were too low to herald the success of coeducation across the entire campus, overall the *Tribune* declared that "during these few years of trial, many questions in regard to women's capacity for sustained and heavy intellectual labor . . . have been practically settled." Referencing Harvard professor Edward Clarke, an outspoken critic of coeducation, the *Tribune* offered the female students at Michigan as a "living refutation of Dr. Clarke's theory."[54] In 1878, President Bascom of the University of Wisconsin, where women made up approximately one-quarter of the student population, reported finding it "very strange" that, rather than constituting a new threat, student life was more consistent with the "confinement" to which young women were already accustomed.

By contrast, Bascom argued, the academic setting was more difficult for male students who, "sun-browned and apparently robust do not endure the violent transition as well as women." Citing a comparison of student absences by gender, Bascom affirmed coeducation: "The young women do their work with less rather than greater labor than the young men, and certainly do not fall below them in any respect as scholars. . . . The young women whose health was primarily the ground of criticism, have improved in strength rather than deteriorated since they have been with us."[55] Clarke claimed that the consequences of a "mismatched education"—where women were forced away from a natural, "periodic" academic schedule and forced into a "persistent" college structure, suitable only for men—would only be detected after the folly of college had past. If subjected to a biologically inappropriate organizational form of higher education, women would discover his "truth" too late. Critics like Clarke used the threat of future infertility to undermine advances for women's equality.

Julia Ward Howe denounced Clarke's scare-tactics. Rather, she countered, the restrictions placed on women enervated their natural capabilities—both physical and intellectual. To this end, she noted the corset was far more likely to impair reproductive function than coeducation. Howe called out the amplification of "collegiate rigor" as a test to exclude women: "Boys as well as girls break down under severe study, men as well as women. . . . Let milder and more humane regime be devised and enforced. No one loses health through the lessons of wisdom wisely explained. It is the hurried, undigested (also indigestible) tuition which nauseates and fatigues!"[56] In short, Howe argued that constructing the collegiate environment to produce stress, insecurity and competition harmed women and men.

The debate over women's access to elite education reflected the growing influence of white nationalism. Clarke warned that the "persistent" exertion required by an academic schedule fitted to the masculine physiology would rob women their future "duty and compensating privilege" to "nurse a race." During the late nineteenth century, medical professionals increasingly sought to link policy governing women's reproduction with racial politics, including white dominance.[57] These maneuvers were equally present in education reform. Political actors treated elite women's reproductive capacity as a limited resource. "If the education of the sexes remains identical, instead of being appropriate and special . . . then the sterilizing influence of such a training, acting with tenfold more force upon the female than upon the male, will go on, and the race will be propagated from its inferior classes. The stream of life that is to flow into the future will be Celtic rather than American."[58] Furthermore, Clarke argued that, unlike working class girls whose "boisterous" upbringing made them more robust, affluent women required an educational setting that reflected the "delicacy" of their home environment. His critics mocked that his attentions and concerns for women would be better applied to women working in manufacturing, and as clerks, teachers, maids, and mothers where women were not at liberty to rest during menstruation.[59] Clarke's arguments claimed that the physical demands of women's unique biological determinates were specific only to affluent, "native" white women whereas more robust peasant women— and particularly those from Ireland—were equipped with unassailable fertility.

In short, Clarke did not argue that women of the middle and upper classes should not be educated. Rather, he argued that women's education should fit their biologically determined development. Restricting women's access to elite higher education served to prioritize women's position as mothers, and served particular goals of preserving the racial hierarchy. Sex-designed colleges incorporated Clarke's warnings into

FIGURE 5. Dining room of Haven House, 1904. Courtesy of Katherine Elizabeth McClellan, Smith College Archives, Smith College.

their design. Pervasive supervision over health and tightly controlled femininity were all woven into the colleges' physical environment and their extracurricular program. In 1884, administrators from Berea, Oberlin, Smith, Wellesley, and Harvard convened in New York City to discuss the future of "the higher education of women."[60] This group was convened by the Congregational Club, uniting many important figures from the AMA. In his address, Reverend Laurenus Seelye, president of Smith College, reminded his audience that "the higher education of women is no longer a hope, it is a realization." Accepting that women had proven their "capacity for intellectual rigor," education leaders debated how to educate women despite the "perils" facing female students who "cannot endure as easily as the average man the strain of prolonged mental effort." The answer was to counter the rising trend of gender co-education by creating separate campuses to accommodate elite women. Rather than "remove the peril by giving up education" for women, new colleges were created to "conduct education with increasing respect for sanitary laws."[61]

At Smith College, the height between steps was exceptionally shallow; stairs were considered potentially hazardous to the reproductive organs and so they were minimized whenever possible. Students lived and dined in houses, in part, to mimic a more familial atmosphere while also facilitating constant supervision. Above each door was a transom window so that the house matron could always ensure that lights out was strictly enforced, thus ensuring that the students were well-rested and not studying too late at night. Vassar College, founded in 1861, considered the "health of the student . . . a prime object of attention" and to that end, "great care is taken to the sanitary regulations of the College, as respects hours for rising and retiring, the warming and ventilation of rooms, choice and preparation of food." Students were assigned an "hour of ease" after instructional time ended. Students were encouraged to take part in appropriate forms of "invigorating exercise" and for this purpose the campus included graveled walking trails, with boating in the summer and skating in the winter, as well as a "well-furnished gymnasium" to use in times of inclement weather.[62]

Though sex-designed colleges were few, their design suggested that, more broadly, women required a unique and appropriate form of education. This would shape the practices selected for women's continued incorporation in higher education. Increasingly, critics of coeducation foregrounded the debate using a logic that established the primacy of women's reproductive capacity over their potential for other forms of societal contribution. This also helped to overshadow earlier concerns that college-educated women would compete against men in the labor market. As the next section describes, this activation of difference moved from intellectual discourse to produce of a new organizational form.

Competition and Quality Control:
Policing Status and Gender

During the early 1880s, a new type of organization developed to monitor the boundaries of what constituted a college education. In the 1880s and 1890s, a new form of organization sought to shape the rapidly developing field of higher education. These organizations, however, sought to monitor and evaluate colleges based on academic rigor. Whereas the AMA and anti-caste colleges viewed students' moral and social development—including a spirit of inclusivity—as an important outcome of higher education, this new model sought to impose academic rigor as primary measure of educational quality. As the field of higher education rapidly populated, there was also a wide range of quality and types of schools that called themselves colleges. Beyond this, as access for women increased—albeit incrementally—many were concerned that women were admitted but not eligible for the full benefits of higher education.

In 1881, two young Bostonians, recently graduated from college and frustrated by the lack of professional opportunities they found for educated women, banded together to create a network for other young college graduates. Many of the founders of ACA shared experiences of having faced hostility during their undergraduate years as the first generation of women to attend public higher education. These women were not mobilizing to expand women's enrollment in higher education. The problem, the founders of the ACA decided, was not that there were too few opportunities for women to attend college; but rather that there were too many schools that called themselves colleges for women, but were incomparable in rigor to men's higher educational opportunities.

The ACA faced a challenge of commensuration. How did a ladies course at Oberlin compare to liberal arts training at Wellesley or the University of Michigan? Other schools seemed to offer a rigorous education like the Decatur Institute (now Agnes Scott College) or Mount Holyoke Seminary (now Mount Holyoke College), but did institutes and seminaries qualify as colleges? No less crucial, how did women fare at coeducational public universities? Did the ability to enroll translate into equal opportunity? Perhaps not, but being on the same campus might be critical for being able to demonstrate inequality.

Emerging organizations frequently increase in variation as the population increases.[63] As new variations grew out of the old—as coeducation turned to segregation—the actors behind these new colleges legitimated new organizational forms by consecrating difference. Critics responded to women's access to coeducation with new and searing questions. Should women be educated *as women*, or should they transgress the separate spheres and lay claim to forms of knowledge, disciplines, and professions largely denied them? College organizations advanced sex-segregation as an innovative solution to circumnavigate structural constraints and respond to limitations.

How did women's higher education develop as a separate sphere? Traditional accounts place women's colleges at the vanguard of women's access to higher education. Closer examination of the timing of organizational emergence reveals that women's colleges were instead a response to increasing pressure to push women out of coeducational universities. While very small numbers of women were able to enroll in male colleges and universities since the 1840s, the uniquely open moment in higher education after the Civil War increased the options for women. Their claim to access, however, was complicated by the prevalent logics at work in the democratization of higher education. The call for mass higher education—beginning with the 1862 Morrill Act—positioned the purpose of higher education as directed to voters and workers. Women did not fall easily into either category. Early coeducation was followed by calls for segregation and organizational pressure to provide a biologically appropriate form of education in place of coeducation. Women's colleges had to assure critics that affluent white women could maintain their reproductive potential *and* graduate from college. No concerns, however, were voiced that either education or work would threaten black women's reproductive capabilities. In contrast to the logics of education for voters and workers, the segregation of women's education was tied to sexual politics.

To avoid allegations that college-educated white women were inferior in achievement to men, the ACA attempted to dispel any critiques by tightening their circle to only the most exclusive colleges. The first generation of white women college students united to develop strict measures of college quality. Frustrated by marginal treatment and disappointing postgraduate opportunities, the ACA launched a movement to evaluate colleges and universities comparatively and with regard to their depth of commitment to female students. This movement, together with pressures to stratify the field of higher education by merit, prioritized a new organizational form—women's colleges.

Given the rapid praise the press lavished on coeducational universities, the ACA viewed their project as preventing the inability, willful or not, of administrators to claim coeducation despite vast limitations. The ACA made it their mission to tighten the standards for what constituted a college education and not allow finishing schools to repackage themselves as colleges without a thorough change in curriculum, faculty, and facilities. Their concern was that the rapid demand for women's education would quickly flood the landscape with inferior colleges. As the next chapter will show, there are important parallels between the control over curriculum and status among predominately black colleges and women's colleges. A similar struggle was evinced by Horace Bumstead, president of Atlanta University, and by the faculty and students at Howard who protested when new administrators attempted to weaken the intellectual quality of the university. For the promise of increasing access to college education to remain meaningful, women in the ACA and activists at Howard alike mobilized to ensure that academic standards were maintained. The story of the ACA is important for shedding light on the importance of the era in the rise of higher education as a competitive field.

The ACA's initial membership circle included graduates from Oberlin, Vassar, Wellesley, Smith, Boston University, Cornell, Michigan, and Wisconsin. This initial group was not subject to any application or selection process. The early members shared a common dismay in post-collegiate life and a privileged social network in the Boston area. College had been intellectually exciting, filled with an expectation that they were educating themselves for a purpose. After graduation, many described isolation and frustration as they found themselves highly educated but denied a professional outlet for their ambition and capabilities.

Their collective experiences had convinced them "that if women were not to be fed at a second table, so to speak, a body of women of standing and achievement (had to) organize."[64] Their work was to ensure commensurability between higher educational opportunities for men and women. From the wide spectrum of educational opportunities available to women, the ACA attempted to simplify a messy and complicated field into a discernible normative system. The ACA had particular goals; simple access to some form of education was insufficient. The ACA persisted in refining standards to keep women's higher education in line with men's higher education. As Espeland and Sauder argue, "Where self-fulfilling prophecies operate primarily by changing behavior in relation to altered expectations, commensuration works mainly by transforming cognition; it changes the locus and form of attention, both creating and obscuring relations among entities."[65] The ACA became deeply involved in not only developing a metric for ensuring equivalency for women's educational opportunities with those of men, but in developing a structure through which to evaluate the rapidly expanding field of U.S. higher education. It was not until Andrew Carnegie launched the Foundation for the Advancement of Teaching and took over much of the ACA's evaluative work that the ACA restricted its concern to solely adjudicating colleges based upon their commitment to women's participation in higher education. Commensuration transforms qualities into quantities along a shared metric, and it is this process that permits the measurement of seemingly intangible experiences such as "learning" and "equality." It is a means of policing merit once the logics for its adjudication have been established and lending a legitimizing objective veil to subjective distinctions.

The growth of the ACA propelled the growth of privately coordinated watchdog organizations in higher education. Prior to this there was very little oversight. The Bureau of Education, a federal organization that grew out of the federal government's involvement in higher education during Reconstruction, produced a few reports but suffered severe under-funding. Further, the Bureau of Education merely recorded the existence of colleges and universities. It did not evaluate quality. The National Association of Land Grant Colleges was founded in 1887. By 1900, the presidents of the University of Chicago, Harvard, Columbia, Johns Hopkins, and the University of California convened to charter the Association of American Universities. Comparing U.S. PhD-granting institutions to their state-regulated European competitors, the presidents sought to demand greater uniformity among colleges calling themselves universities.[66] At the time, there were no standards to differentiate the naming of colleges or universities. For example, Oberlin debated whether it should be called a university in March of 1896. The debate, as recorded in the Board of Trustees minutes, did not reflect on accompanying changes that might be necessary to finances, curriculum, programs of study, faculty hiring, or any other changes that might be expected for a college to transform into a university. Oberlin faculty sensibly and overwhelmingly voted against the change since it would only be a change in name, and not in practice.[67]

The ACA accepted certain compromises in order to make demands for elevating the standards of college available to women. They countered arguments based in biological determinism while recognizing the barriers to women's professional liberty. An ACA regional chapter—the Western Department of the American Association of College Alumnae—began collecting data on the health of alumnae children to counter arguments of higher infant mortality. While acquiescing that college graduates had fewer children, the chapter denied fears that college education had "diminish[ed] women's fitness for conjugal relation." It countered that as the "large patriarchal families" decreased in size, they increased in fitness and vitality."[68] Despite some protests, the ACA argued that alumnae would be wise to build their careers in education, health, and social services, where they would be less likely to compete against men. The ACA cautioned that higher education only threatened "domestic and social life when it promises the women who aspire to it what is not in its power to confer."[69] In short, the ACA counseled that colleges should prepare women for fields that might prove receptive to women applicants and avoid competition in the labor market.

As described in chapter 4, private foundations provided enormous financial support to select colleges. The allocation of these funds was directed toward particular interests. Rockefeller's GEB also culled a select number of institutions to support based on Rockefeller's goal of investing in urban education—to give cities the power that comes from a powerful university. But urban life had largely been deemed unacceptable for young women of the upper class. The colleges designed to accommodate beliefs about women's particular health and social needs were most often located in rural areas. Though Rockefeller gave small donations to women's colleges, his most generous donations went to support higher education in the cities and to universities that barred admission to women.[70] Indeed, between 1902 and 1915, the Rockefeller Foundation for Higher Education only funded Spelman College (then Institute), which at that time provided vocational rather than intellectual training, and to teacher training programs and industrial education programs for poor women.[71] Though among elite colleges women matched men in academics, the colleges were largely unable to attract financial support from the country's largest and most influential funding agency. While white women were still discursively depicted as in competition with white men for academic achievement, they were removed from the pathways to elite professional status offered by elite colleges and universities.

College Networks and Social Closure

The ACA first created standards for member colleges to purge finishing schools that threatened the status of women's higher education. Prestige is relational and as such women felt that association—even perceived similarity—could tarnish the educational possibilities for all if some women's education remained inferior. "Immediately there arose the question of how to judge the standard of these institutions, how to evaluate the degrees they conferred, and, in the case of coeducational institutions, how to assure one's self that every opportunity, intellectual and personal, should be open to women equally with men."[72] Initially, however, the ACA Executive Committee decided that any woman graduated from any college, university, or scientific school should be admitted. This early practice of the ACA resulted in considerable slippage between the individual alumna and the college from which she graduated. If initial applicants to membership presented in accordance with the unspoken requirements of the ACA Executive Committee, other applicants from the same college would, in the future, be eligible. The graduate wholly represented the college. Equating social standing with college quality, of course, opened the door wide for social prejudices. As the qualifications for membership increased, the new requirements ensured *de facto* segregation without ever having to write a policy of racial discrimination.

After its first year, the ACA recognized it needed a policy and the first Committee on Admission of Colleges took up the work.[73] By 1886, the ACA determined it could not exert control over all colleges educating women, but its list would certify members as embodying "exceptional intellect or attainment." By 1889, the Executive Committee agreed on a set of minimum standards for member colleges. These standards included that faculty should only teach at the college level and not also instruct at the preparatory level, admission standards be comparable to other member colleges, and that the college or university had awarded at least twenty-five women graduates degrees in arts, philosophy, science, or literature. The first requirement posed a challenge for many colleges since preparatory and college divisions at many colleges often overlapped. The second requirement addressed ladies courses, a degree which by its very name suggested second-rank status. The committee found the final requirement necessary to draw attention to the many colleges and universities that were, in theory, coeducational though tiny numbers of women were graduated.

By 1895, the ACA launched another evaluative committee for the "unification of collegiate standards." This required college presidents and other educational authorities to provide a self-evaluation and state their view of the standards colleges and universities should maintain in common. The report that followed proposed a new metric for evaluating the quality of colleges with two unequivocal rules for exclusion. The new criteria for evaluation prioritized academic resources over all other criteria. Many anti-caste colleges had previously asserted their value based on the unique mixture of students from different backgrounds, making a case that college was itself an experience. As DuBois described, anti-caste colleges had been "social settlements" where the great product of education was one of interaction.[74] As social settlements, their charge was to bring together people from different backgrounds who would not have the chance to interact in other settings. High school education for blacks was extraordinarily limited. Even by 1915, states rarely had more than two high schools open for black students.[75] As such, many colleges traditionally educating blacks had high school preparatory divisions on site. The ACA criteria regarding preparatory divisions, as such, evinced *de facto* discrimination.

The ACA's new determinants focused on the educational qualifications of the faculty and the financial resources of the college—endowments, buildings and equipment, and available income. The ACA wanted to ensure that women students would not be shunted off to teaching assistants or restricted to courses taught by the lowest-ranking faculty. The ACA bemoaned that there "were too many examples of too many courses of instruction offered in proportion to the teaching force, too large a proportion of the instruction . . . given by young teachers on temporary contracts and far too little by the well-paid of large acquirements and experience."[76] As colleges aligned their practices with the changing demands, the ACA continued to revise and elevate its membership criteria. This time the endowment, salaries by professorial rank, and total property value should be the average of the current member colleges; colleges offering preparatory programs or which granted honorary doctoral degrees were excluded from consideration. For colleges to meet the standards set by the ACA, they needed to comply with the general practices and logics of high-status colleges and universities. Having to financially afford ACA requirements largely excluded colleges enrolling many self-supporting poor students, thereby excluding many traditionally black colleges.

More controversial criteria—women's inclusion in organizational decision-making and faculty positions—seemed unlikely to be adopted by the majority of colleges. For instance, by its twenty-fifth anniversary, the ACA favored women on faculty and the Board of Trustees. It could not, however, issue this as one of its standards since none of the most elite colleges had women on their board and few had female instructors or professors. Thus, the most transformative criteria were made as recommendations, rather than criteria that would exclude colleges or universities from ACA membership. Only resource-rich colleges could meet the strict demands and high bar set by the ACA.

In 1905, Andrew Carnegie launched his Foundation for the Advancement of Teaching. By 1910, the ACA determined that "the standardization of courses in academic and financial matters (will) now be left to other agencies, and that the maintenance of suitable conditions for women in those institutions which admit them will henceforth receive special emphasis." With that, the ACA accepted those colleges and universities included on Carnegie's list. In addition, the ACA added its own membership requirements that the colleges have a "reasonable recognition of women in the faculty and student body, with material provision for their intellectual and social needs," comparable salaries for male and female faculty, and added recognition for those colleges with women on the Board of Trustees.[77]

The ACA's intent was to extract the highest standards for women's collegiate education and to diminish those who offered anything less than an education comparable to the best colleges available to men. Fearing that inferior schools would diminish the status of women's education writ large, the ACA's goal was to strictly limit the types of programs that qualified as a college education. The ACA's 1891 report articulated its goal of "holding the standard of collegiate education for women so high that the influence of the Association may be felt not only by all college women, whether within the Association or not, by all collegiate interests in the country." This was nowhere considered as acutely necessary as in the South where, in 1903, the ACA counted "more than 140 Southern institutions bearing the name 'college for women,' with not more than two of them doing four years of college work." The ACA charged that many of these were merely preparatory or finishing schools masking as colleges.[78] The ACA laid down procedures regulating college practices regarding hiring, tenure, admissions, and denying membership to colleges that also offered preparatory programs. This resulted in a wide range of colleges aligning practices and leaving little space for local-level variation. The ACA proved an important disciplinary force that shaped the rise of comparative evaluations for higher education.

As higher education increasingly diversified its forms to adapt to competitive pressures within the expanding field of higher education, women's education, too, diversified—within coeducational colleges and universities and through the categorizing and commensuration of sex-segregated educational opportunities. This chapter illustrates the power of organizational activation in shaping the field of higher education; this shaped not only access but also gave rise to two new organizational forms in higher education. First, colleges designed for the particular health needs of elite women constituted a new differentiated form of higher education. With the population of new colleges rapidly expanding, a new private evaluation body, the ACA emerged to commensurate quality among colleges. As higher education increasingly became a competitive field, reformers demanded new controls for inclusion as a college or university. Marginal access—and its disappointments—spurred a new form of higher education designed for women. Further, the quest to ensure that access provided fair treatment inspired evaluative college rankings.

This raises an important question about what might have been had the anti-caste movement focused its energies differently. If the AMA had targeted its efforts to forcing inclusive practices in public universities, and not claimed extra-democratic authority, what might have happened? Of course, it is nearly impossible to perfectly predict the path not taken. We might, however, expect that had private funds not intervened, taxpayers might have protested—as they did in Michigan—paying for duplicate systems of education. Or perhaps, if there had been greater control on the number of colleges that opened—especially if these had been under the authority of the state—we might have seen greater ability to police the quality of higher education.

CHAPTER SIX

A Scarcity of Great Men
Educating Leaders at Howard and Oberlin

> We have here an argument for the development of the highest
> susceptibilities of the negro race. Inspiration comes from the
> summit, not from the valley. The world need not have dread
> of a people who aspire.
>
> —HOWARD UNIVERSITY PROFESSOR KELLY MILLER
>   IN THE *WASHINGTON POST*, May 10, 1903

> We want to have the world feel that they have an interest
> in Oberlin.
>
> —OBERLIN COLLEGE TRUSTEE, March 1896

As the relevance of the shared network among anti-caste AMA colleges
declined, individual colleges faced new challenges. Each had received
acknowledgement of their special position in the burgeoning field of
higher education through newspaper coverage and through ties to politicians and powerful cultural actors. But their standing thus far had
largely been built on their success in racial coeducation. As the field of
higher education demanded that colleges diversify beyond the old abolitionist base, Oberlin and Howard took similar paths of claiming elite
status and crafting an organizational persona built around male leadership. To increase their competitive advantage, administrators at Oberlin
and Howard reconsidered the purpose of college, aligned changes to
curriculum, and fashioned enrollment to increase their legitimacy. This
chapter investigates the retrenchment process at Oberlin and Howard:
how college students, faculty, and administrators navigated the uncertain
times in a changing—and troubling—political and legal climate. Anti-
caste colleges, seeking to increase their status and prestige, crafted an
ideal type of student to secure their organizational position in the
emergent field of competitive higher education.

Howard and Oberlin, too, differentiated themselves from other
colleges by claiming a unique advantage in their ability to educate
male leaders. Recall that when Howard University was founded in
1866, its trustees declared their intent to "make the Howard University a

University indeed, as broad and catholic as it is possible for an institution to be—no less so than Harvard, Dartmouth, Yale, Oberlin, or any other institution of worth in this country," which would "be open to all persons without distinction of race, sex or former condition."[1] But as professional organizations—the American Medical Association, for example—discriminated against black and white Howard graduates, the university increasingly struggled to enroll white students. In Howard's case, this meant building a redoubt for black intellectuals. Oberlin pushed for elite status, and abandoned its anti-caste heritage to do so.

Oberlin College: Educating Great Men

Can it be that the present generation of students and instructors have cut themselves loose from the past history and traditions on which its present prosperity rests? Oberlin during its early history stood out from other colleges for two fundamental principles, the higher education of women and the brotherhood of man, including the black man. These two ideas gave her friends and prestige in every state in the nation and in many foreign countries. It is because of these that Oberlin has a national reputation instead of being a small, local Ohio college. Its liberal progressive policy has attracted students, friends, and money and so has made its present success possible.

—Anonymous Oberlin graduate, in DuBois,
   The College-Bred Negro American, 1910

In 1834, Oberlin College promised abolitionist Lewis Tappan to provide coeducational education in exchange for Tappan's much-needed financial assistance. Oberlin was not the first college to admit black students. It was the first to write an explicit policy of interracial coeducation. The college gained its national reputation because of this rare inclusivity. Oberlin transformed from a peculiar college known for its radicalism and piety to an institution that promoted its distinctive brand of moral leadership in the higher education landscape. By the mid-1880s, Oberlin students grew increasingly diverse with regards to their political, social, and religious beliefs. During these years, for the first time, students began to use a market logic when deciding where to attend college. A broader field of options existed and prospective students compared schools by social networks, cost, and prestige value. An 1891 news article, authored by an Oberlin student, compared the cost of education among elite colleges and Oberlin, finding that "the education given at Oberlin may not be of the highest quality but the cost is low enough."[2] The college increasingly attracted students who had compared Oberlin to a range of other colleges while making their decisions. Trustees, however, hoped to transform the College and enter into competition with exclusive liberal arts colleges of the Northeast.

Changes in Student Enrollment and Donors

Despite strong ties to Berea, Oberlin increasingly positioned itself as unique rather than as part of a broader movement for coeducation. In fact, its earliest students "prided themselves on being a peculiar people."[3] Oberlin promoted its position as singular: "Oberlin is the only college in the United States where there is absolutely no caste. No man is above his brother.... Nor does it matter whether the 'brother' is white or black, for although Oberlin was not founded as a college for blacks, yet there was never any 'color line.'"[4] While Berea, Howard, and Oberlin all enacted policies to foster interracial cooperation, both Berea and Howard adopted color conscious strategies when it became clear that addressing issues of race was necessary to realize their broader mission. Berea and Howard adapted their admissions policies and actively promoted interracial cooperation on faculty and administration. Oberlin, by contrast, insisted that leaving an open door to qualified candidates of any racial background would suffice.

Oberlin had long been sustained through generous donations. Its initial success was dependent on its commitment to coeducation, and this political mission drew donations from across the United States and from British abolitionists. It is not an exaggeration that without donations from abolitionists, the college would likely have shuttered. In its earlier years, Oberlin students were most often the children of abolitionists who decided to attend the college because it shared their religiously grounded politics. Oberlin's low tuition and numerous scholarship opportunities allowed even poor students to work their way through college. Students often took their high school and collegiate education at Oberlin. As described in chapter 4, however, by the late 1870s, a host of factors undermined the continued relevance of racial coeducation in the eyes of many potential donors. While a few sizable donations from elderly abolitionists still trickled in, it was clear that Oberlin faced a daunting challenge.

By the late 1880s, trustees were forced to confront the difficulties in raising funds from alumni. Many alumni wrote pleading letters to encourage the college to cultivate a plan for financial independence. So many Oberlin alumni were themselves engaged in charitable work that they had little reserve to give back to the college. Most Oberlin graduates fell into two occupations: teachers and preachers. These professions were considered the necessary foundation for developing communities, whether in international missions or domestically in the South or the West. Alas, many were teachers; they were paid low wages and dedicated themselves to raising funds for their own schools. Other graduates in the missionary field were equally unlikely to have the financial reserve to donate to their alma mater. Oberlin had proven successful in stimulating generations of dedicated and often quite selfless workers, but that success posed a serious challenge to the college's fundraising abilities. At its March 1893 meeting, the Board of Trustees recognized that the limited professional pursuit of their graduates, combined with the declining number of families sharing its particular theological and political beliefs, presented dire economic challenges for the future of the college.

As more and more colleges were founded, Oberlin administrators decided that the college needed to narrow its focus. Oberlin used the growing number of colleges to legitimate its retreat from coeducation. Former Ohio governor Jacob Cox was invited to deliver an address for the fiftieth anniversary of the college. In his address, he articulated the college's historic commitment to coeducation as temporary, claiming its mission "was to educate the intelligence and the conscience of the people till legislation and governmental action in behalf of freedom should be the necessary response of legislator and ruler to an imperative popular demand."[5] As many colleges were now open to blacks and women, Oberlin no longer had any special imperative to open its doors to all. This varied greatly from Oberlin's message in its earlier years, in which inclusion of blacks and women was pronounced essential to its purpose.

Adapting to the Emerging Field of Higher Education

By the early 1890s, Oberlin began to align its organizational practices to match its "competition." The board described the field through the range of choices available: students could attend a free college (like Ohio State University or a private school with an inclusive scholarship program), modestly priced colleges like Denison ($30 annual tuition), or pay dearly for an elite education at the University of Chicago ($125). No longer content to replace faculty by hiring Oberlin graduates or others within the anti-caste network, the board discussed the need to recruit nationally competitive faculty. In evaluating faculty salaries, Oberlin solicited comparative salary information from Princeton, Chicago, Harvard, and Yale.[6] Changes in the field pressured Oberlin to align with one of two financial models: family-supported tuition or a combination of donations and student self-support through work-study programs. In debating a tuition hike, the Board of Trustees recognized that doing so would fundamentally change the character of the college.

The board majority selected expensive midwestern universities—Northwestern University and University of Chicago—as their ideal competition. President Fairchild recognized this would finalize their shift to the market-driven field of education: "We are going to be subjected to a good deal of competition. The average expense (of college) is very low. . . . If our tuition is put up we will have to compete with a much more active competition than in the past."[7] Oberlin's board raised tuition the following year, deliberately deciding not to keep pace with free or low-tuition colleges but to pursue elite status. By 1898, the board established its class of competition as Cornell, Syracuse, University of Chicago, Amherst, Williams, and Western Reserve. The board also strategized price-setting, stating that "people take you for what you hold yourself to be worth."[8] To maintain enrollment and gain legitimacy more broadly, Oberlin's board repeatedly voted to mirror enrollment patterns of the Northern elite schools. In 1894, Oberlin aligned the degrees, certificates, and courses of study to match competitors' offerings and even voted to retroactively grant bachelor's degrees to alumni who had studied in a variety of outmoded programs. The board hoped this would encourage the allegiance—and generosity—of its alumni. The board approved changing the degrees awarded to alumni who graduated more than ten years prior. As colleges converged in awarding bachelor's degrees, Oberlin did away with its wide range of other degree programs.

The academic requirements for entering Oberlin were rigorous. Students were expected to have knowledge of classical languages and sat for examinations covering particular texts and mathematical skills. This requirement demanded that students either attended a high caliber high school or possessed the capability to study Latin and Greek independently. In 1886, the Oberlin College Annual Report argued that "it is not unreasonable to say that the advantages offered the general student here are equal to those of any school west of New England."[9] For students raised in Oberlin, attending the preparatory division provided this foundation. But colleges did not necessarily share similar requirements, and this reduced the number of colleges competing for the same students. Describing her path to Oberlin, a student in 1889 remarked that her high school prepared students to attend Yale, Harvard, Amherst, and Smith.[10] During the 1870s, the University of Michigan was the first to take action to standardize expectations for high school preparation as part of the admissions process. But it was not until the second decade of the twentieth century that standardized tests became more common and colleges became selective in their admissions.[11]

Entrance requirements aside, colleges differed in their approach to the certification of knowledge. It was not uncommon, however, for students to sit for separate exams for each college they desired to enter. In 1877, for instance, students applying to Vassar College took a three-day examination on campus. Applying to a school with such requirements essentially entailed a preparatory education that dovetailed with the expectations of a specific college. Other colleges, such as Williams and Vassar Colleges, both protested the desirability of moving to an admissions process where the connections between high school preparation and college selection were not as tightly bound. These colleges claimed that more general requirements would weaken the rigor of the college. Colleges like Williams and Vassar worried that general admissions tests and qualifications would also undermine the legitimacy of *social* networks in admissions.[12] There were, of course, other reasons why college control of admissions requirements and testing mattered. At Oberlin, the entrance requirements emphasized classical languages and philosophy. This partly stemmed from Oberlin's tradition of preparing male students for the ministry. Because the majority of its students had arrived directly from its preparatory division, it was a relatively streamlined—if demanding—process.

To increase the potential applicant pool, the board began to alter entrance requirements around the turn of the century. Oberlin boasted that "for years it has been more difficult to enter Oberlin than to enter Harvard or Yale, not because the standard was higher, but because the demands were not in harmony with the work of the best preparatory schools."[13] Still, during the 1880s and 1890s, high schools and colleges prepared for this tremendous change. By 1899, the matter of a uniform college admissions exam came before the Association of Colleges and Secondary Schools of the Middle Atlantic States and Maryland. By 1901, the first College Board examinations were held; within the decade, elite colleges of New England had adopted a new standard for admissions.[14]

One consequence of its increasingly national applicant pool was that students no longer necessarily shared Oberlin's social beliefs about race and social equality. Social ties were important for maintaining Oberlin's unique commitment. On campus, a small group of white Oberlin students even protested sharing dining tables and dormitories with black students. Though alumni and faculty alike decried that bigotry was not in line with the "Oberlin principle," the campus was clearly susceptible to social splintering. In the student newspaper, a black student argued that the separation was not by choice among black students: "We expect to endure some slights here, to meet some prejudice, but when it comes to a separate table at the Ladies Boarding Hall in liberal Christian Oberlin, it is more than we ever conceived of."[15] The white student protestors reasoned that "at other colleges" in the North they would not have to share social spaces. The dean of women mobilized support for integrated dining and vigorously advocated for maintaining integrated dormitories.[16] In describing the college in an article for the *Chicago Tribune*, one Eastern student denied the presence of "large numbers" of black students.[17] The student reported a black student population of around "one-thirteenth" the campus population, similar to elite schools. In fact, the Oberlin yearbook throughout the 1890s pictures fewer than ten black students enrolled in the senior class, of which there were strikingly more women than men. These students pose with classmates in various group photographs of activities or boarding houses.

Still, contrary to the student whose opinion reached the readers of the *Tribune*, few Eastern colleges had anywhere close to the proportion of black students as Oberlin. As described in chapter 5, women's colleges were even more conservative. For example, Vassar and Smith enrolled one black woman each during the 1890s. As wealthier white students arrived, the campus commitment had dropped and the college claimed that providing minimal access for exceptionally well-qualified black students was sufficient. But the very spirit of coeducation as *mutually* beneficial had eroded. Whereas previous generations were proud of Oberlin's coeducational program, some of the new students no longer valued racial coeducation or the political engagement that had so long been a traditional part of Oberlin's identity.

In addition to aligning with northeastern colleges on matters of academic admissions criteria and tuition, the board also began to mirror elite schools with regard to policies and practices around race. It quietly redistributed resources to more closely resemble the enrollment patterns of the elite New England schools where very few minorities were admitted. Most visibly, Oberlin allowed its substantial scholarship fund for black students to run fallow, reduced its commitment to gender coeducation, and increased its enrollment of white men with new scholarships. Between the mid-1880s and the dawn of the twentieth century, Oberlin changed in ways that rendered it barely recognizable to many devoted alumni.

The Avery Trust had provided a substantial endowment to provide scholarships for black students. While other black students were able to attend Oberlin through the generosity of individual donors, the Avery Trust guaranteed the tuition of fifty black students. The trust stated that if, at some future date, the college should cease to use the trust to award scholarships to blacks, the funds would revert to the Avery family. In the early 1890s, the board addressed challenges from black townspeople that the trust was improperly managed.[18] Although members of the town's black community petitioned the Board of Trustees to voice their concern that the college was not fairly administering a large scholarship fund for black students, the board continued to allow the scholarship fund to go untapped.[19]

When Oberlin's black enrollment dipped to rates equal to its prewar numbers, the Oberlin College Annual Report attributed the shift to the expansion of black educational opportunities nationwide. "Colored students find it possible to attend good colleges and universities to-day, where in former years it would not have been possible to matriculate, and schools nearer the students' homes, by attending which a considerable saving of money is effected."[20] This was hardly a realistic option for a comparable education. Frequently, these other schools provided industrial training rather than a collegiate curriculum. As described in chapter 4, Southern colleges were woefully ill-funded compared to those in the North. Further, Northern colleges very rarely admitted more than a handful of black students per decade. Despite this, the president of Atlanta University was compelled to remind the U.S. commissioner of education of the many barriers black students faced despite the lack of formal, written restrictions. "It is sometimes said that any bright negroes in the South who want a college education can come to Northern colleges and get it. This may be true as regards the very brightest who can feel the attraction of an educational opportunity a thousand miles away and obtainable there only at high cost."[21] Oberlin had long been that beacon and, despite protests from alumni and Oberlin townspeople, the Board of Trustees largely ignored challenges of their stewardship of the Avery Trust.

By the start of the new century, it was clear that Oberlin saw its earlier anti-caste model of coeducation as a historic contribution, made for extraordinary times. The old commitment no longer structured the atmosphere of campus life. Reflecting on its changed strategy, Oberlin relayed in the Annual Report of 1900 that the college had contributed "an incalculable service for the higher life of the country. . . . It opened its doors to students, irrespective of race, and was foremost in the Antislavery agitation which led up to the Civil War and the act of Emancipation. . . . Oberlin rejoices in the increasing educational opportunities open to colored students of this country, and takes just pride in looking back upon the contributions which Oberlin College has been able to make to this great work."[22]

During the 1890s the Board of Trustees deliberated over how best to secure a foothold for Oberlin as an elite college. The character of the board itself changed as many of the older members passed away, others found the new business mindset troubling. In debating whether to accept a new member of the board, an "old guard" trustee argued, "We shall make a mistake if we should bring to this position here a man, our own graduate or any other, simply because they have wealth or are likely to have wealth or influence if they have not other qualification. If Oberlin were to place its interests in the hands of men careless of its great history, I should lose my own special interest in it very largely." Despite the single protest, the wealthy new trustee was put up for the vote.[23] The college increasingly sought enrollment from white men by investing in athletics and merit scholarships. Women and blacks were still permitted to enroll but their place in the college was secondary. While the college denied that individual students were racist, they supported white students' exclusionary practices, in part to ensure that other white students would enroll. The board's decisions proved successful. Enrollment grew faster between 1885 and 1905 than in all previous decades. Between 1835 and 1895, the college (preparatory and college divisions) added approximately

FIGURE 6. Calisthenics in Warner gym, 1920. Courtesy of Oberlin College Archives.

ten students per decade. In 1835, the college enrolled 110 students and by 1895 boasted 439 students. As a result of the dramatic changes initiated by the Board of Trustees, by 1905, the college enrolled 714 students, and by 1908 this included students from every state and international students from Peru, Canada, Austria, and Micronesia.

Recall that Oberlin had offered donors the opportunity to support students through "subscription" scholarships; many students had supported their education by working—often as teachers—during academic holidays.[24] Self-sufficiency had long been a cherished value of the college. By the 1890s, however, Oberlin further retreated from its anti-caste commitment to poor students. Oberlin initiated a fundraising campaign to provide scholarships to "reward merit rather than premiums for poverty."[25] Oberlin made new financial scholarships available to "benefit needy and worthy young men," which were only awarded to white men. Oberlin hoped to attract male students and, to this end, Oberlin dedicated an impressively large (and rare) $50,000 gift from an alumnus to build a new men's gymnasium.

Oberlin's president, Dr. Barrows, articulated that the "old college" man of the nineteenth century—focused on scholarship and religious piety—needed to be remade for the times of "opulence and luxury . . . when great men were scarce (and) personality is more sacred than things and institutions."[26] Oberlin set forth crafting new "college men"— Protestants who played football, jockeyed in debate tournaments, and possessed an appropriate moral fortitude to "handle" wealth.[27] Oberlin

College's new campaign was meant to secure their status as on par with elite Eastern liberal arts colleges.[28]

By 1899, Oberlin launched a campaign to position itself as a center for training "great men" to take on national and international leadership roles. As Oberlin's president Barrows described, Oberlin would cultivate "men who not only know how to be gentlemen, but appear like gentlemen in a world of growing taste and refinement."[29] Depicting Oberlin as uniquely poised to shape leaders in the developing U.S. colonial realm, president Barrows encouraged alumni to view colonialism as a new stage in Oberlin's "service" to oppressed peoples. Barrows invited Reverend Dr. Gordon of Boston to speak with alumni, reminding them that those who "feared revolutionary imperialism" adopted this view from their comfortable positions; they believed the United States "a smug little place by itself, with plenty of bread, plenty of butter, [and] . . . have never shown a desire to send out anything for the elevation of mankind."[30] Barrows launched a campaign to articulate Oberlin's unique history as not limited to national concerns.

Barrows encouraged a view of colonialism as a new phase of racial uplift. He argued that Oberlin students could take on leadership roles in U.S. colonial endeavors in the same way they had through abolitionist and Reconstruction-era projects. Oberlin's history of religious piety gave evidence that it was uniquely prepared to develop moral leaders. The trustees and the president articulated that Oberlin's long history of training preachers and teachers for the Southern field and international mission work situated the college perfectly for raising the next generation of diplomatic envoys and colonial leaders. And indeed by 1918 another Oberlin president, Henry Churchill King, was appointed by Woodrow Wilson to colead a commission to investigate "French, British, Arab, and Zionist proposals for the division and governance in the Eastern Mediterranean area." King published a booklet on the topic, and the cover image of that document nicely illustrates Oberlin's early twentieth-century view of its educational mission and its interpretation of the agenda of American empire.[31] The cover illustration shows a parade of white men with banners held high, and the banner in the foreground reads: "The Fight for Character."[32] These new political positions, however, were only open for men. Though Oberlin did not explicitly evict female students, increasingly women were excluded from scholarships and from the center of the college mission. The new model Oberlin student was a white gentleman prepared for political leadership.

Oberlin had long focused its attention on national matters. Its students were abolitionists who trained to teach and preach in poor Southern communities or missions abroad, and the college had always seen campus life as deeply intertwined with adult and civic responsibility. But by 1890—with dramatic and frightening changes underway—Oberlin retreated. Outside Oberlin, the retrenchment of civil rights for blacks was deepening. In 1890, Mississippi became the first state to institute a literacy test to screen voters, which effectively disfranchised the majority of the state's black citizens. It would take other Southern states a few more years to follow suit. Yet the early 1890s also saw important social movement mobilization; there was increasing pressure on whites to recognize that equal rights on paper were anything but in blacks' daily lives. By 1892, Ida B. Wells launched her campaign against the terror threatening blacks when she published *Southern Horrors: Lynch Law and in All Its Phases.* A small group of black civic leaders decided the time was right to push against the recent 1890 Louisiana Separate Car Act. Full of hope, they launched their protest in June of 1892 by sending Homer Plessy—who by all accounts appeared white and was one-eighth black—to board a whites-only train car. Surely, the ridiculousness of draconian racial categorization would be revealed. In decades past, Oberlin administrators and faculty would have written newspaper columns, made public speeches, and put their national reputation and expertise to use in fighting injustice. This did not happen. Oberlin administrators and faculty were now cited in the newspapers or invited to lecture on their academic expertise, and students were allowed to prioritize campus hijinks over social responsibilities.

Elsewhere, on the New England college scene, athletics were gaining popularity. In 1890, Smith College built a new gymnasium and, in 1893, this was the site of the first women's basketball tournament. The physical education instructor made a few modifications to the game to reduce the physicality of the game. Women's basketball quickly gained popularity and teams were soon formed at Oberlin. At Oberlin, as at Smith, teams were organized by class since intercollegiate athletics had yet to gain wide popularity. A few miles away from Smith College, two black players—William Henry Lewis and William Tecumseh Sherman Jackson—joined the Amherst College football team.[33] They were two of the three black students enrolled on campus.[34] In short, though the political arena was electric, on campuses students were increasingly learning to see student life as separate from the political.

Whereas previous generations had all engaged in shared labor and pious religious devotion, leisure was for the first time introduced to campus life. When students were dependent on the college for scholarships and low tuition, the college had greater authority to act *in loco parentis* and determine how students should spend their time. While there were some literary societies, the town as a whole supported collegiate life and the distinctions between the preparatory division, the college, and the religious life of the community were opaque. As Oberlin increased its efforts to compete for students outside the old abolitionist network, the college grew wealthier and whiter and students interacted more often with same-age peers. Student life increasingly prioritized intercollegiate events and connections. College sports and debate societies connected Oberlin to students at other colleges. The campus increasingly looked to its relationships with other colleges to define its purpose. Previously, Oberlin's connections were largely limited to other anti-caste schools. Intercollegiate coordination had predominately focused on the political and religious work of the college as an organization, and involved only faculty, administrators, and alumni. These ties had not emphasized relationships among students. During the late 1880s, Oberlin students increasingly participated in intercollegiate activities—debate and sports—that offered greater contact with students on other campuses.

Absent external rankings or formal ties forged through sports, Eastern colleges had used their social ties to other colleges to convey their position in the field. In this way, colleges expanded the boundaries of their organizational reach into the broader field of higher education. Anti-caste colleges had previously defined their importance in terms of future services for graduates—particularly through teaching in freedmen's schools or missionary work. To obtain such success did not require connections with other colleges, but required connections with donors who would pay for salaries or help build new schools and churches. But as Oberlin increased the enrollment of students who were reliant on their families for tuition, rather than donors, student interests increasingly focused on intercollegiate social connections. Many of the college newspapers—Yale's *Courant*, for example—were devoted to publishing student poetry and fiction. The literary societies that had been popular on campuses in previous decades were finding new ways to reach students at other campuses. In 1877, Vassar's student paper, the *Miscellany*, began to regularly publish a new column devoted to listing the number of other colleges subscribing to the Vassar paper. Student newspapers sent clippings of their campus news to other colleges, giving students a sense of life on other campuses. Details included information on school colors, campus traditions, and elective societies. These newspaper articles also helped shape the field of elite higher education, informing students of the colleges they should pay attention to while overlooking or dismissing others. Absent the rise of rankings, students gained a sense of status by association. Student newspapers at predominately white schools, unsurprisingly, paid scarce attention to schools enrolling more than a few black students.

As Oberlin sports teams began to travel to compete against other colleges, they confronted even more overt racial hostility. Oberlin's sports teams had to decide whether to find hotel lodging that would accommodate all players or whether white students could stay in fine lodgings where black players were not permitted. For a few years the team elected to lodge together. In part, the increasing wealth of Oberlin students shaped these decisions. White athletes preferred the opulence of establishments like the Great Southern Hotel—with its domed ceiling and pink marble lobby—in Columbus, Ohio. Such hotels, however, barred black patrons. Black athletes could only stay at the YMCA or no-frills hotels. The black players protested by refusing to play unless the team confronted discrimination together. By 1910, the college president defended its decision that black students should make their own hotel arrangements if they continued to participate in collegiate athletics. The president declared that forcing white players to stay in the inferior lodgings available to black players would threaten the team's competitive ability. First-class lodging was necessary if "a fair competition with other colleges would be secured." Even more than this decision, interim president Root's language conveyed that coeducation had become a dream forgotten: "This arrangement, it should be understood, was not due to any opposition on the part of our boys to the colored men."[35] In other words, competition had replaced cooperation as the central logic that guided and unified the actions and ideals on campus.

Opposition from Many Sides

The retreat from coeducation was met with substantial resistance. The college was attacked in the press—particularly the *Cleveland Plain Dealer*—

for its increasingly hostile displays toward its black students. The *Plain Dealer* assessed the situation simply: "Oberlin College Turns on the Negro."[36] The college was accused of segregating bible studies, dormitories, and dining tables. Alumnae, in particular, frequently wrote to the college to protest that the coeducational spirit of Oberlin had been destroyed because administrators refused to discipline white students.

The burden of integration was increasingly placed on black students. Julia Wilson, who sponsored the tuition for several black students to attend Oberlin, wrote President Fairchild to protest that black students reported feeling ostracized. Her intent in sponsoring their education at Oberlin—rather than Fisk College—was to ensure that they were guaranteed the highest quality education and learned to "mingle as men of equal power and standing with the best elements of the white race." Wilson deferred that Oberlin's academic quality was superior to other options, but she cautioned that the informal curriculum might prove disastrous if the current climate went unchecked. In its earlier years, Oberlin had viewed its campus as a model where students would learn the habits of social equality. Wilson and others now feared that exposing black students to antagonistic whites would produce feelings of anger and bitterness. In other words, interracial contact—unless guided by proactive, thoughtful administrators and faculty—could not only fail to bring about greater understanding, experiences of discrimination might create interracial hostility. She cautioned the lasting deleterious effects that would follow if Oberlin failed to bring white students into the college's tradition of social equality: "I do not think you imagine, however, how keenly and how painfully they feel any treatment which sets them on one side as 'colored,' nor do you know how intensely such treatment reacts in prejudicing their minds against white men."[37] In her 1885 letter to the college, leading black educational reformer Mary Church Terrell made clear that the Oberlin from which she graduated had indeed retreated from its mission. Terrell wrote the college president to protest that segregated dormitories had ostracized her daughter. She reminded the college that "I was accorded the same treatment at Oberlin College at that time as any white girl.... Outward manifestations of prejudice against colored students would not have been tolerated for one minute by those in authority at that time."[38] By 1904, black Oberlin students founded separate literary societies with black townspeople as a means to "narrow the breach" and create a discussion forum to counter rising racism.[39] Still, campus life—dormitories, athletics, and other activities—grew increasingly segregated. Though Oberlin did not exile students or refuse all black applicants, it was clear that black students were no longer considered integral to the college's mission, nor even very welcome.

The changing field of higher education—and the rise of industrial colleges for blacks—permitted Oberlin to retreat from its commitment to interracial education. As Oberlin shifted away from viewing its primary network as religious, and as it drew ever more on the practices of socially selective colleges and universities, status replaced service as the college's goal. The competitive nature of higher education had dramatic consequences for Oberlin's model. Whereas Oberlin's anti-caste commitment originally included racial coeducation, access for women, and an emphasis on educating poor students, by the mid-1880s, Oberlin's trustees advised retreating from all three of these commitments. Most importantly, the increasing segregation was part of broader changes to bolster Oberlin's competitive advantage. Oberlin was developing a particular educational program for a particular type of student. Oberlin modeled itself on elite Ivy League schools but drew upon its "moral" heritage to cast Oberlin as ideal preparation for leaders in the burgeoning U.S. colonial empire.

Howard University: A Redoubt for Black Elites

Howard University's founding was motivated by political concerns, as discussed in chapter 3. Its founders—even its most conservative founders—believed that coeducation and support for a black elite mattered for state security. There was early goodwill for establishing Howard as a high caliber university. In this way, Howard—like many of the colleges founded after the Civil War and supported by the AMA—had a political intention imprinted in its foundation. Its mission dedicated the university to a particular political vision and its charter, authorized by the U.S. Congress, declared its colorblind mission to "serve youth." But like Berea, Howard was from the start deliberately "color conscious"— to borrow from legal scholars Anthony Appiah and Amy Gutman—in organizing the university.[40] Howard's earliest organizers ensured that blacks and whites were represented on faculty and among trustees, and closely monitored student behaviors. Its first president, General O. O. Howard (1865–1872) firmly believed that the best educational opportunities were those shared by blacks and whites. From its inception, Howard was challenged in its quest to be inclusive (both in race and gender) and gain recognition for its programs as comparable with the very best colleges in the country.

Howard claimed that it provided a general education and its doors were open to all, though the press consistently framed it as a university for black students. To maintain its anti-caste mission, Howard needed to enroll students across the color line. Echoing sentiments of others in the anti-caste movement, Howard president William Weston Patton (1877–1889) urged the public to not only consider Howard diverse in terms of "races" but stressed that blacks were "not to be regarded as an indistinguishable mass of colored humanity, somewhat as one might look upon a flock of black sheep. They have their individual distinctions of body and mind, as marked as any among the whites."[41] Within the AMA network, the university was described in a manner that was consistent with the founders' intent. As a leading anti-caste newspaper publisher and close friend to the university, Henry Field, described the university as a "natural outgrowth of emancipation. . . . The University has no mention of color or race in its charter, but it is open to all races and to both sexes: yet its intention is to ensure the best advantages of education to the colored people."[42] Indeed, Howard was most often described as an excellent opportunity for "colored citizens to (obtain) an education which may fit them for the full privileges and high responsibilities of their new position."[43] In other words, while many within the AMA hoped Howard would enroll more than a token number of white students, even supporters viewed it as a university primarily for black students.

The challenge for Howard during the nineteenth century was, in many ways, one of determining the extent of conciliations the university would make to retain white students. The university enrolled white students, as well as Native Americans and students sponsored by missions in East Asia. Supportive journalists opined that higher education for blacks was a matter of "great national importance. And we hail with satisfaction that this work is already well under way at Washington."[44] Journalists asserted higher education as important for educating blacks for new roles as *citizens* and voters, and for important positions in developing and modernizing Southern community life: teachers, preachers, and doctors. Some of the founders envisioned Howard graduates carrying these skills to predominately black communities in the South or as missionaries to Africa.

By the mid-1880s, the university had largely retracted its race-neutral efforts. Observers noted, "Howard University might as well claim to be the National University for the Freedmen of the United States,"[45] and anointed it the "Negroes' Harvard."[46] Major news outlets like the *Chicago Tribune*, the *Washington Post*, and the *New York Times* effectively categorized the university as occupying a unique position among U.S colleges and universities. Before rankings, colleges and students largely appraised their status position through college networks. Howard was often favorably compared to predominately white schools. Most often, Howard was compared to Cornell because both were founded in the same year, featured labor opportunities for students who needed to work to afford college, and offered a rigorous academic curriculum. According to the *Washington Post*, although Cornell attracted "the cream of the white race," and Howard students "were from the despised and downtrodden, ... Howard University [had] a member of Congress in its Alumni ... and the Minister to Liberia. I don't believe Cornell has done any better."[47] Through comparisons to other colleges, the ever-expanding and changing field of higher education was made more legible. Still, Howard was treated as a special case by the media. Howard was not once mentioned in the same news article with another predominately black college until 1896. Both Oberlin and Berea were compared to other AMA-affiliated predominately black schools. When Howard was finally aligned with other predominately black schools, it was not in reference to the academic dimensions of the university. Rather, a journalist praised the mobilizing efforts of black students at predominately white elite schools (Cornell, Howard, Oberlin, Wellesley, Williams, and the University of Pennsylvania) and predominately black schools (Atlanta, Fiske, and Howard) in forming a joint association for the study of racial injustice.[48] Indeed, despite Oberlin's strategic campaign to achieve elite status, Howard University was just as often compared by the media to the dominant elite universities of the Northeast.

Challenges over Representation in Administration

During his presidency, General Howard was largely commended for his policy of appointing blacks to controlling positions. After Howard's departure and as the university developed into a larger organization, the question of how to adjudicate coeducation and racial cooperation at the level of faculty and administration grew more contentious. Increasingly, Howard's black leaders favored a faculty and administration that more closely mirrored student demographics. One dean stated, "that it is far better that Howard University should be blotted out of existence than that colored youths should there be taught to look upon themselves as inferiors, which must always be the case when they are educated in schools where they alone are governed, and can never have any share in the governing power."[49] The *Washington Post* frequently endorsed expanding black autonomy and authority for the university. This sentiment was often opposed by religious organizations that had long constituted an important support network for Howard.

The issue of representation—and the particular knowledge and experience that black candidates would offer—was raised with the search for each new president. As the trustees debated over presidential candidates, two main issues arose. First, presidential searches illuminated key differences in the meaning of integration and the reliance of the university on external sources for funding and legitimacy. John Mercer Langston, Oberlin graduate and Howard law professor, served as the interim president when General Howard stepped down in the wake of charges of financial mismanagement. Black and white trustees supported Langston as a candidate for the presidency. A great rancor arose when Howard was replaced with the white Reverend Whipple of the AMA. Some of the protest was based on the fear that Whipple, a Congregationalist, would exert too strong a denominational influence. Whipple was selected for his social networks and the potential funds they might attract. Ultimately, white trustees largely voted against Langston, fearing that a black president would struggle to raise capital from white donors.[50]

Langston charged that the white trustees no longer believed in providing professional education to black students. He suggested that white trustees were decreasingly interested in the medical, law, and theological departments. Langston was not alone in suggesting that the trustees were actively trying to force out professors from these departments, and his charges were underscored by the fact that the trustees had failed to issue payroll to these departments. Instead, in 1874, the trustees made the professional departments "self-supporting," which reduced faculty to obtaining direct payments from their students, most of whom were working while attending college. The theology department was funded by the AMA because federal funds could not be applied to religious education. Unlike efforts at Oberlin to restructure its financial model by attracting students who could pay their own tuition, by and large Howard already attracted the wealthiest students it was likely to enroll. The consequence of starving out several of the law faculty was that no students were graduated between 1879 and 1881. Beginning in 1879, funds from Congress eased the financial situation.

In 1877, Howard trustees again elected a white president, W. W. Patton. The quarrel this time was not over the chosen candidate. Raised by radical abolitionists, Patton had been a lecturer at Oberlin College and penned "the John Brown Song" in 1861 as a tribute to a fallen martyr. In 1862, he led a committee to petition President Lincoln for black emancipation. Patton was committed to Howard's intellectual tradition and a strong advocate for social equality.[51] Though a fine candidate, many had felt the hour had arrived for Howard's administration to better reflect the student population. Nor would Howard have been the first college with a black president, though colleges with black presidents were not considered Howard's academic rivals. In many cases, this was due to a predominately industrial curriculum while others—like Wilberforce, for instance—offered some similar programs but not the full range of academic programs Howard offered.[52] Upon leaving Congress in 1871, Hiram Revels was appointed president of Alcorn University—the first black college to receive Morrill Act funding. Allen College and Paul Quinn, which were affiliated with the African Methodist Episcopal Church, also had black presidents. In the 1877 election, General O. O. Howard sent in his support for Francis Cardozo, one of the two black candidates in competition with Patton. Educated in Scotland and a former AMA agent, Cardozo was a committed integrationist.

Trustee Frederick Douglass declared, "that it was due to the colored race to select a colored man for President." Douglass was one of many blacks growing agitated with white paternalism. He addressed a black audience in 1875: "We have been injured more than we have been helped by men who have professed to be our friends. We must stop these men from begging for us. . . . We must stop begging ourselves. If we build churches, don't ask white people to pay for them. If we have banks, colleges and papers, do not ask other people to support them. Be independent. . . . I am here to-day to offer and sign a declaration of independence for the colored people of these United States."[53] Douglas noted that though Howard still educated whites—primarily in the medical department— the university's core constituency was black students. The board's continued resistance to black leadership signaled that integration on paper mattered more than the development of the university for black autonomy. The *Chicago Daily Tribune* reported, that "the color line was pretty sharply drawn on the informal ballot."[54] Despite these challenges, Howard historian Rayford Logan describes Patton's election as far less "acrimonious" than previous presidential decisions.[55]

Another white Congregationalist, Jeremiah Rankin—a former AMA Executive Board member—was appointed president after Patton's death; he held office from 1890 to 1903. During Rankin's administration, the university refused pressures to create agricultural and industrial training; instead, Rankin authorized a new bachelor of science degree program. Five black trustees were added to the board, including former congressman John R. Lynch and former senator Blanche Bruce. During Rankin's tenure, he reported educating a total of 5,676 students; student totals increased from 365 in 1889 to 700 by 1900.[56] And in an effort to increase its standing in the broad field of higher education, Rankin and the Executive Committee voted in 1896 to pay for membership to the Association of Colleges and Schools in the Mid-Atlantic States.[57] Rankin's administration pressured for congressional funding increases and pushed to increase Howard's academic reputation even as pressure mounted to restrict education for blacks to manual labor training.

Though there had been strong support for a black president since the mid-1870s, Howard's previous white presidents had strong ties to abolitionist and anti-caste circles. John Gordon, president of Howard University from 1903–1906, was different. Black students and faculty alike reported that he would not acknowledge their presence when passing on campus. The *New York Times* reported on an investigation into the animosity toward Gordon and found that "the main cause for the trouble was the refusal of Dr. Gordon to meet his fellow teachers socially."[58] Journalists supported Howard students in pressing for an administration that would recognize the gap between its philosophical commitments and the failure of colorblind policies to combat discrimination. In 1905, the *Washington Post* endorsed a black president for Howard on the justification that the university enrolled a majority of black students: "Why should not the race have an unrestricted opportunity to assert itself and illustrate whatever virtues and capacities it may possess?"[59]

Debates over Integration and the Purpose of Black Education

There were three principle arguments for integration during the nineteenth century. The first and most conservative position held that through integrated schools whites would exert a "civilizing influence." A second argument claimed that separate educational tracks could not lead to equal status. This was a key sentiment among blacks who were part of integrationist projects. A third argument charged that interracial coeducation would exert a mutually beneficial environment for blacks and whites. After General Howard's administration, this third coeducational argument was rarely referenced in adjudicating policy at the university.

A fourth position was not espoused in public discourse, but raised in contentious policy deliberations. White students were needed to maintain Howard's legitimacy as a leading university. At Howard, the tension around racial integration hinged on how best to ensure that integration included blacks in positions of authority and influence, that white students were not favored in classrooms or for awards, and that a Howard education would continue to educate students in racial cooperation. But Howard was in a peculiar position. The administration worried that if white students were not granted deferential treatment, white students would cease to enroll. White trustees felt it critical to maintain some semblance of integration to maintain the status of the university. Increasingly, black trustees and faculty argued that the cost for such legitimacy was too high.

Blacks composed one-third of the medical class, and the faculty were displeased that whites consistently voted for white valedictorians. As a result, in 1881, the medical department initiated a merit-based selection of its valedictorian by awarding the status to the student with the highest exam results. When some white students protested the selection, the university informed the press that despite this recent event, "the best feeling has always prevailed between them and the white students showed their good feeling to their colored fellow students by electing for two consecutive years a colored president of the class."[60] In previous years, only members of the graduating class were eligible to vote but all students were able to cast a ballot in this election. A white student interviewed by the *Washington Post* reported that the selection was unfairly made to "secure the good will of assistance of these influential men and get the necessary appropriations."[61] The student charged that to secure continued appropriations the faculty felt coerced by Congress to favor black students. This story was interpreted quite differently by the faculty, the *Washington Post* reporter, and supporters outside the university. Just as members of the ACA were motivated by the frustration that mixed-gender education too often meant that women were "served at a second table," black students at Howard protested that prizes and honors should go first to whites.

The importance many of Howard's white supporters placed on its integrated character often produced disproportionate advantages for white students. A prominent activist within the Niagara Movement, Ida Bailey, called the press out for overlooking that white students regularly exploited Howard by using it as an inexpensive stepping-stone before transferring to a more prestigious, white university "where they could graduate and gain a little better social standing." Bailey challenged the *Washington Post's* rosy depiction of Howard as a fully coeducational university.[62]

Outside Howard, there were growing pressures to limit black education. Uplift ideology took center stage in 1881 when Booker T. Washington organized Tuskegee Institute for industrial education. Uplift ideology argued that colleges should elevate the moral character of blacks through education rather than develop intellectuals. Education in this model was a form of social discipline grounded in specific beliefs about the path to equality. Uplift ideology assumed economic stability would engender civic equality. Whereas anti-caste advocates argued that white society needed recalibration to align with republican ideals of governance, uplift ideology focused on blacks' adaptation to white society. It held that blacks, while disadvantaged by the conditions of slavery, could be *made* equal to whites. This did not require change on the part of whites. Instead, blacks should prove their value by accomplishment and, rationally, whites would accord blacks equal opportunities. Uplift ideology attached industrial education to many freedmen's schools. Originally, manual labor programs on campus were instituted to protect students' physical health or for poor students to afford college, akin to current work-study programs. By the 1880s, industrial skills became the centerpiece of many school curriculums.[63]

By the late 1890s, uplift ideology advocates abandoned the original intent that through education blacks and whites could reach equal status.[64] When Washington delivered the *Atlanta Compromise* speech, he denounced the initial success of black politicians as wrong-headed: "In the first years of our new life we began at the top instead of at the bottom; that a seat in Congress or the state legislature was more sought than real estate or industrial skill." For Howard students and faculty, this must have been a painful blow. Howard took pride in educating elites and graduates assumed responsibility for using their education to improve the conditions for blacks despite enormous obstacles. Washington capitulated the goal of social equality when he said, "It is at the bottom of life we must begin, and not at the top, . . . The wisest among my race understand that the agitation of questions of social equality is the extremist folly." Though no longer a staunch advocate for social equality, the AMA responded to the rising opposition to black education: "And here let us say, that the white people of the South make no greater mistake than when they imagine that it is a dangerous thing to educate the colored people. On the contrary, we believe that the facts make it manifest that it is by these educated men that their race will be guided wisely and safely through this great crisis, and that if a war of races is to be avoided, these educated colored men will be a grand factor in averting it."[65]

In his 1904 inaugural address, new president John Gordon outlined his intention to defend Howard from pressures to convert to industrial education. Gordon declared that Howard's purpose was to educate a black leadership class. This was a shift from the anti-casteist mission of coeducation.[66] Within a year, Gordon moved to increase industrial education. Already on shaky ground, this decision placed him at odds with black faculty who strenuously objected to the erosion of liberal arts at Howard. Many worried that Gordon's promotion of industrial education was a starting point for a thorough change in the intellectual rigor offered by the university. The *New York Times* reported that faculty and students wholly rejected Booker T. Washington's strategy for racial uplift through industrial education. Instead, the Howard community and its network of supporters "insist that there shall be one institution in the South where a colored boy or girl may get a classical education."[67]

By the following year, 700 students walked out in protest during one of his speeches, and the African Methodist Episcopal church declared, "It cannot be emphasized too strongly that there is no objection to Dr. Gordon because he is a white man. We welcome all our white brethren. . . . But there is no room in our schools and colleges for the 'Lily White' educator of the Gordon type who insults the manhood of the race."[68] Lily White Republicans constituted a political bloc of Conservatives mobilizing within the Republican Party to undermine black gains in civil rights and oust blacks from the party. Protestors saw a similar trend at work in Gordon's efforts at Howard.

Activating Ethnographic Expertise as a Resource

Howard's leadership failed to convince the media to adopt its favored frame of multiracial and colorblind campus relations. After nearly two decades of attempting integration through colorblind discourse, Howard leaders adopted a new strategy by claiming ethnographic capital for their expertise in race relations. The anti-caste tenets were increasingly viewed as counter-productive because by focusing on the social construction of race, anti-casteists failed to secure a strategy to counter the rising discrimination and violence blacks experienced. The civil rights retrenchments of the latter 1880s—hallmarked by lynchings, labor exploitation, and widespread voter disfranchisement—were increasingly difficult to ignore. Still, many of the white trustees and supporters believed that good manners and hard work would quell the violence. With increasing evidence that Howard students would face racial discrimination, no matter how great their academic preparation, the university transitioned to race-conscious organizing to address racial injustice.

Howard leaders activated racial status as a resource and their expertise provided entrée to politicians and philanthropic foundations. In particular, by claiming knowledge of a largely hidden world of black elites, Howard's position as an elite college for blacks allowed it access to important politicians. Unlike Berea or Oberlin, Howard had an arsenal of black board members empowered by past political and social movement experience. Howard counted John Mercer Langston, Francis Cardozo, Frederick Douglass, and Reverend Henry Garnet among its Board of Trustees.[69] Howard's elite advanced to power in the political sphere. John Mercer Langston left the university to become commissioner of agriculture before winning election to Congress. His ties to Howard remained strong. Howard professor and Oberlin alumnus, Richard Greener, represented a delegation of black citizens who met with Senator Windom to discuss the proposal that blacks migrate from the hostile conditions of the South to the West.[70] At the "largest assemblage of colored people ever seen" in New York City, Howard's reverend Garnet read a series of resolutions approving black westward-migration as a response to "the unparalleled atrocities of their former masters . . . and the Federal protection withdrawn from them."[71] President McKinley visited Howard's campus and invited students to the White House.

When Oberlin graduate and Howard professor Langston won a seat in Congress, he announced his determination for full national inclusion: "Men used to give us rights. We will help to give the rights now. . . . This is our government to aid and our fellows to save . . . even, until the blood shall run in streams, if necessary, till by the comingling of white men's blood and black men's blood our country shall be the grandest and our Government the greatest and most lasting the world has ever seen."[72] Professors regularly wrote articles or were cited in the *Washington Post* and spoke on the lecture circuit. Howard's political influence was growing stronger, quite contrary to the old fears that Howard's reputation would descend without a noticeable enrollment of white students.

If Howard had failed to attract white students who might otherwise attend Harvard, Dartmouth, or Yale, as the founders hoped, Howard alumni found connections with black students at those institutions.[73] Denied access to their own alumni associations, black graduates united in a common cause of promoting social justice and shared professional encouragement. Howard alumni joined with black alumni from Atlanta, Fisk, Cornell, Howard, Oberlin, Wellesley, Williams, and the University of Pennsylvania to create a joint association dedicated to promoting social justice and shared professional encouragement.[74] By 1900, Howard was viewed as an important point of entrée to the black intellectual and political life of the nation. Howard aligned with the role the press and observers had long considered its rightful category, that of a black university, and accessed the ability to address racial injustice by claiming particular expertise in race relations.

During the 1890s, Howard and its alumni increasingly spoke out on racial injustice—particularly aided by sociology professor Kelly Miller.[75] Trustees, faculty and students alike increasingly stepped forward to address racial inequalities. Miller actually changed disciplines in order to focus on race. As the first and last black PhD graduated from Johns Hopkins during the nineteenth century, Miller joined Howard's faculty as a mathematics professor. Finding himself increasingly compelled to study racial injustice, he became Howard's first sociology professor. Unlike Berea or Oberlin, Howard had an arsenal of black board members with deep political and social movement experience.[76] Howard professors and administrators were regularly quoted as race relations experts. Howard professor Kelly Miller spoke out against the limited education options for blacks promoted by followers of Booker T. Washington. Kelly helped radicalize the university to defend its pledge to educate students as intellectuals, and not manual laborers, against growing pressure to adopt uplift ideology. The conversion to race-consciousness did not signal an acceptance of segregation but a new resource to accomplish the goal of black inclusion. Howard affiliates were politically active and promoted egalitarian race relations, if not anti-caste ideals. Howard cultivated black elites and fought discrimination, whether in the press, by external organizations, or on campus.

But many argued for a segregated path to future integration and to consider legal rights as a means to eventual social integration. When Senator Hoar spoke to a graduating class of Howard lawyers, he counseled graduates to remember that they had achieved constitutional rights "whereas the forces arrayed against them were only temporary."[77] Despite mounting evidence, many white allies failed to heed the warning signs of rights retrenchment. Their faith in legal rights impaired their ability to see that social discrimination could erode legal rights. Howard students were strictly limited in their abilities to protest. The administration's Executive Committee voted in 1884 that no classroom space could be used for activities that critiqued the university.[78] The university clamped down on student speech and protest largely in fear of losing congressional funding and private donor support. The challenge of pleasing particular constituencies with particular accounts of Howard's aims was delicate, and the administration worried that protest could alienate key backers.

Howard differentiated itself by claiming its campus as a last redoubt for a black elite. In doing so, it also regularly affirmed the moral character and tradition of the university. As other traditionally black colleges increasingly added industrial programs and as black students faced increasingly hostile conditions on predominately white campuses, Howard fought back. Kelly Miller insisted that Howard University mattered politically, even if it no longer enrolled many white students: "In a republic like ours it is essential to elevate to high station men of moral enthusiasm and righteous disposition."[79] Miller maintained that Howard provided a necessary niche for both the black community and the nation more broadly.

Increasingly, Howard University engaged in politics and gained access to leading politicians. While professors at Oberlin College were quoted in the media for their academic expertise, Howard professors were cited as experts for their ethnographic capital and commented frequently on race relations. In public lectures on the failure of Reconstruction, John Mercer Langston affirmed the foregone option of Republican Tutelage for the South, citing "the wrong political education of the South" as the prime reason for Southern instability. Langston decried that the ideological shift required for true political union had not been diffused: "The central and controlling idea of the Government of this country, as expressed by Abraham Lincoln, has never possessed the people of the South."[80] Frederick Douglass, then marshal of Washington, D.C., introduced Howard president Patton to U.S. president Hayes. Patton was pleased to find "another of Time's curious reversal of former ideas," acknowledging that his introduction to the highest political office was made possible through his social ties with a black man. At other times, President McKinley visited Howard's campus and President Roosevelt invited Howard sophomores to a reception at the White House.

Howard claimed expertise and legitimacy as a bridge organization connected to white elites and black society. Howard was able to gain funds on the basis that its faculty were also uniquely positioned to produce the scholarship on the history of race and its implication in the United States. While most foundations were funding segregated industrial education for blacks, Howard was awarded substantial resources as a site for academic inquiry into black history. Because of its history, location, and vocal faculty, the Rockefeller family saw Howard as the best site to support black intellectuals. In its allocation of funds, Rockefeller's GEB rarely supported black elites.[81] Berea-educated historian Carter G. Woodson established the Association for the Study of Negro Life and History with significant funding from the Rockefeller family.[82] The establishment of this center can be understood as another manifestation of Howard's political presence.

In addition to the scientific racism studies pursued in many universities—including Harvard's professor Shaler—professors at Columbia University were writing a white supremacist history revisionist history of the Civil War that would later come to be known as the Dunning School. As Khalil Muhammad details, Shaler and others crafted a narrative that linked blackness with criminality and immorality while casting white ethnic groups as capable of reform.[83] The Dunning School at Columbia recast Reconstruction with a particularly troublesome set of characters: "The shiftless, poor white scalawags; the greedy carpetbaggers; the ignorant, deluded, sometimes vicious Negroes; and the noble, courageous and chivalrous Southrons who fought and won the battle for White Supremacy."[84] Howard faculty founded the American Negro Academy, a consortium of black intellectuals united against vicious assaults by whites. Through scholarship, they promoted a "talented tenth" in scholarship and the arts. These historians and scholars endeavored to use academic knowledge to counter white supremacist accounts rising from elite white universities and broader political culture.[85]

Howard had a complicated set of historical narratives. For most of its early years, its administration insisted on retaining anti-caste discourse even as the university failed to achieve the diverse enrollment and coeducational practices intended by its founders. As the university increasingly moved away from the anti-caste model in its discursive strategy, it gained greater strength in advocating for black intellectuals. Kelly Miller championed a middle ground between the promotion of a "talented tenth" and the "compromise" of industrial education. Miller guarded Howard's reputation zealously. As the *Washington Post* described, Miller repelled Thomas Dixon's racist portrayals of blacks in his trilogy—*The Leopard's Spots* (1902), *The Clansman* (1905), and *The Traitor* (1907); this trilogy formed the basis for the movie *Birth of a Nation*. In *The Leopard's Spots*, Dixon charged that no amount of education could render blacks the equal of whites. Following a lengthy description of blacks' accomplishments, Miller challenged: "If you could show that the negro was incapable of mastering the intricacies of Aryan speech, that he could not comprehend the intellectual basis of European culture, or apply the apparatus of practical knowledge, that he could not be made amenable to the white man's code or appreciate his spiritual motive, your case would be proved. But in default of such demonstration, we must relegate your eloquent pronouncement to the realm of generalization and prophecy, an easy and agreeable exercise of the mind, in which the romancer ever delights to indulge."[86]

Miller spoke before the American Social Science Association and a range of political and civic organizations. Blacks' self-sacrifice and political devotion to republican governance were frequent themes. "In every national crisis," Kelly told a group of social scientists gathered in New York, "the negro has illustrated his patriotism anew."[87] Miller devoted himself to the sociological study of black criminalization as well. He exposed the manipulation of crime statistics to distort public perceptions of blacks. This refuted Dixon's claim, of course, that the expenditure of financial resources on black education was futile. To counter the "leopard's spots" hypothesis, Miller demonstrated that white and black college graduates were equally likely to commit crimes.[88]

Unlike the majority of AMA schools, and much of education available to blacks in the South, Howard University never bowed to the demands that blacks be granted only industrial education. While Berea bent to the new trend of uplift education, albeit for poor whites, Howard maintained an emphasis on professional and liberal arts education.

Despite Howard's race-neutral self-promotion, Howard supporters and commentators consistently depicted the university with the special mission of educating black leaders. By 1900, this had become reality. The deep political experience of black board members and faculty, combined with a majority black student population, produced stronger resistance to colorblind policy at Howard than at Oberlin.

Education for Leadership

As Oberlin and Howard made their case for national prominence and asserted their unique position in the field of higher education, both drew heavily on the role of ethnographic experts to assert their knowledge of particular groups. They also evinced what Gary Alan Fine calls reputational entrepreneurs.[89] Reputational entrepreneurship controls the memory of historical figures and events through motivation narrative facility and institutional placement. Such entrepreneurs "transform persons into morals" as a means of accelerating or retarding social change. In order to wield these types of expertise, college leaders had to create narratives that were at minimum plausible to external audiences. They needed to manufacture credible narratives that fit the expectations of both past supporters (including their own alumni) and the audiences they hoped to attract.

Oberlin effectively recast its earlier anti-caste heritage as a historical necessity; it had been a moral leader by including blacks during an era hallmarked by the immorality of slavery. Its founders had articulated that Howard would be as rigorous as any Northeastern university but democratic and welcoming to all. Its message resonated with the broader public best when it articulated the university's specialty in educating black leaders for black communities. For instance, Kelly Miller argued against those who charged that blacks did not require higher education. Declaring Howard graduates rendered a "patriotic service," Miller proclaimed "when knowledge has been acquired, it is always applied to the point where the need is greatest and the call is loudest."[90] Neither Oberlin nor Howard educated students solely for their own individual edification or professional training. Rather, their graduates were endorsed for their potential to right injustice and champion the downtrodden. Reputational entrepreneurs for both Howard and Oberlin produced an account of past events that credibly positioned them to take on a new set of organizational goals.

By the turn of the twentieth century, Howard and Oberlin emphasized their goal as one of producing leaders. Unlike Berea, Oberlin and Howard continued to enroll small numbers of women but—as discussed in greater length in chapter 5—college administrators were involved in directing women to "better opportunities" elsewhere. Howard and Oberlin increasingly described their mission as training leaders. Both shared a foundational goal of producing teachers and preachers. Oberlin initially espoused a particularly radical theological doctrine and hoped that its graduates would popularize the beliefs in the West. As abolition grew, Oberlin students often taught and pastored in the South. Founded more than thirty years after Oberlin, Howard initially saw its mission to send teachers and preachers to the South. Other supporters hoped that Howard graduates would also work as missionaries in various parts of Africa. In reality, smaller numbers of Howard graduates pursued their careers in the South. Alumni reports, however, reveal that most stayed in Washington, D.C., some sought less hostile professional conditions in the West, and a small number ventured abroad as missionaries.[91]

The U.S entree into colonial empire offered both Oberlin and Howard an important discursive connection between their changing missions and the changing political environment. Oberlin's president Barrows and its Board of Trustees articulated that Oberlin could fill a much-needed moral training ground to staff new colonial projects. This built upon Oberlin's long heritage of education and missionary work, both abroad and in the South, and it also opened doors to new professional tracks that were separate from religious and low-paid services. To encourage new funding and enrollment streams, Oberlin needed to overcome its prior reputation as a radical college, and simultaneously develop a future alumni base that could afford to donate back to the college.

The colonial project abroad also provided a needed opening for Howard to articulate its desire for increased autonomy. Referencing the impulse for moral leaders in the colonial empire, Howard professor Kelly Miller argued: "In order to acquaint our newly acquired step-children in the distant seas with the beneficence of American institutions, we "send forth the best we breed" to rule over them. The same wholesome example should be held up to the backward race within our own gates by placing men of the highest character and purpose in places of national authority."[92] Miller argued that the United States had fundamentally failed blacks during Reconstruction by allowing the "carpetbag adventurer" and the "unrepentant rebel" to be "political schoolmasters" for the South, thus there was "little opportunity for [blacks] to learn the importance of good citizenship." Miller urged that greater care be used in preparing leaders for the colonies, and that no better leaders would be found than those graduated from Howard University.

Kelly Miller urged greater investment in Howard as a site of leadership development for racial uplift. Writing for the *Washington Post*, he claimed "no other school in the entire country is so deeply and potently felt within the sphere of its influence. . . . We should judge an institution not by its brilliant prospectus, paper courses, and prophetic programmes but by the men whom it sends out into the world and the work they do and the worth they manifest."[93] Howard, Miller argued, did not produce graduates who worked to accumulate wealth; graduates were lawyers, doctors, and teachers with a deep sense of civic purpose. Oberlin and Howard graduates were focused on advancing a moral and political agenda. These occupations were not individual accomplishments but lawyers "rendered a patriotic service" in defending the rights of his client, while the doctors were "apostles of good health and sanitary living, thus increasing the vital capacity, and consequently, the economic efficiency of the country's greatest laboring class." And above all, Howard graduates were "advocates of peace and good will between the races." Professor Miller made a case for Howard as the preeminent American training center for educating black male leaders. As he wrote in 1905, "A truly great man always transcends the petty distinctions of party, of caste, or class, and gives himself to the undivided welfare of his country, and, if he be a genius, to the service of the whole human race. The negro as an American citizen glories in all the high ideals which Theodore Roosevelt holds up and sustains."[94]

Howard and Oberlin claimed their expertise not only on knowledge about groups, but about managing relationships between groups and stewarding lower-status groups to a higher status. As Gary Alan Fine has argued, control over reputation is not an end in itself, but a means to situate issues of the present in light of the "lessons" of history.[95] It is a strategic endeavor. The administration at Howard and Oberlin drew from their institutional histories and discursive repertoires to refashion their campuses in ways that aligned with the new and shifting expectations of higher education. Colleges specialized in terms of ethnicity. Whether focusing on mountain whites, black elites, or white leaders with intercultural competence to manage new projects in the colonial field, a masculinist discourse of "leadership" pervaded discussions about the purpose of education. Colleges and universities were living, changing organizations. The actors within the administration—and the pressures they created and responded to—actively pushed the boundaries of higher education. At times, presidents like James Fairchild at Oberlin or General Howard at Howard viewed the work of the college or university they governed as in service to the nation. Fairchild, in his 1866 inaugural address, described that the best motivation for students was to "live in sympathy with the movements of the world, and feel its claims," and in doing so, that student "is most likely to give himself earnestly to a preparation for his work."[96]

CHAPTER SEVEN

A New Constituency for Berea

> It was a great disappointment to find that the old friends of
> Berea had almost entirely forgotten the Institution and become
> interested in Hampton Institute and other schools in the
> South. . . . I there made up my mind that I must create a new
> constituency depending little upon the old one.
>
> —RECOLLECTION OF BEREA COLLEGE PRESIDENT
>   W. G. FROST, 1910 (Oberlin College Archives, Record
>   Group 21, 92–93)

> A man may be our brother though he be black or red or yellow.
> He is none the less our brother because he is of our own race
> and nationality. Newest of the forms of work of the American
> Missionary Association, that which it does for the mountaineers
> is not the least important.
>
> —W. E. BARTON TO THE AMA, *The American Missionary*,
>   April 1868, 180

During the 1890s the boundaries between the forms of higher education
available to black and white students were drawn with increasing clar-
ity. Colleges educating black students faced enormous financial pressure
to focus on industrial education and minimize—or better yet, eliminate—
the traditional liberal arts foundation of a college education. Berea's administration proposed crossing these divides to offer industrial education
to poor whites. The organizational differentiation strategy pursued by
President William Goodell Frost ended Berea's long-standing commitment to radical coeducation, but not without a fight by Berea students
and alumni.

Frost was not the first Berea College president to encourage attention
to poor whites, and indeed, overcoming class and race barriers was at the
heart of the anti-caste mission. A decade before President Frost, Berea's
president Fairchild suggested in 1883 that a subsection of poor Southern
whites could be an accessible new population of interest for the AMA.
In his address to the annual meeting of the AMA, Fairchild revived a

familiar call to include poor whites as part of the Southern reform effort. Poor whites were reviled for their unwillingness to participate in reform programs, viewed as a dangerous, violent, and ignorant element. Berea College argued for distinguishing between poor Southern whites and mountain whites. The college depicted eastern Kentucky—and the mountain whites found there—as a politically unique region in the South claiming that many in eastern Kentucky sided with the Union during the Civil War.

Although it never seceded, Kentucky was central to the Civil War. Presidents of both the United States and the Confederate States were Kentuckians. That most famous of abolitionist works, *Uncle Tom's Cabin*, which Abraham Lincoln famously suggested helped start the war, highlighted the cruelty of slavery in Kentucky. Lincoln retained the border states—Kentucky among them—by excluding "states not in rebellion" from the abolition of slavery outlined in the Emancipation Proclamation of 1862. As noted Reconstruction historian C. Vann Woodward argued, "Despite Kentucky's failure to secede and join the Confederacy, no state below the Ohio River presented a more solidly Confederate-Democrat front in the decade after Appomattox."[1] To position Kentucky as isolated from the war was incongruous to Americans in the nineteenth century.

As this chapter will show, Berea College launched a new cultural category—the Appalachian—and a new organizational form of mountain education. The first section of this chapter provides a historical context of the representations of poor whites after the Civil War. This is followed by an analysis of the group-making strategies used by Berea College.[2] This chapter highlights the role of organizations in packaging ideas and meanings about race as a meaningful social division. This is two-fold. By attending to the work of organizations, we are able to see organizational actors activate racial boundaries to further their interests. To put poor whites at the center of a major fundraising campaign, Berea's president had to convince skeptical donors of their moral worth. Berea's president Frost claimed ethnographic capital—that "unique gift of understanding the natives"—as a means to claim legitimacy and activate particular narratives about people in the Appalachian Mountains and the purpose of a college education. Frost envisioned that by defining a particular constituency, he could command a sphere of influence and determine populations of both students and donors.

While higher education dramatically expanded after the Civil War, this expansion led to comparisons between colleges. Because many colleges, AMA colleges in particular, depended on private donations for financial support, colleges increasingly turned to differentiation strategies to make themselves appealing to donors. Whereas Oberlin College and Howard University made administrative choices to closer align with the dominant model of elite higher education, Berea endeavored to create something new. Architects of higher education more broadly—and anti-casteists more particularly—conceived of the college campus as a site where individuals could be transformed. As discussed previously, if—as Max Weber imagined—higher education should become a site for the consecration of the elite, social mobility occurred because individuals were changed by their education. By contrast, Berea's president Frost, like the architects of industrial education for blacks, envisioned matching the form of higher education to the expectations for a particular group. Such plans claimed the knowledge to specify the "fundamental nature" of groups and allocate educational opportunities accordingly. Of course, this was not without its challenges. To understand the difficulty of Berea's endeavor, the next section offers historical context for poor whites from the end of the Civil War through the 1880s.

Historical Context: Poor Whites after the Civil War

The aftermath of the American Civil War called into question the social organization of the South. During the early years of Reconstruction, the new state of West Virginia, eastern Kentucky and Tennessee, and western North Carolina were hailed as a region of Union loyalists during the Civil War, and journalists and the AMA regularly presented the inhabitants of the region as morally superior to other Southern whites. Hailing from eastern Tennessee, President Andrew Johnson lauded Unionist poor whites as an essential cornerstone in rebuilding the South. As described in chapter 2, President Johnson's Reconstruction program claimed that Northern migrants, German immigrants, and Unionist poor whites of the Southern Appalachian region constituted the "new race of thorough Union men" who would revive the South.[3] Abolitionists had argued for more than a century that the institutional effects of slavery undermined the humanity of all those—white and black, master, poor white, and enslaved—who lived under its influence. Journalists even described poor whites as victims of slavery: "The effect of two centuries of slavery on the 'poor whites' of the South has been terrible. When the war began they numbered four million, just about as numerous as the slaves—showing that to make a chattel of a black man required that a white man should be ruined. Shut out from the rich lands and impressed with the plantation idea that all manual labor degrades free people."[4] In short, this argument held that the importation and enslavement of black laborers had shut out poor whites from anything other than subsistence farming. Recognizing this difficulty of the work ahead, the AUC was founded in 1864 to provide aid to Southern "refugees" who had been loyal to the Union.

President Johnson and many benevolent aid organizations, including the AUC and the AMA, distinguished between a binary of "poor Southern Whites" and Southern oligarchs. Commissioner of the federal agency charged with administrating Reconstruction, General Howard endorsed the AUC in 1865: "Everything that you, as a commission, can do to facilitate industrial pursuits, to encourage education, and meet the wants of the suffering among the poor white people, who have been degraded by slavery, is collateral with my specialty, and meets my hearty sympathy and support alone." The AUC, like the AMA, was an anti-caste organization that recognized "no distinctions of caste or color, proffering its assistance to all men upon the score of a common humanity alone."[5] But poor whites across the South largely refused AMA or AUC programs between 1865 and 1867. There were numerous reasons why Northern donors and the national AMA organization rejected Southern whites from their programs, given the broader mission of the organization, as will be discussed in greater depth in this chapter. Frustrated by white resistance to reform efforts, the AMA and AUC jettisoned poor whites from their missions after 1870. In the 1870s, when the Berea-based campaign for mountaineers was first launched, the AMA had a clearly articulated mission that focused on the "most wronged and oppressed" and an important criterion for this was that the oppressors were white. The AMA articulated that blacks depended upon voluntary associations for education and other social provisions because the planter class remained a dominating force in Southern states.

Southern poor whites were often the object of much scorn, and considered stubbornly troublesome. As the *New York Times* opined in 1866, "For all his faults and defects, the Irishman will work. He will go thousands of miles to procure employment, by which he can better his own circumstances, and elevate his family in the social scale, as well as assist his needy relatives. But the poor white in Dixie refuses to toil or spin, no matter how needy he may be."[6] Poor whites were vilified as ignorant, uneducated, and unlikely to break their allegiance to the Democratic Party.

Poor blacks and poor whites were set in competition against one another. As blacks increasingly rose in educational attainment, whites resented the challenge to their status. Almost immediately after the war, journalists compared the two groups: "Comparatively little destitution or hunger is reported to exist among the blacks because both men and women have sought for work and obtained it, and are therefore self-supporting. They are hard at it plowing and hoeing corn and cotton, either for wages or for a share of the crop, and their employers furnish them with food in part payment for their labor. . . . The 'poor whites,' are shockingly improvident and thriftless. They utterly refuse to hire out to the planters and work for wages. They still look upon labor as disreputable and degrading."[7] Benevolent organizations, including the AMA, reported frustration with poor whites throughout the South. Unlike blacks, who eagerly enrolled in AMA schools, poor whites largely rejected Northern efforts.

By the 1880s, poor whites were regularly charged with the rising white-on-black violence: "These midnight attacks on colored people are made by what is known as 'poor white trash,' and the better class of citizens are awakening to the fact that they must be put down."[8] In the mid-1880s, it seemed hard to imagine a less worthy cause to champion. In 1887, the New York Times described a West Virginian: "He has a few acres of ground, a few sticks of corn, and a shanty in some hollow hereabout, where he gets food enough to escape starvation and breeds gaunt children to grow up and follow in his footsteps. He is 'poor white trash.' . . . He unquestionably is trash. There never was a fitter name for a more melancholy article."[9] Together with a few other regional AMA members, President Frost set out to challenge the dominant representations of poor whites as a monolithic and dangerous class by claiming that the poor whites of Appalachia were fundamentally different. As one journalist opined in response to the rapidly growing mobilization of AMA affiliates in support of mountain whites, this group—eastern Kentuckians—were "a strange people indeed to be held up as the highest type of American chivalry!"[10]

Blending an Abolitionist Heritage
with White Redemption at Berea

Berea initially succeeded in attracting donations by framing the college as a cure for slavery's mutual harm. The years after 1877 came to be called Redemption. During this time, the planter class returned to the national fold as an unrepentant prodigal son, and former Confederate states regained political autonomy. As historian David Blight argued, the time between the election of Rutherford Hayes in 1877 and the *Plessy v. Ferguson* decision (163 U.S. 537 (1896)) was characterized by a reunion of Southern and Northern whites who agreed to memorialize the war as a shared national tragedy. Northern whites lowered the "bloody shirt" and quieted their calls for extracting punishment from the South. Whites united over the devastation on both sides of the Mason-Dixon line, and came to a subtle agreement that the cost of the war had not been worth its gains.[11] It was during this historical moment that Berea College's president Fairchild pleaded that mountain whites were worthy of social investment. Fairchild justified their deservedness for aid because of their chosen isolation from the institution of slavery. This opened the possibility of innocence in the South. Fairchild depicted mountain whites as the less successful brother to the slave-holder.

> Slavery had no use for a self-respectful, laboring white man. The badge of manual labor was a badge of servile degradation. Of two brothers one would chance to get a little start, own a few slaves and all society would spur him onward. The other, less fortunate at the start, would slip away to some mountain hamlet and lead an uneventful, unambitious life and bring up a large family in utter ignorance. He plodded on his way, working only as necessity compelled him, instinctively hating slavery, slave-owners and slaves. Thus slavery rejected not simply this broken mountainous country, but the large class of whites which inhabited this region. If the North cares to dignify physical labor in the South, if it feels the need of a class that has a natural love for free republican institutions, if it cares to have the common-school system take rooting in the soil, if it desires a class of whites that shall be the wise, consistent friends of the colored people, perhaps it may find that this large body of whites rejected by slavery will prove the effective agency under the divine planning for this.[12]

Fairchild urged the AMA to consider mountain whites as part of the organization's moral mission. At the college level, transitioning to a focus on mountain whites seemed difficult to many. One trustee described Berea's new challenge as one of discipline: "The difficulty is going to be to get these shrewd, horse-swapping Scotchmen of Eastern Kentucky to enter any course where the advantages to be gained are very far in the future."[13] These students were often described as undisciplined, unruly, and uninterested in formal education. But there was some hope. As a Berea professor stated, "The mountaineer does not take kindly to institutional life. This disinclination is rapidly changing."[14] These complaints that poor whites were recalcitrant and hostile to education were similar to the familiar complaints from reform workers and journalists since the Civil War.

Reformers set about defining the boundaries to distinguish "mountaineers" from other poor whites by imploring their donor base to consider the political attitudes, rich natural resources of the region, and the excitement of a new venture in advancing a new mission for the AMA. Their work was complicated by journalist reports that linked poor whites in the mountains to poor whites in other parts of the South. In both cases, journalists regularly described a violent population notable for deviation from bourgeoisie norms and practices familiar to New England Protestants. Although organizations like the BRFAL and the AUC failed in previous efforts to incorporate poor whites into their education and reform programs, the new Appalachian project at Berea College offered a new highly targeted approach that resonated with rising xenophobic fears in the Northeast. A decade after President Fairchild introduced mountain whites as a group of concern, the AMA promoted the "discovery" of mountain whites to counter waning support for its traditional focus on interracial coeducation and, increasingly, education in colleges serving majority-black students.

Inventing Anglo-Saxon Appalachia

When Frost accepted the presidency at Berea in 1890, he was on sabbatical from his faculty position at Oberlin and making an extended tour of German universities. Frost, like several other Oberlin faculty, was intrigued by the burgeoning public school system and the German research university model that was gaining attention and favor by American academics. Frost would have been privy to the rapidly developing social changes in Bismark's Germany, where religious organizations, such as the *Innere Mission*, were party to developing a collaborative national social welfare state.[15] While abroad, Frost may have felt quite disconnected from the social changes happening back home and, upon arriving in Berea in 1892, was quite surprised by what he found. By all indications, Frost—a professor of classics at Oberlin and the son of two staunchly ab-olitionist Oberlin alumni—appeared an apt choice. Frost described the importance of his Oberlin experience in motivating his move to Berea: "Anti-slavery training made me ambitious to prove that Berea which had taken the bold step of admitting colored students just as a Northern or European school would do could be made a real success on that basis."[16]

Shortly after his arrival, however, the challenge of the new position became clearer. Frost described his inaugural fundraising trip to points North, including the "old abolitionist centers" of Cleveland and Cincinnati in Ohio, Utica and Syracuse in New York, and Boston "where our best friends were supposed to be." But Frost reported "a great disappointment to find that the old friends of Berea had almost entirely forgotten the Institution and become interested in Hampton Institute and other schools in the South. . . . I there made up my mind that I must create a new constituency depending little upon the old one."[17] Rather than change the funding model as trustees decided to do at Oberlin, Frost changed the college's population to attract Northern donors with xenophobic fears of changing U.S. demographics. Frost's shift in policy stemmed from a desire to differentiate the college and launch it onto the national stage.

In 1892, President Frost addressed the Ohio Teachers Association in Cincinnati, Ohio: "I am here to announce the discovery of a new world, at least a grand new subdivision. Have you ever heard of Appalachian America? Just as our western frontier has been lost in the Pacific Ocean, we have discovered a new pioneer region in the mountains of the Central South."[18] Few had, as yet, heard of Appalachian America—it had indeed just been discovered, creatively packaged, and marketed to philanthropists in the North and Midwest. Frost coined the term "Appalachia" as a new cultural category, and not merely a geographical term. Frost proclaimed his ethnographic capital of mountain whites: "no people need a friendly interpreter more than the American highlanders, and as the President of Berea College, I have had exceptional opportunities, and it has been my special duty to study their character, and all that can be known of their history."[19] Claiming ethnographic expertise, however, was—as might be expected—less directed to students and local residents than it was intended to signal authority and legitimacy to third-party organizations and Northern donors.[20] Others within the AMA were inspired by Frost's efforts and saw the potential for reinvigorating an enervated organization. Reverend Mills announced at the 1893 annual meeting of the AMA that "service for these American Highlanders will keep alive the romance of missions. They were patriots unsurpassed in the [American] revolution and in the rebellion [Civil War], and their sturdy stock will furnish patriots for every crisis to come. They are of high origin, have a high home, evidence high capability, and must have a high destiny. It is a gilt-edged investment for our American churches to incorporate these American whites in the great commonwealth."[21]

Though the college enrolled slightly more black than white students, its commitment to racial coeducation quickly diminished. The administration highlighted the mountain region as the special focus of the college even while enrolling students from across the nation, from as far as Oregon and Rhode Island. Frost's vision for Berea was to build an industrial college—akin to those endorsed by Booker T. Washington—on the doctrine of uplift ideology. Journalists echoed his message that the education of poor whites should follow the trend in uplift education available to blacks: "The poor white boy of the South needs the same opportunity for industrial training which so many have gladly extended to the negro by such institutions as Hampton and Tuskegee."[22] Although black students continued to enroll until 1903, no mention was made in the college's publicity materials of its anti-caste history or integrated classrooms after 1895.

Frost attempted to shift boundaries by linking mountain whites to the New England pilgrim. It was a bold move to position a discursively degraded group in relation to the highest status of whiteness. Frost advocated viewing mountain whites as a type of "lost cousin" to the Anglo-Saxon pilgrims of New England. In an 1899 *Harper's Weekly* article, Frost argued that Appalachians should inspire "more than antiquarian interest" for they were "part and parcel of the nation." He suggested, "when we consider the separate elements of the nation, the 'mountaineer' must not be overlooked as he certainly belongs to the category native born." Frost cast a positive light on the characteristics of mountaineer as *ur*-American, making the "value of such a population sufficiently evident."[23]

Frost cleverly tapped into the growing interest in foreign colonies. He drew on a number of colonial tropes to make his case for Berea, appealing to donors who might otherwise be tempted with international projects. Frost used a number of tropes—geographical remoteness, antiquated manners, and linguistic variance—to differentiate Appalachian whites from the suspect category of poor whites. President Frost gauged that greater intrigue might be gained by providing a new frontier, a new site for domination, and a new wilderness to tame. With each passing year, President Frost described Eastern Kentucky as increasingly remote. By 1898, on another publicity trip to New York City, he told his audience, Berea was no longer simply geographically remote but from another time: "It took only a little while to convince me that the 300 miles I had traversed to reach them was a longer journey than if I had gone to Europe, for I had taken a step from the present age back to the seventeenth century."[24] Berea had long experimented with a host of creative frames to promote the college. Whether framed as remote and therefore innocent from slavery, home to Union heroes, or a site of rich geological resources, the college tied its descriptions to the changing interests of donors.

Frost influenced professors of both social and natural science to aid in his campaign. An *American Journal of Sociology* article by S. S. Mac-Clintock refuted claims that mountain whites descended from "the indentured class, the poor white trash of Virginia," insisting that "no other equal area in the United States has such a homogenous Anglo-Saxon population as this. . . . It is a case of arrested development in civilization and a most interesting one. It must be studied as such. President Frost has aptly termed the inhabitants 'our contemporary ancestors.'"[25] Mac-Clintock and Frost both urged academics to devote further research into Appalachia as a "living time-capsule." Another AMA member authored three books describing the social ecology of the region and urging external investment in Appalachian education. New immigration streams and black northward migration were met with increasing hostility in Northern cities. By appealing to nativist prejudices, Frost aligned the college's program with increasingly popular trends in racial attitudes. Frost's innovation did not merely disseminate extant stereotypes. He actively created a new narrative to recast the stigma attached to feuding mountaineers and poor whites. He created a powerful motivational account to inspire donors to educate a group that had, until recently, been written off as "poor white trash."

Academics found Berea a useful example to support their claims that race symbolized meaningful differences in development. The valorization of Appalachia and its construction as a site of arrested development, intersected with the increasing popularity of these views. Frost's framing of Appalachia stirred the imagination in literature, created intrigue in the burgeoning social sciences, and dovetailed with a scientific narrative. One of Frost's most renowned supporters was Harvard professor Nathaniel Southgate Shaler. Shaler was a former student of Harvard professor Louis Agassiz who had helped bring polygenism, or the belief that different races evolved separately, into mainstream American science in the mid-nineteenth century. This belief opposed integration, arguing that it crossed "two races of men" whose development occurred on separate tracks. For Appalachian advocates within the AMA, this idea provided a rationale for understanding even a vilified subsection of whites as more deserving of aid than blacks. For instance, AMA-affiliate Reverend Lathrop argued in 1889 that isolation had "stranded" the Appalachians.

> Here are nearly two millions of people, scattered here and there over this great Cumberland Plateau, who because of their inaccessibility, their poverty and indifference, have been largely passed by until recently. The great tides of missionary effort have swirled and risen to the east, the south and the west, but have reached only a little way up into the caves and valleys of this great island plateau, which towers a thousand feet above the surrounding country. The inevitable effects of isolation, of intermarriage, of stagnation and neglect in mental and spiritual matters, has brought about a condition of things which calls for the aid and sympathy of all good Samaritans . . . left alone in their mountain fastnesses, left behind in the march of human progress, they have been a nation of Robinson Crusoes, deteriorating and retrograding from the inevitable nature of mankind when left to itself.[26]

This view articulated that the work of Reconstruction failed because the educational forms did not pair with racial development: slavery stunted the predetermined development trajectory of poor whites by exiling them from a bifurcated society that recognized only those either enslaved or enslaving others. Mountaineers—and later Appalachians— were presented as a people apart, though the historical record indicates that owning fewer than five slaves was not uncommon in eastern Kentucky. Appalachia presented a novel challenge to academics who argued that racial development explained and justified white supremacy. Using their logic, how could "degenerate" whites have fallen so far from their genetic destiny? Shaler and his sympathizers argued that poor whites had been neglected while blacks had received greater attention. To Frost, this was the basis for a new fundraising campaign.

Appalachian experts advanced the racist idea that "racial stock" served as a prophylactic against social degradation, and that the Anglo-Saxon had withstood decades of neglect and social isolation. Frost introduced a claim that Appalachian whites were descended from the same "stock" as New England puritans and that social, cultural, and political values were transferred between the generations. Appalachian experts frequently relied on genealogical narratives to convince upon the broader community of the AMA and philanthropic donors of the worthiness of mountain whites. "The fact is, this is the same blood good middle-class English blood that makes our New England people what they are, *and blood tells*. Of course there are some real poor whites here that are akin to the crackers . . . but the real mountaineer is not of this class."[27] As this new claim took hold, increasingly specific elaborations were made to produce an origin myth for the "true mountaineer." Experts argued that when "blood tells," the same valor and virtue expected of New England Pilgrims could be awakened in the mountaineers. Though their potential might have languished, experts asserted that their lineage made them worthy of social aid.

Defeating Popular Imagery of the "Outlaw" Mountaineer

Frost and his disciples still had to counter the glaring problems of the region. News reports about the region focused on ignorance and violence. Media descriptions matched Thorstein Veblen's characterization of a barbaric, predatory, and uncivilized community with "a more or less consistent attitude of plundering and coercion on the part of the fighting body, and this animus is incorporated into the scheme of life of the community."[28] On every metric, journalists found mountain whites failing in their performance of what historian Gregory Smithers calls the "standards of whiteness" that prevailed in the nineteenth century. In no small part, poor whites were treated with contempt for "fail[ing] to hold up the color line."[29] By refusing to adhere to a particular set of cultural rules, poor whites were living evidence against the white supremacist narrative that color shaped morality.

The college—and later other "mountain experts"—argued that eastern Kentucky constituted a particular cultural region that suffered delayed development because it had not embraced slavery. This developmental lag then reduced the region to crime and poverty. To present this case, Frost and other "ethnographic experts" drew from social theory of the time—Thorstein Veblen and Herbert Spencer, for example— to explain that social development progressed in stages of civilization. Experts argued that the region's stagnated social development left its residents behind the comparative development of new immigrants. The mountain region was depicted "not only a refuge of the oppressed, but for the refugees of the law. In the mountains of Kentucky especially there is a large percentage descended from outlaws [and] . . . it is not necessary to say that neighborhood and family quarrels are many and furious. In many places it is impossible to carry on a school with success on account of these family feuds and brawls."[30]

To argue that race was destiny, as some contemporary social scientists claimed, Appalachian experts needed to explain why this "lost" group of white Anglo-Saxon protestants were better known for their murderous feuds than for their virtue. Newspapers regularly covered "clan wars," most famously those between the Hatfields and the McCoys. To counter these negative representations, experts contextualized the violence and lawlessness as a rational response to disrespect for formal governance learned under the uncivilized and barbaric rule of slavery. Rebelliousness, violence, and even intemperance, were rendered as virtues demonstrating an independent spirit shared by pioneers and revolutionaries of early eras in U.S. history. Some alleged that the "true mountaineer" descended from indentured servants and yet, "still had enough of the Anglo-Saxon spirit about him to make him an unsatisfactory chattel."[31] Under the rule of an unjust oligarchy, disrespect was a rational response. Experts argued that mountain whites had developed a laudable set of characteristics in opposition to the slave-holding South. This opposition constituted their distinctiveness and their value: "These mountain folks, though poor and ignorant, are to be distinguished from the so-called poor whites of the low countries, who had had ground out of them much of their self-respecting manhood. The mountaineers have had pluck enough left in them to keep up a feud with the slaveholders aristocracy."[32] It was this rebellious spirit—now problematized—that permitted mountain whites to maintain their distinctive nature despite contact with the institution of slavery.

Casting murders as feuds, or reciprocal violence amongst equals, repelled attention to the political nature of the conflicts. As scholars have described, the feuds often took place among the educated and those in political power.[33] Instead of reporting the crimes as political—or, at the very least, indicative of the need for better governance—violence between known parties was construed as further evidence of a "backwards" and "peculiar" people languishing in a state of arrested development and in need of moral intervention. Yet the translation of murder into feud did more than construct stereotypes about a mythical Appalachia; these narratives also served to sanctify criminal acts. This process of sanctification or redemption emphasized that the story and the history could exculpate the offender. Not only do narratives matter for individual acquittal, but as this case shows, powerful narratives can also exculpate an entire group of people. Rebelliousness and violence were translated as "pluck" or "grit" and as evidence of a pioneering spirit handed down through generations.[34]

Reformers drew on imagery of the pioneering spirit of the "good American" to impose boundaries between poor whites and mountain whites. In an article for the *American Journal of Sociology*, one sociologist used the story of an Appalachian child to describe the pioneering history of the United States: "Sarepta Gabbard is quite unconscious of her pedigree but this daughter of Bud's, the Union veteran, Palestine the moonshiner, Daniel the backwoodsman, David the Indian fighter, and Adam the revolutionary soldier, as she rides timidly into Berea . . . will be a job and a problem to her teachers."[35] The selected historical archetypes were given to vice and violence, but the author encouraged other sociologists to interpret this lineage as possessing heroic character traits. Such descriptions drew upon a number of tropes to present Appalachia as a region of Union support, rugged individualism, yet mixed with sufficient need so as to compel Northern actors to contribute to funds for "saving" mountain whites.

Academics and Appalachian experts alike encouraged activating racial boundaries rather than the moral and political boundaries that had been the foundation of anti-caste campaigns for black citizenship in the immediate aftermath of the war (as described in chapter 2). Social boundaries are often conceptualized as bright, tightly maintained and impermeable, or more nebulous or "blurry."[36] Yet the nature of these

boundary distinctions changed over time; the meanings of the boundaries depended on the experts' interpretations. The case of Berea College
illustrates how organizations can use boundary-making strategies—
including narratives that activate ideas that link value assessments to
racial hierarchies—to further their interests and cultivate resource streams.
In drawing a bright line between mountain whites and poor whites,
experts imposed criteria of a particular genealogy and geographic residence as defining characteristics.[37] Contrarily, good works or moral
character did not make the supplicant more or less deserving. Furthermore, this particular form of whiteness was only accessible if awarded
membership by ethnographic experts, experts who used burgeoning
social science methodologies—surveys and socio-linguistics—to draw
boundaries and grant membership. In doing so, particular forms of
education and aid were matched to newly defined groups.

Motivation for Aid

As the AMA diversified its efforts, the organization increasingly supported projects that were exclusive to particular groups. AMA affiliates
in the West generated increasing Eastern support for projects targeting
Chinese immigrants and Native Americans. Around the same time, Berea
found declining support for its mission of integrated education. One of the
most prominent officers in the AMA, Stanley Lathrop, suggested that the
AMA increasingly turn its attention to a yet needier client, the mountain
whites. Lathrop drew on the imagery presented in numerous AMA magazines, conferences, and through inter-member contact to articulate the
need for an uplift program for white Appalachia. Though organizations
like the BRFAL and the AUC had both failed in their efforts to incorporate poor whites into their education and reform programs, the Appalachian project offered a highly targeted new approach with broad appeal
in a climate of rising xenophobia.

Nativist appeals fed into the larger political trends in racial attitudes
in the North. By the 1890s, politicians and Northern newspapers expressed fear of "Africanization," or a belief that blacks were gaining too
much power and influence. Despite the postwar outpouring of sympathy
for the exodus, fifteen years later blacks were depicted as a "plague" in
the North: "The black man multiplies, swarms, spreads and overruns
every locality . . . like the frogs of Egypt."[38] In 1896, legislative bills and
rulings like Plessy v. Ferguson legally encoded the already culturally

practiced doctrine of separate but equal, signaling the legal and political blockade of integration. "Ascriptive Americanism," or the belief that only whites deserved citizenship, was an old belief—and by the end of the nineteenth century, this racist notion triumphed over a variety of boundary experiments. Northern progressive-era reforms, including settlement houses and public health campaigns, focused on environmental issues associated with urban poverty. These campaigns explained white and white-ethnic poverty as the result of inadequate living conditions and poor schools; black poverty was explained in terms of racial difference.[39]

Frost created interest in the idea of the Appalachian mountaineer and simultaneously exerted strict control of his invention. Frost kept close tabs on depictions of mountain whites, and was quick to pen scathing rebuttals when politicians, journalists, or novelists described Appalachia in less than sympathetic terms. Why were Northerners motivated to champion—discursively and financially—a far-away rural people? First, Northerners viewed the region as rich in political and material resources. With the first arrival of British coal mining in 1883, Northern industrialists quickly assessed the region's wealth in both coal and timber and treated the region as an internal colony.[40] Appalachian experts quickly tapped into the importance of the new coal mining operations. In 1884, Reverend Roy addressed the AMA through its national journal: "In native material resources is it not superior to this grand New England which has spread out her tent to cover the continent with her ideas and her institutions? As New England herself is gradually changing by the forces of migration and immigration, so may not these sunnier and richer hills and mountains take on slowly the forces of a new and mighty civilization."[41] This call for donations emphasized natural resources and played on the growing Northern xenophobia towards new immigrants.

In addition to nativist or white supremacist arguments, Northern investment was also encouraged for political interests. Mountaineers could be counted on to vote Republican. Blacks faced such rampant voter intimidation that Republican whites needed to find another Republican base in the South. The *Chicago Tribune* lauded the "hardy mountaineers," who despite "belong[ing] to the poor-white-trash class of the South" could always be relied upon to vote against the Democratic Party.[42] As hostility towards blacks increased, states increasingly found new ways to challenge the expanded electorate. Mountain whites were understood as the only white Republicans in the South and, as literacy requirements increasingly shaped voter eligibility, uplift for these whites was considered politically important. For these reasons, Reverend Roy encouraged the AMA to include mountain whites within its work in the South: "While the Association has free access, with its school and church process to all classes of both races at the South, do not its traditions, its spirit, its methods lay upon it a peculiar obligation to take hold of these unlettered, depressed, but worthy mountain people? We are debtors to them because they were largely Union men."[43]

Experts implored their donor base to consider the political attitudes, rich natural resources of the region, and the excitement of a new venture in advancing a new mission for the AMA. Above all these, however, they redeemed the mountaineers for their Anglo-Saxon purity. Experts launched a set of broad configurations of what mountaineers represented, though at this stage they were largely negatively defined by what they were not: poor whites or new immigrants. Berea's new message resonated with Northern audiences, evidenced by increased enrollment, donations, speaking engagements, and connections to important social and political figures of the day.

Tools and Strategies for Consecrating a New Group

Success for group-making projects is generally measured by the degree to which powerful actors change policies and allocate resources. In other words, a campaign's success is measured by the institutionalization of its discursive tools and the adoption of new meanings associated with the group or cultural object.[44] Violence in eastern Kentucky during the late nineteenth and early twentieth century was made into a powerful symbolic narrative. The sensationalist accounts produced by experts—and reproduced more broadly by journalists and distributed by Northerners— created tales that were "often erroneous, exaggerated and self-serving."[45] Appalachian experts aligned their narratives to tap into a growing Northern xenophobia. They were able to incorporate even the most heinous of crimes into a narrative of white moral superiority by depicting vices among mountain whites as virtues.

By changing the mission of the school and "discovering" a new pioneer region, President Frost attracted renewed interest to Berea College. To accomplish the transformation of land and people into "region" and "pioneer stock," President Frost campaigned to journalists, social scientists, literati, and politicians. Frost's management of ethnographic capital allowed him to lecture at Carnegie Hall and Cooper Union, and gain written endorsements from political figures, including Theodore Roosevelt. Perhaps equally important is that he attracted the interest of key academics, including Harvard anthropologist Nathan Shaler, in the rising scientific racism movement, who bequeathed Berea $250,000. Frost launched an academic journal to secure a place for Appalachians as a legitimate social category for scientific study; social science journals, including the *American Journal of Sociology*, published articles citing Frost. President Frost published articles in *Harper's Magazine*, *Ladies Home Companion*, *Outlook*, *Atlantic Monthly*, *American Monthly Review of Reviews*, and the *New York Times*. In addition to promoting Appalachia at Carnegie Hall in New York City, he also spread the word at dinner parties attended by Harvard professors and Woodrow Wilson.[46]

In 1895, AMA connections secured Frost a meeting with then-New York City police commissioner Theodore Roosevelt. In 1897, Roosevelt gave an address in New York City to garner support for Frost's Appalachian campaign: "Where shall we find better elements to build upon, or better encouragement for the use of all the instruments of education that shall enable such a people to make of themselves all they are capable of?"[47] A few years later, Berea publicity materials boasted an endorsement from President Roosevelt. Other supporters included Rockefeller's GEB and Helen Gould, daughter of railroad baron Jay Gould and later a member of the Russell Sage Board, who chartered a special train to bring friends to visit Berea College.[48]

In addition to finding legitimating academic and political partners, Appalachia needed mapping to become a separate entity. In 1893, John Hall published "The Mountain Whites of the South." The monograph was the first to specify the qualifications of mountain whites by combining ethnic spatial claims. Hall legitimated mountain whites for Northern investment by sketching a causal relationship between the institution of slavery and the denigration of Scotch-Irish mountaineers. Hall argued that mountain whites had suffered "greater injury" from slavery than blacks; he argued that blacks were "saved" by slavery from "savagery" while mountain whites were denied resources to stay on pace with their coethnics.[49]

In 1901, Robert F. Campbell published a booklet titled "Classification of Mountain Whites," which used Frost's claims to build a categorization schema of three types of mountain whites in the Appalachian region. The first order of Appalachians were those living in the fertile valleys who "compare favorably with any population on the globe." The locations Campbell provided were towns central to the "breadbasket of the Confederacy." He boldly argued that even Southern whites with ties to the Confederacy could be redeemed through Appalachian Anglo-Saxon heritage. Next were the "higher grade" of mountain people, who preserved the "characteristics that mark the Scotch-Irish wherever they are found, . . . hardy, hospitable, honest and intelligent . . . in native force . . . they are in no way inferior, but rather superior, to many more highly favored representatives of the same race. Their very isolation has saved them from many of the subtle evils that are poisoning the streams of a higher civilization."[50] Despite promotions by Fairchild, Frost, and others, many knew of eastern Kentucky primarily from reports of nationally publicized violence in the region—particularly the Hatfield-McCoy feud of the 1880s. Campbell separated the worthy Appalachian from "a third and lower grade found in the Appalachian mountains, . . . [who is] shiftless, ignorant and apparently without aspirations." Campbell asserted, "it would be just as fair for one to describe the typical dweller in the slums of New York, and then declare with a wave of the hand that there are 'millions of him' in that great city." Instead, Campbell claimed that these mountain dwellers were ethnically distinct from the Appalachian of Anglo-Saxon stock. The "third grade" were comprised of "descendants of bound white servants and criminals transported from Great Britain, and the propagation of the scum that floated across from Germany and other continental countries to the new world." It was this third grade that had earned Appalachia its negative reputation for clan-feuding, moonshining, and depravity.[51] Campbell, Frost, and others excluded the more troubling tales from the geographic region of Appalachia by claiming that the moonshiners and feudists were a separate category of poor whites, ethnically and culturally distinct from the cultural category of Appalachians, or Anglo-Saxon mountaineers.

These boundary distinctions garnered resources from important funding agencies. In 1908, Theodore Roosevelt, concerned by the rise of immigration and the "immorality" of urban growth, launched a national survey—the Committee on Country Life—to improve prospects for rural Americans. This, however, benefited only whites. W. E. B. DuBois requested that the committee also investigate the "system of peonage," including "practical slavery," operating in the South, but his request to include rural blacks in the study was denied.[52] In 1909, John D. Rockefeller created the Sanitary Commission for the Eradication of Hookworm

Disease. The campaign medicalized white poverty by claiming that rural Southern whites were not lazy but infested with a disease.[53] This crusade addressed the challenge that poor Southern whites failed to meet expectations of white racial development and helped Berea garner support for mountain whites.

At that same time, the Russell Sage Foundation provided funding to John C. Campbell to conduct a cultural survey of the region between 1908 and 1909. In 1917, Russell Sage published its guide to the 265 Appalachian counties in Alabama, Georgia, Kentucky, North Carolina, South Carolina, Tennessee, Virginia, and West Virginia; residence in these counties became Berea's new admissions guidelines. By 1911, the number of students seeking admission to Berea was so great that "the trustees amended the Constitution to make the southern mountain region Berea's special field; and in 1915, the College ruled that students from outside the mountain region would be admitted in special cases only."[54] This latest policy required clarifying the geographic boundaries of Appalachian America, and the college adopted John C. Campbell's map for this purpose. The scope of Appalachia continued to expand through the 1960s until Appalachia covered nearly all nonmajority black portions of the South, eventually extending as far as New York.[55]

Berea College and Appalachian Education

Under Frost, a new region was discovered and marked with clearly delineated racial and cultural boundary lines. A new population in need of philanthropic services identified. Further, an interracial school that had been established in a slave-holding state as a blatant challenge to an unjust system was now the representative school for a region. This region became the last pioneer stronghold, an ancient enclave of the Anglo-Saxon, or as President Frost liked to call the it, "our contemporary ancestors."[56]

Though still enrolling a sizeable number of black students, by 1900, Berea represented itself as serving only white, mountain youth; there was no mention of its original commitment to anti-caste education or mixed-race education. The college was remade on the industrial model proposed by Booker T. Washington and in 1900 announced: "This College now stands before the public as the representative school for the mountains, as Hampton and Tuskegee stand as the representative institutions for the colored people."[57] Frost encouraged others to see mountain whites in competition with blacks for scarce resources. White student enrollment quadrupled during the first decade of Frost's administration. By 1903, blacks constituted only 16 percent of Berea students. In 1904, Berea College was the only institution affected when the Kentucky State Legislature passed the Day Law forbidding the "coeducation of the races." One judge declared the legislation "a blessing to Berea College." Oberlin's president wrote Frost a letter of congratulations.[58]

Market-logic shaped not only student decisions—as we saw in the case of Oberlin College—but also directly shaped fundraising strategies in higher education.[59] In the early 1900s, Berea College's new publicity slogan was "work that wins," promising that the return on an investment in Appalachian whites would be greater than that of money donated to black schools. This investment was tied specifically to cultivating "good" citizens in line with nativist visions of an ethnically pure America. A 1910 Berea College publicity brochure featured a quote from the well-known Harper's Magazine journalist, Julian Ralph: "To know that men of the race of Shakespeare, Burns, Queen Bess and Danie O'Connor, to the number of 2,000,000 lack the schools which we boast are the bulwarks of our greatness—to know that men who bear the very names and blood of Patrick Henry, Andrew Jackson, Clay, Sumpter, Boone, scores of the best names in our history, languish here for the barest chance to renew the triumphs of these founders and leaders of our nation—is that not cause for shame? The value of these people is greater than ever just now when we have drained the old world of its best and most adventurous blood, and are taking in a less easily assimilated immigration."[60]

Championing Appalachian students as an under-served group proved popular; by the end of the nineteenth century, a new wave of benevolent agencies helped create a distinct "mountain" field. Some colleges followed Berea's lead by shifting their mission to focus on Appalachia's "Anglo-Saxon stock." For instance, Presbyterians transformed their three established colleges in Tennessee into institutions focused on mountain whites.[61] This campaign even attracted General O. O. Howard. General Howard had long championed racial integration. While president of Howard, he insisted that integration was more than merely demographic. While he demanded that the faculty and Board of Trustees be representative, Howard ensured that the fundamental principle of integration—of shared power at every level—extend to all aspects of the university. General Howard helped found Lincoln Memorial University in eastern Tennessee in 1897. How did a staunch advocate for black civil and social

BEREA * COLLEGE

In Lincoln's state — for Lincoln's people.

Berea, Ky., May 10, 1899.

ABE LINCOLN STUDYING BY THE CABIN FIRE.

FIGURE 7. In Lincoln's state for Lincoln's people, 1899. Courtesy of Berea College Special Collections and Archives, Berea, Kentucky.

rights join the campaign for Appalachia? O. O. Howard was persuaded by arguments that linked the mountaineer mythology with Republican loyalty. In his personal writings, he reflected that his dedication to mountain uplift stemmed from his affection for President Lincoln.[62] The charter for Lincoln Memorial University declared it "shall ever seek to make education possible to the children of the humble common people of America, among whom Abraham Lincoln was born."[63]

The Appalachian campaign was not limited to the college setting. Northerners founded rural settlement houses and adapted the model for a rural, Appalachian population. In 1900, the Berea Board of Trustees launched a new initiative of "settlements," though as the board noted, "The word "settlement" is used not as a *name* to be applied to these efforts but as a descriptive term for our own convenience—locally in the mountains they will simply be called "that thar School on Fish Creek that Berear College is a backing of."[64] In 1902, Katherine Petit and May Stone founded the first rural settlement house, the Hindman Settlement House in Knott County, Kentucky.[65] Less than a decade after their survey of the Appalachian region, John C. Campbell's widow founded the John C. Campbell Folk School in North Carolina, dedicated to the preservation of mountain culture. Frost's strategy spurred a new cultural category and diffused an organizational form of donation-funded mountain schools to match.[66]

To coordinate the efforts of the numerous missionaries and educators arriving in the region, the Russell Sage Foundation organized the first Annual Conference of Southern Mountain Workers in 1912. The conference built on Frost's efforts to create the Appalachians as a culturally distinct group with shared ethnic ties to Northern whites of English descent. Leaders in the conference beseeched reform agencies to "not try to make the mountaineers into 'nice little northerners.' We must not project upon them anything that might be all right for us, but not for their environment."[67] During the 1919 annual conference, there was a moment in which two of the eminent leaders of the Appalachian movement debated the potential for individuality. John C. Campbell asked if mountain whites might not be considered first as individuals and second as residents of the Appalachian region: "Shall the schools of the mountains be based on the needs of the mountain country, or on the needs of the individual person in the mountains?" President Frost answered, "Education should be adapted to the needs of the mountain people as a whole, and not to the individual."[68] In an era noted for its focus on rugged individualism, a stigmatized category of people had been transformed from traitorous "poor whites" to needy "mountain whites" and finally as "Appalachians" and worthy Anglo-Saxons. Frost made clear that groups of people had particular educational needs.

Resistance to Segregation

The 1883 Supreme Court decision, which overturned the 1875 Civil Rights Bill promising equal access to private facilities, had allowed private organizations like the American Medical Association to discriminate against doctors educated at Howard University. This decision had important implications for Berea as well, though Berea's case proved more complex. In 1904 the Kentucky State Legislature passed the Day Law to ban integrated private higher education. Berea College was the only school affected by this law. The case moved on to the Supreme Court, but by that time, Berea's commitment to coeducation had largely passed and their focus on educating mountain whites had taken hold.

In contrast to Oberlin, white and black Berea students protested the rising exclusion of black students. Students continued to live together in dorms without incident. Students still came from Northern states—most often Ohio, though some as far as Oregon and Rhode Island—and all reports suggested that the spirit of coeducation persisted despite Frost's attempts to divert resources towards poor whites. Just before the Kentucky State Legislature undertook the Day Law to outlaw interracial education, one faculty advisor described to the trustees the atmosphere in the male dormitory: "I report with pleasure an exceedingly good spirit between colored, mountain, and northern men. This has been true throughout the year. There has been no serious disorder, nor any outbreak of race or sectional feeling.... Here throughout the year, the Negro, the Mountaineer, and the Northerner fraternized in the most cordial way.... The three kinds of students have associated daily, in the most brotherly way."[69] Whereas students at Oberlin protested continued integration in dining halls by pointing out that such social "sacrifices" would not be asked of them at other Northern colleges, Berea students protested the administration's pointed efforts to decrease coeducation. Student protestors were joined by alumni and many town residents.

The news also mobilized Berea supporters far from campus. Alumnus Frank L. Williams, an esteemed educator, mobilized fellow alumni and current students against the segregationist practices of President Frost. In a personal letter to Frost, Williams accused Frost of not valuing the college's tradition of coeducation, as evidenced by policies that prioritized poor whites and alienated black students.[70] In 1903, Booker T. Washington also wrote a personal letter to Frost accusing him of promoting the hateful idea that "the white man should be educated before the Negro is educated."[71] White and black students alike agitated against Frost's new initiatives for mountain education. A letter from fifty black students to Frost demanded he defend coeducation: "Berea College was founded upon these principles, opposition to sectarianism, slave-holding castes, and every other wrong institution or practice, we believe—(a) That the college should be run on these principles, (b) That any form of separation whatsoever will be fostering and encouraging those principles against which this institution was established."[72] Frank Williams and several fellow educators passed a resolution at the Kentucky State Teachers' Association in 1907 titled, "President Frost's Betrayal of the Colored People in his Administration of Berea College." In 1908, the case went before the U.S. Supreme Court. The court ruled in favor of "the power of a state over its own corporate creatures."

Much of the political dissent during Reconstruction stemmed from the enduring American debate over the autonomy of states and the reach of the federal government. In his dissent, Justice Harlan laid bare the implications of the court's decision: "Further, if the lower court be right, then a state may make it a crime for white and colored persons to frequent the same marketplaces at the same time, or appear in an assemblage of citizens convened to consider questions of a public or political nature, in which all citizens, without regard to race, are equally interested. Many other illustrations might be given to show the mischievous, not to say cruel, character of the statute in question, and how inconsistent such legislation is with the great principle of the equality of citizens before the law."[73]

Supreme Court Justice John Marshall Harlan's dissent importantly touched upon the changing logics of the era. He not only refuted that separate could be equal but also inveighed that inequality in the private sphere would surely have spillover effects in the public sphere. In other words, Harlan argued that symbolic status—as evidenced by treatment in broader social life—inevitably shaped access to political rights. He asked, "Have we become so inoculated with prejudice of race than an American government, professedly based on the principles of freedom and charged with the protection of all citizens alike, can make distinctions between such citizens in the matter of their voluntary meeting for innocent purposes simply because of their respective races?" Justice Harlan had also provided the lone dissent in Plessy v. Ferguson. Born to a Kentucky slaveholding family, Harlan embodied the personal transformation the anti-caste mission had hoped possible for white Southerners. As he described so eloquently, however, the dominant logic guiding American institutions was increasingly one of racial hierarchy rather than of national solidarity.

Berea students and alumni who doubted President Frost's commitment to coeducation were proved correct when Frost responded to the Supreme Court decision, saying "It does not, however, greatly affect us at this time." Frost had different intentions for the college. Berea College, following the 1904 Day Law, helped to secure a new school for black students who were then exiled to a campus outside Louisville. To this effort, Berea provided $200,000, much of it raised by alumni who grieved the demise of coeducation. To provide for the new segregated school, black alumni mobilized to rally funds. Frost described this effort as "a great hardship" on top of "our urgent work for the mountaineers." Frost noted the generosity of alumni and black Kentuckians: "Toward this fund the colored people of Kentucky are subscribing very liberally, hoping to have a school of their own at an early day."[74] However, alumni, faculty, and concerned black leaders like Booker T. Washington urged that black Kentuckians did not want what Frost called a "school of their own." Many black families had been a part of Berea for generations and heartbreakingly described the new school as an "exile."

The Invention of Appalachia:
An Effect of Intercollegiate Competition

As higher education became a competitive field, colleges marketed their offerings to targeted groups. Private actors in the nonprofit sector often make claims about what constitutes a valued or worthy subject for social remediation programs. As social aid increasingly takes on the characteristics of a capitalist market, nonprofit actors differentiate among possible clientele as a means to carve their specialty niche in the crowded market of the needy.[75] This is also true for the educational field. Actors in nonprofit sectors exist in a state of constant and unrelenting pressure to secure funding, ambidextrously drawing on multiple logics to attract funds from a range of differently motivated funders.[76]

Because the AMA needed to raise donations from Northern audiences, the organization differentiated its mission and aims in ways that would resonate with its potential donors—and many within the AMA feared that racial coeducation no longer attracted donations. This placed increasing competitive pressure on regional projects. Not only did they compete against external organizations, but AMA affiliates in Kentucky competed against affiliates in California, the Dakotas, and New York for resources and reputation. In determining the "most oppressed," AMA affiliates needed to make their case for why their particular constituencies deserved aid more than other groups. In doing so, AMA members activated ideas about the capacities and value of particular groups. At Berea, this created a tension between experts seeking funds and missions, and the consequences of the pressure to create new markets for philanthropy. This allows us to see how organizations not only differentiate in response to resource demands, but also create new fields—populated by activating "new" cultural categories—to increase their organization's ability to draw status and resources.

The invention of "the Appalachian" at Berea College as a distinct category of Southern whites helped Berea maintain its status as a unique, mission-driven college during a period of enormous changes. Race is not biological or natural and yet, the degree to which actors are enabled or constrained in defining, choosing, or activating racial identities remains under-theorized, particularly for whites.[77] Prejudice is often conceived of as an outcome of racial homophily—where "birds of a feather flock together"—but how people understand and attach meaning to racial identities are neither inherent nor natural.[78] Rather, meanings can be attached to ascriptive characteristics strategically, and this attachment can be strategically accomplished by organizations that activate racial meanings to further their interests.

Whiteness has been understood as "embodied racial power," and as a racial structure that is "almost invisible."[79] Poor white trash is a complication of whiteness that poses a challenge to accounts of hegemonic whiteness. The production of meanings about race, ethnicity, class, and gender are both unstable and politically contested; this is true for poor whites as well as other groups. Ideas about groups do not *emerge ex nihilo*. The rendering of whiteness as elastic obscures the organizing force of ethnic entrepreneurs—here reformers—who actively shape meanings about race. Meanings about race depend on how individuals are categorized by others (particularly those with greater power), individual self-identification, and the changing dynamics of both of these processes over time.

The creation of a new cultural category of redemption-worthy whites began in the hills of Eastern Kentucky and spread to the majority-white regions of many Southern States—Alabama, Georgia, Mississippi, North Carolina, South Carolina, Tennessee, and West Virginia. Essentially, only Louisiana, Texas, and Florida could not claim "Appalachian" status. Thus, while the college restricted its enrollment policy to only admit Appalachians, by mapping Appalachia as the white South, it accomplished *de facto* segregation. The invention of the Appalachian white as a heretofore overlooked category of southern whites, and the use of national origin myths to establish their purity and isolation from the evils of slavery, offered up a redeemable symbolic space within the white South—a space from which symbolic legitimacy was extended to other, previously reviled groups of southern whites. Appalachia-entrepreneurs cultivated ethnographic capital by carefully monitoring the media's application of the "Appalachian" category. Appalachia promoters substituted cultural and ethnic specificity (Anglo-Saxon) for the previously valorized trait of "loyalty" as criteria for redemption.

By 1917, Berea positioned itself as a source of great patriotism: "Never before did America have more need of Americans; and nowhere in America is there so large a reservoir of undeveloped and unspoiled American life."[80] Since its founding, Berea had claimed that its work served the Union. It first articulated the college as a site of political service by educating blacks and whites in a spirit of coeducation. Later it elevated a denigrated group—poor whites—by claiming a particular subsection (the mountaineers) as unlike white Southerners because of their Union loyalties, evidenced through Union service. By the early twentieth century, however, Berea rooted its patriotism solely in racial terms. Berea College had transformed from the most successful site of interracial coeducation to a mythic token for white nationalism. Berea, more than Howard or Oberlin, effectively transformed ideas into actions.

Conclusion

From Coeducation to the Consecration of Difference

> The prejudices of the whites, descending through generations,
> imbibed by individuals in infancy, and strengthened by
> universal sentiment, practice, and association of ideas cannot
> be easily and soon overcome, and are not, so far as feeling is
> concerned, wholly within the power of volition, so as to be
> annihilated at will. They will vanish gradually in the presence
> of increasing evidence of a noble manhood. Developed
> intellectual power, the higher education, success in industrial
> pursuits, the acquirement of wealth and culture and character,
> will cause them to disappear.... When I deposit a gold coin on
> the table, it commands a certain degree of respect.... Will the
> result not be analogous, when the colored man shall be seen to
> have an intrinsic value equal to that of the white man? When
> one shall no longer associate him with the ideas of bondage,
> pauperism, and barbarism, but those of freedom, prosperity,
> intelligence, and culture; when he shall not only carry in his
> person the stamp of American citizenship, but shall come out
> from a university training a scholar and a gentleman, like a
> glittering coin from the die.
>
> —PRESIDENT PATTON, "Inaugural Address to Howard
> University," *The American Missionary*, January 1878, 16

President Patton's inaugural speech raises deep sociological questions: How can prejudice be overcome? How is the status of group determined? Is it through the demonstration of political loyalty? And what assures the stability of rights? Certainly, governments are charged with policing deliberate and overt efforts to deny citizens equal access to certain social provisions, yet laws are often inadequate for maintaining hard-won victories for greater inclusion. From emancipation to the present, the quest for equality in educational opportunity has been blocked by the particulars of managing implementation. This book has explored what happens when private organizations—such as the AMA—

assert their primacy as the rightful agents to resolve these democratic challenges.

At the end of the Civil War, the United States faced the daunting challenge of rebuilding a broken social order. There were—and are—a host of possibilities for reorganizing social hierarchies and determining the political and symbolic power. Social orders need not be based on race or ethnicity any more than they are determined by religion or divine right, though all of these arrangements have prevailed in different times and places. Anti-casteists envisioned building an inclusive new America. Their work was grounded in religious faith and the belief that only individual transformations could realize meaningful social change. This was in essence the original anti-caste challenge and goal—to replace the imposition of racial caste with egalitarian cooperation.

There were, of course, diverse opinions about the promise of emancipation and the best path to national stability.[1] As described in chapter 2, some Republicans optimistically imagined that blacks' political loyalty to the Republican Party—the Party of Lincoln and emancipation—would ensure their value to policy-makers. Like the black leaders who, shortly before the war ended, counseled General Sherman and Secretary of War Edwin Stanton to support land redistribution and homesteading, Booker T. Washington argued that economic security would develop the base from which blacks could gain traction as true citizens. In its early years, the anti-caste movement offered a radical strategy: Whites had to learn to respect blacks as equals and this could only come through sustained integrated education. The imperative of interracial coeducation was that blacks could not *prove* that they deserved equal status. Rather, eradicating prejudice required a thorough reeducation of whites.

From the outset, the AMA proposed that organized efforts were necessary to achieve integration. To create peace, only interracial coeducation could integrate political and social institutions. Indeed, AMA agents often spoke out against the inadequacy of legal-rational institutions to address moral questions.

Even the most experimental or progressive colleges are situated within a particular historical and political context. By examining the implementation of the anti-caste vision in three colleges, we saw that the return of segregation was not primarily the result of conditions *within* the colleges but a response to external pressures. Activists, political elites, college administrators, and students operated in a rapidly transitioning, deeply contentious, and sometimes violent political environment. The AMA depended on the continued interest of donors, on legislation that protected graduates from discrimination by professional organizations, and on law-makers who would refuse to tolerate violence and intimidation by whites against blacks. The colleges were vulnerable to the shifting interests of donors and lacked the stability afforded to state institutions. The rapid development of higher education in the South, including colleges providing industrial education for blacks, opened some doors but also signaled the emergence of a competitive, comparative field of higher education.

Educational organizations generate categories, allocate status, and influence group boundaries. They do not do so under conditions of their own choosing and the logics of these boundaries and of status and "merit" are deeply contested and activated to serve particular organizational interests. In the cases at hand, it is clear that the changes in strategy by the AMA, commensuration work by the ACA, and the rise of philanthropy had important impacts on the shape of higher education. More generally, it is difficult to estimate the number of colleges, seminaries, and institutes that have shuttered or changed course because of their shifting environments. As a specialist in the U.S. Office of Education explained, even the "serious student of [college closures] has usually been forced willy-nilly into a stuff of a few dead trees without any definite idea of the total number in the forest."[2] What is clear is that the history of early efforts for interracial coeducation should dispel the optimism of a neat linear, upward trajectory of progress. Industrial education was not a first step toward expanding educational opportunities for blacks; nor were women's colleges pioneers in advancing women's education. Rather, these forms of education emerged through status conflict and to preserve higher education as a restricted social space controlled by elites. New educational forms were developed in response to the changing racial order. Embedded in this period of organizational innovation and change were deep fears about the legitimacy of merit, the fragility of status, and dilemmas of civic inclusion.

A Competitive, Differentiated Field

Merit and the Purpose of College

For women and black students of either sex, early access was achieved with much less resistance than expected. Social commentators positioned higher education in Washington, D.C., as a quasi-natural experiment to compare whites and blacks: Howard's proximity to white institutions "afford(s) favorable opportunities to compare the results of the collegiate training of white men and black men."[3] Another observer found "no difference . . . in capacity between the whites (pinks they should be called), blacks, and browns."[4]

As the radicalism of Reconstruction faded, so too did the hope for universal and immediate equality. Anti-caste colleges had been promoted as a third space where the rules and logics of political and social life could be suspended. Campuses appeared to be separate spaces, organized around idealism. Often separated from town by gates or other markers, students were frequently governed by collegiate authorities rather than municipal or state legal systems, as they are today. For these reasons, the founders of AMA-affiliated colleges imagined that their campus communities would offer space to resolve misconceptions around race before graduating students into that more complicated world. The purpose of these colleges had not been to fuel competition over achievement, but rather for students to learn to live the ideals needed to realize a diverse democracy.

As seen at the beginning of this chapter, President William Patton of Howard University put forth an idea that we now take for granted: educational achievement promises social mobility. In this vision, a college degree would both certify the bearer's accomplishments and demand respect. Educational achievement, Patton argued, would be the objective metric that would, at last, offer blacks unquestionable intrinsic respect—like the "gold coin on the table." College could be a proving ground to achieve the rights of citizenship. Other options—land redistribution, military occupation, and Northern colonizers—were rejected in favor of education as the best hope for renewing the Union. Reformers had failed to anticipate the backlash that such an emphasis on education might generate, or that hard-won victories could be undermined.

As college administrators, journalists, and policy-makers concentrated on using education to convince whites of blacks' merit, and as the number of black college graduates increased, blacks were nevertheless barricaded from professional organizations, social and cultural spaces, and political rights. What the AMA had not anticipated was the broader reaction to its project, nor the paradox that status recognition would—inverse to their expectations—raise, not lower, barriers. Once whites recognized the achievements of blacks and/or women, restrictions and barriers were quickly erected. Given the limited successes of each group, as measured in enrollment, graduation, and professional achievements, it appears that the threshold for being perceived as a status threat to white men was not especially high. Nearly every success in undermining the color line was met with great resistance. Representative Joseph H. Rainey (South Carolina, Republican) described the quandary to Congress: "Just as soon as we begin to assert our manhood and demand our rights we are looked upon as men not worthy to be recognized, we become objectionable, we become obnoxious, and we hear this howl about social equality."[5] As described in chapter 6, the American Medical Association very quickly moved to bar black doctors. It also barred whites who learned in interracial classrooms and laboratories, a not so subtle message to those who would cross the color line. These actions by private organization, not only the Supreme Court decisions of the 1880s, enforced the racialized status order.

This reminds us that to understand integration—and its challenges—we need to look beyond formal legal structures and beyond the interpersonal relationships emphasized by contact theory. We need to consider how prejudice gets built into organizational environments, and develop and implement policy that defends against retrenchment. Whether in repealing the Civil Rights Act of 1875 or the Voting Rights Act of 1965, too often history demonstrates a knee-jerk impulse in U.S. social policy to derail programs promoting equality when they prove effective.[6]

One imagines President Patton nodding in ascent to Max Weber's postulate that as democracy takes hold and replaces outmoded caste hierarchy with bureaucratic procedures, education can create a merit-based bureaucracy.[7] But Weber also warned that higher education might merely become a new caste system, an argument that has been further developed by Pierre Bourdieu and many others. As we have seen, the attempt to use education to replace the outmoded caste systems in nineteenth-century United States failed because of the obligation hoarding of reformers, the emergence of a competitive field, and the unwillingness of whites to give up the spoils of injustice. A more fully bureaucratic system of higher education might have placed control of higher education in the hands of the state, thus reducing competition between colleges.[8]

Differentiation, Rating, and Ethnographic Expertise

The largely forgotten histories of interracial coeducation at Berea, Oberlin, and Howard show how organizational development and racial categorization are linked. As colleges increasingly came into competition with one another, they pursued strategies of differentiation. As Emily Barman has written, this is a common process among nonprofit organizations, in which they assert their uniqueness as a means to maintain limited resources in a crowded field.[9] Nonprofit organizations must often persuade potential donors of the legitimacy of their unique missions and the necessity of their programs. This same set of pressures came to bear as colleges came into competition with one another. In this case, colleges' differentiation strategies relied heavily on activating race, ethnicity, and gender as important distinctions. In particular, administrators linked target groups with different purposes of education. This resulted in specially designed forms of education: sex-designed colleges for affluent white women and industrial colleges for blacks and Appalachians. Collegiate sports and merit scholarships were added to attract white men to college life; classical languages, originally important for religious scholarship, were maintained as part of elite curricula even as the Protestant colleges and universities produced fewer clergy. Because few women or blacks attended high schools where they could study Greek and Latin, their use in admissions was a *de facto* barrier that few challengers could surmount.

Higher education in the United States became quite diversified, with minimal external oversight. The complete absence of state control over how colleges were founded and evaluated helped to make higher education a competitive field. As more colleges were founded, access increased dramatically, but the value of a college degree depended heavily on the status of the college. Professional organizations, charities, and private evaluation systems—what we would now think of as "rating" systems—shaped the field in ways that individual colleges, or even networks of them, could not ignore. As we saw in chapter 5, the ACA was the first organization to attempt a comparative evaluation of colleges. Its work tied the status of a particular college to the social status of the students in attendance, rather than other criteria. The anti-caste colleges began to articulate their missions, and each developed a new and distinct form of education deemed appropriate for the particular group it educated. The colleges not only identified targeted populations to enroll, but also actively constructed and consecrated particular meanings for new, carefully demarcated groups. While some practices were made uniform in growing higher education—such as the conferring of bachelor's degrees—colleges also differentiated their missions to match their sources of financial support and the changing legal-political dynamics.

Higher education became an arena to "curate" groups of people as colleges empowered "ethnographic experts" to strategically draw boundaries, activate meanings about race and sex, and match narratives about groups to emergent organizational forms. As described in chapters 5, 6, and 7, administrators and faculty paid attention to donor interests as they decided how to depict their students. Should they focus on industrial education or the liberal arts? Should they assure elite families of their daughters' reproductive futures with specially designed campuses? Should they appeal to nativist fears with homespun stories from Appalachia? As their answers married organizational forms with clusters of people, new cultural meanings about categories and groups—including the new category of Appalachia—were consecrated. Moreover, women, mountaineers, and blacks were all prescribed limited forms of higher education. Theoretically, this illustrates the co-constitution of cultural logics and material resources. In addition, it is important to remember that these changes were, in large, produced by private organizations, rather than solely by the state. Practically, this means that contrary to the Morrill Act's push for mass education, as higher education was developing into a demarcated field, with its own rules, logics, and norms. Some kind of college was appropriate for all, but access to prestige decreased.

This unequal field was not accepted by all. Responding to the debates about differentiated definitions, Horace Bumstead, the president of Atlanta University—an AMA affiliate—suggested, "If the term 'higher education' needs definition, let me say what I have in mind—such education as an average white boy gets when he 'goes to college.' I mean a curriculum in which the humanities are prominent and in which intercourse with books and personal contact with highly educated teachers constitute the chief sources of power." Bumstead, a Yale graduate who studied in Germany before accepting the presidency at Atlanta University, had little patience for those who used semantic debates to deny blacks a quality education.[10] Indeed, the ACA described its earlier dilemma in evaluating colleges as a confrontation of "choosing between a broad and generous spirit of fellowship and a policy of rigid discrimination" as though these were inherently and necessarily mutually exclusive. Difficult decisions had to be made to ensure a reasonable standard, claimed the ACA.[11]

Despite wide recognition of deep segregation in higher education, most college administrators upheld the notion of elite universities as colorblind meritocracies. Brown University reprimanded W. E. B. DuBois for his efforts to collect enrollment data by race, countering that the "constant effort of the college should be to ignore such distinctions and replace them with the distinctions of ability and character. It is possibly for this reason that we have never kept any record of race distinctions among our alumni."[12] And despite its flaws, the ACA's efforts to demand evidence of the quality and availability of education access for women proved instrumental in tempering inflated accounts of gender equality. By 1904, Harvard professor Hugo Münsterberg described the idyllic atmosphere on women's college campuses and praised the students who "in all the colleges of the country outdo the men in their studies, win the highest prizes, attend the most difficult lectures, the old slander about deficient brain substance and mental incapacity can no longer serve as a pretext for closing the university to competing womanhood."[13] As described in chapter 6, Howard students were also widely praised for their academic accomplishments and compared favorably to students at Cornell and other prestigious universities. However, much praise was lavished on women and black college graduates, and with acknowledgement that these colleges offered an enormous freedom to students during their time on campus, both women and blacks remained almost wholly excluded from most professions and political life.

The Morrill Act aided public universities, but they had failed to implement racial integration and, most also failed to substantively include women. The second Morrill Act in 1890 sought to rectify this, but rather than forcing public universities to develop integration programs, federal funding was awarded to private "historically black colleges and universities." The act recognized that the historically black colleges and universities had often begun with a spirit of inclusivity, but policymakers reasoned that integration had been tried and had failed. By the 1890s, "black codes"—usually produced at the local level—subordinated black labor to an economic system benefiting Southern and Northern whites and rampant white-against-black brutality rendered the anti-caste hopes of earlier decades nearly inconceivable to latter generations.[14] In 1896, the U.S. Supreme Court ruled in favor of the principle of separate but equal in the case of Plessy v. Ferguson, using a similar logic that integration had failed. The majority opinion held that social equality could not be secured through legislation, but required "natural affinities, a mutual appreciation of each other's merits and a voluntary consent of individuals," and it argued that this affinity most naturally occurred along racial lines.

As colleges communicated their ideas about the fitness of education for particular groups, ideas about differentiation in forms of citizenship were consecrated and made natural. This can be seen in the language of the AMA itself. By 1898, the AMA was promoting the idea that "the passionate fervor of the Negro, the silent persistence of the Indian, the patient purpose of the Chinaman, are as important to the greatness of this nation as the conscious imperialism of the white man. This society's [the AMA] mission is to help to blend them in one and make the grand resultant the self-poised benignant, resistless force of a free nation to make a free humanity."[15] By the end of the nineteenth century, the anti-caste dream had passed and the AMA no longer fought to eradicate old status hierarchies based on color or work toward building interracial cooperation.

The anti-caste movement had initially sought to redefine citizenship and social status. But as colleges pursued strategies to maintain or increase their own status, competition engendered a highly stratified higher education field that did not prove a universalizing force for social and political participation. Noted historian Horace Mann Bond, the son of Berea and Oberlin graduates, reminds us of the degree to which meanings about race have shaped U.S. institutions: "We may now agree that [Reconstruction] involved social, economic, and political redefinition of the *status* of varied economic and racial groupings. The shape of future institutions was to be molded, superficially by the partisan elements, fundamentally by the social and economic forces which gave those elements strength and direction."[16]

As this book has emphasized, integration requires more than just legal interventions, compositional shifts, or the building of interpersonal relationships. It requires a plurality of institutional infrastructures. Furthermore, to explain segregation by invoking homophily ignores the social and political processes by which groups are defined as similar or different. Integration requires organized actors to sustain it, yet we can also find the cause of segregation in the purposeful actions of people who make organizational decisions. The integration we can envision today extends far beyond what the AMA could have imagined.[17] On one hand, the pathways to resegregation documented here remind us that hard-won social movements can be quickly rescinded. On the other hand, these cases should undermine our tendency to take the twenty-first century's deeply fractionalized, segregated field of education for granted and inspire vigorous and sustained efforts for educational equality.

Notes

Archive Abbreviations Used in the Notes

ARC   Amistad Research Center at Tulane University, New Orleans, La.

BCA   Berea College Archives, Berea, Ky.

GMBC   George J. Mitchell Department of Special Collections & Archives at Bowdoin College, Brunswick, Me.

HUA   Howard University Archives, Washington, D.C.

NARA   National Archives and Records Administration, Washington, D.C.

OCA   Oberlin College Archives, Oberlin, Ohio

RAC   Rockefeller Archive Center, Sleepy Hollow, N.Y.

SCA   Smith College Archives, Northampton, Mass.

UKSC   University of Kentucky Special Collections Research Center, Lexington, Ky.

Chapter One

1. C. Clifton Penick, "Berea College, Kentucky," *Christian Union*, July 5, 1888.

2. For a history of British anti-caste activism, see Bressey, *Empire, Race and the Politics of Anti-Caste*.

3. Karl Marx, "The Prussian State," *New York Tribune*, October 28, 1851.

4. "A Class Struggle," *New York Times*, April 29, 1865.

5. Haynes, *Noah's Curse*.

6. Stamatov, *The Origins of Global Humanitarianism*.

7. General Howard, "Education of the Colored Man," 1868 Speech, O. O. Howard Papers, GMBC.

8. Zelizer, *The Purchase of Intimacy*.

9. Farrow, Lang, and Frank, *Complicity*; Harris, *In the Shadow of Slavery*.

10. Educated Labor or Our Duty to the Americo-African Race, Annual Report of the American Missionary Association, 1867, ARC, 1.

11. Hirschman, "Rival Interpretations"; Patterson, "Slavery"; Patterson, "Freedom, Slavery, and the Modern Construction of Rights."

12. Fairchild, *Berea College*, 63.

13. Fairchild, *Oberlin*, 27.

14. Katz, "From Voluntarism to Bureaucracy"; Skocpol, Ganz, and Munson, "A Nation of Organizers"; Skocpol and Crowley, "The Rush to Organize."

15. DuBois, "The Freedmen's Bureau"; Lieberman, "The Freedmen's Bureau"; McFeely, *Yankee Stepfather*.

16. Annual Report of the American Missionary Association, 1867, ARC.

17. Fairchild, *Berea College*, 66.

18. "Berea College," *New York Times*, February 2, 1878.

19. Bourdieu, *Distinction*, 481.

20. Such romances often attracted scorn. When a "pretty American girl with fluffy blond hair" employed by the Howard University library married a Japanese student, she was pilloried in the press when he left her. See "Sad Jap Romance of American Girl," *Chicago Daily Tribune*, April 10, 1904.

21. While fewer blacks attended Oberlin and fewer whites attended Howard than the equal representation at Berea, Oberlin and Howard still enrolled more minority students than do most selective colleges in the twenty-first century.

22. "Commencement Week at Oberlin: The Social Problem Solved," *Chicago Tribune*, August 29, 1865.

23. "Article 6," *The Independent*, July 3, 1884.

24. Bailey, *Neither Carpetbaggers Nor Scalawags*; Davis, *We Will Be Satisfied*; Foner, *Freedom's Lawmakers*; Brundage, *Lynching in the New South*; Doyle, *The Etiquette of Race Relations*; Gerteis, *Class and the Color Line*; Tolnay and Beck, *A Festival of Violence*; Wells-Barnett, *The Red Record*; Woodward, *The Strange Career of Jim Crow*.

25. Mische, "Projects and Possibilities," 696.

26. Blight, *Race and Reunion*; Lemann, *Redemption*.

27. "Education," *New York Times*, August 13, 1865.

28. These archives are the Amistad Research Center, Tulane University, New Orleans, La.; The Avery Research Center for African American History and Culture, College of Charleston, S. Car.; Berea College Archives, Berea, Ky.; George J. Mitchell Special Collections, Bowdoin College, Brunswick, Me.; Moorland-Spingarn Research Center, Howard University, Washington, D.C.; Oberlin College Archives, Oberlin, Ohio.; The Rockefeller Archive Center, Sleepy Hollow, N.Y.; Smith College Archives and Sophia Smith Collection, Smith College, Northampton, Mass.; Special Collections of University of Kentucky Libraries, Lexington, Ky.

29. Gamson and Modigliani, "Media Discourses"; Schudson, *Discovering the News*; Skrentny, "Policy-Elite Perceptions"; Steensland, "Moral Classification"; Washburn, *The African American Newspaper*.

30. Tunnell, *Crucible of Reconstruction*.

31. Skowronek, *Building a New American State*; Skocpol, *Protecting Soldiers and Mothers*; Skocpol and Crowley, "The Rush to Organize."

32. See Hallett, "The Myth Incarnate"; Hallett and Fine, "Group Culture"; and Hallett and Ventresca, "Inhabited Institutions."

33. For an organizational account of race and higher education in the twentieth century, see Rojas, *From Black Power*.

34. Woodward, *Origins of the New South*, 446.

35. Coates, *Between the World and Me*, 7.

36. Wimmer, "Elementary Strategies"; Wimmer, "Herder's Heritage."

37. Wray, *Not Quite White*; Gans, "'Whitening'."

38. Winant, "Race and Race Theory"; Winant, "White Racial Projects."

39. Benford and Snow, "Framing Processes and Social Movements"; Steensland, "Why Do Policy Frames Change?"

40. Bourdieu, "What Makes a Social Class?"; Wacquant, "Symbolic Power and Group-Making." See also DiMaggio, "Culture and Cognition," for further elaboration on schemas in cultural processes.

41. Lainier-Vos, *Sinews of the Nation*; Saperstein, Penner, and Light, "Racial Formation in Perspective"; Smajda and Gerteis, "Ethnic Community."

42. Katznelson, *When Affirmative Action was White*; Katznelson and Weir, *Schooling for All*; Keyssar, *The Right to Vote*.

43. Alexander, *The New Jim Crow*; Orfield, *Schools More Separate*; Moody, "Race, School Integration, and Friendship Segregation"; Logan, Oakley, and Stowell, "School Segregation"; Saatcioglu and Carl, "The Discursive Turn."

44. Annual Report of the American Missionary Association, 1870. ARC.

45. Ibid.

46. "Colleges in the United States," *New York Times*, December 8, 1873.

47. Somers, *Genealogies of Citizenship*; Skrentny, *The Minority Rights Revolution*.

48. Haney-Lopez, *White by Law*; Loveman, "The Modern State"; Loveman and Muniz, "How Puerto Rico Became White"; Steensland, "Moral Classification"; Marx, *Making Race and Nation*; Hochschild and Powell, "Racial Reorganization"; Fox and Guglielmo, "Defining America's Racial Boundaries."

49. Solomon, "The Oberlin Model"; Solomon, *In the Company of Educated Women*; Anderson, *The Education of Blacks in the South*.

50. Meyer, Ramirez, Frank, and Schofer, "Higher Education as an Institution."

51. Schofer and Meyer, "The Worldwide Expansion."

52. Renzulli, "Organizational Environments."

53. Snyder, *120 Years of American Education*, 64.

54. Meyer, Ramirez, Frank, and Schofer, "Higher Education"; Alon, "The Evolution of Class Inequality."

55. Goldberg, *Citizens and Paupers*; Skocpol, *Protecting Soldiers and Mothers*.

56. Gerth and Mills, *From Max Weber*, 243.

57. Bourdieu, *The State Nobility*.

58. Ibid., 103.

59. Khan, *Privilege*.

60. Though certainly "public Ivies"—Michigan, Berkeley, Wisconsin—are part of the education of the elite, fewer than 2 percent of current college students attend the 225 top-tier private liberal arts schools. See Ferrall, *Liberal Arts at the Brink*.

61. DiMaggio and Powell, "The Iron Cage Revisited"; Fligstein, "Social Skill."

62. Emirbayer and Johnson, "Bourdieu and Organizational Analysis."

63. Bordin, *Women at Michigan*; Campbell and McCammon, "Elizabeth Blackwell's Heirs"; Weiss and Miller, "The Social Transformation"; Mitchell, Armstrong, and Arum, "Sieve, Incubator, Temple, Hub"; Cobb, "The First Hundred Years"; Karabel, "Status-Group Struggles"; Lamb, *Howard University Medical Department*; Peitzman, *A New and Untried Course*. On organizations' resource dependence, see Pfeffer and Salancik, *The External Control of Organizations*.

64. Lasser, *Educating Women and Men*; Geiger, *To Advance Knowledge*; Reuben, *The Making of the Modern University*; Penner and Saperstein, "How Social Status Affects Race."

65. Bonilla-Silva, *Color-Blind Racism*; Lewis, "What Group?"

66. Bonilla-Silva, "Rethinking Racism", 469.

67. Allport, *The Nature of Prejudice*; Steinman, "Settler Colonial Power."

68. Most recently, scholars have considered how to build "substantive inclusion." This requires that group affiliations are acknowledged, recognized, and valued. Importantly, substantive inclusion runs directly counter to color-blind ideology, and measures how actors interpret situations as exclusionary or inclusive. To support substantive inclusion, administrative and faculty can acknowledge when and where racial hierarchies are built into academic understandings of merit. These can be remedied by strengthening diversity in curriculum, actively teaching students skills for engaging in contentious dialogue, and hiring tenure-track faculty who are assured academic freedom. For further reading, see Carter, *Stubborn Roots*; Carter, "Race and Cultural Flexibility."

69. Moody, "Race, School Integration and Friendship Segregation"; Reardon, Grewal, Kalogrides, and Greenberg, "Brown Fades"; Tyson, *Integration Interrupted*.

70. Orfield and Lee, *Brown at 50*, 12.

71. Massey and Denton, "The Dimensions of Residential Segregation"; Crowder, Pais, and South, "Neighborhood Diversity."

72. Becker, "Making Inclusive Communities"; Berbrier, "Half the Battle"; Berbrier, "Making Minorities"; Benhabib, *The Claims of Culture*; Binder, *Contentious Curricula*; Brubaker, *Ethnicity without Groups*; Wells, Holme, Revilla, and Atanda, *Both Sides Now*; Goldsmith, "Schools, Neighborhoods or Both?"; Goldsmith, "Schools' Role"; Horton, "Black Education at Oberlin."

73. Lainier-Vos, *Sinews of the Nation*; Krause, *The Good Project*; Johnson, Dowd, and Ridgeway, "Legitimacy as a Social Process"; Johnson, *Backstage at the Revolution*.

74. Lamont and Molnar, "The Study of Boundaries"; Lamont and Bail, "Sur les frontières."

75. Loveman, "The Modern State"; Loveman and Muniz, "How Puerto Rico Became White."

76. Bloemraad, *Becoming a Citizen*; Brubaker, *Nationalism Reframed*; Calhoun, "Nationalism and Ethnicity"; Smith, *Civic Ideals*; Smith, *The Ethnic Origins of Nations*; King and Smith, "Racial Orders"; Glenn, *Unequal Freedom*.

77. Southern states continued to mobilize against integration in the 1950s. For an organizational account, see Irons, *Reconstituting Whiteness*.

78. Keyssar, *The Right to Vote*.

79. Katznelson and Weir, *Schooling for All*, 8; Hochschild and Scovronick, *American Dream*.

80. Guinier and Torres, *The Miner's Canary*; Conway, *Utopian Dream*.

81. Orfield, *Schools More Separate*.

82. These figures obtained from college or university website enrollment data for either the class of 2018 or 2019. It is important to note that selective private

universities compete for students from a national pool, and this draw is important for their reputation as national rather than regional universities in rankings.

83. Carnevale and Strohl, *Separate and Unequal.*

84. *Fisher v. Univ. of Texas at Austin*, 645 F. Supp. 2d 587, 591 (W.D. Tex. 2009); *Fisher v. University of Texas at Austin*, 570 U.S. ___ (2013): 8. The Supreme Court has now determined that diversity in admissions cannot be used to right previous wrongs but rather, as decided in *Grutter v. Bollinger*, racial diversity can be a "plus factor" in scoring individual applicants where it serves the interest of the state. Justice Thomas challenged that state interest in cultivating a diverse set of future leaders has been used in multiple ways; he argued that in the 1950s, "segregationists likewise defended segregation in that it provided more leadership opportunities for blacks."

85. Mabee, "A Negro Boycott."

86. *Fisher v. University of Texas at Austin*, 645 F. Supp. 2d, 591.

87. Logan, Oakely, and Stowell, "School Segregation"; Reardon, Grewal, Kalogrides and Greenberg, "Brown Fades."

88. Soskis, "The Problem of Charity."

89. Many colleges, including Columbia and Cornell, offered students opportunities to earn their tuition and fees through on-campus labor. This "learning and labor" model initiated at Oberlin and carried over to Berea and Howard, was an extension of a larger movement to ensure students "equality of opportunity" access to college and colleges—even the most elite. The industrial education movement, mobilized by Booker T. Washington, shifted the focal point of the black college program from one of self-sustenance to industrial training.

Chapter Two

1. Congressional Globe, 39th Cong., 2nd sess., January 3, 1867, 251–52.

2. Captain Henry Wirz, who commanded the notorious Andersonville Prison, where Union soldiers were held prisoners of war, was brought to military tribunal and eventually hanged. A brutal guerilla fighter from eastern Tennessee, Champ Ferguson, was also hanged.

3. Alexander and Smith, "Citizen and Enemy"; Wagner-Pacifici, *The Art of Surrender*; Wagner-Pacifici and Hall, "Resolution of Social Conflict."

4. Go, *American Empire.*

5. "Negro Courts in Mississippi," *Chicago Tribune*, August 12, 1865.

6. Berlin, *Slaves without Masters*; McIntyre, *Criminalizing a Race*; Nystrom, "Racial Identity and Reconstruction"; Perkins, "The Nineteenth Century Black Women"; Wilder, *Ebony and Ivy.*

7. The 1860 Census documents that one in every thirty Southern whites owned more than twenty slaves, the qualification for classification as a "planter." See Berlin, *Generations of Captivity* for a thorough discussion of regional variations in slavery.

8. Somers, "Citizenship and the Place of the Public Sphere," 589; Somers, *Genealogies of Citizenship*; Glenn, *Unequal Freedom*; Smith, *Civic Ideals.*

9. Benhabib, *The Claims of Culture*; Bloemraad, *Becoming a Citizen.*

10. Hochschild and Powell, "Racial Reorganization."

11. This act played a crucial role in shaping future welfare state development. See Skocpol, *Protecting Soldiers and Mothers*; Orloff, *The Politics of Pensions*; and Goldberg and Alan, *Citizens and Paupers.*

12. "The Freedmen's Bureau: Its Organization and the Progress of its Work," *New York Times*, June 26, 1865.

13. Howard, *Autobiography*, vol. 2.

14. General Oliver Otis Howard to the Annual Meeting of the American Missionary Association, 1868, ARC.

15. Vaughn, *Schools for All.*

16. By 1853, Mann also turned his attention to the potential democratic influence of private colleges. In this spirit, he helped launch Antioch College in Ohio.

17. King, *Separate and Unequal*, 5.

18. Katznelson, *When Affirmative Action Was White.*

19. Zolberg and Woon, "Why Islam is like Spanish"; Lamont and Bail, "Sur les frontières."

20. Keyssar, *The Right to Vote.*

21. "The Conflicting Reports from the Southern States," *New York Times*, January 23, 1866.

22. "South Carolina in Convention," *Chicago Tribune*, December 2, 1865.

23. "The South As It Is," *New York Times*, August 22, 1865.

24. "President Johnson's Speech," *Chicago Tribune*, October 13, 1865.

25. Steinberg, "The Talk and Back Talk," 14.

26. Guterl, *American Mediterranean.*

27. Schurz, *Report on Conditions*, 23.

28. Berezin, "Events as Templates of Possibility"; Lamont and Molnar, "Toward a Comparative Sociology"; Sewell, "Historical Events"; Steensland, *The Failed Welfare Revolution.*

29. Slez and Martin, "Political Action and Party Formation," 63.

30. For this reason, I compare the conservative *New York Times* with articles in the reform-oriented *Chicago Tribune.*

31. Campbell, "Ideas, Politics and Public Policy"; Jacobs and Sobieraj, "Narrative, Public Policy, and Political Legitimacy."

32. "Black Voters," *Chicago Tribune*, July 14, 1865.

33. "The South: The Progress of Material Development," *New York Times*, December 13, 1865.

34. "The Government and the Freedmen," *New York Times*, June 6, 1865.

35. "Employers for the Freedmen," *New York Times*, June 18, 1865.

36. Freedmen solicited counsel both in securing any labor contracts and in negotiating the terms of employment. Many Southerners were resistant to both. Powell, *New Masters*, 115; Hahn, *A Nation under Our Feet.*

37. "Negro Will Not Work," *Chicago Tribune*, May 22, 1865.

38. "The Freedmen's Home Farm: Jeff Davis' Old Plantation," *New York Times*, August 22, 1865.

39. "Abandoned Plantations," *Chicago Tribune*, September 24, 1865.

40. Potter and Schamel, "The Homestead Act"; Shanks, "The Homestead Act."

41. Schurz, *Report on Conditions*, 14.

42. Ibid.

43. Ibid., 125.

44. "Land for the Freedmen," *Chicago Tribune*, December 29, 1865.

45. "How To Make Slaveholders Pay Wages," *Chicago Tribune*, July 18, 1865.

46. "Land for the Freedmen," *Chicago Tribune*, December 29, 1865.

47. "Abandoned Plantations," *Chicago Tribune*, September 24, 1865.

48. Foner, *Reconstruction*, 246.

49. Colby, "The Freedmen's Bureau," 221.

50. Schurz, *Report on Conditions*, 26.

51. "Negro Troops at the South," *Chicago Tribune*, August 28, 1865.

52. "How to Make Slaveholders Pay Wages."

53. "Reducing Our Armies," *Chicago Tribune*," July 31, 1865.

54. "How to Make Slaveholders Pay Wages."

55. "Our Charleston Correspondent," *New York Times*, May 22, 1865.

56. "The Personnel of Reconstruction," *Chicago Tribune*, April 27, 1865. See Lamont and Bail, "Sur les frontières."

57. See Lamont and Bail, "Sur les frontières."

58. "Proceedings of the Colored National Convention Held in Rochester, July 6th, 7th, and 8th, 1853, Rochester," Frederick Douglas Project: Claims of our Common Cause, 1853, accessed July 3, 2015, http://rbscp.lib.rochester.edu /4368.

59. "Wendell Phillips on Negro Suffrage and the War," *New York Times*, June 10, 1865.

60. "The Suffrage in Mississippi," *Chicago Tribune*, June 18, 1865.

61. "A Fallacy Exposed," *Chicago Tribune*, July 12, 1865.

62. "Southern Statesmanship," *Chicago Tribune*, June 15, 1865.

63. "Wendell Phillips."

64. "South Carolina in Convention," *Chicago Tribune*, December 2, 1865.

65. "Negro Suffrage in the South," *Chicago Tribune*, May 19, 1865.

66. "Negro Suffrage: Letter from John Stuart Mill," *Chicago Tribune*, September 22, 1865.

67. "A Class Revolution," *New York Times*, April 29, 1865.

68. "Editorial Article 2," *Chicago Tribune*, March 2, 1865.

69. New Granada is now Columbia and Panama.

70. DuBois, *Black Reconstruction*, 88–90.

71. United States Congress, *Report of the Joint Committee*, 172.

72. "Education Follows the Flag," *Chicago Tribune*, April 3, 1865.

73. "What We Owe to the New South: The Prevalence and Density of Popular Ignorance," *New York Times*, June 24, 1865.

74. "Answers to Questions: How to Develop the Negro Race," *New York Times*, November 12, 1865. Italics in the original.

75. "Answers to Questions."

76. "Education of the Negroes," *The New York Times*, November 15, 1866.

77. "The National Bureau of Education," *Chicago Tribune*, March 24, 1866.

78. "Education—Public Schools," *Chicago Tribune*, May 20, 1865.

79. "Our Reconstruction Policy," *Chicago Tribune*, April 18, 1865.

80. "A Dominant Fact in the Southern Situation," *New York Times*, August 10, 1865.

81. Annual Report of the American Missionary Association, 1866, ARC.

82. "Education Follows the Flag," *Chicago Tribune*, April 3, 1865.

83. Annual Report of the American Missionary Association, 1870. ARC.

84. "What We Owe to the New South: The Prevalence and Density of Popular Ignorance," *New York Times*, June 24, 1865.

85. "The Education of Freedmen," *New York Times*, May 21, 1865.

86. "Educational Convention," *New York Times*, August 10, 1865.

87. Archival records of Howard's involvement in teacher hiring and retention are found in the American Missionary Collection, May 1866–June 1868, Box 22, Washington, D.C., ARC. Correspondence, Freedmen's Bureau Period, May 1865–Spring 1874, O. O. Howard Collection, M91.3, GMBC.

88. There were limitations, however, on allocating funds to religious education. As such, colleges organized by churches could receive funds for general operating costs but not for theological programs. Since many of the voluntary societies were sponsored by religious organizations, this sometimes proved challenging.

89. Butchart, *Schooling the Freed People*, 80; Jones, *Soldiers of Light and Love*.

90. Anderson, *The Education of Blacks in the South*; Butchart, *Schooling the Freed People*.

91. Annual Report of the American Missionary Association, 1865, ARC.

92. Ibid., 19, 21.

93. "The Freedmen's Schools," *Harper's Weekly*, October 3, 1868.

94. Butchart, *Schooling the Freed People*, 80.

95. Clemens, "From City Club to Nation State," 82.

96. See Thelin, *A History of American Higher Education*.

97. Padgett and Powell, *The Emergence of Organizations and Markets*.

98. Snyder, *120 Years of American Education*, 64.

99. Soysal and Strang, "Construction of the First Mass Education System," emphasized the expansion of higher education as a result of the interaction of social institutions and competition between state, church, and "societal groups." Yet, Soysal and Strang restricted their analysis to the national level to capture "the symbolic construction of a unified national system of education" (277). By limiting their analysis, they failed to capture racialized competition, and may have missed an important motivational factor and mechanism for legitimating high-status groups. While higher education expansion has largely been studied at the state level, investigating the within-country struggles may be important for highlighting competition prior to diffusion.

100. Snyder, *120 Years of American Education*; DuBois and Dill, *The College-Bred Negro American*, 100.

101. Act of July 2, 1862 (Morrill Act), Public Law 37–108, Enrolled Acts and Resolutions of Congress, 1789–1996, Record Group 11, General Records of the United States Government, NARA.

102. Notably, Representative Justin Smith Morrill, author of the legislation, was from Vermont.

103. Katz, *The Irony of Early School Reform*.

104. Holt, *Black Over White*.

105. The Ku Klux Klan later claimed responsibility for Benjamin Randolph's 1868 murder. Randolph was gunned down while campaigning for reelection.

106. Snider, *Light on the Hill*.

107. Fairchild, *Oberlin*, 27.

108. American Union Commission, *American Union Commission*.

109. Thurston Chase, "Report of the Richmond Agent to Sept. 1, 1865," *New York Times*, September 17, 1865.

110. Though Washburn enrolled very few black students, its white students defended integration well into the 1890s. For instance, students joined in protest when a rival white school refused to play Washburn's baseball team, which included black athletes. See Article III, The Articles of Association in the Incorporation of Lincoln College, 1865, University Archives, Mabee Library, Washburn University.

111. The medical profession had yet to become a prestigious field. See Starr, *The Social Transformation of American Medicine*.

112. The Fourteenth Amendment, or Equal Protection Clause, passed in 1868, and the Fifteenth Amendment extended citizenship in 1870.

113. Marshall, *Citizenship and Social Class*.

Chapter Three

1. Karabel, *The Chosen*; Stevens, *Creating a Class*.

2. Allport, *The Nature of Prejudice*.

3. Beard, *The Providence of God*, 16.

4. Beard, *A Crusade of Brotherhood*.

5. Ibid., 23.

6. Acts 17:26, Fiftieth Annual Report of the American Missionary Association, 1896, ARC, 103.

7. Correspondence of Reverend Samuel Hunt to Reverend Michael Strieby, May 17, 1866, American Missionary Association Collection, Box 112, Document 89912, ARC.

8. Tenth Annual Report of the American Missionary Association, 1856, ARC.

9. E. H. Fairchild, "The South," *Chicago Daily Tribune*, August 9, 1880.

10. Fairchild, *Berea College*.

11. Ibid., 63–66.

12. C. C. White Leigh, "Colored Slaves," *Harper's Weekly*, January 30, 1864, 71.

13. Twenty-Fifth Annual Report of the American Missionary Association, 1871, ARC.

14. Black, "Berea College," 271.

15. Fairchild, *Oberlin*, 27. The nineteenth century term "literary" is synonymous with "academic."

16. Black, "Berea College," 269.

17. Fairchild, *Oberlin*, 32.

18. Ibid., 57.

19. Oberlin College Annual Report, 1899, OCA, 53.

20. Fairchild *Oberlin*, 7.

21. These colleges included Antioch, Dartmouth, Bowdoin, Brown, Knox, Middlebury and Yale.

22. Between 1816 and 1867, the American Colonization Society transported around 13,000 emigrants from the United States to Liberia. The American Colonization Society did not disband until 1964. See the African-American Mosaic: A Library of Congress Resource Guide for the Study of Black History and Culture, accessed April 27, 2016, https://www.loc.gov/exhibits/african/afam002.html; *The Liberator*, January 10, 1835, 5–6. For more on the Lane Rebels, see Baumann, *Constructing Black Education*.

23. Fairchild, *Oberlin*, 20, 23.

24. Ibid., 57.

25. Fairchild, *Oberlin*, 52. Emphasis added.

26. Oberlin College Board of Trustees, Minutes of the Meeting of the Board, June 26, 1866, Record Group Board of Trustees II, 1834–1906, vol. 1, OCA.

27. Oberlin College Board of Trustees, Minutes of the Meeting of the Board, June 26, 1866 and August 26, 1867, Record Group Board of Trustees II, 1834–1906, vol. 1, OCA.

28. *Cleveland Plain Dealer*, March 3, 1862 in Blodgett, "John Mercer Langston."

29. *Lorrain County News*, February 19, 1862 in Blodgett, "John Mercer Langston."

30. Woodward, *Origins of the New South*, 6.

31. Despite this, Clay did not grant manumission to the enslaved persons at his Whitehall plantation until 1844.

32. Annual Report of the American Missionary Association, 1856, ARC.

33. "A Journey to Virginia in December, 1859," Oberlin Thursday Lectures, Addresses, and Lectures, 1898, OCA, 158–59.

34. Fee, *Autobiography*, 146, 154.

35. Ibid., 183.

36. "Kentucky Kuklux Again," *New York Times*, April 17, 1871.

37. Records of the Education Division of the Bureau of Refugees, Freedmen, and Abandoned Lands, 1865–1871, Rolls 20–21, M803, NARA.

38. "Life's Battle Begins," *Chicago Daily Tribune*, June 25, 1885.

39. *Kentucky Register* articles quoted in "Article 2," *The Independent*, August 21, 1873.

40. "An Appeal for Aid to a Kentucky College," *New York Times*, March 9, 1868.

41. "Gen. Howard and the Howard University," *New York Times*, August 26, 1867; "Article 5," *Friends' Review: A Religious, Literary and Miscellaneous Journal*, August 22, 1868; "Literary Institutions," *The Independent*, August 27, 1878.

42. Woodword, *Origins of the New South*, 320–25.

43. John Francis Cook et al. to the Honorable Senators and Members of the House of Representatives in Congress Assembled, December 1865, 39A-H4, Committee on the District of Columbia, Petitions & Memorials, ser. 582, 39th Cong., U.S. Senate, Record Group 46, NARA.

44. Moore, *Leading the Race*.

45. Tasso Corben, "Washington in Mid-Summer," *The Independent*, August 12, 1869. See also, "A Visit to Howard University," *Zion's Herald*, June 28, 1877.

46. Like at Howard, many white students enrolled in the Straight University Law School. In a report to the AMA, the university reported that thirty of its fifty law students were white. W. S. Alexander, "The Freedmen: Straight University, New Orleans," *American Missionary* 36, no. 8 (August 1882): 234.

47. O. O. Howard, "Howard University," *The Independent*, June 24, 1869.

48. Ibid.

49. Records of the Assistant Commissioner for the District of Columbia, Bureau of Refugees, Freedmen, and Abandoned Lands, 1865–1869, Microfilm Publication M1055, Roll 21, Miscellaneous Reports and Lists, NARA.

50. "Howard University: From Our Own Correspondent," *New York Times*, July 8, 1873.

51. Allport, *The Nature of Prejudice*; Goffman, *Aylums*.

52. Binder, "For Love and Money," 568.

53. Tyson, *Integration Interrupted*; Carter *Stubborn Roots*.

54. Oberlin College Catalogue, 1908, OCA.

55. International student enrollment reflected the colleges' connection to missionary work.

56. Here a "class" is best translated for modern readers as a "group." Annual Circular to Alumni and Friends, 1880, OCA.

57. Fairchild, *Oberlin*, 28.

58. Ibid., 27.

59. Fewer than twenty-five students graduated from the college course. Cowles, Catalogue and Record of Colored Students, Office of the Secretary, Oberlin College, OCA.

60. Annual Report of the American Missionary Association, 1856, ARC.

61. "An Appeal for Aid to a Kentucky College," *New York Times*, March 9, 1868.

62. Annual Reports of Faculty and Officers to Trustees, Comments of Trustees, June 16, 1880, BCA.

63. Report of L. V. Dodge to Trustees, June, 1891, BCA.

64. "Berea College, Kentucky," *The Independent*, November 20, 1879.

65. Annual Reports of Faculty and Officers to Trustees, Comments of Trustees, June 16, 1880, BCA.

66. "Berea College Endowment," *New York Times*, May 8, 1881.

67. O. O. Howard, "Howard University," *New York Evangelist*, December 26, 1872.

68. C. Churchill, "Howard University," *The Independent*, February 10, 1870.

69. Ibid.

70. M. E. Strieby, "Howard University," *Christian Union*, February 26, 1873.

71. William W. Patton, "The Colored Race," *Chicago Daily Tribune*, May 27, 1877.

72. C. Churchill, "Howard University."

73. Moldow, *Women Doctors in Gilded Age Washington*, 37–41; Howard University Alumni Catalogue, 1867–1896, HUA.

74. Henry M. Field, "Howard University," *New York Evangelist*, February 27, 1879.

75. Board of Trustees Minutes, 1853, OCA.

76. Jackson-Coppin, *Reminiscences of School Life*, 19.

77. "Wellington Rescuers," *Chicago Tribune*, July 11, 1874.

78. Francis L. Cardozo taught Latin at the university from 1870 until June 1872. Frederick Douglas was a member of the Howard Board of Trustees from 1870 to 1876. Reverend Garnet was a member of the Howard Board of Trustees from 1867 to 1869. He was the first African American elected to the board. Oberlin graduate John Mercer Langston was a professor of law in the Howard University law department from 1868 to 1875. He served as the department's dean from 1870 to 1875. From 1873 to 1875, Langston was the university's vice president and acting president. Dyson, *Howard University*.

79. "Literary Institutions," *The Independent*," August 27, 1868.

80. Though individual alumni information is not consistently available for all three colleges, a Howard University publication reveals that most alumni pursued careers in the North, with a small number each year locating in the South. Howard lawyers were most likely to remain in Washington, D.C., and approximately 20 percent of theology students pursued international mission work. Alumni Catalogue of Howard University, 1867–1896, HUA.

81. "Literary Institutions."

82. Ibid.

83. Jackson-Coppin, *Reminiscences of School Life*, 15.

84. Ibid., 15

85. Ibid., 14.

86. "A Case of Too Much Zeal," *The Washington Post*, June 2, 1895.

87. Professor Howard Murray, Report to the Trustees, 1901, BCA.

88. Jackson-Coppin, *Reminiscences of School Life*, 20

89. Alumni File, Record Group 28, OCA, 206.

90. Collegiate athletics appeared on some campuses by the mid-1880s, but did not fully take hold at Berea, Howard, and Oberlin until the 1890s.

91. Wilson, *Berea College*, 44.

92. Little, "The Extra-Curricular Activities"; Moore *Leading the Race*. It should be noted that the archives for Berea and Oberlin have better records for their literary societies, whereas information on Howard's societies comes from the *Washington Post*.

93. Jackson-Coppin, *Reminiscences of School Life.*

94. Letter from to Alfred V. Churchill, January 21, 1941, Anna Julia Cooper Alumni File, RG 28, Box 206, OCA.

95. Applegate, *The Most Famous Man in America.*

96. "Education at the South," *New York Times*, January 26, 1869.

97. Fairchild, *Berea College*, 63.

98. "Education Follows the Flag," *Chicago Tribune*, April 31, 1865.

99. C. Clifton Penick, "Berea College, Kentucky," *Christian Union*, July 5, 1888.

100. "Article 6," *The Independent*, July 3, 1884.

Chapter Four

1. "Colleges in the United States," *New York Times*, December 8, 1873.

2. Swing, *James Harris Fairchild*, 223.

3. In his inaugural address, Fairchild described the impact of the Civil War on the college: "In a school thus kept in sympathy with the great movements of the day, it was impossible that the call of the country, in the hour of its peril, should not meet an earnest response; and so we parted with our young men, in scores and hundreds, glad of the spirit of Christian patriotism that was in them, and sorrowing most of all that the faces of many of them we should see no more." Swing, *James Harris Fairchild*, 222.

4. John Mercer Langston assembled volunteers for the Fifty-Fourth Massachusetts, the first black regiment, and Giles Shurtleff, an Oberlin alumnus and future trustee of the college, led the "Monroe Rifles," a troop of Oberlin students. Fairchild, *Historical Sketch*, 22.

5. For a discussion of the early nineteenth century college curricula, see Rudolph, *The American College*, 110–26.

6. Bishop, *A History of Cornell*, 74.

7. "Colleges in the United States," *New York Times*, December 8, 1873.

8. Alumni Catalogue of Howard University, 1867–1896, HUA.

9. The Commissioner of Education Reports did not record data by race or ethnicity.

10. During the 1870s, for instance, blacks were massacred in both South Carolina and New Jersey. Theodore Davis, "The Patenberg Massacre," *Harper's Weekly: A Journal of Civilization*, October 12, 1872, 796.

11. C. H. Richards, "Protection by Development," AMA Annual Conference, 1878, ARC.

12. "The Freedmen," *The New York Times*, August 20, 1865.

13. Hallett and Fine, "Group Cultures," 10.

14. Steinmetz, "The Devil's Handwriting."

15. Holt, *Black over White*; Hahn, *A Nation under Our Feet.*

16. Turkel, *Heroes of the American Reconstruction*, 161. DuBois, *Black Reconstruction*, 420–428; Hahn, *A Nation Under Our Feet.*

17. "Time Works Wonders," *Harper's Weekly*, April 9, 1870, 232.

18. "The Colored Conventions: The Demand for Education to be Vigorously Pushed," *New York Times*, December 14, 1883; Giozzo, "John Jones and the Black Convention Movement."

19. Representative Alonso Ransier (R-FL), 1.2 Cong., rec. 1311–1314, 1874.

20. Congressional Record, vol. 2, part 1, 43rd Cong., 1st sess., 1874, 565–67.

21. Annual Report of the American Missionary Association, 1872, ARC.

22. Congressional Record, vol. 2, part 1, 43rd Cong., 1st sess., 1874, 565–67.

23. Ibid. A fierce advocate for civil rights, Charles Sumner died in 1874.

24. Cain, "All We Ask Is Equal Laws," 565–67; See also, Hine, "Black Politicians in Reconstruction"; Lynch, *The Facts of Reconstruction*; Ransier, "Civil Rights" *Congressional Record*, House, 43rd Cong., 1st sess., February 7, 1874, 1314; and Rankin, "The Origins of Black Leadership."

25. Congressional Record, House, 43rd Cong., 1st sess., February 3, 1875, 982.

26. "Editorial," *Harper's Weekly*, December 20, 1871.

27. "Protection by development," speech delivered by C. H. Richards to the Annual Meeting of the American Missionary Association, 1878, ARC.

28. Franklin, *Reconstruction after the Civil War*.

29. The Civil Rights Cases, 109 U.S. 3, 1883, U.S. Supreme Court.

30. T. Thomas Fortune, "The Civil Rights Decision," *N.Y. Globe*, October 20, 1883, in Lado, "A Question of Justice."

31. Civil Rights Cases, 109 U.S. 3, 1883, U.S. Supreme Court.

32. Congressional Record, vol. 2, part 1, 43rd Cong., 1st sess., 565–67.

33. Cable, *The Silent South*, 26.

34. The United States Bureau of Education, *Report of the U.S. Commissioner of Education 1901–1902*, vol. 1 (Washington, D.C.: Government Printing Office), 201–24.

35. William Lloyd Garrison, "Results of Emancipation," *The Independent*, January 13, 1870.

36. "Colored Law Graduates," *Washington Post*, May 29, 1894.

37. Davis, "*We Will Be Satisfied.*"

38. Cable, *The Silent South*, 26.

39. "To Aid Fleeing Negroes," *New York Times*, April 24, 1879.

40. "New Homes for Freedmen," *New York Times*, January 23, 1879.

41. "A Great Exodus of Negroes," *New York Times*, August 12, 1880.

42. "The Old Year," *Chicago Daily Tribune*, January 1, 1880.

43. Foner, *Reconstruction*.

44. Richardson, *Christian Reconstruction*, 21, 223.

45. U.S. Senate, *Report and Testimony of the Select Committee of the United States Senate to Investigate the Causes of the Removal of the Negroes from the Southern States to the Northern States*, Senate Report 693, part I, 46th Cong., 2nd sess., part I (Washington, D.C.: Government Printing Office, 1880), 93–98.

46. Douglass, 1880, quoted in Aptheker, *Woman's Legacy*, 724.

47. Painter, *Exodusters*; Jack, *The St. Louis African American Community*.

48. Letters from Reverend Burdett to Reverend Strieby, May 1877, AMA Box 57: 45243, ARC.

49. Burdett was born into slavery in 1829 and departed for Kansas in 1878. Reverend Gabriel Burdett to Reverend Michael Strieby, August 2, 1877, Box 57, Folder 1877, Document 45256, ARC.

50. Ibid.

51. The United States Bureau of Education. *Report of the U.S. Commissioner of Education*, vol. 1 (Washington, D.C.: Government Printing Office, 1901), 195–96.

52. Twenty-Fifth Annual Report of the American Missionary Association, 1871, ARC, 85.

53. Annual Report of the American Missionary Association, 1867, ARC.

54. Cunningham, "Mobilizing Ethnic Competition."

55. Henry Ward Beecher to the Annual Meeting of the American Missionary Association, 1870, ARC.

56. For discussions of the changing demographics and the rise of cultural institutions, see DiMaggio, "Cultural Entrepreneurship"; Beisel, *Imperiled Innocents*; Douglas, *Jim Crow Moves North*.

57. In the 1857 Dred Scott case, Chief Justice Roger Taney argued that, unlike enslaved blacks, American Indians could become citizens. By 1868, however, American Indians were explicitly excluded from the Fourteenth Amendment.

58. Annual Report of the American Missionary Association, 1871, ARC. See also, Glasrud, *Brothers to Buffalo Soldiers*.

59. Annual Meeting of the American Missionary Association, 1874. ARC.

60. "How to Make Slaveholders Pay Wages," *Chicago Tribune*, July 18, 1865.

61. Annual Report of the American Missionary Association, 1871. ARC.

62. Ibid.

63. "Appeal from Executive Board National Equal Rights League," *The Liberator*, December 23, 1864.

64. American Missionary Association Annual Report, 1874. ARC.

65. Speech of General Oliver Otis Howard to the American Missionary Association Annual Meeting, 1867. ARC.

66. Douglas, *Purity and Danger*.

67. *American Missionary Magazine*, vol. 32, issue 5, May 1878, ARC, 130.

68. *American Missionary Magazine*, vol. 32, issue 8, August 1878, ARC, 227.

69. Lamb, *Howard University Medical Department*; DuBois, *The College-Bred Negro American*.

70. Lathrop, "*The South.*"

71. Rankin, "The Origins of Black Leadership"; Moore, *Leading the Race*; Kelley, *Right to Ride*.

72. Black Press Archives, Moorland-Spingarn Research Center at Howard University.

73. Olzak and Shanahan, "Racial Policy and Racial Conflict."

74. Jewell, *Race, Social Reform*.

75. Annual Meeting of the American Missionary Association, 1877, ARC.

76. J. P. Thompson, "The Freedmen: Two Simple Rules," *American Missionary*, vol. 32, issue 1, January 1878, ARC, 15.

77. *American Missionary Magazine*, vol. 32, issue 6, June 1878, ARC, 162.

78. American Missionary Association Annual Meeting, 1878, ARC.

79. Michael Strieby, "The Freedmen: Providential Calls," *American Missionary*, vol. 33, issue 12, December 1879, ARC, 374.

80. Sauder and Lancaster, "Do Rankings Matter?"

81. Peabody Education Fund, *Proceedings*. Like Rockefeller's General Education Board, the Peabody Foundation comprised both Southern and Northern men. It included a former Oberlin student, Reverend H. B. Whipple.

82. Painter, *Exodusters*, 107. Painter identifies Atticus Haygood and George W. Cable as the two leading "white experts on black people."

83. Barrows, *John Henry Barrows*, 56.

84. Moses, "Black Messiahs and Uncle Toms," 95.

85. There is no record of the exact itinerary for this trip at the RAC and it is unlikely that documentation of it has been preserved. Discussions of this trip appear in the 1901 Trustee Minutes for the General Education Board and were confirmed by newspaper coverage.

86. Clemens, "From City Club to Nation State," 381.

87. Organization of the Preliminary Conference, January 15, 1902, General Education Board Minutes, 1902–1906, Box 23, RAC.

88. Special Meeting of the General Education Board, February 7, 1907, General Education Board Minutes, Box 23, RAC.

89. Minutes of the Board of Trustees Meetings, 1903–1930, General Education Board Minutes, RAC.

90. LSRM Series 3.8, Interracial Relations, Box 96, Folder 966, Association for the Study of Negro Life and History, RAC.

91. Review of Board of Trustee Minutes, 1900–1918, General Education Board, RAC.

92. Executive Committee, General Education Board Minutes, April 9, 1909, Box 23, Board of Trustees Minutes, RAC.

93. Letters between Dr. Wallace Buttrick, Secretary, General Education Board and P. P. Claxton, Commissioner of the U.S. Department of the Interior, General Education Board, Series 1, Subseries 2, Box 264, Folder 2727, RAC. Claxton invited Buttrick, GEB; Dr. Wickliffe Rose, Southern Education Board, Secretary of the Rockefeller Sanitary Commission and General Agent of the Peabody Educational Fund; Mr. Starr Murphy, no agency listed; Dr. James Dillard, Jeanes Fund and Slater Fund; John Glenn, Russell Sage Foundation; and James Bertram, Carnegie Corporation.

94. Letter from Frederick T. Gates to William H. Taft, President of the United States, January 25, 1911, General Education Board Minutes, Box 2, Folder 28, Frederick T. Gates Collection, General Education Board, RAC.

95. Minutes of the Annual Meeting of the Board of Trustees, January 23, 1906, General Education Board Minutes, Box 23, RAC.

96. Minutes of the Executive Committee, March 27, 1906, General Education Board, Box 23, RAC.

97. Clemens, "From City Club to Nation State," 379.

98. Harlan, *Separate and Unequal*, 86.

99. Bourdieu, *Language and Symbolic Power*, 127.

100. Podolny, *Status Signals*.

101. Douglas, *Purity and Danger*.

102. Barman, "Asserting Difference."

103. Report of the Commissioner of Education, vol. 2 (Washington, D.C.: U.S. Government Printing Office), 1631–33, 1696–98.

104. The General Education Board, An Account of Its Activities, 1902–1914, RAC, 193.

105. For a more elaborate history of Northern foundations and Southern public education, see Anderson and Moss, *Dangerous Donations*; Walters and James, "Schooling for Some."

106. Clemens, "From City Club to Nation State," 82.

107. Bourdieu, *The State Nobility*; Gieryn, "A Space for Place."

108. Solomon, *In the Company of Educated Women*, 96.

109. Horowitz, *Alma Mater*.

110. Karabel, *The Chosen*.

111. Jencks and Riesman, *The Academic Revolution*; Wechsler, *The Qualified Student*; Lifschitz, Sauder, and Stevens, "Football as a Status System."

Chapter Five

1. "Colleges in the United States," *New York Times*, December 8, 1873.

2. Lifschitz, Sauder, and Stevens, "Football as a Status System."

3. Horowitz, *Alma Mater*, 56.

4. Bradley and Charles, "Uneven Inroads"; Bradley, "The Incorporation of Women."

5. Stille, *History of the United States Sanitary Commission*, 179.

6. Minor v. Happersett, 88 U.S. 21 Wall., 162, (1874).

7. "Colleges in the United States," *New York Times*, December 8, 1873.

8. Butchart, *Schooling the Freedpeople*.

9. Peitzman, *A New and Untried Course*, 112.

10. Fee, Brown, Lazarus, and Theerman, "Medical Education for Women."

11. Münsterberg, *The Americans*, 568.

12. "Will Cure Many Ills," *Washington Post*, May 11, 1897.

13. Aptheker, *Woman's Legacy*, 100; Morantz-Sanchez, *Sympathy & Science*, xviii.

14. Solomon, *In the Company of Educated Women*, 84.

15. "Colleges in the United States," *New York Times*, December 8, 1873.

16. Barnes, "Crossing the Invisible Line."

17. Bordin, *Women at Michigan*, 4.

18. "Coeducation Abolished," *Chicago Daily Tribune*, June 29, 1885. See also Munroe, *The University of Delaware*.

19. Minutes of the Board of Trustees, March 4–5, 1896, Series III, Document Files Supporting Minutes of the Board, Box 4, OCA.

20. Perkins, "The African-American Female."

21. DuBois, *The College-Bred Negro American.* The predominately black colleges surveyed by DuBois were Biddle, Lincoln, Atlanta Baptist College, Virginia Union University for men, and Spelman and Hartshorn Memorial for women.

22. Cooper, *A Voice from the South,* 75.

23. Anna Julia Cooper was a tireless reformer, educator, and classics scholar. Educated at Oberlin, she continued her education later in life at the Sorbonne in Paris, where she became the first black woman to earn a doctorate in history.

24. Perkins, "The African-American Female."

25. Goldin and Katz, "Mass Secondary Schooling," 382.

26. Frances Hazen, "Young Women," *Oberlin Students' Monthly,* May 1859, Student Life Records (Publications), Record Group 19/00/1, Box 1, OCA, 267

27. Ibid.

28. Swing, *James Harris Fairchild,* 162.

29. Ginzberg, "The 'Joint Education of the Sexes'," 71.

30. Cravath, *Autobiography,* 1901, Student File of Samuel A. Cravath, OCA.

31. Conway, "Perspectives on the History," 6.

32. Higginson, *Common Sense about Women.*

33. Benford, Robert D., and David A. Snow, "Framing Processes and Social Movements."

34. "The Women's Medical College," *New York Times,* February 28, 1870.

35. The Vacancy in the Board of Trustees, *Vassar Miscellany,* April 1, 1872.

36. "The Woman Workers of Russia," *Woman's Work: A Journal Devoted the Employments of Women* 1, issue 6, Schlesinger Library, Radcliffe Institute, Cambridge, Mass. (May 1885): 2.

37. Rosenberg, *Changing the Subject,* 22.

38. Ibid., 25.

39. "The Harvard Annex," *Cornell Daily Sun,* January 31, 1881.

40. "College Annexes," *Chicago Daily Tribune,* July 12, 1885.

41. May Wright Sewall, "The Domestic and Social Effects of the Higher Education of Women," (read before the Western Association of the Association of Collegiate Alumnae, Ann Arbor, Mich., December 10, 1887): 5 http://purl.dlib .indiana.edu/iudl/inauthors/VAB1846.

42. See Archer and Blau, "Class Formation in Nineteenth-Century America"; Abbott, *The System of Professions.*

43. Münsterberg, *The Americans,* 5.

44. Flexner, *Medical Education;* Morantz-Sanchez *Sympathy & Science.*

45. Cooper, *A Voice from the South,* 71.

46. Horowitz, *Alma Mater,* 38.

47. The Vacancy in the Board of Trustees, *Vassar Miscellany,* April 1, 1872.

48. Collins, *Black Feminist Thought.*

49. Goodman, "The Manual Labor Movement"; Higginson and Mann, "The Murder of the Innocents."

50. Palmieri, *In Adamless Eden,* 55; Clarke, *Sex in Education,* 121.

51. Clarke, *Sex in Education,* 121.

52. "The Education of Girls," *New York Times,* November 6, 1877.

53. Dall, "Chapter Five," 107.

54. "Michigan University: Result of Six Years of Co-Education of the Sexes," *Chicago Daily Tribune*, February 20, 1875.

55. Citing the university president's annual report, "Coeducation: Views of the President of the University of Wisconsin," *New York Times*, January 4, 1878.

56. Howe, *Sex and Education*, 9–10.

57. Beisel and Kay, "Abortion, Race, and Gender."

58. Clarke, *Sex in Education*, 121–40. For an argument about how efforts to control women's reproduction brought together concerns over both religion and race, see Wilde and Danielsen, "Fewer and Better Children."

59. Elmore, "Chapter Twelve," 174–82.

60. "City and Suburban News," *New York Times*, May 20, 1884.

61. Reverend Seelye's 1884 speech was published as a pamphlet in 1888. Sophia Smith Collection, Writings About Smith College, 1884–1886, Folder IX, SCA.

62. "The Vacancy in the Board of Trustees", *Vassar Miscellany*, January 1, 1877; Thirteenth Annual Catalogue of the Officers and Students of Vassar College, 1877–1878, Vassar College Archives.

63. Aldrich, *Organizations Evolving*.

64. Talbot and Rosenberry, *The History*, 80.

65. Espeland and Sauder, "Rankings and Reactivity," 16.

66. For a history, see Hawkins, *Banding Together*.

67. There is no record of why faculty members voted against becoming a university. It appears that the faculty were wary of the increasing corporate character of the Board of Trustees and the changes it wanted to bring to Oberlin.

68. Sewall, "The Domestic and Social Effects," 9–10.

69. Ibid., 18.

70. Statement of Appropriations, 1906–1944, General Education Board, Box 336, Folder 3534, RAC.

71. Watson and Gregory, *Daring to Educate*.

72. Talbot and Rosenberry, *The History*, 20.

73. Ibid., 63–67. The Committee was led by Alice Freeman (Michigan 1876), Florence Cushing (Vassar 1874), and Margaret Hicks (Cornell 1878, B. Arch 1880).

74. DuBois, *The College-Bred Negro American*.

75. Graphic Review, General Education Board Southern Program, 1902–1935, Series VI, General Education Board, RAC.

76. Talbot and Rosenberry, *The History*, 63–72.

77. Ibid., 82.

78. Ibid., 49.

Chapter Six

1. "Gen. Howard and the Howard University"; Howard University Charter, 1866, HUA.

2. "The Cost of an Education," *Chicago Tribune*, October 25, 1891.

3. Shumway and Brower, *Oberliniana*, 85.

4. Ibid., 174.

5. Jacob Dolson Cox, "Jubilee Address," in Shumway and Brower, *Oberliniana*.

6. Minutes of the Oberlin Board of Trustees Meeting, February 27, 1895, OCA.

7. Minutes of the Oberlin Board of Trustees Meeting, June 17, 1895, OCA.

8. Minutes of the Oberlin Board of Trustees Meeting, March 1898, OCA.

9. Oberlin College Annual Report, 1886, OCA.

10. "Oberlin College: A Sketch by a Student," *The Hartford Courant*, July 9, 1889.

11. Wechsler, *The Qualified Student*.

12. Exchanges, *Vassar Miscellany*, October 15, 1877.

13. Many of the most elite private preparatory schools were founded between the mid-1870s and 1900. "Oberlin College: Election of Seven New Trustees," *New York Tribune*, March 17, 1900.

14. Fuess, *The College Board*.

15. *Oberlin Review*, March 3, 1883, 137.

16. Baumann, *Constructing Black Education*, 75.

17. "The Cost of an Education," *Chicago Tribune*, October 25, 1891.

18. Annual Reports of Oberlin College from the 1890s, OCA.

19. Minutes of the Oberlin Board of Trustees Meeting, June 20, 1892; Report on the Avery Fund. Prepared by J. H. Fairchild. September 15, 1892. Series III. Document Files Supporting Minutes of the Board, RG Board of Trustees, Box 3, 1886–1896, OCA.

20. Annual Report of Oberlin College, 1899, OCA.

21. Bumstead, "Higher Education of the Negro," 224.

22. Annual Report of Oberlin College, 1900, OCA.

23. Minutes March 4–5, 1896, Series III, Document Files Supporting Minutes of the Board, Box 4, OCA.

24. In many places, and especially in the agricultural South, primary schools were open for only few months a year, which made this arrangement possible.

25. "The Cost of an Education," *Chicago Tribune*, October 25, 1891.

26. "Scarcity of Great Men," *Chicago Tribune*, January 17, 1899.

27. Ibid.

28. Oberlin College Annual Report, 1886, OCA.

29. Barrows, *John Henry Barrows*, 402.

30. "Oberlin's President Dined," *Boston Advertiser*, May 25, 1899; President Barrows' Clippings, OCA.

31. For further reading on American empire building during the late nineteenth century, see Go, *American Empire and the Politics of Meaning*.

32. Oberlin College Archive Digital Exhibit, "Controversial Diplomacy," November 1998.

33. Albright, "A Slice of History."

34. Massachusetts Senator Hoar, who counseled Howard students that "the forces against them were only temporary," provided Jackson's scholarship. See Albright, "A Slice of History."

35. "Professor Root's statement of facts about *colored students*," June 20, 1910, 260-E Records of the Board of Trustees, OCA.

36. Baumann, *Constructing Black Education*, 95.

37. Julia Wilson to President James Fairchild, March 16, 1882, Fairchild Papers, OCA.

38. Baumann, *Constructing Black Education*, 101.

39. Ibid., 75. See Waite, *Permission to Remain*.

40. Appiah and Gutman, *Color Conscious*.

41. William W. Patton, "The Colored Race," *Chicago Daily Tribune*, May 27, 1877.

42. Henry M. Field, "Howard University," *New York Evangelist*, February 27, 1879.

43. "Colleges for Colored People," *American Educational Monthly*, May 1875. Berea College, Fisk University, Alcorn University, and Straight University, however, were all praised for opening their doors to students "without distinction of sex or race."

44. "Educate the Freedmen," *Chicago Tribune*, August 16, 1868.

45. "Correspondence," *New York Evangelist*, May 27, 1880.

46. "The Negroes' Harvard," *Washington Post*, April 14, 1884.

47. Ibid.

48. "Colored Students Studying Sociology," *Washington Post*, November 15, 1896.

49. "Educational," *Zion's Herald*, October 14, 1875.

50. "Howard University," *Chicago Daily Tribune*, April 26, 1877.

51. Patton did not, however, view women as equal to men. After "the anti-female suffragist," Patton declared in a public lecture that women were weaker in intellectual capacity. Susan B. Anthony confronted Patton, saying she thought his mother should spank him. The *Chicago Daily Tribune* ran a lengthy critique of Anthony, claiming that this exchange demonstrated her maternal instinct and suggested gleefully that it was Anthony who should have been spanked more often. "Mme. Anthony's Remedy," *Chicago Daily Tribune*, January 30, 1885.

52. Colleges with black presidents prior to 1877 include Alcorn University (1871) and Alabama A&M (1875).

53. McPherson, "White Liberals and Black Power," 1358.

54. "Howard University," *Chicago Daily Tribune*, April 26, 1877.

55. Logan, *Howard University*, 79.

56. These figures were not disaggregated from the preparatory division.

57. Logan, *Howard University*, 129.

58. "May Quit Howard University," *New York Times*, May 20, 1905.

59. "Justice for Howard University," *Washington Post*, December 29, 1905.

60. "Negro Valedictorian," *Washington Post*, February 3, 1881.

61. Ibid.

62. Ida Bailey, *Washington Post*, March 20, 1903. The Niagara Movement was founded in 1905 by W. E. B. DuBois and William Trotter, a leading newspaper editor, to protest what they saw as Booker Washington's accommodationist uplift ideology. The group, comprised of leading black teachers, clergy, and business owners protested segregation. Following a deadly 1908 riot, the organization helped develop the interracial National Association for the Advancement of Colored People. See Giddings, *Ida*, 453–529.

63. Tuskegee, for instance, offered programs of study or majors, but did not offer trades.

64. Washington, *The Story of My Life and Work*.

65. "The Southern Situation: Some Suggestive Facts," *American Missionary Magazine*, February 1890, 35–37, ARC.

66. Inaugural Address of the Rev. John Gordon, March 30, 1904, Reference Files, HUA.

67. "May Quit Howard University."

68. "Hissed by Students," *Washington Post*, December 9, 1905. For more on how student social movement pressure can result in organizational change, see Rojas, *From Black Power*.

69. Clifford L. Muse, "Howard University's Founders and Supporters: The Military and Abolitionist Connection," accessed March 18, 2011, http://www .huarchivesnet.howard.edu/0008huarnet/muse1.htm; Dyson, *Howard University*.

70. "New Homes for Freedmen," *New York Times*, January 23, 1879.

71. "To Aid Fleeing Negroes," *New York Times*, April 24, 1879.

72. "Cheers for Langston," *Washington Post*, September 25, 1890. After Langston's election, Virginia would not send another black representative to Congress until 1972.

73. "Gen. Howard and the Howard University," *New York Times*," August 26, 1867.

74. "Colored Students Studying Sociology."

75. Woodson, "Kelly Miller."

76. For detailed biographies see Logan, *Howard University*.

77. "Colored Law Graduates," *Washington Post*, May 29, 1894.

78. Logan, *Howard University*, 104.

79. Kelly Miller, "Uplifts Whole Race," *Washington Post*, December 14, 1902.

80. "Southern Pacification," *New York Times*, April 18, 1877.

81. Laura Spelman Rockefeller's father had aided refugee slaves en route to Canada; Spelman Seminary (now college) was aided by a generous donation in her memory.

82. The Laura Spelman Rockefeller Memorial Fund awarded $25,000 for the "study of the negroes part in the Reconstruction Period and the activities of the free negroes before the Civil War." Letter from W. S. Richardson to Carter G. Woodson, February 16, 1922, LSRM Series 3.8 (Interracial Relations), Box 96, Folder 966, RAC.

83. Muhammad, *The Condemnation of Blackness*.

84. Bond. "Social and Economic Forces," 290.

85. Dyson, *Howard University*.

86. "Negro Repels Attack," *Washington Post*, September 3, 1905.

87. "The Negro as a Political Factor," *New York Times*, November 16, 1902.

88. Muhammad, *The Condemnation of Blackness*, 96.

89. Fine, *Difficult Reputations*.

90. Miller, "Uplifts the Whole Race."

91. Union Alumni Association, Alumni Catalogue of Howard University with List of Incorporators, Trustees, and Other Employees, 1867–1896, 1896, HUA.

92. Miller, "Uplifts the Whole Race."

93. Ibid.

94. Kelly Miller, "Roosevelt and the Negro," *Washington Post*, December 25, 1902.

95. Fine, *Difficult Reputations*.

96. Swing, *James Harris Fairchild*, 226.

Chapter Seven

1. Woodward, *Origins of the New South*, 6.

2. Barth, "Introduction"; Bourdieu, "What Makes a Social Class?"; Brubaker, *Ethnicity without Groups*.

3. "Our Reconstruction Policy," *Chicago Tribune*, April 18, 1865.

4. "Editorial Article 2," *Chicago Tribune*, March 2, 1866.

5. American Union Commission, *American Union Commission*, 3; "American Union Commission," *Harper's Weekly*, October 21, 1865.

6. "Affairs in the South," *New York Times*, April 8, 1866.

7. "The Southern Poor," *Chicago Tribune*, May 30, 1867.

8. "Poor White Trash To Be Put Down," *New York Times*, February 26, 1884.

9. "Life at White Sulphur," *New York Times*, September 2, 1887.

10. "Letters on the South," *New York Evangelist*, May 27, 1886.

11. Blight, *Race and Reunion*.

12. Address of C. G. Fairchild to the American Missionary Association, *American Missionary*, vol. 37, issue 12, December 1883, ARC, 391–93.

13. Annual Report to the Board of Trustees of Berea College, 1906, BCA.

14. Report of Professor Howard Murray Jones to the Trustees of Berea College, 1901, BCA.

15. Bayreuther, *Geschichte der Diakonie*; Sevelsted, "Doctrine and Discipline." For observations by Oberlin faculty touring Germany, see G. White, "Impressions of Germany," *Oberlin Review*, March 4, 1890.

16. W. G. Frost, Record Group 21, 1910, OCA, 88.

17. W. G. Frost, Record Group 21, 1910, OCA, 92–93.

18. W. G. Frost, Speeches and Publicity, 1892, BCA.

19. "Hints from the Mail Bag," *New York Times*, January 19, 1901.

20. Barman, *Contesting Communities*; Jacobs and Sobieraj, "Narrative, Public Policy, and Political Legitimacy"; Jenkins, "Resource Mobilization Theory"; Karabel, "Status-Group Struggle"; Hsu, "Market Ventures, Moral Logics."

21. Charles Mills, "Annual Meeting: Report on Mountain Work," *American Missionary*, vol. 47, issue 12, December 1893, ARC, 401–02.

22. "Study of Race Problems," *New York Times*, March 13, 1900.

23. Frost, "Our Contemporary Ancestors."

24. "In Kentucky's Mountains," *New York Times*, December 12, 1898.

25. MacClintock, "The Kentucky Mountains."

26. Lathrop, "The South."

27. L. E. Tupper, "The South," *American Missionary*, vol. 44, issue 9, September 1890, ARC, 273.

28. Veblen, "The Barbarian Status of Women."

29. Ibid., 507; Smithers, *Science, Sexuality and Race*; Wray, *Not Quite White*, 82.

30. "Helping Mountain Whites," *New York Times*, November 27, 1892.

31. "The Poor Whites of the South," *New York Times*, May 10, 1896.

32. J. Roy, "Addresses: Mountain Work," *American Missionary*, vol. 38, issue 12, December 1885, ARC, 397.

33. "Kentucky Feuds: The Leaders Are Often Educated Men," *Los Angeles Times*, August 1, 1899; Hutton, *Bloody Breathitt*.

34. Smith, "From Vice to Virtue."

35. MacClintock, "The Kentucky Mountains," 5–6.

36. Zolberg and Woon, "Why Islam is like Spanish."

37. Fox and Guglielmo, "Defining America's Racial Boundaries"; Fox, *Three Worlds of Relief.*

38. "Delano and the Southern Problem: The Evanston Baptist Begins a Series of Addresses on his Impressions." *Chicago Daily Tribune*, January 28, 1895.

39. Muhammad, *The Condemnation of Blackness.*

40. Caudill, *Night Comes to the Cumberlands*; Gaventa, *Power and Powerlessness.*

41. J. Roy, "Addresses: Mountain Work," *American Missionary*, vol. 38, issue 12, December 1885, ARC, 397.

42. "Bright Star of Hope," *Chicago Daily Tribune*, October 29, 1894.

43. Roy, "Addresses: Mountain Work," 402.

44. Weitzer, "The Social Construction of Sex Trafficking."

45. Billings and Blee, *The Road to Poverty*, 134.

46. Office of Information (Development) Publications, "Berea College, 1878–1919," Record Group 5.23, Box 7, Folder 1, BCA.

47. "Roosevelt at Trinity," *Berea Quarterly*, February 1897, BCA, 10–11.

48. "Miss Gould in Cincinnati," *New York Times*, June 3, 1900.

49. Hall, *The Mountain Whites*, 17.

50. Campbell, *Classification of Mountain Whites*, 4.

51. Ibid., 7.

52. Ellsworth, "Theodore Roosevelt's Country Life Commission," 163.

53. Ettling, *The Germ of Laziness.*

54. Berea College Catalogue, 1915, BCA.

55. Guidelines for Funding Appalachian Projects, Development Districts, and Research, 1969, Box 124, Folder 2, Appalachian Regional Commission Archives, UKSC.

56. Berea College Board of Trustees Records, 1915, BCA.

57. Annual Report of Berea College, 1902, BCA.

58. Bernstein, "Plessy vs. Lochner"; Bigglestone, "Oberlin College and the Negro Student."

59. Hsu, "Market Ventures, Moral Logics."

60. Office of Information Publications, "Berea College 1878–1919," Record Group 5.23, Box 7, Folder 1, BCA; Julian Ralph, "Letter from Theodore Roosevelt to Julian Ralph," *Harper's Magazine*, November 23, 1895. Note that novelist Julian Ralph wrote extensively for *Harper's Magazine*.

61. Hall, *The Mountain Whites*.

62. O. O. Howard Collection, M91.11: Religious and Educational Work, 1857–1902, Records, BCA.

63. Russell Sage Foundation, 1899–1911, Lincoln Memorial University, Series 10, Box 83, Folder 785, RAC.

64. Prudential Committee, Report to the Board of Trustees of Berea College, 1900, Record Group 2, Box 9, BCA.

65. Stoddart, *Challenge and Change*.

66. Notable legacies from this movement are Alice Lloyd College, the Williamsburg Institute (now University of the Cumberlands), the Highland Research and Education Center, and the University of Pikeville.

67. Russell Sage Foundation, Early Office Files 169T, Southern Highland Division—Reports, etc., 1910–1917, IV 4 B1.3, Box 16, Folder 136, RAC.

68. Ibid.

69. Report of Professor Howard Murray Jones to the Trustees of Berea College, 1901, BCA.

70. Frank L. Williams et al., "President Frost's Betrayal of the Colored People in his Administration of Berea College," 1902–1905, Vertical Files: Day Law III, BCA.

71. Letter from Booker T. Washington to Frost, February 12, 1903, Frost Correspondence—1903 (L–Z), Record Group 3.03, Box 6 Presidents, BCA.

72. Letter to President Frost, March 28, 1904, W. G. Frost Chapters, RG 3.03 Box 23/6, BCA.

73. Berea College v. Kentucky, 211 U.S. 45 (1908). This case was argued April 10 and 13, 1908; it was decided November 9, 1908.

74. "Berea Loses Suit," *Berea Citizen*, November 12, 1908, RG 12.13, BCA.

75. Barman, *Contesting Communities*.

76. Binder, "For Love and Money."

77. Gans, "'Whitening'"; Wray, *Not Quite White*.

78. Wimmer and Lewis, "Beyond and Below Racial Homophily."

79. Bonilla-Silva, *Racism Without Racists*, 346–57; Lewis, "What Group?"

80. Dr. Barton for the Committee on Resolution to Donors, Annual Meeting of the Board of Trustees, June 6–7, 1917, 331–33, BCA.

Conclusion

1. Foner, *The Fiery Trial*.

2. Badger, "Colleges that Did Not Survive," 306.

3. "Washington in Mid-Summer," *The Independent*, August 12, 1869.

4. "The Colored People in Washington," *New York Evangelist*, April 21, 1870.

5. Congressional Record, Forty-Third Congress, vol. 2, 1st sess., 1874, 75.

6. On the voting rights case *Shelby County v. Holder* in 2013, The Supreme Court invalidated the formula used to determine which states are covered by Section 5 of the Voting Rights. For more see, The Brennan Center for Justice at New York University Law School, August 4, 2015, http://www.brennancenter.org/analysis /voting-rights-act-resource-page.

7. Weber, *Economy and Society*, 998.

8. Weber, "The 'Rationalization' of Education and Training."

9. Barman, *Contesting Communities*.

10. Bumstead, "Higher Education of the Negro," 224. During the Civil War, Horace Bumstead served in the Union Army as a major for a black regiment, the Forty-Third Regiment of U.S. Colored Troops.

11. Talbot and Rosenberry, *The History*, 63–69.

12. DuBois, *The College-Bred Negro American*, 53.

13. Münsterberg, *The Americans*, 566.

14. Tolnay and Beck, *A Festival of Violence*.

15. "A. E. Dunning in Concerning Human Rights," *American Missionary*, vol. 52, no. 4, December 1898, 203, ARC.

16. Bond, "Social and Economic Forces," 291.

17. See Paschel, "The Right to Difference."

Bibliography

Abbott, Andrew. *The System of Professions: An Essay on the Division of Expert Labor*. Chicago: University of Chicago Press, 1988.

Albright, Evan. "A Slice of History." *Amherst Magazine*, Winter 2007, 14–15.

Aldrich, Howard. *Organizations Evolving*. Thousand Oaks, Calif.: SAGE Publications Inc., 1999.

Alexander, Jeffrey, and Philip Smith. "Citizen and Enemy as Symbolic Classification: On the Polarizing Discourse of Civil Society." In *Where Culture Talks: Exclusion and the Making of Society*, edited by M. Fournier and M. Lamont, 289–308. Chicago: University of Chicago Press, 1993.

Alexander, Michelle. *The New Jim Crow: Mass Incarceration in the Age of Colorblindness*. New York: The New Press, 2012.

Allport, Gordon W. *The Nature of Prejudice*. Cambridge, Mass.: Perseus Books, 1954.

Alon, Sigal. "The Evolution of Class Inequality in Higher Education: Competition, Exclusion, and Adaptation." *American Sociological Review* 74 (2009): 731–55.

American Union Commission. *American Union Commission: Its Origin, Operations and Purposes*. New York: Sanford, Harroun and Company, 1865.

Anderson, Eric, and Alfred A. Moss. *Dangerous Donations: Northern Philanthropy and Southern Black Education, 1902–1930*. Columbia: University of Missouri Press, 1999.

Anderson, James. *The Education of Blacks in the South, 1860–1935*. Chapel Hill: University of North Carolina Press, 1988.

Appiah, K. Anthony, and Amy Gutmann. *Color Conscious: The Political Morality of Race*. Princeton: Princeton University Press, 1998.

Applegate, Debby. *The Most Famous Man in America: The Biography of Henry Ward Beecher*. New York: Three Leaves Press, 2006.

Aptheker, Bettina. *Woman's Legacy: Essays on Race, Sex, and Class in American History*. Amherst: University of Massachusetts Press, 1982.

Archer, Melanie, and Judith R. Blau. "Class Formation in Nineteenth-Century America: The Case of the Middle Class." *Annual Review of Sociology* 19 (1993): 17–41.

Badger, Henry. "Colleges that Did Not Survive." *Journal of Negro Education* 35 (1966): 306–12.

Bailey, Richard. *Neither Carpetbaggers Nor Scalawags: Black Officeholders During the Reconstruction of Alabama 1867–1878*. Montgomery: New South Books, 2006.

Barman, Emily. "Asserting Difference: The Strategic Response of Nonprofit Organizations to Competition." *Social Forces* 80 (2002): 1191–222.

————. *Contesting Communities: The Transformation of Workplace Charity.* Stanford: Stanford University Press, 2006.

Barnes, Sarah. "Crossing the Invisible Line: Establishing Co-Education at the University of Manchester and Northwestern University." *History of Education* 23 (1995): 35–58.

Barrows, Mary. *John Henry Barrows: A Memoir.* New York: Fleming H. Revell Company, 1904.

Barth, Fredrik. "Introduction." In *Ethnic Groups and Boundaries: The Social Organization of Cultural Difference,* edited by Fredrik Barth, 9–38. London: Allen & Unwin, 1969.

Baumann, Roland. *Constructing Black Education at Oberlin College: A Documentary History.* Athens: Ohio University Press, 2010.

————. *Geschichte der Diakonie und Inneren Mission in der Neuzeit.* Berlin: CZV-Verlag, 1983.

Beard, Augustus Field. *A Crusade of Brotherhood: A History of the American Missionary Association.* New York: Pilgrim Press, 1909.

————. *The Providence of God in the Historical Development of the Negro.* New York: American Missionary Association, 1895.

Becker, Penny Edgell. "Making Inclusive Communities: Congregations and the 'Problem' of Race." *Social Problems* 45, no. 4 (1998): 451–72.

Beisel, Nicola. *Imperiled Innocents: Anthony Comstock and Family Reproduction in Victorian America.* Princeton: Princeton University Press, 1997.

Beisel, Nicola, and Tamara Kay. "Abortion, Race, and Gender in Nineteenth-Century America." *American Sociological Review* 69 (2004): 498–518.

Benford, Robert D., and David A. Snow. "Framing Processes and Social Movements: An Overview and Assessment." *Annual Review of Sociology* 26 (2000): 611–39.

Benhabib, Seyla. *The Claims of Culture: Equality and Diversity in the Global Era.* Princeton: Princeton University Press, 2002.

Berbrier, Mitch. "'Half the Battle': Cultural Resonance, Framing Processes, and Ethnic Affectations in Contemporary White Separatist Rhetoric." *Social Problems* 45 (1998): 431–50.

————. "Making Minorities: Cultural Space, Stigma Transformation Frames, and the Categorical Status Claims of Deaf, Gay, and White Supremacist Activists in Late Twentieth Century America." *Sociological Forum* 17 (2002): 553–91.

Berezin, Mabel. "Events as Templates of Possibility: An Analytic Typology of Political Facts." In *The Oxford Handbook of Cultural Sociology,* edited by Jeffrey C. Alexander, Ronald Jacobs, and Philip Smith, 613–35. New York: Oxford University Press, 2012.

Berlin, Ira. *Generations of Captivity: A History of African-American Slaves.* Cambridge, Mass.: Harvard University Press, 2009.

————. *Slaves without Masters: The Free Negro in the Antebellum South.* New York: The New Press, 2007.

Bernstein, David Eliot. "Plessy vs. Lochner: The Berea College Case." *Journal of Supreme Court History* 25 (2000): 93–111.

Bigglestone, W. E. "Oberlin College and the Negro Student." *Journal of Negro History* 56 (1971): 198–219.

Billings, Dwight B., and Kathleen M. Blee. *The Road to Poverty: The Making of Wealth and Hardship in Appalachia*. Cambridge, U.K.: Cambridge University Press, 2000.

Binder, Amy J. *Contentious Curricula: Afrocentrism and Creationism in American Public Schools*. Princeton: Princeton University Press, 2002.

———. "For Love and Money: One Organization's Creative and Multiple Responses to a New Funding Environment." *Theory and Society* 36 (2007): 547–71.

Bishop, Morris. *A History of Cornell*. Ithaca, N.Y.: Cornell University Press, 1962.

Black, Isabelle. "Berea College." *Phylon Quarterly* 18 (1957): 267–76.

Blight, David W. *Race and Reunion: The Civil War in American Memory*. Cambridge, Mass.: Harvard University Press, 2001.

Blodgett, Geoffrey T. "John Mercer Langston and the Case of Edmonia Lewis: Oberlin, 1862." *Journal of Negro History* 52 (July 1968): 201–18.

Bloemraad, Irene. *Becoming a Citizen: Incorporating Immigrants and Refugees in the United States and Canada*. Berkeley: University of California Press, 2006.

Bond, Horace Mann. "Social and Economic Forces in Alabama Reconstruction." *Journal of Negro History* 23 (1938): 290–348.

Bonilla-Silva, Eduardo. *Racism without Racists: Color-Blind Racism and the Persistence of Racial Inequality in America*. New York: Rowman & Littlefield, 2003.

———. "Rethinking Racism: Toward a Structural Interpretation." *American Journal of Sociology* 62, no. 3 (1997): 465–480.

Bordin, Ruth. *Women at Michigan: The Dangerous Experiment, 1870s to the Present*. Ann Arbor: University of Michigan Press, 2001.

Bourdieu, Pierre. *Distinction: A Social Critique of the Judgment of Taste*. New York: Routledge, 1986.

———. *Language and Symbolic Power*. Cambridge, Mass.: Harvard University Press, 1991.

———. *The State Nobility: Elite Schools in the Field of Power*. Stanford: Stanford University Press, 1998.

———. "What Makes a Social Class? On the Theoretical and Practical Existence of Groups." *Berkeley Journal of Sociology* 32 (1987): 1–18.

Bowers, William L. "Country-Life Reform, 1900–1920: A Neglected Aspect of Progressive Era History." *Agricultural History* 45, no. 3 (1971): 211–21.

Bradley, Karen. "The Incorporation of Women into Higher Education: Paradozxical Outcomes?" *Sociology of Education* 73, no. 1 (2000): 1–18.

Bradley, Karen, and Maria Charles. "Uneven Inroads: Understanding Women's Status in Higher Education." *Research in the Sociology of Education and Socialization* 11 (2004): 63–91.

Bressey, Caroline. *Empire, Race and the Politics of Anti-Caste*. London: Bloomsbury, 2013.

Brubaker, Rogers. *Ethnicity without Groups*. Cambridge, Mass.: Harvard University Press, 2004.

———. *Nationalism Reframed: Nationhood and the National Question in the New
Europe*. Cambridge, U.K.: Cambridge University Press, 1996.

Brundage, W. Fitzhugh. *Lynching in the New South: Georgia and Virginia,
1880–1930*. Champaign: University of Illinois Press, 1993.

Bumstead, Horace. "Higher Education of the Negro—its Practical Value." Vol. 1,
Report of the Commissioner of Education. Washington, D.C.: U.S. Government
Printing Office, 1903.

Butchart, Ronald. *Schooling the Freed People: Teaching, Learning, and the Struggle
for Black Freedom, 1861–1876*. Chapel Hill: University of North Carolina Press,
2010.

Cable, George Washington. *The Silent South: Together with the Freedmen's Case in
Equity and the Convict Lease System*. New York: C. Scribner's Sons, 1885.

Cain, Congressman Richard Harvey. "All We Ask Is Equal Laws, Equal
Legislation and Equal Rights." *Congressional Record* 2, no. 1 (1874): 565–67.

Calhoun, Craig. "Nationalism and Ethnicity." *Annual Review of Sociology* 19
(1993): 221–39.

Campbell, John. "Ideas, Politics, and Public Policy." *Annual Review of Sociology*
28 (2002): 21–38.

Campbell, Karen, and Holly McCammon. "Elizabeth Blackwell's Heirs: Women
Physicians in the United State, 1880–1920." *Work and Occupations* 32 (2005): 290.

Campbell, R. F. *Classification of Mountain Whites*. Hampton, Va.: Hampton
Institute Press, 1901.

Carnevale, Anthony, and Jeff Strohl. *Separate and Unequal. How Higher Education
Reinforces the Intergenerational Reproduction of White Racial Privilege*.
Washington, D.C.: Georgetown Public Policy Institute, 2013.

Carter, Prudence. "Race and Cultural Flexibility among Students in Different
Multiracial Schools." *Teachers College Record* 112 (June 2010): 1529–74.

———. *Stubborn Roots: Race, Culture and Inequality in U.S. and South African
Schools*. New York: Oxford University Press, 2012.

Caudill, Harry M. *Night Comes to the Cumberlands: A Biography of a Depressed
Area*. Boston: Little, Brown, and Company, 1962.

Clarke, Edward H. *Sex in Education; Or, a Fair Chance for the Girls*. Boston:
James R. Osgood and Company, 1875.

Clemens, Elisabeth. "From City Club to Nation State: Business Networks in
American Political Development." *Theory & Society* 39 (2010): 377–96.

Coates, Ta-Nehisi. *Between the World and Me*. New York: Spiegel and Grau, 2015.

Cobb, W. Montague. "The First Hundred Years of the Howard University
College of Medicine." *Journal of the National Medical Association* 59 (1967):
408–20.

Colby, Ira. "The Freedmen's Bureau: From Social Welfare to Segregation."
Phylon 46 (1985): 219–30.

Collins, Patricia Hill. *Black Feminist Thought: Knowledge, Consciousness, and the Politics of Empowerment.* Boston: Unwin Hyman, 1990.

Conway, Jill Ker. "Perspectives on the History of Women's Education in the United States." *History of Education Quarterly* 14 (1974): 1–12.

———. *Utopian Dream or Dystopian Nightmare? Nineteenth Century Feminist Ideas About Equality.* Ann Arbor: University of Michigan Press, 1987.

Cooper, Anna Julia. *A Voice from the South.* New York: Oxford University Press, 1990. First published 1892 by The Aldine Printing House.

Crowder, Kyle, Jeremy Pais, and Scott J. South. "Neighborhood Diversity, Metropolitan Constraints, and Household Migration." *American Sociological Review* 77 (2012): 325–53.

Cunningham, David. "Mobilizing Ethnic Competition." *Theory & Society* 41 (2012): 505–25.

Dall, Caroline. "Chapter Five." In *Sex and Education: A Reply to Dr. E. H. Clarke's "Sex in Education,"* edited by Julia Ward Howe, 87–108. Boston: Roberts Brothers, 1874.

Davis, Hugh. *"We Will Be Satisfied With Nothing Less": The African American Struggle for Equal Rights in the North During Reconstruction.* Ithaca, N.Y.: Cornell University Press, 2011.

DiMaggio, Paul. "Cultural Entrepreneurship in Nineteenth-Century Boston, Part I: The Creation of an Organizational Base for High Culture in America." In *Rethinking Popular Culture: Contemporary Perspectives in Cultural Studies,* edited by Chandra Mukerji and Michael Schudson, 374–97. Berkeley: University of California Press, 1991.

———. "Culture and Cognition." *Annual Review of Sociology* 23 (1997): 263–87.

DiMaggio, Paul, and Walter Powell. "The Iron Cage Revisited: Institutional Isomorphism and Collective Rationality in Organizational Fields." *American Sociological Review* 48 (1983): 147–60.

Douglas, Davison M. *Jim Crow Moves North: The Battle over Northern School Desegregation, 1865–1954.* Cambridge, U.K.: Cambridge University Press, 2005.

Douglas, Mary. *Purity and Danger: An Analysis of Concepts of Pollution and Taboo.* New York: Routledge Classics, 2008. First published 1966 by Routledge.

Doyle, Bertram Wilbur. *The Etiquette of Race Relations in the South: A Study in Social Control.* Chicago: University of Chicago Press, 1937.

DuBois, W. E. B. *Black Reconstruction: An Essay toward a History of the Part Which Black Folk Played in the Attempt to Reconstruct Democracy in America, 1860–1880.* New York: The Free Press, 1992. First published, New York: Harcourt, Brace and Company, 1935.

———. "The Freedmen's Bureau." *Atlantic Monthly,* March 1901.

DuBois, W. E. B., and Augustus Dill, eds. *The College-Bred Negro American.* Atlanta: Atlanta University Publications, 1910.

Dyson, Walter. *Howard University, The Capstone of Negro Education: A History, 1867–1940.* Washington, D.C.: The Graduate School, Howard University, 1941.

Ellsworth, Clayton S. "Theodore Roosevelt's Country Life Commission." *Agricultural History* 34 (1960): 155–72.

Elmore, Maria A. "Chapter Twelve." In *Sex and Education: A Reply to Dr. E. H. Clarke's "Sex in Education,"* edited by Julia Ward Howe, 174–82. Boston: Roberts Brothers, 1874.

Emirbayer, Mustafa, and Victoria Johnson. "Bourdieu and Organizational Analysis." *Theory & Society* 37 (2008): 1–44.

Espeland, Wendy, and Michael Sauder. "Rankings and Reactivity: How Public Measures Recreate Social Worlds." *American Journal of Sociology* 113 (2007): 1–40.

Ettling, John. *The Germ of Laziness: Rockefeller Philanthropy and Public Health in the New South.* Cambridge, Mass.: Harvard University Press, 1981.

Fairchild, Edward H. *Berea College, Ky.: An Interesting History.* Cincinnati: Elm Street Printing, 1875.

———. *Historical Sketch, Oberlin College.* Springfield, Ohio: Republic Printing Co., 1868.

Fairchild, James H. *Oberlin: Its Origin, Progress and Results.* Oberlin: Butler, 1860.

Farrow, Anne, Joel Lang, and Jenifer Frank. *Complicity: How the North Promoted, Prolonged, and Profited from Slavery.* New York: Ballantine Books, 2005.

Fee, Elizabeth, Theodore M. Brown, Jan Lazarus, and Paul Theerman. "Medical Education for Women, 1870." *American Journal of Public Health* 92 (2002): 363.

Fee, John G. *The Autobiography of John G. Fee.* Chicago: National Christian Association, 1891.

Ferrall, Victor. *Liberal Arts at the Brink.* Cambridge, Mass.: Harvard University Press, 2011.

Fine, Gary Alan. *Difficult Reputations: Collective Memories of the Evil, Inept, and Controversial.* Chicago: University of Chicago Press, 2001.

Flexner, Abraham. *Medical Education in the United States and Canada.* New York: Carnegie Foundation for the Advancement of Teaching, 1910.

Fligstein, Neil. "Social Skill and the Theory of Fields." *Sociological Theory* 19 (2001): 105–25.

Foner, Eric. *The Fiery Trial: Abraham Lincoln and American Slavery.* New York: W. W. Norton & Company, 2010.

———. *Freedom's Lawmakers: A Directory of Black Officeholders during Reconstruction.* New York: Oxford University Press, 1993.

———. *Reconstruction: America's Unfinished Revolution, 1863–1877.* New York: HarperCollins, 1988.

Fox, Cybelle. *Three Worlds of Relief: Race, Immigration, and the American Welfare State from the Progressive Era to the New Deal.* Princeton: Princeton University Press, 2012.

Fox, Cybelle, and Thomas Guglielmo. "Defining America's Racial Boundaries: Blacks, Mexicans, and European Immigrants, 1890–1945." *American Journal of Sociology* 118 (2012): 327–79.

Franklin, John Hope. *Reconstruction after the Civil War.* Chicago: University of Chicago Press, 1994.

Frost, W. G. "Our Contemporary Ancestors in the Southern Mountains." *Atlantic Monthly,* March 1899, 311–20.

Fuess, Claude. *The College Board, Its First Fifty Years*. New York: Columbia University Press, 1950.

Gamson, William, and Andre Modigliani. "Media Discourse and Public Opinion on Nuclear Power: A Constructionist Approach." *American Journal of Sociology* 95, no. 1 (1989): 1–37.

Gans, Herbert. "'Whitening' and the Changing American Racial Hierarchy." *DuBois Review* 9 (2012): 267–79.

Gaventa, John. *Power and Powerlessness: Quiescence and Rebellion in an Appalachian Valley*. Urbana: University of Illinois Press, 1982.

Geiger, Roger. *To Advance Knowledge: The Growth of American Research Universities, 1900–1940*. New York: Oxford University Press, 1986.

Gerteis, Joseph. *Class and the Color Line: Interracial Class Coalition in the Knights of Labor and the Populist Movement*. Durham, N.C.: Duke University Press, 2007.

Gerth, Hans, and C. Wright Mills. *From Max Weber: Essays in Sociology*. New York: Galaxy Books, 1958.

Giddings, Paula J. *Ida: A Sword Among Lions*. New York: HarperCollins, 2008.

Gieryn, Thomas. "A Place for Space in Sociology." *Annual Review of Sociology* 26 (2000): 463–96.

Ginzberg, Lori. "The 'Joint Education of the Sexes': Oberlin's Original Vision." In *Educating Men and Women Together*, edited by Carol Lasser, 67–80. Urbana: University of Illinois Press.

Giozzo, Charles. "John Jones and the Black Convention Movement, 1848–1856." *Journal of Black Studies* 3, no. 2 (1972): 227–36.

Glasrud, Bruce A., ed. *Brothers to the Buffalo Soldiers: Perspectives on the African American Militia and Volunteers, 1865–1917*. Columbia: University of Missouri Press, 2011.

Glenn, Evelyn Nakano. *Unequal Freedom: How Race and Gender Shaped American Citizenship and Labor*. Cambridge, Mass.: Harvard University Press, 2002.

Go, Julian. *American Empire and the Politics of Meaning: Elite Political Cultures in the Philippines and Puerto Rico*. Durham, N.C.: Duke University Press, 2008.

Goffman, Erving. *Asylums: Essays on the Social Situations of Mental Patients and Other Inmates*. New York: Penguin Press, 1961.

Goldberg, Chad Alan. *Citizens and Paupers: Relief, Rights and Race, from the Freedmen's Bureau to Workfare*. Chicago: University of Chicago Press, 2007.

Goldin, Claudia, and Lawrence Katz. "Mass Secondary Schooling and the State: The Role of State Compulsion in the High School Movement." In *Understanding Long Run Economic Growth*, edited by Dora Costa and Naomi Lamoreaux, 275–310. Cambridge, U.K.: Cambridge University Press, 2011.

Goldsmith, Pat António. "Schools' Role in Shaping Race Relations: Evidence on Friendliness and Conflict." *Social Problems* 51 (2004): 587–612.

Goldsmith, Pat Rubio. "Schools, Neighborhoods, or Both? Race and Ethnic Segregation and Educational Attainment." *Social Forces* 87 (2009): 1913–43.

Goodman, Paul. "The Manual Labor Movement and the Origins of Abolitionism." *Journal of the Early Republic* 13 (Autumn 1993): 355–88.

Guinier, Lani, and Gerald Torres. *The Miner's Canary: Enlisting Race, Resisting Power, Transforming Democracy.* Cambridge, Mass.: Harvard University Press, 2002.

Guterl, Matthew. *American Mediterranean: Southern Slaveholders in the Age of Emancipation.* Cambridge, Mass.: Harvard University Press, 2008.

Hahn, Steven. *A Nation under Our Feet: Black Political Struggles in the Rural South from Slavery to the Great Migration.* Cambridge, Mass.: Harvard University Press, 2003.

Hall, John. *The Mountain Whites of the South.* Pittsburgh: J. McMillin Publishing, 1893.

Hallett, Tim. "The Myth Incarnate: Recoupling Processes, Turmoil, and Inhabited Institutions in an Urban Elementary School." *American Sociological Review* 75 (2011): 52–74.

Hallett, Tim, and Gary Alan Fine. "Group Cultures and the Everyday Life of Organizations: Interaction Orders and Meso Analysis." *Organization Studies* 35 (2014): 1773–92.

Hallett, Tim, and Marc Ventresca. "Inhabited Institutions: Social Interactions and Organizational Forms in Gouldner's Patterns of Industrial Bureaucracy." *Theory and Society* 35 (2006): 213–36.

Haney-Lopez, Ian. *White by Law: The Legal Construction of Race.* New York: New York University Press, 2006.

Harlan, Louis. *Separate and Unequal: Public School Campaign and Racism in the Southern Seaboard States, 1901–1915.* New York: Atheneum, 1968.

Harris, Leslie M. *In the Shadow of Slavery: African Americans in New York City, 1626–1863.* Chicago: University of Chicago Press, 2003.

Hawkins, Hugh. *Banding Together: The Rise of National Associations in American Higher Education, 1887–1950.* Baltimore: Johns Hopkins University Press, 1992.

Haynes, Stephen. *Noah's Curse: The Biblical Justification of American Slavery.* New York: Oxford University Press, 2007.

Higginson, Thomas Wentworth. *Common Sense about Women.* Boston: Lee and Shepard, 1881.

Higginson, Thomas Wentworth, and Horace Mann. "The Murder of the Innocents." *Atlantic Monthly,* September 1859, 345–56.

Hine, William C. "Black Politicians in Reconstruction Charleston, South Carolina: A Collective Study." *Journal of Southern History* 49, no. 4 (1983): 555–84.

Hirschman, Albert O. "Rival Interpretations of Market Society: Civilizing, Destructive, or Feeble?" *Journal of Economic Literature* 20 (1982): 1463–84.

Hochschild, Jennifer, and Brenna Powell. "Racial Reorganization and the United States Census 1850–1930: Mulattoes, Half-Breeds, Mixed Parentage, Hindoos, and the Mexican Race." *Studies in American Political Development* 22 (2008): 59–96.

Hochschild, Jennifer, and Nathan Scovronick. *The American Dream and the Public Schools.* New York: Oxford University Press, 2003.

Holt, Thomas C. *Black over White: Negro Political Leadership in South Carolina during Reconstruction.* Urbana: University of Illinois Press, 1977.

Horowitz, Helen Lefkowitz. *Alma Mater: Design and Experience in the Women's Colleges from Their Nineteenth-Century Beginnings to the 1930s.* New York: Knopf, 1984.

Horton, James Oliver. "Black Education at Oberlin College: A Controversial Commitment." *Journal of Negro Education* 54 (1985): 477–99.

Howard, Oliver Otis. *Autobiography.* 2 vols. New York: Baker and Taylor, 1908.

Howe, Julia Ward, ed. *Sex and Education: A Reply to Dr. E. H. Clarke's "Sex in Education."* Boston: Roberts Brothers, 1874.

Hsu, Carolyn. "Market Ventures, Moral Logics, and Ambiguity: Crafting a New Organizational Form in Post-Socialist China." *Sociological Quarterly* 47 (2006): 69–92.

Hutton, T. R. C. *Bloody Breathitt: Politics and Violence in the Appalachian South.* Lexington: University of Kentucky Press, 2013.

Irons, Jenny. *Reconstituting Whiteness: The Mississippi State Sovereignty Commission.* Nashville: Vanderbilt University Press, 2010.

Jack, Bryan. *The St. Louis African American Community and the Exodusters.* Columbia: University of Missouri Press, 2007.

Jackson-Coppin, Fanny. *Reminiscences of School Life and Hints on Teaching.* Philadelphia: AME Book Concern, 1913.

Jacobs, Ronald, and Sarah Sobieraj. "Narrative, Public Policy, and Political Legitimacy: Congressional Debates about the Nonprofit Sector, 1894–1969." *Sociological Theory* 25, no. 1 (2007): 1–25.

Jencks, Christopher, and David Riesman. *The Academic Revolution.* Garden City, N.Y.: Doubleday, 1968.

Jenkins, J. Craig. "Resource Mobilization Theory and the Study of Social Movements." *Annual Review of Sociology* 9 (1983): 527–53.

Jewell, Joseph. *Race, Social Reform, and the Making of a Middle Class: The American Missionary Association and Black Atlanta, 1870–1900.* Lanham, Md.: Rowman & Littlefield, 2007.

Johnson, Cathryn, Timothy Dowd, and Cecilia Ridgeway. "Legitimacy as a Social Process." *Annual Review of Sociology* 32 (2006): 53–78.

Johnson, Victoria. *Backstage at the Revolution: How the Royal Paris Opera Survived the End of the Old Regime.* Chicago: University of Chicago Press, 2008.

Jones, Jacqueline. *Soldiers of Light and Love: Northern Teachers and Georgia Blacks, 1865–1873.* Athens: University of Georgia Press, 1980.

Karabel, Jerome. *The Chosen: The Hidden History of Admission and Exclusion at Harvard, Yale, and Princeton.* Boston: Houghton, 2005.

———. "Status-Group Struggle, Organizational Interests and the Limits of Institutional Autonomy: The Transformation of Harvard, Yale and Princeton, 1918–1940." *Theory and Society* 13 (1984): 1–40.

Katz, Michael. "From Voluntarism to Bureaucracy in American Education." *Sociology of Education* 44, no. 3 (1971): 297–332.

————. *The Irony of Early School Reform: Educational Innovation in Mid-Nineteenth Century Massachusetts.* New York: Teachers College Press, 1968.

Katznelson, Ira. *When Affirmative Action Was White: An Untold History of Racial Inequality in Twentieth-Century America.* New York: W. W. Norton, 2005.

Katznelson, Ira, and Margaret Weir. *Schooling for All: Class, Race, and the Decline of the Democratic Ideal.* New York: Basic Books, 2005.

Kelley, Blair L. M. *Right to Ride: Streetcar Boycotts and African American Citizenship in the Era of Plessy v. Ferguson.* Chapel Hill: University of North Carolina Press, 2010.

Keyssar, Alexander. *The Right to Vote: The Contested History of Democracy in the United States.* New York: Basic Books, 2000.

Khan, Shamus. *Privilege: The Making of an Adolescent Elite at St. Paul's School.* Princeton: Princeton University Press, 2012.

King, Desmond. *Separate and Unequal: African Americans and the U.S. Federal Government.* New York: Oxford University Press, 1997.

King, Desmond, and Rogers Smith. "Racial Orders in American Political Development." *American Political Science Review* 99 (2005): 75–92.

Krause, Monika. *The Good Project: Humanitarian Relief NGOs and the Fragmentation of Reason.* Chicago: Chicago University Press, 2014.

Lado, Marianne. "A Question of Justice: African-American Legal Perspectives on the 1883 Civil Rights Cases." *Chicago-Kent Law Review* 70 (1995): 1123–95.

Lainier-Vos, Dan. *Sinews of the Nation: Constructing Irish and Zionist Bonds in the United States.* Cambridge, U.K.: Polity Press, 2013.

Lamb, Daniel S. *Howard University Medical Department, Washington, D.C.: A Historical, Biographical, and Statistical Souvenir.* Washington, D.C.: Howard University Medical Department, 1900.

Lamont, Michèle, and Christopher Bail. "Sur les frontières de la reconnaissance. Les catégories internes et externes de l'identité collective." *Revue Européenne des migrations internationales* 21 (2005): 61–90.

Lamont, Michèle, and Virag Molnar. "The Study of Boundaries in the Social Sciences," *Annual Review of Sociology* 28 (2002):167–95.

————. "Toward a Comparative Sociology of Valuation and Evaluation." *Annual Review of Sociology* 38 (2012): 201–21.

Lasser, Carol, ed. *Educating Men and Women Together: Coeducation in a Changing World 1833–1908.* Urbana and Chicago: University of Illinois Press, 1987.

Lathrop, S. "The South: Ten Years at the Front." *The American Missionary* 43 (1889): 103–05.

Lemann, Nicholas. *Redemption: The Last Battle of the Civil War.* New York: Farrar, Straus & Giroux, 2006.

Lewis, Amanda. "What Group? Studying Whites and Whiteness in an Era of Colorblindness." *Sociological Theory* 22, no. 4 (2004): 623–46.

Lieberman, Robert. "The Freedmen's Bureau and the Politics of Institutional Structure." *Social Science History* 18, no. 3 (1994): 405–37.

Lifschitz, Arik, Michael Sauder, and Mitchell Stevens. "Football as a Status System in U.S. Higher Education." *Sociology of Education* 87 (2014): 204–19.

Little, Monroe. "The Extra-Curricular Activities of Black College Students 1868–1940." *Journal of Negro History* 65 (1980): 135–48.

Logan, John, Deidre Oakley, and Jacob Stowell. "School Segregation in Metropolitan Regions, 1970–2000: The Impacts of Policy Choices on Public Education." *American Journal of Sociology* 113 (2008): 1611–44.

Logan, Rayford W. *Howard University: The First Hundred Years: 1867–1967.* New York: New York University Press, 1969.

Loveman, Mara. "The Modern State and the Primitive Accumulation of Symbolic Power." *American Journal of Sociology* 110 (2005): 1651–83.

Loveman, Mara, and Jeronimo O. Muniz. "How Puerto Rico Became White: Boundary Dynamics and Inter-Census Racial Reclassification." *American Sociological Review* 72 (2007): 915–39.

Lynch, John R. *The Facts of Reconstruction.* Indianapolis: Bobbs-Merrill Co., 1913.

Mabee, Carleton. "A Negro Boycott to Integrate Boston Schools." *New England Quarterly* 41 (1968): 341–61.

MacClintock, S. "The Kentucky Mountains and Their Feuds." *American Journal of Sociology* 7 (1901): 1–28.

Marshall, T. H. *Citizenship and Social Class and Other Essays.* Cambridge, U.K.: Cambridge University Press, 1950.

Marx, Anthony W. *Making Race and Nation: A Comparison of South Africa, the United States and Brazil.* Cambridge, U.K.: Cambridge University Press, 1988.

Massey, Douglas, and Nancy Denton. "The Dimensions of Residential Segregation." *Social Forces* 67 (1988): 281–315.

McFeely, William S. *Yankee Stepfather: General O. O. Howard and the Freedmen.* New Haven: Yale University Press, 1968.

McIntyre, C. *Criminalizing a Race: Free Blacks under Slavery.* New York: Kayode, 1993.

McPherson, James M. "White Liberals and Black Power in Negro Education, 1865–1915." *American Historical Review* 75 (1970): 1357–86.

Meyer, John W. "The Effects of Education as an Institution." *American Journal of Sociology* 83 (1977): 55–77.

Meyer, John W., Francisco O. Ramirez, David John Frank, and Evan Schofer. "Higher Education as an Institution." In *Sociology of Higher Education*, edited by P. Gumport, 187–221. Baltimore: Johns Hopkins University Press, 2007.

Mische, Ann. "Projects and Possibilities: Researching Futures in Action." *Sociological Forum* 24 (2009): 694–704.

Moldow, Gloria. *Women Doctors in Gilded Age Washington: Race, Gender, and Professionalization.* Urbana: University of Illinois Press, 1987.

Moody, James. "Race, School Integration, and Friendship Segregation in America." *American Journal of Sociology* 107 (2001): 679–716.

Moore, Jacqueline. *Leading the Race: The Transformation of the Black Elite in the Nation's Capital, 1880–1920.* Charlottesville: University Press of Virginia, 1999.

Morantz-Sanchez, Regina Markell. *Sympathy & Science: Women Physicians in American Medicine.* Chapel Hill: University of North Carolina Press, 2000.

Moses, Wilson. *Black Messiahs and Uncle Toms: Social and Literary Manipulations of a Religious Myth*. (Revised Edition) The Pennsylvania State Universty, 1993.

Muhammad, Khalil. *The Condemnation of Blackness: Ideas about Race and Crime in the Making of Modern Urban America*. Cambridge, Mass.: Harvard University Press, 2011.

Munroe, John A. *The University of Delaware: A History*. Newark: University of Delaware Press, 1986.

Münsterberg, Hugo. *The Americans*. New York: Dodd, Meade and Co., 1904.

Nystrom, Justin. "Racial Identity and Reconstruction: New Orleans's Free People of Color and the Dilemma of Emancipation." In *The Great Task Remaining Before Us*, edited by Paul A. Cimbala and Randall M. Miller, 122–39. New York: Fordham University Press, 2010.

Olzak, Susan, and Suzanne Shanahan. "Racial Policy and Racial Conflict in the Urban United States, 1869–1924." *Social Forces* 82 (2003): 481–517.

Omi, Michael, and Howard Winant. *Racial Formation in the United States: From the 1960s to the 1980s*. New York: Routledge, 1986.

Orfield, Gary. *Schools More Separate: Consequences of a Decade of Resegregation*. Cambridge, Mass.: Harvard Civil Rights Project Report, 2001.

Orfield, Gary, and Chungmei Lee. *Brown at 50: King's Dream or Plessy's Nightmare?* Cambridge, Mass.: The Civil Rights Project at Harvard University, 2004.

Orloff, Ann Shola. *The Politics of Pensions: A Comparative Analysis of Britain, Canada, and the United States, 1880–1940*. Madison: University of Wisconsin Press, 1993.

Padgett, John, and Walter Powell. *The Emergence of Organizations and Markets*. Princeton: Princeton University Press, 2012.

Painter, Nell Irvin. *Exodusters: Black Migration to Kansas after Reconstruction*. New York: W. W. Norton & Co., 1976.

Palmieri, Patricia. *In Adamless Eden: The Community of Women Faculty at Wellesley*. New Haven: Yale University Press, 1997.

Paschel, Tianna. "The Right to Difference: Explaining Colombia's Shift from Color-Blindness to the Law of Black Communities." *American Journal of Sociology* 116 (2010): 729–69.

Patterson, Orlando. "Freedom, Slavery, and the Modern Construction of Rights." In *The Cultural Values of Europe*, edited by Hans Joas and Klaus Wiegandt, 115–51. Liverpool: Liverpool University Press, 2008.

———. "Slavery." *Annual Review of Sociology* 3 (1977): 407–49.

Peabody Education Fund. *Proceeding of the Trustees of the Peabody Education Fund, 1867–1914*. Boston: Press of John Wilson and Son.

Peitzman, Steven J. *A New and Untried Course: Woman's Medical College and Medical College of Pennsylvania, 1850–1998*. New Brunswick: Rutgers University Press, 2000.

Penner, Andrew, and Aliya Saperstein. "How Social Status Affects Race." *Proceedings of the National Academy of Sciences* 105 (2008): 19628–30.

Perkins, Linda. "The African-American Female 'Talented Tenth' A History of African American Women in Seven Sister Colleges." *Harvard Educational Review* 67 (Winter 1997): 718–56.

———. "The Nineteenth Century Black Women and Racial 'Uplift' Prior to Emancipation." In *The Black Woman: Cross Culturally*, edited by Filamena Steady, 317–35. Cambridge, Mass.: Schenkman Publishers.

Pfeffer, Jeffrey, and Gerald Salancik. *The External Control of Organizations: A Resource Dependence Perspective*. New York: Harper and Row, 1978.

Podolny, Joel. *Status Signals: A Sociological Study of Market Competition*. Princeton: Princeton University Press, 2008.

Potter, Lee Ann, and Wynell Schamel. "The Homestead Act of 1862." *Social Education* 61 (1997): 359–64.

Powell, Lawrence. *New Masters: Northern Planters during the Civil War and Reconstruction*. New Haven: Yale University Press, 1980.

Rankin, C. "The Origins of Black Leadership in New Orleans during Reconstruction." *Journal of Southern History* 40 (1974): 417–40.

Reardon, S. F., E. Grewal, D. Kalogrides, and E. Greenberg. "Brown Fades: The End of Court Ordered School Desegregation and the Resegregation of American Public Schools." *Journal of Policy Analysis and Management* 31 (2012): 876–904.

Renzulli, Linda. "Organizational Environments and the Emergence of Charter Schools in the United States." *Sociology of Education* 78 (2005): 1–26.

Reuben, Julie. *The Making of the Modern University*. Chicago: University of Chicago Press, 1996.

Richardson, Joe M. *Christian Reconstruction: The American Missionary Association and Southern Blacks, 1861–1890*. Athens: University of Georgia Press, 1986.

Rojas, Fabio. *From Black Power to Black Studies: How a Radical Social Movement Became an Academic Discipline*. Baltimore: Johns Hopkins University Press, 2007.

Rosenberg, Rosalind. *Changing the Subject: How the Women of Columbia Shaped the Way We Think About Sex and Politics*. New York: Columbia University Press, 2003.

Rudolph, Frederick. *The American College and University: A History*. Athens: University of Georgia Press, 1962.

Saatcioglu, A., and Jim Carl. "The Discursive Turn in School Desegregation: National Patters and a Case Analysis of Cleveland, 1973–1998." *Social Science History* 35 (2011): 59–108.

Saperstein, Aliya, Andrew Penner, and Ryan Light. "Racial Formation in Perspective." *Annual Review of Sociology* 39 (2013): 359–78.

Sauder, Michael, and Ryon Lancaster. "Do Rankings Matter? The Effects of U.S. News & World Report Rankings on the Admissions Process of Law Schools." *Law and Society Review* 40 (2006): 105–34.

Schofer, Evan, and John Meyer. "The Worldwide Expansion of Higher Education in the Twentieth Century." *American Sociological Review* 70 (2005): 898–920.

Schudson, Michael. *Discovering the News: A Social History of American Newspapers*. New York: Basic Books, 1978.

Schurz, Carl. *Report on Conditions in the States of South Carolina, Georgia, Alabama, Mississippi, and Louisiana to the 39th U.S. Senate*. Washington, D.C., 1865.

Sevelsted, Anders. "Doctrine and Discipline: A Genealogy of the Religious Voluntary Roots of Danish Welfare." Paper presented at the conference of the Social Science History Association, Baltimore, November 15, 2015.

Sewall, May Wright. "The Domestic and Social Effects of the Higher Education of Women. Read before the Western Association of Collegiate Alumnæ, at Ann Arbor, Mich., Dec. 10, 1887." Indiana Authors and their Books. http://purl.dlib.indiana.edu/iudl/inauthors/VAB1846, (retrieved June 2, 2014).

Sewell Jr., William. "Historical Events as Transformations of Structures: Inventing Revolution at the Bastille." *Theory and Society* 25, no. 6 (1996): 841–81.

Shanks, Trina Williams. "The Homestead Act: A Major Asset-Building Policy in American History." In *Inclusion in the American Dream: Assets, Poverty, and Public Policy*, edited by Michael Sherradan, 20–41. New York: Oxford University Press, 2005.

Shumway, A., and C. Brower. *Oberliniana. A Jubilee Volume of Semi-Historical Anecdotes Connected with the Past and Present of Oberlin College, 1833–1883.* Cleveland: Home Publishing Company, 1883.

Skocpol, Theda. *Protecting Soldiers and Mothers: The Political Origins of Social Policy in the United States.* Cambridge, Mass.: The Belknap Press of Harvard University Press, 1992.

Skocpol, Theda, and Jocelyn Elise Crowley. "The Rush to Organize: Explaining Associational Formation in the United States, 1860s–1920s." *American Journal of Political Science* 45 (2001): 813–29.

Skocpol, Theda, Marshall Ganz, and Ziad Munson. "A Nation of Organizers: The Institutional Origins of Civic Voluntarism in the United States." *American Political Science Review* 94 (2000): 527–46.

Skowronek, Stephen. *Building a New American State: The Expansion of National Administrative Capacities, 1877–1920.* Cambridge, U.K.: Cambridge University Press, 1982.

Skrentny, John D. *The Minority Rights Revolution.* Cambridge, Mass.: Harvard University, 2002.

———. "Policy-Elite Perceptions and Social Movement Success: Understanding Variations in Group Inclusion in Affirmative Action." *American Journal of Sociology* 111 (2006): 1762–815.

Slez, Adam, and John Levi Martin. "Political Action and Party Formation in the United States Constitutional Convention." *American Sociological Review* 72 (2007): 42–67.

Smajda, Jon, and Joseph Gerteis. "Ethnic Community and Ethnic Boundaries in a "Sauce-Scented Neighborhood." *Sociological Forum* 27 (2012): 617–40.

Smith, Anthony D. *The Ethnic Origins of Nations.* London: Basil Blackwell, 1986.

Smith, Christi M. "From Vice to Virtue: Racial Boundaries and Redemption Narratives in Late 19th Century Appalachian Feuds." *Race and Justice* 6, no. 2 (2016): 146–69.

Smith, Rogers M. *Civic Ideals: Conflicting Visions of Citizenship in U.S. History.* New Haven: Yale University Press, 1997.

Smithers, Gregory D. *Science, Sexuality and Race in the United States and Australia, 1780s–1890s.* New York: Routledge, 2008.

Snider, William. *Light on the Hill: A History of the University of North Carolina at Chapel Hill.* Chapel Hill: University of North Carolina Press, 1992.

Snyder, Thomas, ed. *120 Years of American Education: A Statistical Portrait.* Washington, D.C.: U.S. Department of Education, 1993.

Solomon, Barbara. *In the Company of Educated Women.* New Haven: Yale University Press, 1985.

———. "The Oberlin Model and Its Impact on Other Colleges." In *Educating Men and Women Together*, edited by Carol Lasser, 83–101. Urbana: University of Illinois Press, 1987.

Somers, Margaret R. "Citizenship and the Place of the Public Sphere: Law, Community, and Political Culture in the Transition to Democracy." *American Sociological Review* 58 (1993): 587–620.

———. *Genealogies of Citizenship: Markets, Statelessness, and the Right to Have Rights.* New York: Cambridge University Press, 2008.

Soskis, Benjamin. "The Problem of Charity in Industrial America, 1873–1915." PhD diss., Columbia University, 2010.

Soysal, Yasemin Nuhoglu, and David Strang. "Construction of the First Mass Education System in Nineteenth-Century Europe." *Sociology of Education* 62 (1989): 277–88.

Stamatov, Peter. 2015. *The Origins of Global Humanitarianism: Religion, Empires, and Advocacy.* Cambridge, U.K.: Cambridge University Press, 2015.

Starr, Paul. "Social Categories and Claims in the Liberal State." *Social Research* 50 (1992): 263–295.

———. *The Social Transformation of American Medicine: The Rise of a Sovereign Profession and the Making of a Vast Industry.* Chicago: University of Chicago Press, 1982.

Steensland, Brian. *The Failed Welfare Revolution: America's Struggle over Guaranteed Income Policy.* Princeton: Princeton University Press, 2008.

———. "Moral Classification and Social Policy." In *The Handbook on the Sociology of Morality*, edited by Steven Hitlin and Stephen Vaisey, 455–68. New York: Springer, 2010.

———. "Why do Policy Frames Change? Actor-Idea Coevolution in Debates over Welfare Reform." *Social Forces* 86, no. 3 (2008): 1027–54.

Steinberg, Marc. "The Talk and Back Talk of Collective Action: A Dialogic Analysis of Repertoires of Discourse among Nineteenth-Century English Cotton Spinners." *American Journal of Sociology* 105 (1999): 736–80.

Steinman, Erich. "Settler Colonial Power and the American Indian Sovereignty Movement: Forms of Domination, Strategies of Transformation." *American Journal of Sociology* 117 (2012): 1073–130.

Steinmetz, George. "The Devil's Handwriting": Precolonial Discourse, Ethnographic Acuity, and Cross-Identification in German Colonialism." *Comparative Studies in Society and History* 45 (2003): 41–95.

Stevens, Mitchell L. *Creating a Class: College Admissions and the Education of Elites.* Cambridge, Mass.: Harvard University Press.

Stevens, Mitchell L., Elizabeth Armstrong, and Richard Arum. "Sieve, Incubator, Temple, Hub: Empirical and Theoretical Advances in the Sociology of Higher Education." *Annual Review of Sociology* 34 (2008): 127–51.

Stille, Charles. *History of the United States Sanitary Commission: Being the General Report of its Work during the War of the Rebellion.* Philadelphia: Lippincott & Co., 1866.

Stoddart, Jess. *Challenge and Change in Appalachia: The Hindman Settlement School.* Lexington: University of Kentucky Press, 2002.

Swing, Albert. *James Harris Fairchild, or Sixty-Eight Years with a Christian College.* New York: Fleming H. Revell Co., 1907.

Talbot, Marion, and Lois Rosenberry. *The History of the American Association of University Women, 1881–1931.* Boston: Houghton Mifflin, 1931.

Thelin, John R. *A History of American Higher Education.* Baltimore: Johns Hopkins University Press, 2011.

Tolnay, Stewart, and E. M. Beck. *A Festival of Violence: An Analysis of Southern Lynchings, 1882–1930.* Champaign: University of Illinois Press, 1995.

Tunnell, Ted. *Crucible of Reconstruction: War, Radicalism, and Race in Louisiana, 1862–1877.* Baton Rouge: Louisiana State University Press, 1984.

Turkel, Stanley. *Heroes of the American Reconstruction: Profiles of Sixteen Educators, Politicians, and Activists.* Jefferson, N.C.: McFarland and Company, 2005.

Tyson, Karolyn. *Integration Interrupted: Tracking, Black Students, and Acting White after Brown.* New York: Oxford University Press, 2011.

United States Bureau of Census. "Historical Statistics of the United States, Colonial Times to 1970." Washington, D.C.: Government Printing Office, 1949.

United States Congress. *Report of the Joint Committee on Reconstruction.* 1st sess., 39th U.S. Congress. Washington, D.C.: Government Printing Office, 1866.

Vaughn, William. *Schools for All: The Blacks & Public Education in the South, 1865–1877.* Lexington: University Press of Kentucky.

Veblen, Thorstein. "The Barbarian Status of Women." *American Journal of Sociology* 4 (1898): 503–27.

Wacquant, Loïc. "Symbolic Power and Group-Making." *Journal of Classical Sociology* 0, no. 0 (2013): 1–18.

Wagner-Pacifici, Robin. *The Art of Surrender: Decomposing Sovereignty at Conflict's End.* Chicago: University of Chicago Press, 2005.

Wagner-Pacifici, Robin, and Meredith Hall. "Resolution of Social Conflict." *Annual Review of Sociology* 38 (2012): 181–99.

Waite, Cally. *Permission to Remain Among Us: Education for Blacks in Oberlin, Ohio, 1880–1914.* Westport: Praeger Publishers, 2002.

Walters, Pamela Barhouse, and David R. James. "Schooling for Some: Child Labor and School Enrollment of Black and White Children in the Early Twentieth-Century South." *American Sociological Review* 57 (1992): 635–50.

Washburn, Patrick. *The African American Newspaper: Voice of Freedom*. Evanston: Northwestern University Press, 2006.

Washington, Booker T. *The Story of My Life and Work*. New York: Cosimo Books, 2007.

Watson, Yolanda, and Sheila Gregory. *Daring to Educate: The Legacy of the Early Spelman College Presidents*. Sterling, Va.: Stylus Publishing, 2005.

Weber, Max. *Economy and Society: An Outline of Interpretive Sociology*. Berkeley: University of California Press, 1978.

———. "The 'Rationalization' of Education and Training." In *Max Weber: Essays in Sociology*, translated by H. H. Gerth and C. Wright Mills, 240–43. New York: Oxford University Press, 1991.

Wechsler, Harold S. *The Qualified Student: A History of Selective College Admission in America*. New Brunswick: Transaction Publishers, 2014. First published 1977 by John Wiley & Sons.

Weiss, Richard, and Lynn Miller. "The Social Transformation of American Medical Education: Class, Status, and Party Influences on Occupational Closure, 1902–1919." *Sociological Quarterly* 51 (2010): 550–75

Weitzer, R. "The Social Construction of Sex Trafficking: Ideology and Institutionalization of a Moral Crusade." *Politics & Society* 35 (2007): 447–75.

Wells, Amy Stuart, Jennifer Jellison Holme, Anita Tijerina Revilla, and Awo Korantemaa Atanda. *All Sides Now: The Story of School Desegregation's Graduates*. Berkeley: University of California Press, 2009.

Wells-Barnett, Ida. "The Red Record Tabulated Statistics and Alleged Causes of Lynching in the United States." Project Gutenberg, 2005. Downloaded from https://archive.org/stream/theredrecord14977gut/14977.txt, on June 4, 2015.

Wilde, Melissa, and Sabrina. Danielsen. "Fewer and Better Children: Race, Class, Religion, and Birth Control Reform in America." *American Journal of Sociology* 119 (2014): 1710–60.

Wilder, Craig Steven. *Ebony and Ivy: Race, Slavery, and the Troubled History of America's Universities*. New York: Bloomsbury Press, 2013.

Wilson, Shannon. *Berea College: An Illustrated History*. Lexington: University of Kentucky Press, 2006.

Wimmer, Andreas. "Elementary Strategies of Ethnic Boundary Making." *Ethnic and Racial Studies* 31 (2008): 1025–55.

———. "Herder's Heritage and the Boundary-Making Approach. Studying Ethnicity in Immigrant Societies." *Sociological Theory* 27 (2009): 244–70.

Wimmer, Andreas, and Kevin Lewis. "Beyond and Below Racial Homophily. An Exponential Random Graph Model of Social Networks among College Students." *American Journal of Sociology* 116 (2010): 583–642.

Winant, Howard. "Race and Race Theory." *Annual Review of Sociology* 26 (2000): 169–85.

———. "White Racial Projects." In *The Making and Unmaking of Whiteness*, edited by Birgit Brander Rasmussen, Eric Klinenberg, Irene J. Nexica, and Matt Wray, 97–112. Durham, N.C.: Duke University Press, 2001.

Woodson, Carter G. *Education of the Negro Prior to 1861*. New York: Putnam Sons, 1915.

——. "Kelly Miller." *Journal of Negro History* (1940): 137–38.

Woodward, C. Vann. *Origins of the New South, 1877–1913*. Baton Rouge: Louisiana State University Press, 1951.

——. *The Strange Career of Jim Crow*. Oxford: Oxford University Press, 1955.

Wray, Matt. *Not Quite White: White Trash and the Boundaries of Whiteness*. Durham, N.C.: Duke University Press, 2006.

Zelizer, Viviana A. *The Purchase of Intimacy*. Princeton: Princeton University Press, 2007.

Zolberg, Astride, and Long Litt Woon. "Why Islam Is like Spanish: Cultural Incorporation in Europe and the United States." *Politics & Society* 27 (1999): 5–38.

Index

Abbot, Andrew, 126

Abolitionists and abolitionism: and anti-caste movement, 2, 3–4, 173; emancipation as goal of, 3; as international movement, 47; emotionally persuasive campaigns of, 53; and higher education, 60, 64, 73, 175, 193; mobilization of, 65–66, 73; on fallacy of color as signifier of moral character, 69; and AMA, 122; and women's activism, 145; on institutional effects of slavery, 208–9

Adams, John Quincy, 66

Adults, access to citizenship rights, 31

Africa, 203

African Methodist Episcopal Church, 51, 192, 196

African students, at Howard University, 86

The Afro-American, 128–29

Agassiz, Louis, 216

Alabama: black voting rights in, 23; exemptions for white voters in, 23; and land redistribution, 41; state-supported higher education in, 56; Appalachian counties of, 225, 232

Alabama A&M University, 265n52

Alcorn University, 192, 265nn43, 52

Alexander, Michelle, 13

Allen College, 192

Allport, Gordon, 85

American Anti-Slavery Society, 65–66

American Association of University Women, 27

American Baptist Home Missionary Society, 51

American capitalism, feudalism compared to, 3

American caste system: race as marker in, 2, 13, 14, 34, 68, 112; AMA's focus on dismantling of, 15, 28. *See also* Anti-caste movement

American Colonization Society, 254n22

American Institute of Instruction, 52

American Journal of Sociology, 215, 219, 223

American Medical Association, 19, 156, 228, 238

American Missionary Association (AMA): in anti-caste movement, 3, 4–5, 10, 28, 59, 68, 105, 106, 109, 130, 242; and racial coeducation, 3, 4, 5–6, 8, 9, 12, 50, 52, 71, 106, 113, 126, 127–28, 173, 212, 231, 235; and interpersonal transformation, 5; moral ideals of, 5, 10, 67, 69, 111, 123, 126, 134, 163, 212, 235; affiliated colleges of, 8, 14, 51–52, 58–59, 67–68, 71, 72, 77, 80, 82–83, 88, 105–7, 109, 111, 122, 127–28, 136, 147, 172, 173, 231, 237, 255n46; primary schools founded by, 8, 14, 15, 67, 131; obligation hoarding of, 10, 54, 138; national organization of, 11; and cultural beliefs around race, 13, 67; on education as reparation, 13–14, 15, 33, 106, 124–25; on social relief as reparation, 13–14, 15, 33, 122; and citizenship of blacks, 14–15, 24, 123, 124, 125, 127; on influence of education, 19; funding of higher education, 27, 68, 72, 102, 105, 106, 133, 137, 231; state circumnavigated

Berea College (cont.)
88, 89, 207, 213, 226, 231; planned
interracial residential community
of, 78; and anti-caste education, 79,
80, 85, 89, 101, 138, 206, 214, 225;
mission of, 79, 85, 96; and poor
whites, 81, 140, 206–8, 211–12;
enrollment strategies of, 86, 87,
88–89, 91, 94, 175, 265n43; administrators of, 91, 92, 95, 101, 119, 120,
162, 197, 206, 227, 229; learning and
labor programs of, 93–94, 99, 158;
donors to, 94, 107, 140, 211, 215, 217,
222, 223; preparatory division of, 94,
103; professions of alumni, 95, 101;
dormitories of, 97; extracurricular
activities of, 97–99, 100; literary
societies of, 97–99, 100, 256n92;
egalitarianism at, 99, 101; William
Frost's lecture on, 99; commencement exercises of, 100; shifts in
educational landscape, 107; and
black migration, 119–20; distancing
from AMA, 122; General Education
Board's donation to, 132–33;
exceptionalism of, 136, 141;
industrial training of poor whites,
140, 206; physical activity for
students, 158; and industrial
education, 201, 214, 225; and
ethnographic capital, 207, 213–14,
218, 220, 222–23, 232; and white
redemption, 211–12; and colonialism, 215; and natural sciences, 215;
and social sciences, 215, 216–17,
220, 222, 223; political influence
of, 222–23; and Day Law banning
integration, 226, 228, 230; collegiate athletics at, 256n90
Bertram, James, 260n93
Biddle College, 262n21
Binder, Amy, 85–86
Biological determinism, 159, 161–62,
165, 167–68
Birth of a Nation (film), 201

Bismarck, Otto von, 213
Black athletes, civil rights of, 186
Black codes, 36, 123, 124, 241
Black criminalization, 200, 201
Black elites: and Howard University,
6, 7, 188–202; in Washington, D.C.,
98; success of, 128; and social
movements, 197
Black middle class, 64, 129
Black migration: to North, 107,
117–21, 215, 220–21; to West, 107,
118, 119, 120, 197; U.S. Senate's
investigation of, 118, 119
Black personhood, Northern expectations of, 53
Blacks: industrial colleges for, 6, 7, 27,
133, 137, 138, 140, 180, 188, 193, 195,
199, 200, 201, 206, 208, 214, 236, 239,
249n89; voting rights of, 13, 14–15,
43–44, 45, 49, 146; civil rights of,
19–20, 30, 31; citizenship rights of,
23, 24, 34–35, 61, 204; and land
redistribution, 30, 32, 33, 37, 38–41,
44, 49, 235; education of, 45, 48–50,
130–35; alliance with poor whites,
48; education as means of white
control over, 48–49, 131; poor
whites' morality compared to, 53;
preference for black teachers, 53–54;
higher education opportunities for,
55, 60, 65, 100, 115–16, 137, 140–41,
152, 153, 156, 180–81, 195, 206, 210,
236–37, 240; political power of, 57,
108–9, 118, 197–200, 220, 221;
narratives of economic and political
worth of, 61; and Booker T.
Washington's uplift ideology, 71;
land ownership of, 78; civic
associations of, 81, 82; intellectual
capacity of, 100; violence against,
105, 109, 115, 117, 118, 121, 124, 128,
129, 184, 197, 210, 236; AMA linking
other groups to, 127; achievements
of, 128–29, 197–99, 237–38, 241;
high school education for, 170; poor

whites in competition with, 210.
See also Black elites

Black veterans, benefits for, 116
Blake, Lillie Devereaux, 153–54
Blight, David, 211
Bond, Horace Mann, 242
Bonilla-Silva, Edward, 20
Boston University, 115
Bourdieu, Pierre, 5, 11, 18, 135, 238
Bowdoin College, 115, 254n21
Brazil, 47
Brown, John, 77, 192
Brown, William, 14
Brown University, 94, 144, 153, 254n21
Bruce, Blanche, 108, 193
Bumstead, Horace, 165, 240, 270n10
Burdett, Gabriel, 72, 119–20, 259n49
Bureau of Education, 167
Bureau of Refugees, Freedmen, and
   Abandoned Lands (BRFAL): and
   education in South, 4, 32, 33, 51,
   52–55, 102, 131, 138; AMA coordinat-
   ing placement of teachers in schools
   of, 5; closing of, 13–14; and North-
   ern tutelary governance of South,
   30, 52; creation of, 32; and land
   redistribution, 40–41; and Union
   Army, 41; demand for black teachers
   in South, 53–54; AMA working
   with, 67; faculty of AMA-affiliated
   colleges working in, 72; in Kentucky, 79; enforcement of legal
   protections, 112; loss of support
   for, 122; and poor whites, 212, 220
Burlingame-Seward Treaty (1868),
   124
Butler, Benjamin, 111–12
Buttrick, Wallace, 260n93
Buttrick, William, 132

Cable, George Washington, 100, 115,
   116–17, 131
Cain, Harvey, 110, 111–12, 115
California: AMA missions for
   Chinese immigrants in, 107, 122–23;

measures against Chinese immi-
   grants, 124
Campbell, John C., 225, 227–28
Campbell, Robert F., 223–24
Camp Nelson refugee camp, Ken-
   tucky, 72, 78, 119
Canada, 182
Capitalist contributions, to higher
   education, 28
Capitalist logics, and social reform,
   132
Cardozo, Francis L., 93, 192, 197,
   256n78
Carnegie, Andrew, 166, 170–71
Carnegie Foundation, 19
Carnegie Foundation for the Advancement of Teaching, 156, 166,
   170–71
Catholics, education projects in
   South, 10
Change: and culture, 67; macro-level
   social change, 85, 106–7; in legal
   system, 108–17; and individual
   transformation, 235
Chicago Daily Tribune, 265n51
Chicago Tribune: on Oberlin College,
   6, 92, 179; on BRFAL, 30; on land
   redistribution, 39; on military occupation, 43; on voting rights, 45; on
   education, 49, 51; on Berea College,
   79; on college commencement
   activities, 99–100; on racial
   coeducation, 100; on black migration, 118; on black rights, 124;
   on Harvard University, 154; on
   women's higher education, 154, 160;
   on Howard University, 190, 192;
   on Appalachian whites, 221; and
   Reform Republicans, 250n30
Children, access to citizenship rights,
   31
China, 86, 124
Chinese immigrants: AMA missions
   for, 107, 122–23, 127, 220, 242;
   federal treaties concerning, 124

Committee on Country Life, 224

Compromise of 1877, 113

Conference for Education in the South (CES), 131–32

Congregational Club, 162

Congregationalists, 10, 191, 193

Connecticut, state-support higher education in, 56–57

Connecticut insurance companies, 2–3

Conservative Republicans: Reconstruction policies of, 30–31, 33, 34–35; and Northern immigrants' management of Southern agriculture, 37–38; on land redistribution, 40; on segmented citizenship rights, 40, 61; on voting rights, 44, 45, 46, 48, 61; on education for blacks, 48, 61, 62; on subservient status of blacks, 48; on social equality, 112; Lily White political bloc of, 196

Contact theory: and interpersonal interaction as key to overcoming prejudice, 20–21, 65, 68, 85, 238; interracial contact compared to coeducation, 26; as solution to problem of racial segregation, 65

Convention of Colored Men, 109

Conway, Jill Ker, 151

Cook, John Francis, 81–82

Cooper, Anna Julia, 99, 150, 156–57, 262n23

Cooper Institute, 99

Cornell, Ezra, 104

Cornell University, 8, 57, 95–96, 104, 110, 154, 177, 190, 198

Cowles, Henry, 88

Cox, Jacob Dolson, 92, 176

Cravath, Erastus, 119

Cultural sociology, and contestation around racial meanings, 21

Culture: beliefs about race, 13, 67; and change, 67; and interracial cooperation, 68; as repertoire, 68

Curry, J. M. L., 131, 132

Dartmouth College, 154, 254n21

Davis, Jefferson, 38, 108

Davis Bend Plantation, 38

Decatur Institute (now Agnes Scott College), 164

De facto discrimination, 170

De facto segregation, 10, 65, 232, 239

De jure segregation, 10, 65

Democratic Party: and Southern planter class, 44; view of blacks, 74; and poor whites, 210

Democratic societies: and education as arena for merit, 17–18, 28, 238; education as key power in shaping, 28, 49; as representative, 31; Jacksonian democratic ideals, 94

Demographic changes, 107, 121, 123, 213

Denison College, 176

Dillard, James, 260n93

DiMaggio, Paul, 18

Dix, Morgan, 153–54

Dixon, Thomas, 201

Doctrine of Social Equality, 3

Dodge, V. I., 89

Douglas, Mary, 127, 136

Douglass, Frederick, 93, 119, 192, 197, 200, 256n78

Dred Scott case (1857), 259n57

DuBois, W. E. B., 150, 169–70, 224, 241, 262n21, 265n62

Dunning School, 200

East Asia, immigrants from, 107, 121, 122

Eastern Europe, immigrants from, 107, 121

Easton, John, 83

Eaton, John, 102

Economic growth, and access to higher education, 17

Education: primary education, 8, 14, 15, 52, 53, 57, 58, 67, 130, 133, 137, 264n24; infrastructure of, 9; role of education in Reconstruction, 12,

Education (cont.)
16–17, 30, 32, 35, 37, 38, 41, 45, 48–50, 61, 80; and social status, 12, 15, 19, 22; as reparation for former slaves, 13–14, 15, 33, 106; and merit through educational achievement, 17–18, 28, 48; and citizenship, 22–24; desegregation and resegregation in twentieth century, 24, 26; and voting rights, 45, 46, 47, 48; as means of discipline, 48, 61, 62; and white control over blacks, 48; public-private partners in South, 50–55; freedmen's schools, 51, 57, 62, 128, 146, 185, 195; adult education, 52, 53; and black teachers, 53–54, 120; and Northern teachers, 53, 54, 95, 146; public campaigns for school funding, 53–54; high school education, 54, 57, 94, 133, 134, 137, 148, 170, 175, 178, 264n13; access to, 57, 111–12; black representation on local boards of education, 109; and legal system changes, 109; and philanthropic foundations, 130–35; equality in educational opportunity, 234. *See also* Gender coeducation; Higher education; Racial coeducation

Egalitarianism: and anti-caste movement, 5, 7, 20, 28, 63, 69, 105, 111, 115, 129, 219, 235; implementation of reforms, 11

Elites: and higher education, 17–18, 19, 94, 95–96, 154–55, 158, 177, 208; state consecration of, 18; liberal arts education for, 27; and state funding of education, 57; and education in South, 62; demographic changes as status threat to, 123; jurisdiction in domains of state policy, 141; private preparatory schools for, 264n13

Emancipation: and anti-caste movement, 3–4; black Americans' reaction to, 7; as legal recategorization of enslaved persons, 14; Southern planter class's resistance to, 40; military occupation for enforcement of, 42; post-emancipation social relations, 53; and Howard University, 189; promise of, 235

Emancipation Proclamation, 47, 76, 192, 207

Emirbayer, Mustafa, 18

Enslaved persons: counted as three-fifths of a person, 2, 44; reparations for, 13–14; status transformation of, 14; range of skin shades, 69–70; slave owners' raping of enslaved women, 69; American debt to former slaves, 106

Enslavement of blacks: and anti-caste movement, 2–4, 47, 69; biblical "Curse of Ham" as justification for, 2; corruption of U.S. political, legal, and social institutions, 2–3; slavery as shared historical condition, 2; as economic domination, 3; U.S. reckoning with specter of, 12; and logic of race as marker of status inequality, 13; and rules governing citizenship, 22; slavery as barrier to modern governance, 34; international support for abolition of, 47; European feudalism compared to, 49; effect on poor whites, 59, 77, 208–9, 211–12, 216–17, 219, 223; and social construction of race, 68–69; AMA on, 69, 126, 127; institutional effects of, 208–9. *See also* Reparations

Equal accommodations, denial of, 114

Equal Protection Clause of Fourteenth Amendment, 25, 253n112

Equal Rights League, 116

Espeland, Wendy, 166

Ethnic boundaries: role of organizations in, 11, 19; and absence of state control over elite higher education, 18; organizational actors attaching meanings to, 22; and citizenship rights in Europe, 23; and Appalachian whites, 223

Europe: revolutions of 1848 in, 2, 47; and citizenship based on ethnic heritage, 23; class politics in, 47; feudalism in, 49

External organizations: resistance to racial coeducation, 19, 107; mediation of status contests, 107. *See also* Benevolent organizations; Philanthropic foundations; Professional organizations

Fairchild, Charles, 72

Fairchild, Edward H.: on caste prejudice, 69; on color-coded social hierarchy, 70; at Oberlin College, 72; as president of Berea College, 72; on racial coeducation, 78–79, 99; and donors, 80; and poor whites, 206–7, 211–12; and Appalachian whites, 224

Fairchild, James H.: on racial coeducation, 68, 73–74; as president of Oberlin College, 72; on enrollment strategies, 87, 187; inaugural address of 1866, 103, 205, 257n3; on women's higher education, 151; and market-driven field of higher education, 177

Fee, John, 70–71, 72, 77–79, 88, 99, 119

Fee, Matilda, 78

Fee, Tappan, 78

Feminism, 145, 146, 149, 158

Ferguson, Champ, 249n2

Feudalism: and anti-caste movement, 2, 3; U.S.'s break from, 3; vestiges of, 47; enslavement of blacks compared to, 49

Field, Henry, 189

Fifteenth Amendment, 14, 253n112

Fine, Gary Alan, 106, 202, 204

Finney, C. G., 92

Fisher, Abigail, 25

Fisher v. the University of Texas–Austin (2012), 25

Fisk University, 8, 149, 187, 198, 265n43

Fisk University Jubilee Singers, 72, 119

Flexner Report, 19, 156

Fligstein, Neil, 18

Florida: and land redistribution, 41; state-supported higher education in, 56

Foreign Anti-Slavery Society, 66

Former Confederates: voting rights of, 14–15, 44–45; trials of, 29, 249n2; Andrew Johnson's pardoning of, 36, 45; claiming abandoned lands, 41

Former Confederate States: requirements for readmission to Union, 9, 16, 29, 32–33, 108; lack of material resources contributed for education, 55; constitutions of, 108; land redistribution in, 117; political autonomy of, 211

Fortune, T. Thomas, 114

Fourteenth Amendment, 14, 23, 25, 114, 124, 253n112, 259n57

France, 47–48

Frank Leslie's Illustrated, 147

Franklin, Benjamin, 57

Franklin, John Hope, 113

Freedmen: education as compensation for unrequited labor and military service, 32, 80, 124–25; freedmen's schools, 51, 57, 62, 128, 146, 185, 195; BRFAL providing support for schools in South, 53

Freedmen's aid societies, 53

Freedmen's Village, Arlington, 82

Free persons of color, in New Orleans, 50–51

French Bourbons, 47

in-groups and out-groups, 12; cultural deservedness of, 24; and mountain education, 28, 207, 212, 228; political rights of, 61, 62; and colleges' dependency on donors, 107, 122; AMA's focus on particular groups, 126, 136, 231; General Education Board's organizing education to match groups, 132; and competition in higher education, 138, 208, 236; and ethnographic expertise, 202, 204, 220, 240; and defining Appalachian whites, 222–25, 227–28; determination of status quo, 234

Grutter v. Bollinger (2003), 249n84

Gutman, Amy, 188

Habitus, college campuses disrupting, 5

Hadley, Arthur, 116

Haiti, 108

Hall, John, 223

Hallett, Tim, 85, 106

Hampton Institute, 8, 133, 140, 213, 214, 225

Hampton University, 60

Harlan, John Marshall, 229–30

Harper's Ferry, West Virginia, 77

Harper's Magazine, 223, 226, 269n60

Harper's Weekly, 53–54, 69–70, 108, 112, 214

Hartshorn Memorial College, 262n21

Harvard Civil Rights Project (now at UCLA), 20

Harvard University: black enrollment in, 8, 24, 110, 115–16; and Berea College's preparatory division, 94; annex for women, 144, 153, 154–55; administrators of, 162; and Association of American Universities, 167; faculty of, 177; high school preparation for, 178; scientific racism studies at, 200

Hatfield-McCoy feud, 218, 224

Hayes, Rutherford B., 113, 129, 131, 200, 211

Haygood, Atticus, 131

Hazen, Frances, 150–51

Hemmings, Anita Florence, 150

Higginson, Thomas, 158

Higginsworth, Thomas, 152

Higher education: as political training ground, 6, 8; practice of racial integration, 8, 9, 11, 16, 17, 21, 26; symbolic status of, 8; competitive environment of, 9, 12, 15, 16, 17, 21–22, 23, 26, 27, 55, 105, 107, 136, 138, 139–40, 141, 156, 166, 172, 173, 175, 176, 177, 188, 231–33, 236–43, 252n99; and Protestant organizations, 10; distinctions between forms of, 15–16, 19, 25, 132, 141, 158, 206, 207, 208, 236, 239–40, 242; expanding field of, 15–20, 55–56, 58, 140, 141, 173, 176–83, 185, 208, 252n99; and enrollment increases, 16, 55; and national reunification, 16; access to, 17, 25, 26, 55, 57, 60, 115–16, 142, 152, 157–58, 180–81; and bureaucratization of merit, 17–18, 24, 165, 167, 236; and elite universities, 18–19, 95–96, 154–55, 158, 162, 177, 247n60; as organizational field, 18–19, 102–3; and anti-caste movement, 19, 20, 24, 58, 65, 70, 71, 79, 82–83, 101, 103, 138–41, 142, 163, 169, 208, 238, 239; forms of, 19, 55, 68, 81, 122, 139, 145; inclusive forms of, 19; ranking and rating of, 19, 21, 27, 141, 163–68, 172, 239–40; research universities, 19; purpose of, 21, 138; racial segregation of, 24–26, 55, 131, 135, 137, 138, 241; dual pathways of, 25; as foundational for pluralistic society, 25–26; commensuration as governing mechanism, 27, 107, 138, 143, 144, 164, 166–67, 171, 172, 236; social change through, 28; federal

Muhammad, Khalil, 200
Münsterberg, Hugo, 155–56, 241
Murphy, Starr, 260n93

Napoleon I (emperor of the French),
    51
National Association for the Advance-
    ment of Colored People, 265n62
National Association of Land Grant
    Colleges, 167
National Bureau of Education, 102,
    104
National Equal Rights League, 125
National Freedmen's Relief Associa-
    tion, 70
National Woman Suffrage Associa-
    tion, 154
Native Americans: citizenship rights
    of, 23; at Howard University, 86;
    military action against, 112–13; and
    AMA, 122, 123–26, 127, 220, 242;
    voting rights of, 124
Nativism, 215, 220, 221, 226
New Grenada, 47
New Hampshire, state-support higher
    education in, 56–57
New Jersey, violence against blacks in,
    105, 257n10
New Orleans, Louisiana: blacks
    fleeing rural plantations for, 50–51;
    free persons of color in, 50–51;
    Union occupation of, 50–51
New York: state-supported higher
    education in, 57; donations to AMA
    colleges, 58; women's voting rights
    in, 146
New York Central College, 75
New York City, 3, 37, 215
New York Globe, 114
New York Medical College for
    Women, 147
New York Press Club, 154
New York Times: on civil War, 2; on
    Berea College, 5, 89, 99; on blacks
    compared to European serfs, 34; on

Northern immigrants' management
    of Southern agriculture, 37–38;
    on poor whites, 46, 209–10; on
    education of blacks, 49; on O. O.
    Howard, 84; on college commence-
    ment activities, 99–100; on women's
    higher education, 146, 148, 159; on
    Howard University, 190, 193, 196;
    William Frost's articles in, 223; and
    Conservative Republicans, 250n30
Niagara Movement, 195, 265n62
Noblesse de robe, 18
North: dependence on Southern
    economy, 37; education system in,
    49, 50; private higher education in,
    56, 57; state-supported higher
    education in, 56–57, 136–37, 148;
    black migration to, 107, 117–21,
    220–21; social prejudice in, 115–16;
    discriminatory codes passed in, 123;
    xenophobic fears in Northeast, 212,
    213, 220, 221, 222. See also Reunifica-
    tion of North and South
North Carolina: black voting rights
    in, 23; exemptions for white voters
    in, 23; state-supported higher
    education in, 56; effects of Civil
    War on, 208; Appalachian counties
    of, 225, 227, 232
Northern elites, and rights packages
    of Reconstruction policy, 36–37
Northfield College, 147
Northwestern University, 148, 177

Obama, Barack, 28
Oberlin College: and AMA leader-
    ship, 6; black enrollment in, 6, 73,
    74, 75, 76, 86–88, 95, 96, 100, 149,
    174, 176, 179, 180, 181, 187–88, 228,
    246n21; male leadership, 6, 27,
    173–74, 183, 202, 203, 204–5; and
    racial coeducation, 6, 15–16, 22, 27,
    58, 65, 73, 74, 76, 96, 100, 104–5, 110,
    127, 149, 174, 175, 176, 179, 181,
    186–88, 228, 229, 238–39; student

Organizational logics, of philanthropic foundations, 131

Otterbein College, black students recruited by, 60

Outlook, 223

Page, Inman, 94

Panama, 47

Patriotism, as qualification for voting rights, 45

Patton, William Weston, 90–91, 189, 192–93, 200, 234, 237, 238, 265n51

Peabody, George Foster, 132

Peabody Foundation, 130, 131, 260n81

Peace: and racial coeducation, 3; and reeducation of whites, 5; and Reconstruction policies, 29; military occupation for securing, 42; and egalitarianism, 69

Peck, Henry, 75

Penick, C. Clifton, 1, 5

Perkins, Linda, 150

Peru, 86, 182

Petit, Katherine, 227

Philanthropic foundations: and AMA, 105; and competition in higher education, 107, 236; and industrial philanthropists, 107, 132; and Southern education, 130–35, 137; and women's higher education, 156; and Howard University, 197; and Appalachian whites, 213, 217, 225

Phillips, Wendell, 44

Pieh, Sengbe, 66

Pinchback, P. B. S., 108

Plessy, Homer, 184

Plessy v. Ferguson (1896), 211, 220–21, 230, 241

Podolny, Joel, 136, 137

Police brutality, as new Jim Crow, 13

Political orientation, as social boundary, 22

Polygenism, 158, 216

Pomeroy, Samuel, 93

Poor whites: and anti-caste movement, 4; and stigma of Confederacy, 28; citizenship rights of, 30, 31, 34, 35, 44; education of, 45, 46, 48, 49–50, 51, 209, 212; voting rights of, 45, 46, 50; alliance with blacks, 48, 50, 81; and AMA, 50, 125, 127–28, 206–7, 209, 210; blacks' morality compared to, 53; effects of slavery on, 59, 77, 208–9, 211–12, 216–17, 219, 223; and Berea College, 81, 140, 206–7; industrial education for, 140, 260; historical context of representations, 207, 208–10; as Unionists, 208–9, 215; blacks in competition with, 210; violence against blacks, 210; medicalization of, 224–25; and whiteness, 232. *See also* Appalachian whites

Poverty relief, conflict over role of public and private efforts in, 54, 138–39

Powell, Walter, 18

Power: multi-institutional theories of, 11; symbolic power, 11, 18, 230, 235

Presbyterians, 10, 73, 226

Press: on racial integration of higher education, 8–9; on Reconstruction policies, 36; on land redistribution, 38, 40, 41; on education of freedmen, 54; on interracial colleges, 79, 80; on comparisons in higher education, 141; on Howard University, 189, 190; on poor whites, 212, 214, 217. *See also specific newspapers*

Princeton University, 133, 154, 177

Prisoners, and access to citizenship rights, 31

Private boarding schools, 123

Private organizations: and nation-rebuilding efforts, 9; and racial structures, 11–12; boundaries of, 12; legitimacy of, 12, 14; organizational emergence as count process, 16; colleges founded by, 17, 18, 19, 58;

differentiation and exclusion of blacks, Appalachian whites, and white women from higher education, 19, 238; abandonment of practices of integration, 26; and administration of public goods, 55; legal changes permitting discrimination by, 107; racial discrimination allowed by, 114; and Southern education, 131, 133–34, 139; influence in social institutions, 133–34; and funding for higher education, 137, 139, 168, 240; democratic role of, 234–35

Professional organizations, and competition in higher education, 107

Professions, access to, 19

Property ownership, as qualification for voting rights, 45, 108

Property rights, and Civil Rights Bills, 111

Protestantism: and AMA, 5, 14, 67, 111, 129; and higher education, 10; and Oberlin College, 73, 182

Public health campaigns, 221

Public health crises, as result of Civil War, 7

Public-private sectors: boundaries of, 10–11, 12, 230; and higher education, 18, 19, 24, 55, 56, 137, 139, 247n60, 248–49n82; and education in South, 50–55, 62; and poverty relief, 54, 138–39; and equal accommodations, 114–15; and women, 151

Pullman, George, 119

Quinn, Paul, 192

Race: as marker in American caste system, 2, 13, 14, 34, 68, 112; liminality of in nineteenth-century education, 8; social construction of, 10, 20, 21, 67, 68–69, 197, 231; types

of education projected on, 12, 15; cultural beliefs around, 13, 68; essentialist notions of, 20; organizational actors attaching meanings to, 22; and access to citizenship rights, 31; Reform Republicans on, 42; teachers' beliefs about, 52; meanings of, 68–69, 70, 207, 216, 218, 231–32; as social barrier, 141; and scientific racism, 158, 200, 223

Race relations: industrialists' influence on race relations in South, 107; and AMA, 121–22, 128; and Howard University, 196–202

Racial boundaries: perpetuation of, 12; causal relationship with status boundary processes, 16; organizational actors' activation of, 207, 219–20; of Appalachian region, 225

Racial categories: reinscription of, 7, 232; and absence of state control over elite higher education, 18; and private organizations, 19; and racial social systems, 20; and organizational development, 238–39

Racial coeducation: at Berea College, 1, 5, 6, 15–16, 27, 67–68, 70, 71, 96, 97, 100, 104–5, 110, 127, 175, 206, 214, 220, 225, 228–29, 230, 232–33, 238–39; and AMA, 3, 4, 5–6, 8, 12, 19, 50, 52, 58, 71, 106, 113, 126, 127–28, 173, 212, 231, 235; and anti-caste movement, 3, 5, 21, 24, 26, 58–59, 63, 70, 173, 235; and gender coeducation, 6, 21, 142; and Howard University, 6, 15–16, 27, 71, 100, 104–5, 127, 175, 188–89, 190, 194, 195, 196, 201, 238–39; and Oberlin College, 6, 15–16, 22, 27, 58, 65, 73, 74, 76, 96, 100, 104–5, 110, 127, 149, 174, 175, 176, 179, 181, 186–88, 228, 229, 238–39; shift into segmented system, 6–7, 9; within broader field of higher education, 15–16, 55, 62; resistance from external organizations, 19, 107, 138;

Racial coeducation (cont.)
racial integration distinguished from, 21; benefits of, 25, 52, 60, 68, 110–11, 179, 236; and development of integrated organizations, 26; and primary education, 58; local resistance to, 59, 138

Racial discrimination: legal changes permitting, 107, 114–15, 122; legal changes prohibiting, 110, 111–12; prohibition against in private spaces, 110, 112, 113–15; and ACA, 169, 170; and Oberlin College, 187; and Howard University, 199

Racial equality: debates on college campuses, 98–99; and AMA, 128, 129–30; and racial uplift ideology, 195; and Howard University, 198

Racial formation, theory of, 10–11

Racial hierarchies: debates on, 20; and higher education, 23; and academic understandings of merit, 24, 248n68; Conservative Republicans on retention of, 34–35; and AMA, 67; assumptions of, 71; and women's higher education, 161–62; linking value assessment to, 220

Racial identities, defining of, 10, 231, 232

Racial integration: early struggle for, 12; resistance from external organizations, 19; and contact theory, 20–21; implementation of, 21, 238; and interaction between colleges, 21–22; racial coeducation distinguished from, 21; studies of, 85–86; and Civil Rights Bills, 111, 112; failure of, 241–42; and plurality of institutional infrastructures, 242–43

Racial isolation, measurement of, 21

Racial justice: reparations for injustice, 13–14; and graduates of anti-caste movement colleges, 65; and colorblind language, 69; and Howard University, 198

Racial logics: instability of, 20; race as basis of social status, 106

Racial prejudice: as threat to republican governance, 3, 69; as source of unequal access to education, 17; and contact theory, 20–21, 65, 68, 71, 105; and racial coeducation, 24, 58, 113; education's role in reducing, 48, 71, 99, 100, 126, 127; and individual transformation, 117, 120, 129, 230, 235; AMA's rationality of, 124, 126, 127; W. W. Patton on, 234

Racial schemas, racial coeducation's transformation of, 21

Racial segregation: multilevel analysis of, 11; and schemas imposing hierarchy, 11; of education, 13, 24, 25; legitimatization and normalization of, 16; use of law to combat, 20; of higher education, 24–26; organizational structures of, 26; embedded nature of, 33, 242–43; contact theory as solution to problem of, 65; legal equality contrasted with, 115; and Niagara Movement, 265n62

Racial social systems, and concept of race, 20

Racial structures: and private organizations' nation-rebuilding efforts, 9; definition of, 10; and Protestant organizations in higher education, 10; organizations disrupting or advancing, 11–12; anti-caste movement's dismantling of, 20

Racial uplift: Booker T. Washington on, 71, 195–96, 214, 265n62; and black women's higher education, 150; John Henry Barrows on, 183; Kelly Miller on, 198, 204; and Howard University, 201, 204; and Appalachian whites, 214, 220

Racist beliefs, AMA's belief in education's power over, 19

Radcliffe College, 144

Social development, hierarchy of, 123–24, 129–30, 158, 216, 217, 218, 225

Social equality: and access to higher education, 17; and Conservative Republicans, 112; and AMA, 119, 124, 130; and Oberlin College, 187; and racial uplift ideology, 195–96; and natural affinities, 241–42

Social hierarchy: higher education replacing forms of, 18, 19, 62; education inculcating respect for, 49; and race, 70; at Berea College, 79; women as challengers to, 156; reorganization of, 235

Social integration, potential for realization of, 110, 111–12

Social justice: and AMA, 67, 113; and college campuses, 101; elusiveness of, 115; and Howard University, 198

Social mobility: and access to higher education, 17, 125, 158, 208, 237; resources to build pathways for, 112

Social movements: social problems framed by, 11; of women, 146; and civil rights, 184; and black elites, 197; and Howard University, 198

Social networks: of higher education, 55, 174, 178, 185, 186, 188, 191; of AMA-affiliated colleges, 71, 106; and status hierarchies, 136; college networks and social closure, 168–72

Social order: reorganization of, 30, 235; role of education in, 49

Social problems, framing of, 11

Social relief, as reparation for former slaves, 13–14, 15, 33, 122

Social settlement work, 155, 221, 227

Social status: types of education projected on, 12, 15, 19, 22, 62; interconnectivity of cultural and educational ideals with, 17; poor whites' anxieties concerning, 50; colleges elevating individual social status, 106, 158, 208; race as basis of,

106; role of external organizations in mediation of, 107; and AMA, 130

Social welfare programs: in post-Civil War period, 17; federal government's establishment of social obligation for education, 54; bureaucratization of, 155

Society: moral ideals of, 8; racial integration of, 9

Sorosis, 154

South: AMA primary schools founded in, 8, 14, 15, 67; education system in, 9, 26, 32–33, 47, 48–55, 61–62, 102–3, 108, 130–35; Northern tutelary power over, 30, 33–35, 41, 42, 48, 52, 60, 62, 63, 67, 81, 199–200; morality of groups in, 33, 61, 208; landed aristocracy of, 34; black codes of, 36, 123, 124; modernization of, 48; racial caste system of, 48; rehabilitation of, 49, 68; black teachers in, 53–54, 120; Northern teachers in, 53, 95, 146; state-sponsored higher education in, 56, 57, 108, 136–37; private higher education in, 58, 136–37; Berea College criticized in, 79–80; black migration from, 107, 117–21; industrialists' influence on race relations in, 107; black college graduates migrating to, 120; higher education in, 171, 180, 236; social organization of, 208; peonage in, 224. *See also* Reunification of North and South

South Africa, 13

South Carolina: racial integration of state university, 16, 57; black voting rights in, 23; land redistribution in, 38; higher education in, 56, 57; state-supported higher education in, 56, 57; black political power in, 57, 108; Constitutional Convention of 1868, 57; violence against blacks in, 105, 257n10; Appalachian counties of, 225, 232

South Carolina College, 56

Southern blacks: and anti-caste movement, 4; AMA's educational funding for, 128; General Education Board's education funding for, 132, 133

Southern economy, Northern dependence on, 37

Southern Europe, immigrants from, 107, 121

Southern Homestead Act (1866), 40, 41

Southern middle class, and anti-caste movement, 5

Southern oligarchy, republican governance replacing, 3

Southern planter class: and anti-caste movement, 2, 4; AMA's fear of power of, 10, 15; compensation for loss of property, 13; rights of, 30, 31, 33, 35; poor whites allied with, 31, 48; Reform Republicans on, 34, 61; Conservative Republicans on, 35; in Latin America, 35; and land redistribution, 37, 40, 61; as obstacle to economic revitalization, 39; resistance to black labor, 39, 40, 41, 42; voting rights of, 46; French Bourbons compared to, 47; and education of blacks, 48; political power of, 48, 61, 119, 209; effect of slavery on, 49; access to higher education, 57; and interracial social contact, 114; poor whites distinguished from, 209; and Appalachian whites, 218–19; classification of, 249n7

Southern secession: effect on New York's economy, 3; and absence of common schools in South, 49

Southern states: educational requirements excluding black voters, 23, 248n77; enforcement of constitutional commitments to public education, 26; racist ideologies dominating, 28

Southern values and beliefs, AMA's moral work in transforming, 5

Soysal, Yasemin Nuhoglu, 252n99

Spelman Seminary (now Spelman College), 133, 168, 262n21, 266n81

Spencer, Herbert, 218

Stamatov, Peter, 2

Stanford University, 115, 139

Stanton, Edwin, 235

Stanton, Elizabeth Cady, 154

State constitutions: understanding tests for black voters, 23; of former Confederate states, 108

State expansion, in post-Civil War period, 17

State power: jurisdiction of, 10, 14, 33; and consecration of higher education, 18; and rights of black citizens, 30; strength of, 33; and Reconstruction policy, 36

Status boundaries: causal relationship with racial boundary processes, 16; anti-caste movement's rebuilding ideas on, 20

Status closure, 141

Status hierarchies: and AMA, 127, 130, 136; and higher education, 135–36, 137, 139, 141, 143, 237–38; and poor whites, 210

Status transfers, 135, 137

Steinberg, Marc, 35

Steinmetz, George, 106

Stevens, Mitchell, 141

Stevens, Thaddeus, 29

Stone, May, 227

Stowe, Harriet Beecher, 76, 77, 207

Straight University (now Dillard), 8, 82–83, 255n46, 265n43

Strang, David, 252n99

Strieby, Michael, 72

Student scholarships, as donors' contribution to reparations, 14

Substantive inclusion, 248n68

Sumner, Charles, 25, 31, 111–12, 116

Wellesley College: black enrollment in, 24; grading practices of, 139; administrators of, 157, 162; faculty of, 157; as sex-designed college, 157; liberal arts training of, 164; black alumni of, 198

Wells, Ida B., 184

West: federal resources supporting expansion in, 9; land redistribution in, 39; Union troops deployed to, 43, 113, 123; black migration to, 107, 118, 119, 120, 197; immigrant migration to, 118

Western Reserve College, 177

West Point, 8

West Virginia, 208, 210, 225, 232

Wheeler, W. W., 78

Whig party, 44

Whipple, George, 191

Whipple, H. B., 260n81

White bonded labor, and slavery as shared historical condition, 2

White elites: demographic changes interpreted as status threat, 107; and Southern education, 131

White League, 109

White nationalism, 161, 233

Whites: AMA's reeducation of, 5; exemptions from tests for voting rights, 23; on black students' access to higher education, 115–16; General Education Board's educational funding for, 132; paternalism of, 192; standards of whiteness, 217, 232

White Southerners: symbolic redemption of, 7–12, 211; hostility toward state governing civil rights of blacks, 30, 129; demands for type of government, 33; as threat to political stability, 34; black codes of, 36; resistance to black labor, 38, 39–40, 42, 250n36; military occupation as means of restraining, 42, 43; narratives of economic and political worth of, 61; racial prejudice of, 71, 121, 122, 128; resistance to interracial colleges, 79; voting rights of, 108; masterly inactivity policy of, 109; and "home rule" contests on education, 121–22; political power of, 121; black achievements as status threat to, 129, 238. See also Appalachian whites; Poor whites; Southern planter class; White supremacy

White supremacy: maintaining of, 22; education maintaining, 62; Berea College challenging, 79–80; organizations promoting, 109; and AMA, 128; and policies on women's reproduction, 161; Dunning School, 200; social development as justification of, 217; poor whites as evidence against, 218

Whittier, John Greenleaf, 100

Wilberforce University: black enrollment in, 110; women as students of, 147, 149; industrial curriculum of, 192

Wilder, Douglas, 108

Williams, Frank L., 229

Williams College, 116, 177, 178, 198

Wilson, Julia, 187

Wilson, Woodrow, 183, 223

Winant, Howard, 10

Windom, William, 118, 197

Wirz, Henry, 249n2

Wollstonecraft, Mary, 158

Woman's Congress (1873), 154

Woman Suffrage Association of Missouri, 146

Woman's Work, 153

Women: education of, 6, 15, 143; voting rights of, 23, 142, 146, 152, 165; and access to citizenship rights, 31–32; exclusion from professions, 142, 145; opportunities for professional participation, 145–46, 147, 152–53, 155, 156, 163, 164, 166, 167,

449R00200

Made in the USA
Middletown, DE
14 June 2017